# COMPUTERS IN THE WORKPLACE

# COMPUTERS IN THE WORKPLACE

*Editor*

**Filibert Melsbach**

scitus academics

**Computers in the Workplace**
Edited by **Filibert Melsbach**

This Book is Printed on Acid-Free Paper. ♾



ISBN: 9781681178509
Library of Congress Control Number: 2017948877


SCITUS Academics LLC,
616, Corporate Way, Suite 2, 4766,
Valley Cottage, NY 10989

www.scitusacademics.com

**Notice**



Printed in United States of America.

# Preface

A huge amount of changes are predictable to occur in the workplace during this century. In a nation already populated by small businesses, more and more people will consider entrepreneurial ventures instead of traditional employment. Technology makes it possible to telecommute, work from virtual offices and communicate with businesses and individuals across the globe. Flexible work schedules are popular because so many duties and responsibilities can be accomplished from an employee's home or while the employee is traveling. Computers can do repetitive tasks faster and with fewer mistakes than humans, so the first few decades of the development of the computer for business focused mainly on automating a wide range of industrial processes. The next step brought PCs as productivity tools and entertainment devices to homes and workplaces everywhere. More recent refinements in computers and information technology such as mobile devices have led to a host of business- and consumer-focused "apps" designed to help people to be more organized, efficient and productive. As companies demand more sophisticated technology to help manage their businesses, the cost to develop and produce applications will likely increase. Customized programs that meet the specific needs of a business are becoming more popular as companies engage the services of functional and technology consultants.

This volume discusses the advantages, psychological effects, and sociological implications of the computer in the workplace. The impact of computers on the workplace has been a major source of debate - both in terms of their effects on the quantity and quality of work. It explores how computers have changed the workplace, from robotic computers used in manufacturing and electronic medical records to word processors and computer programming.

# Table of Contents

# CHAPTER 1

# Real-Time Computer Analytical Application in Pressure Transient Analysis of Petroleum Reservoirs

**Faisal Hussain[4], Kanwal K. Pinjani[5]**

[1]*Department of Civil Engineering, Mehran University of E & T, Khaipur Mir's Campus, Khairpur Mir's, Pakistan*

[2]*Department of Mechanical Engineering, Mehran University of E & T, Khaipur Mir's Campus, Khairpur Mir's, Pakistan*

[3]*Department of Civil Engineering, Mehran University of E & T, Jamshoro, Pakistan*

[4]*Department of Petroleum & Natural Gas Engineering, Mehran University of E & T, Khairpur Mir's, Pakistan*

[5]*Water Resources Division, National Engineering Services, Lahore, Pakistan*

## ABSTRACT

Today with certainty, the petroleum industry is fostering sanguinely the fields' development programs for the optimization of reservoir characterization through worth-full appliances of computer analysis techniques. The time element is of prime importance for optimistic petroleum development projects. Therefore, the frontline of "Real-time Analysis" is added into the applications of computer solving techniques for achieving and sketching up the real-time cost effectiveness in analyzing field development programs. It focuses on the phases of real-time well test data acquisition system, real-time secure access to the well test data either on field or in office and real-time data interpretation unit. This interface will yield the productive results for the field of reservoir's pressure transient analysis and wells' systems analysis by following the up-to-date preferred, accurate and effective well test analytical principles with modern real-time computer applications and techniques. It also lays emphasis for the comfort and reliability of data in creating best interpersonal working modes within a reputable and esteemed petroleum development organization.

**Keywords:** Reservoir; Pressure transient; Real-time Analysis; Comfort; Computer applications

# 1. INTRODUCTION

In the mid of eighteenth century when the oil wells were discovered accidentally through water well drilling, it was felt that the oil was the cheapest combustion source. Later the inventions of vehicles and aircrafts indicated that the hydrocarbons will be the environment friendly substance to run the transport across the world. As the energy demand increases with the passage of time, the more and deep wells were explored and produced with a concern over the economical feasibility of those projects. This further exploration and production of hydrocarbons make the field of petroleum engineering into existence which primarily focuses on reservoir engineering management as it mainly evaluates the producible reserves and project's recoverable economic revenues. The reservoir engineering management helps petroleum engineer in characterizing the hydrocarbon reservoirs via analyzing various well tests conducted in the reservoir at the bottom-hole of the well [1,2]. These tests are termed in the petroleum industry as "reservoir's pressure transient tests" while their analysis is known as "reservoir's pressure transient analysis".

As stated above that pressure transient analysis is performed just to characterize the reservoir like to evaluate the physical properties and potential of a reservoir rock in order to produce the hydrocarbons present in it efficiently with maximum recovery. To characterize the reservoir, the basis of pressure transient analysis depends on the graphical interpretation of gradients pressure derivatives versus producible time. This graphical interpretation is obtained via importing the well tests' results. As a reservoir engineer, to fully characterize the reservoir the analytical equations must also be solved optimistically by considering the graphical interpretation results. While the summary of this sketched scenario is not easy to understand nowadays as manually interpreting these graphs and solving the complex analytical equations are unreachable in obtaining the desired results for even a group of various field technicals of petroleum engineering field. This is just because of facing the transient flow into the reservoir as the developments go through into more deep formations while it is of common knowledge that the properties of transient flow remain changeable every time by the reservoir's pressure response with respect to location [1].

## 2. BASIC CONCEPT

The remedy for the effective pressure transient analysis can be solved by introducing the modern pressure transient analysis which is based on the application of computer aided solutions. These solutions are resulted by importing the well tests' data in order to obtain the upscaled graphical interpretation of gradients pressure derivatives versus producible time. Furthermore, an interface for solving the complex analytical equations via importing the up-scaled graphical interpretation results is used to characterize the reservoir [2,3].

No doubt that the phase of interpreting the obtained well tests' results is very important in petroleum industry as it finally makes a company to generate good economical revenues annually via producing these calculated reserves but this phase calculation must be time saving and live for even just calculating the current reservoir volume in order to become accurate in companies annual economic revenues calculations. By introducing this live data interpretation unit, the working technician will come across to know the current heterogeneities of a producing formation which will make them in making the time effective and cost optimistic live well producing decisions [3]. To brief further this phase, it is defining that a real-time data interpretation unit is designed to interpret the live well test data and to solve the analytical complexities for characterizing the reservoir. Furthermore, this unit is also tried to connect by an internet hub just to make the technicians (which are off to the well location or to any location where reservoir characterization and management experts and engineers have their offices) aware of reservoir conditions which will make them in making live correct decisions. This interface will yields the benefits of accessing the well test data at any location without any risk concern or data insecurity, taking time efficient and cost optimistic decisions and maintaining effective interpersonal connections of reservoir and wellsite engineers to monitor and brief the live reservoir conditions [3,4].

In supplementary aspect the concept leads to the main challenge observed during conventional transient testing. That challenge is the rapid interpretation, processing and analysis of data, which is the responsibility of technical authorities or production experts; instead of any as such personnel only wire line experts are present during wire line operation as it is their foremost responsibility. Now the challenge initiates here that how to enhance the level of communication between wire line experts and data processing experts. The conventional technique practiced currently at field is time, cost and energy consuming. It is capable of providing skillful communication medium between on well personnel, field personnel and technical team at head office.

The subject matter is solved by a newly emerging technology of real time interaction **Figure 1**. This technology is purely computer system based as it enclose the application of real-time well test data transmission from wire line tester tool to computer, processing it to assess different parameters, storing the data and meanwhile sending it to other concerned personnel via internet [4].

# 3. WIRE LINE FORMATION TESTER

The universal formation evaluation workflow modules comprises of reservoir mark out by means of seismic information and well-to-well correlations. Further it also includes reserves' volume evaluator—will assist in determination of fluid presence and its productivity. The obtained wire line logs will initially assist endow with fluid type data and productivity. Wire line testing offers proof, comprehensive fluid properties, precise pressure measurements and production evaluation—it's just a way to hunt maximum productivity. Before production of well, formation testing is final evaluation footstep that assist to design well completion and production facilities.

These wire line equipments are either lowers in well by using sonde that is positioned at certain depth. The other method is to attach the equipment with drill pipe/ tubing conveyed by packer.

This one time conducted service of Wire line Formation Tester (WFT) is useful in different domains as to measure the flowing bottom hole pressure, bottom hole flowing rate, permeability of formation, porous opening in producing zone, near well bore parameters, blockage or fractures in reservoir. These testers have also application in determination of assessing reservoir extent and geometry and in investigation of hydraulic communication between wells characteristics and reservoir heterogeneities [5].

The specific operational wire line tester is dart to compute the static pressures of all three permeable layers. Pressure versus depth plots helps in setting up formation

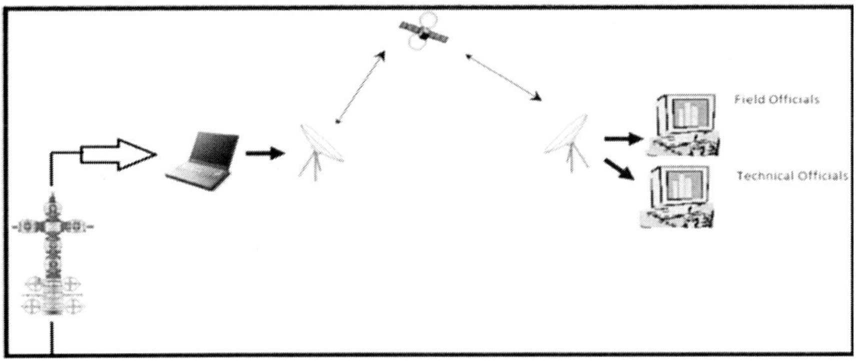


**Figure 1**. Illustration of real time connectivity system.

fluid gradients and categorizes fluid contacts in the reservoir. Primary purpose for testing exploration wells is to obtain a fluid sample, so that reservoir fluid must be characterize as it is in a virgin status; in later stages fluid composition may not exactly match the down hole fluid composition due to higher changes [5].

The same test during the development phase discloses different objectives. Most likely the reservoir deliverability is evaluated and the reservoir fluid is distinguished. Then for relating reservoir characterization to the geological model, operator must understand the hydraulic communications [1,6].

At this arena, formation testing principally consists of open-hole wire line pressure testing. It predominantly assists in evaluating static reservoir pressures, which helps in confirming fluid contacts and fluid density gradients. On this mechanism, different hydraulic slots of reservoir will be determined and coupled with geological model. At this stage, additional development wells are drilled and field production already started. In fresh wells, pressure gradients might already replicate manipulation of production on reservoir pressure. If reservoir simulators were in-placed on those wells, it will assist to predict vertical pressure profiles that confirmed by wireline tester measurements. Observed differences (if any) will help in refining geological model and commence suitable slots in the dynamic model. Reservoirs having large number of stacked layers like deltaic deposits, is considered as crucial stage. Therefore here the wireline pressure measurements are very useful aid to reservoir dynamics characterization as it help out in practically assessing vertical and lateral communications and the volumetric structure of these petite entity accumulations. This appliance contributed to the abrupt approval of first wire-line testing tool. Here the key goal of testing development well is to calculate skin that is resultant of formation damage. Due to dearth of skin, we can turn out the wells at their full potential. But ahead of putting the wells on line, the skin must be corrected if highly detected. One more ground for testing development wells is to organize them for stimulations so that it must be produced economically. This is frequent that operator needs premature revenues on many reservoirs having low productivity. These operators usually pay out massive sum on wide-ranging stimulation operations like hydraulic fracturing in the cases when un-stimulated production rates would be uneconomical. Recovering this investment could take months. Like well testing is in particular imperative to evaluate the productivity put on achieved through quantifying skin, estimating fracture length and its hydraulic conductivity, and appraising financial risks [2,7].

# 4. CONFIGURATION OF WFT MODULE AND DATA ACQUISITION

The WFT string may vary well to well but conventional string comprises of the modules as shown in **Table 1**.

The data revealed from the subsurface survey was further refined and concluded data is shown in **Table 2**.

# 5. DATA PROCESSING.

The input parameters are undergone computation and its given out results are shown in equation (1).

$$\frac{(tp + \Delta t)}{\Delta t} \tag{1}$$

where tp = 72 hr.

Permeability, commonly symbolized as κ shown in equation (2), is a measure of the ability of a porous material such as a rock or unconsolidated material, which is the ability to allow fluids to pass through it. It is of importance in determining the flow characteristics of hydrocarbons in oil and gas reservoirs. For a rock to be considered as an exploitable hydrocarbon reservoir without stimulation, its permeability must be greater than

**Table 1**. WFT tools and their configuration.

| Equipments | Function |
|---|---|
| 1. Electrical power module | Supply electric power to equipments |
| 2. Multi sample module | Collection of high quality fluid sample for PVT analysis |
| 3. Backup for multi sample module | Backup module is attached because limited no. of sample bottles are attached in single module |
| 4. Hydraulic power module | Powering system of assembly |
| 5. Single probe module | It contains pressure gauges, fluid resistivity and temperature sensors |
| 6. Optical fluid analyzer | It measure properties of fluid present in flow line (either reservoir fluid or drilling fluid) |
| 7. Live fluid analyzer | Quantification of the volume fraction of C6 components, essentially liquid HCs and GOR. |
| 8. MRP (Magnetic resonance Porosity) Module | Determination of free vs. bound fluid volume; Detection of hydrates; Measurement of mineralogy-independent porosity; Fluid identification |
| 9. Pump out module | It used to pump unwanted fluid or mud filtrate from formation to the bore hole |
| 10. Hold back hydraulic power module | Backup power system for additional operations |
| 11. Hold back single probe module | Hold back modules are used as backup or for different zone measurement |
| 12. RCI multi tank carriers/1 Gal sample module | Application depends on flow quantity; it is available in H2S and non H2S versions. It contain throttle valve to control flow. |

**Table 2**. Subsurface survey revealed data.

| Parameter | Source | Values received |
|---|---|---|
| Flowrate (q) STB/D | • Pressure transient test | 500 STB/D |
| Total time of test (tp) hours | • Pressure transient test | 72 Hrs |
| Thickness (h) Ft | • Pressure transient test<br>• Core analysis<br>• Well performance<br>• Seismic survey | 22 Ft |
| Oil formation volume factor (Bo) Rb/STB | • Laboratory analysis of reservoir fluid samples | 1.3 Rb/STB |
| Compressibility (Ct) $psi^{-1}$ | • Core analysis<br>• Well logs | $20 \times 10^{-6}$ $psi^{-1}$ |
| Viscosity (μ) cP | • Laboratory analysis of reservoir fluid samples | 1.0 cP |
| Radius of well bore (rw) Ft | • Drilling program | 0.3 Ft |
| Porosity (Ø) % | • Core analysis<br>• Well logs | 2% |
| Bottom hole pressure (Pws) psig | • Pressure transient test | List mentioned below |
| Initial pressure of reservoir (Pi) psi | • To be computed | Required |
| Permeability (k) mD | • To be computed | Required |
| Skin factor (s) | • To be computed | Required |
| Well bore storage capacity (Cs) bbl/psi | • To be computed | Required |

approximately 100 mD (depending on the nature of the hydrocarbon). Because of this reason gas reservoirs with lower permeability are still exploitable because of the lower viscosity of gas with respect to oil.

$$k = 162.6\frac{qB\mu}{mh} \quad (2)$$

Well bore storage can be a concern in wells with two characteristics: wells with a near wellbore limit, or wells with long storage times. For wells that have a near wellbore limit, wellbore storage may mask the pressure transient encountering this limit. This could lead to misinterpretation of the pressure transient test and erroneous characterization of the well. For wells with long storage times (greater than 24 hours for example), the length of the shut-in required to derive useful data from a build-up test may not be economically feasible. Well bore storage is denoted by Cs and is given by equation (3).

$$\mathrm{Cs} = \frac{qB}{24}\frac{\Delta t}{\Delta p} \quad (3)$$

And Skin factor is given by equation (4).

$$s = 1.151\left[\frac{P1hr - Pwf}{m} - \log\left\{\left\{\frac{k}{\varnothing\mu Ctrw^2}\right\} + 3.23\right]\right. \quad (4)$$

## 6. REAL TIME ANALYSIS

A software based approach is followed to develop a simulator which not only compute the required parameters on to the spot but also upload the calculated data on internet. This is second phase of the project which enables real time analysis by well site personnel, headquarter and technical experts. This practice not only saves time and cost of analysis but also provides rapid mode of communication. Though all this activity requires permanent training setup but less effort can result in more.

As in previous phase of project the data was feed to software and it developed the transient test model. Now that generated model is then uploaded to internet, meanwhile all other concerned experts can access the data using internet and their assigned ID. This system not only enables these people to check the data but they can also manipulate the parameters to calculate the impact of analysis. Later the manipulation can be accessed by well site personnel too in order to implement the suggested executions.

The data transmission is practiced by satellite system. The Satellite communication system is a line-of-sight microwave system with a single repeater. The satellite is in geostationary orbit as soon as velocity of satellite is harmonized to the rotary motion of earth at the equator. Due to grand expanse of satellite from earth (i.e.; 22,300 miles) and antenna extent margins that frontier focusing capability, the cone of coverage for a single satellite transmitter can be as outsized as the whole South Asia.

Here the transmission service that originates at a solo summit (single point) from well site and stream to number of summits in unit track like technical officials and headquarters, the bulky district of exposure is best. The extensive holdup between instantaneous, a signal is launch and when it returns to earth at filed stations or at other cities (about 240 millisecond) has no detrimental consequence when the signal is going only unit tracked. Real time coordination usually proceeds as a sequence of signals in unit track that are countered or recognized by signals in the other track. When the delay between the signals being sent and the reply or recognition is long, the communication speed of information becomes leisured. For data packets, huge impediment between technical personnel and rig site crew make the structure undergo giant track of accomplishment for transmission [4,8].

# 7. COROLLARY OF REAL TIME INVESTIGATION

1) The pressure transient test was conducted in 72 hrs and its data analysis was started exactly the termination of operation. The analysis took negligible time and within hour prior choke size was selected and well was put on production as shown in **Figure 2**.

2) The parameters were investigated rapidly after test as shown in Tables 3 and 4 through the output analysis taken from semi-log and log-log determinations given in the Figures 3 and 4 for well test **Table 5**.

3) Multiple access system results more effective and swift communication as compared to transponder based system because flow of data packets is observed from both ends of communication medium.

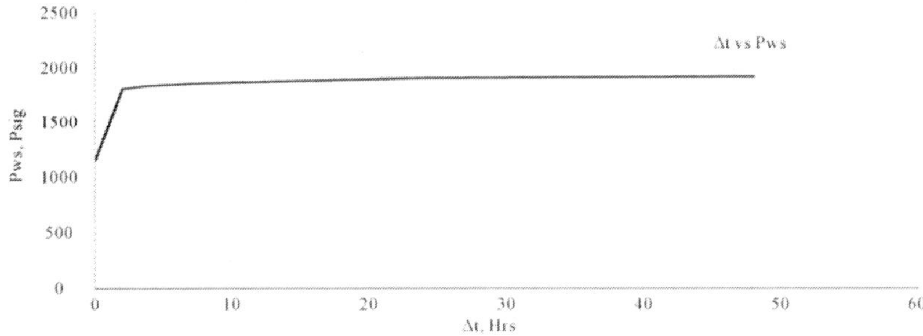


**Figure 2**. Bottom hole pressure vs time plot.

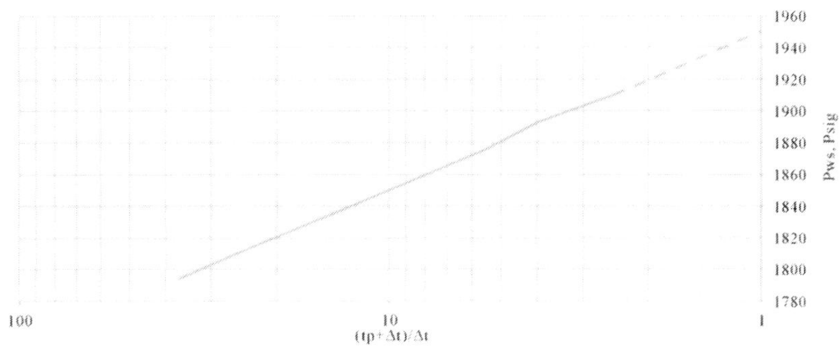


**Figure 3**. Semi-log plot B/Up (producing layer's initial pressure and slope).

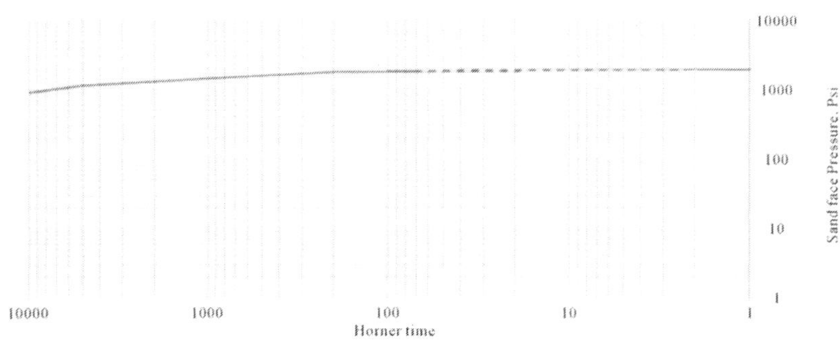


**Figure 4**. Log-log plot B/Up (producing layer permeability plot).

**Table 3**. After test investigated parameters.

| Parameter | Result |
|---|---|
| Slope (m) psi/cycle | 100 psi/cycle |
| Initial pressure of reservoir (Pi) psi | 1950 psi |
| Permeability (k) mD | 48 mD |
| Skin factor (s) | 1.43 |
| Well bore storage capacity (Cs) bbl/psi | 0.68 Bbl/psi |

**Table 4**. Build up test record from producing layer.

| Δt. Hrs | Pws. Psig |
|---|---|
| 0 | 1150 |
| 2 | 1794 |
| 4 | 1823 |
| 8 | 1850 |
| 16 | 1876 |
| 24 | 1893 |
| 48 | 1910 |

## 8. LIMITATIONS OF STUDY

- Suitability of job design remains incompatible to the perforation design and drilling plan. It is required to design the whole operation in series so that equipment size and drilling sections are coordinated.
- Lack of training of well site experts and mobile units result in mismanagement of operation.

| Depth | Lithology | Formation | Stratigraphy/Age |
|---|---|---|---|
| 0 | 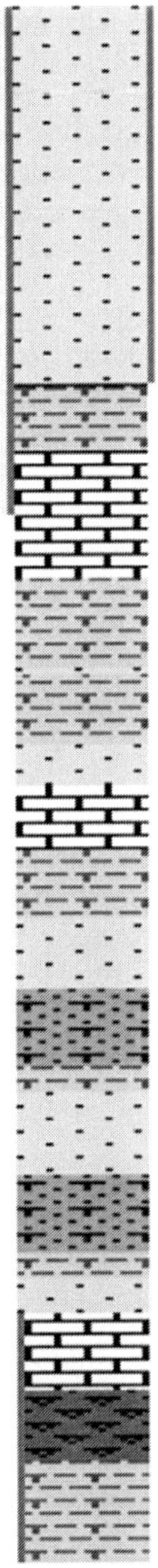 | Alluvium (Sandstone) | Recent |
| 1000 ft | | Siwalik (Sandstone) | Paleocene |
| | | Pirkoh (Limestone) | Pleistocene |
| | | Nari (Clay) | Eocene |
| 2000 ft | | Siwalik (Sandstone) | Oligocene |
| | | Alluvium (Sandstone) | |
| | | Habib rahi (Limestone) | Mid Eocene |
| 3000 ft | | Khirthar (Marl) | Lower Eocene |
| | | Lakhi (Clay) | Upper Cretaceous |
| 4000 ft | | Pirkoh (Limestone) | |
| | | Sirki (Sandstone) | Lower cretaceous |
| 4500 ft | | Ghazi (Shale) | |

**Table 5**. Lithology of well subjected to test.

- The inter connectivity technology is not implemented routinely on fields so it has very limited applications so far. This technology requires promotion in industry so that petroleum industry can make the most of it.
- Limited access to wireless internet, wireless and mobile connectivity and communication systems on well site can consequently delay the job response. The equipment and devise feasibility are priority in this technology.
- For signals like data communications sessions and real time operations—goes in both directions and anticipated to be received at only one other track, the huge district of exposure and the impediment might root troubles.

# 9. CONCLUSIONS

1) WFT dual packer system has proved to be an essential domain for real time analytical application because it enhances the technical scenario of oil and gas fields.
2) The DST, core analysis, well logging and other test data are highly useful in real time planning.
3) Real time analysis provides the means of making onsite and timely decision, which lead to up gradation of technical skills of technical personnel.
4) Satellite system has proved to be a far better option as compared to fiber optic system, because satellite system facilitates wireless and mobile networking even at well sites.
5) NPNS protocol is important for security purpose. By the application of this protocol, variety of operations can be analyzed at a time (real time) with maximum provision of operation and data security.

Faisal Hussain, Kanwal K. Pinjani 6) Real time WFT analysis service is of prime importance for the working environment of Pakistan. Hence it must be promoted and implemented with elevated executions.

# REFERENCES

1. R. Akkurt, M. Bowcock, J. Davies, C. Del Campo and B. Hill, "Focusing on Down Hole Fluid Sampling and Analysis," Oilfield Review, Vol. 18. No. 4, 2006.

2. K. C. Kin, L. Chen, C. Ayan-Schlumberger, L. Q. Xu, J. Cai, S. S. Guo, M. W. Wu, Z. T. Hao, F. X. Pan, Z. J. Tan, H. J. Yang and CNOOC Zhanjiang Ltd., "Comparing Wireline Formation Tester Derived Productivity Index to Drill Stem Test," SPE Asia Pacific Oil and Gas Conference and Exhibition, Brisbane, 18-20 October 2010, Document ID: 130868-MS.
3. R. L. Spross, J. A. Truax, P. F. Rodney and D. D. Gleitman, "Downhole X-Ray Source Fluid Identification System and Method," Patent 8511379, 2012.
4. Schlumberger, "Fundamentals of Formation Testing," 225 Schlumberger Drive, Sugar Land, 2008.
5. P. Weinheber, "Heavy Oil Sampling with Wireline Formation Testers," International Petroleum Conference, Doha, 7-9 December 2011, IPTC 13917.
6. Halliburton, "Wireline and Perforating Services," Pressure Transient Analysis (PTA™), 2009.
7. J. App and C. Ehlig-Economides, "Petroleum Engineering," Pressure Transient Analysis, University of Huston, Huston, 2003.
8. A. Sageev, "Pressure Transient Analysis of Reservoirs with Linear or Internal Circular Boundaries," SGP-TR-65, Stanford Geothermal Program Interdisciplinary Research in Engineering and Earth Sciences, Stanford University, Stanford, 1993.

# CHAPTER 2

# Cloud Computing for Next-Generation Sequencing Data Analysis

**Shanrong Zhao[1*], Kirk Watrous[2], Chi Zhang[1] and Baohong Zhang[1]**

[1] *Early Clinical Development, Pfizer Worldwide Research and Development, Cambridge, MA, USA*

[2] *Business Technology, Pfizer Worldwide Research and Development, Groton, Connecticut, USA*

## ABSTRACT

High-throughput next-generation sequencing (NGS) technologies have evolved rapidly and are reshaping the scope of genomics research. The substantial decrease in the cost of NGS techniques in the past decade has led to its rapid adoption in biological research and drug development. Genomics studies of large populations are producing a huge amount of data, giving rise to computational issues around the storage, transfer, and analysis of the data. Fortunately, cloud computing has recently emerged as a viable option to quickly and easily acquire the computational resources for large-scale NGS data analyses. Some cloud-based applications and resources have been developed specifically to address the computational challenges of working with very large volumes of data generated by NGS technology. In this chapter, we will review some cloud-based systems and solutions for NGS data analysis, discuss the practical hurdles and limitations in cloud computing, including data transfer and security, and share the lessons we learned from the implementation of Rainbow, a cloud-based tool for large-scale genome sequencing data analysis.

**Keywords:** next-generation sequencing, cloud computing, data analysis, workflow, pipeline

# 1. INTRODUCTION

High-throughput next-generation sequencing (NGS) technologies have evolved rapidly and are reshaping the scope of genomics research [1, 2] and drug development [3, 4]. The significant advances in NGS technologies, and consequently, the exponential expansion of biological data have created a huge gap between the computer capabilities and sequencing throughput [5, 6]. Technical improvements have greatly decreased the sequencing costs and, as a result, the size and number of datasets generated by large sequencing centers have increased dramatically. The lower cost also made the sequencing data more affordable to small and midsize research groups. As always, digging out the "treasure" from NGS data is the primary challenge in bioinformatics, which places unprecedented demands on big data storage and analysis. It is becoming increasingly daunting for small laboratories or even large institutions to establish and maintain their own computational infrastructures for large-scale NGS data analysis.

A promising solution to address this computational challenge is cloud computing [7–10], where CPU, memory, and storage are accessible in the form of virtual machines (VMs). In recent years, cloud computing has spread very rapidly for the supply of IT resources (hardware and software) of different nature, and is emerging as a viable option to quickly and easily acquire the computational resources for large-scale NGS data analyses. Cloud computing offers a wide selection of VMs with different hardware specifications and users can choose and configure these VMs to meet their computational demands. With the massive scale of users, cloud computing providers, such as Amazon, are continuously driving costs down, which in turn has led to the use of cloud computing for NGS data analyses attractive within the bioinformatics community. Despite the apparent benefits associated with cloud computing, there are also issues to be addressed. Data privacy and security are particularly important when managing sensitive data, such as the patients' information from clinical genomics studies [11].

The aim of this chapter is to describe the application of cloud computing in large-scale NGS data analysis and to help scientists to understand advantages and disadvantages of cloud computing, and to make an informed-choice on whether to perform NGS analysis on cloud services or to build the infrastructure themselves. It is organized as follows. First, we give a brief introduction to NGS technology, including DNA sequencing, RNA sequencing, and ChIP-sequencing. Secondly, we briefly introduce cloud computing and its services. Thirdly, we summarize and review publicly available cloud-based NGS tools and systems, with some particular emphasis on "Rainbow" [12], a cloud-based tool for large-scale whole-genome sequencing. Finally, we will discuss the challenges and remaining problems related to the full adoption of cloud computing in the NGS data analysis.

# 2. NEXT-GENERATION SEQUENCING

Next-generation sequencing [13] platforms allow researchers to ask virtually any question related to the genome, transcriptome, or epigenome of any organism. It has already profoundly changed the nature and scope of genomic research in the past few years. Sequencing methods differ primarily by how the DNA or RNA samples are obtained (e.g., organism, tissue type, normal vs. affected, experimental conditions) and by the data analysis options used. After the sequencing libraries are prepared, the actual sequencing processes are similar regardless of the method. There are a number of standard library preparation kits from different vendors that offer solutions for whole-genome sequencing (WGS), RNA sequencing (RNA-seq), targeted sequencing (such as exome sequencing, targeted RNA-seq or 16S sequencing), and detection of DNA methylation and protein-DNA interactions. As the number of NGS methods is constantly growing, a brief overview covering the most common methods is presented below.

## 2.1. Genomics

A breakthrough in NGS in the last decade has provided an unprecedented opportunity to investigate the contribution of genetic variation to health and disease [14]. WGS and whole-exome capture sequencing (WES) have emerged as compelling paradigms for routine clinical diagnosis, genetic risk prediction, and rare diseases [15–18]. WGS of tumors [19] is an unbiased approach that provides extensive genomic information about a tumor at the single nucleotide level as well as structural variations such as large insertions, genomic rearrangements, gross deletions, and duplications. Using low-coverage WGS of many individuals from diverse human populations, the 1000 Genomes Project [20] has characterized common variations and a considerable proportion of rare variations present in human genomes. With falling costs, it is now possible to sequence genomes of many individuals for association studies and other genomic analyses [21].

The WGS workflow is depicted in **Figure 1**. A human genome is fragmented into many short pieces that are sequenced by a sequencer. The sequencing step typically generates billions of short reads. All short reads are mapped to a reference genome, and genetic and structural variants can be identified with respect to the reference genome sequence. Human DNA is comprised of approximately 3 billion base pairs. 30× coverage sequencing of a personal genome will produce approximately 100 gigabytes (GB) of nucleotide bases, and its corresponding FASTQ file will be about 250 GB. For a WGS project consisting of 400 subjects, 100 terabytes of disk space is required to store the raw reads alone. Additional space is required for storing intermediate files generated during data analyses. Transferring and processing a dataset of such size would be extremely time-consuming and heavily computation-intensive and thus they pose huge practical challenges in data analyses.

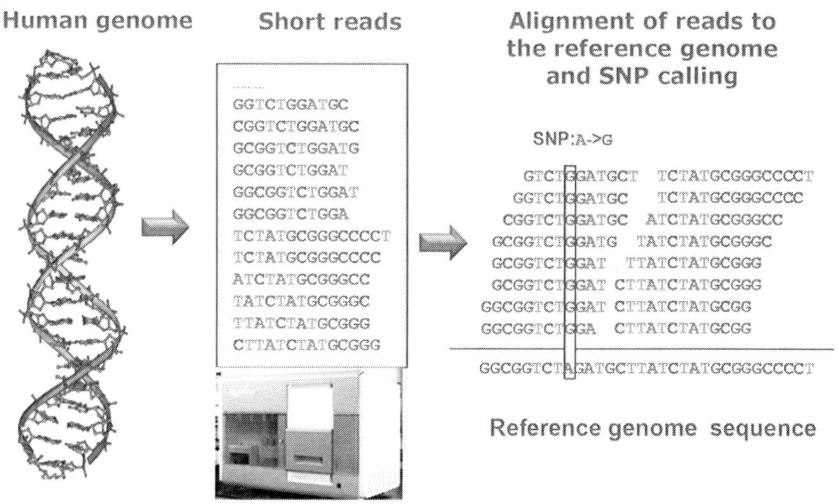


**FIGURE 1.** WGS workflow. A human genome is fragmented and sequenced, and billions of short reads are generated by a sequencer. All short reads are aligned to the reference genome and genetic variants are identified accordingly.

## 2.2. Transcriptomics

RNA sequencing (RNA-seq) has emerged as a powerful technology for transcriptome profiling [22–25]. It allows both quantification of known or predefined RNA transcripts and the capability to detect and quantify rare and novel transcripts within a sample. Compared to microarray, RNA-seq has a broader dynamic range, which allows for the detection of more differentially expressed genes with higher fold-change [26]. It is also superior in detecting low abundance transcripts, differentiating biologically critical isoforms, and allowing the identification of genetic variants. Not only RNA-seq can detect underlying genomic alterations at single-nucleotide resolution within expressed regions of the genome, but also it can quantify expression levels and capture variation not detected at the genomic level, including the expression of alternative transcripts. In the past decade, RNA-seq has become one of the most versatile applications of NGS technology and has revolutionized the researches on transcriptome [27]. As in WGS, RNA-seq generates vast number of short reads that must be computationally aligned or assembled to quantify expression of hundreds of thousands of RNA transcripts. Similar to DNA sequencing, the enormous data from large-scale RNA-seq studies poses a fundamental challenge for data management and analysis in a local environment [28–30]. Consequently, limited access to computational infrastructure and high-quality bioinformatics tools, and the demand for personnel skilled in data analysis and interpretation, remains a serious bottleneck for most researchers.

## 2.3. Epigenomics and Protein-Dna Interactions

While genomics involves the study of heritable or acquired alterations in the DNA sequence, epigenetics is the study of heritable changes in gene activity caused by mechanisms other than DNA sequence changes [31, 32]. Mechanisms of epigenetic activity include DNA methylation, histone modification and more. A focus in epigenetics is the study of cytosine methylation (5-mC) states across specific areas of regulation such as promotors or heterochromatin. Cytosine methylation can significantly modify temporal and spatial gene expression and chromatin remodelling. Two methylation sequencing methods are widely used: whole-genome bisulfite sequencing (WGBS) and reduced representation bisulfite sequencing (RRBS). With WGBS-seq, sodium bisulfite chemistry converts nonmethylated cytosines to uracils, which are then converted to thymines in the sequence reads. In RRBS-seq, DNA is digested with MspI—a restriction enzyme unaffected by methylation status. Fragments in the 100–150 bp size range are isolated to enrich CpG and promotor containing DNA regions. Sequencing libraries are then constructed using the standard NGS protocols.

ChIP-sequencing, also known as ChIP-seq [33, 34], is a method used to analyze protein interactions with DNA. ChIP-seq combines chromatin immunoprecipitation (ChIP) with massively parallel DNA sequencing to identify the binding sites of DNA-associated proteins. It can be used for genome-wide mapping of transcription factor binding sites. Protein-DNA interactions have a significant impact on many biological processes and disease states. The sequence reads generated by ChIP-seq are massive and need to be aligned to reference genome first, and then the locations of protein-DNA interactions are inferred based on enrichment of sequence reads along the genome.

# 3. CLOUD COMPUTING

"Cloud Computing," by definition, refers to the on-demand delivery of IT resources and applications via the Internet with pay-as-you-go pricing. Cloud computing is a model for enabling ubiquitous, on-demand access to a shared pool of configurable computing resources (e.g., networks, servers, storage, applications, and services), which can be rapidly provisioned and released with minimal management effort. With cloud computing, you do not need to make large upfront investments in hardware and spend a lot of time on the heavy lifting of managing hardware. Instead, cloud computing providers such as Amazon Web Services own and maintain the network-connected hardware, and you can provision exactly the right type and size of computing resources you need. You can access as many resources as you need, almost instantly, and only pay for what you request and own. These computing resources include networks, servers, storage, applications, and services. There are several essential characteristics of the cloud computing model.

a. Rapid elasticity: you only allocate resources when you need them, and you are able to dynamically scale-up and -down your allocated resources as your needs change over time.

b. Pay-as-you-go: you only pay when you consume computing resources, and only pay for how much you consume.

c. On-demand self-service: the user can request and manage the computing resources without help from the service providers.

d. Cost-effective: classical computational infrastructure for data processing has become ineffective and difficult to easily scale-up and -down, and cloud computing is a viable and even a cheaper technology that enables large-scale data analysis.

Existing cloud-based services can be classified into four categories or layers (see **Figure 2**). The first one is Infrastructure as a Service (IaaS). This service model is offered in a computing infrastructure that includes servers (typically virtualized) with specific computational capability and/or storage. The user has full control on the operating system and applications that are deployed to, but with limited control, over the network settings. A good example is Amazon elastic compute cloud (EC2), which allows the user to request and manage virtual machines, and Amazon simple storage service (S3), which allows storing and accessing data. The second category of service is Platform as a Service (PaaS) in which the provider offers the customer the authority to create applications using developing tools supported by the provider. PaaS features rapid application development and good scalability, presenting usefulness in developing specific applications for big biological data analysis. Typically, the environment delivered by PaaS includes programming language environments, web servers, and databases. The Amazon Web Services (AWS) software development kit (AWS SDK) and Google App Engine are good examples of this service.

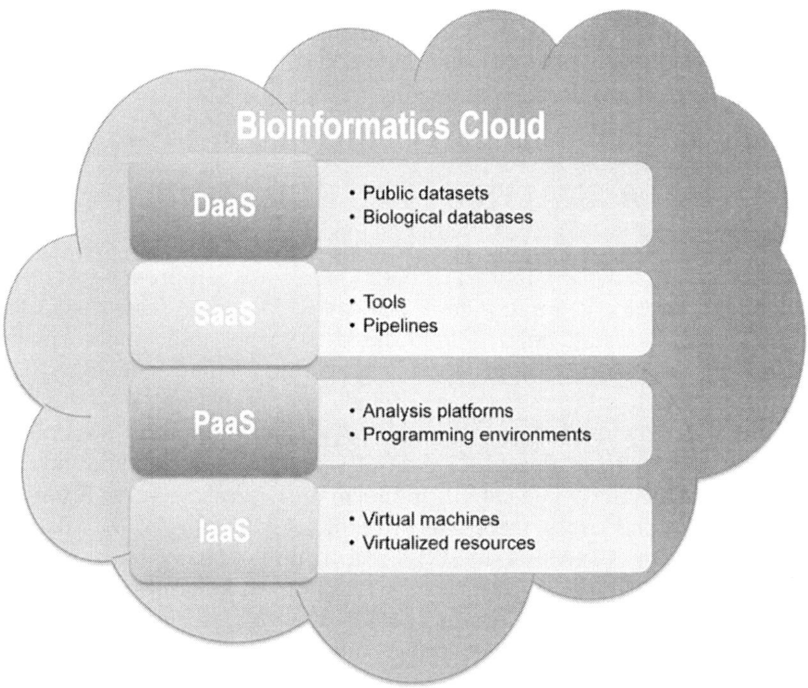


**FIGURE 2.** Illustration of cloud services [8]. Cloud-based services in are grouped into Data as a Service (DaaS), Software as a Service (SaaS), Platform as a Service (PaaS), and Infrastructure as a Service (IaaS).

The third service is Software as a Service (SaaS). SaaS eliminates the need for local installation and eases software maintenances and updates, providing up-to-date cloud-based services for data analysis. Customers do not manage the cloud infrastructure or network components, servers, operating systems, or storage, and can use the applications provided by the cloud provider. Most bioinformatics applications are open-source projects, and difficult to build, configure and maintain, primarily because they lack good documentation and have complex library dependencies. However, as all software applications are installed and configured within the VM, SaaS provides the perfect solution. The fourth layer is Data as a Service (DaaS). Bioinformatics clouds are heavily dependent on data, as data are fundamentally crucial for downstream analyses and knowledge discovery. Due to such unprecedented growth in biological data, delivering Data as a Service (DaaS) via the Internet is of utmost importance. DaaS enables dynamic data access and provides up-to-date data that are accessible by a wide range of devices that are connected over the web. AWS provides a centralized repository of public data sets, including GenBank [35], 1000 Genomes [20], encyclopedia of DNA elements [36], etc., and all public datasets are delivered as services in AWS and thus can be seamlessly integrated into cloud-based applications.

# 4. NGS DATA ANALYSIS ON CLOUD COMPUTING

In recent years, cloud computing offers an alternative approach to quickly and easily acquire computational resources for large-scale NGS data analysis. As a result, many cloud-based services and bioinformatics platforms (see **Table 1**), applications (see **Table 2**), and resources have been developed to address the specific challenges of working with the large volumes of data generated by NGS technology. Cloud computing has created new possibilities to analyze NGS data at reasonable costs, especially for laboratories lacking a dedicated bioinformatics infrastructure. From the perspective of end users, there are three options to analyze NGS data on cloud computing (**Tables 1** and **2**). First, commercial systems such as DNAnexus and Seven Bridges can be used out of box to carry out the entire NGS data analysis. Second, commercial or open bioinformatics platforms are further customized to meet users' computational needs. Third, open-source tools (**Table 2**) can be deployed into the cloud for any customized data analysis.

## 4.1. Commercial Services

Commercial services provide the users with well-established pipelines, user interfaces, and even application programming interfaces (APIs), and can reduce the time and effort required for setting up pipelines for NGS data analysis. For instance, DNAnexus and Seven Bridges offer various customizable NGS data analysis pipelines. In addition, DNAnexus also provides software that can directly upload the sequencing data produced.

**TABLE 1.** Cloud computing services and platforms.

| Name | URL | Description |
|---|---|---|
| BaseSpace | http://basespace.illumina.com | Commercial services |
| Bina | http://www.bina.com/ | Commercial services |
| DNAnexus | http://www.dnanexus.com | Commercial services |
| SevenBridges | http://www.sbgenomics.com | Commercial services |
| Eoulsan | http://transcriptome.ens.fr/eoulsan | Cloud-based platform |
| CloVR | http://clovr.org | Automated sequence analysis |
| Cloud BioLinux | http://cloudbiolinux.org | Virtual machine for bioinformatics cloud computing |
| CloudMan | https://wiki.galaxyproject.org/CloudMan | Cloud-scale Galaxy |
| Globus Genomics | https://www.globus.org/genomics | Cloud-based bioinformatics workflow for NGS analyses |
| GenomeCloud | http://www.genome-cloud.com/ | Analyze genome data |
| COSMOS | http://cosmos.hms.harvard.edu/ | Workflow management system |

**TABLE 2.** Open-source tools for cloud computing.

| Software | URL | Description | Reference |
|---|---|---|---|
| Atlas2 | http://atlas2cloud.sourceforge.net | Genome analysis | [37] |
| CloudAligner | http://cloudaligner.sourceforge.net | Reads mapping | [38] |
| CloudBurst | http://cloudburst-bio.sourceforge.net | Reads mapping | [39] |
| Crossbow | http://bowtie-bio.sourceforge.net/crossbow | Read mapping/SNP call | [40, 41] |
| FX | http://fx.gmi.ac.kr | RNA-seq | [42] |
| Myrna | http://bowtie-bio.sourceforge.net/myrna | RNA-seq | [43] |
| Stormbow | http://s3.amazonaws.com/jnj_stormbow/index.html | RNA-seq | [44] |
| STORMSeq | http://www.stormseq.org/ | Read mapping | [45] |
| GenomeKey | https://github.com/LPM-HMS/GenomeKey | Whole genome analysis | [46] |
| Mercury | https://www.hgsc.bcm.edu/software/mercury | Workflow for genomic analysis | [47] |
| Rainbow | http://s3.amazonaws.com/jnj_rainbow/index.html | Whole genome analysis | [12] |
| PaekRanger | http://ranger.sourceforge.net | ChIP-seq | [48] |
| VAT | http://vat.gersteinlab.org | Variant annotation | [49] |
| YunBe | http://tinyurl.com/yunbedownload | Gene set analysis | [50] |
| BioVLAB-MMIA-NGS | https://sites.google.com/site/biovlab/ | microRNA-mRNA integrated analysis | [51, 52] |
| SURPI | http://chiulab.ucsf.edu/surpi/ | Pathogen identification | [53] |

BaseSpace, launched by Illumina in collaboration with Amazon, is a genomics cloud computing platform that provides NGS data analysis services, such as mapping, de novo assembling, small RNA analysis, library quality control (QC), metagenomics analysis, and data storage. It is designed to bring simplified data management and analytical sequencing tools directly to researchers in a user-friendly manner. BaseSpace provides flexibility and convenience with an array of tools, significantly simplifying the process of yielding meaningful results from NGS data. Bina Technologies offers a service that is composed of a specialized hardware called Bina Box and a cloud service. Bina Box can employ accelerated BWA [54] and GATK [55] for data analyses.

Some commercial services also provide APIs with which the users can manage their jobs or build their own applications. Variant calling on datasets of hundreds or thousands of genomes is time-consuming, expensive, and not easily reproducible given the myriad components of a variant calling pipeline. To address these challenges, the Mercury [47] analysis pipeline was developed on top of the DNAnexus platform. It integrates multiple sequence analysis components across various computational steps, from obtaining patient samples to providing a fully annotated list of variant sites for clinical applications. Mercury is an automated, flexible, and extensible analysis workflow that provides accurate and reproducible genomic results at scales ranging from individuals to large cohorts.

Although a number of cloud-based pipelines are available for analyses of sequencing data in massively parallel DNA sequencing, the majority of them can only identify variants within a single sample. While this approach has enough power for detecting variants in high-coverage sequencing, it performs worse than multiple-sample calling when applied to low-coverage sequencing data. To this end, another scalable DNAnexus-based pipeline for joint variant calling in large samples was developed and deployed to the Amazon cloud. Using this pipeline, Shringarpure et al. [21] identified 68.3 million variants in 2535 samples from Phase 3 of the 1000 Genomes Project. By performing the variant calling in a parallel manner, the data was processed within 5 days at a compute cost of just $7.33 per sample (a total cost of $18,590 for completed jobs and $21,805 for all jobs).

Despite their merits, these commercial services also have several disadvantages. First, the use of a commercial service requires extra expenses for the convenience of NGS data analysis and user-friendly interfaces. Second, compared to open-source tools on the cloud, the commercial services are less customizable with respect to the use of the services and access to the cloud service. Although DNAnexus and Seven Bridges provide APIs to access and control their cloud services, their functionalities are restricted and the users have to request the service provider to set up new application software on their cloud services.

## 4.2. Bioinformatics Platforms

CloudBioLinux [56] is a publicly accessible virtual machine (VM) that is based on an Ubuntu Linux distribution and is available to all Amazon EC2 users for free. It comes with a user-friendly graphical user interface (GUI), along with over 135 preinstalled bioinformatics packages. CloudBioLinux instances provide an excellent environment for users to become familiar with BioLinux and cloud computing. Galaxy is an open, web-based platform for data-intensive biomedical research. Whether on the free public server or your own instance, you can perform, reproduce, and share the entire data analyses. Galaxy Cloud [57], a cloud-based Galaxy platform for the analysis of data at a large scale, is the most used platform for bioinformatics. Unlike commercial software service solutions, users can customize their deployment and have complete control over their instances and associated data. Currently, a public Galaxy Cloud deployment, called CloudMan [57], is provided on the AWS cloud, enables bioinformatics researchers to easily deploy, customize, and share their cloud analysis environment, including data, tools, and configurations. By combining three platforms, CloudBioLinux, CloudMan, and Galaxy, into a cohesive unit, researchers can gain access to more than 135 preconfigured bioinformatics tools and gigabytes of reference genomes on top of the flexible cloud computing infrastructure [56].

Although Galaxy cloud provides a convenient platform for researchers, challenges remain in moving large amounts of data reliably and efficiently and in adding domain-specific tools for specific analyses. To address these challenges, Globus Genomics [58, 59] was developed at the Computation Institute (CI), a joint institute between the University of Chicago and Argonne National Laboratory. Globus Genomics is a cloud-based integrated solution for NGS data analysis. It extends the existing Galaxy workflow system by adding data management capabilities for transferring large quantities of data efficiently and reliably (via Globus Transfer), domain-specific analyses tools preconfigured for immediate use by researchers (via user-specific tools integration), automatic deployment on cloud for on-demand resource allocation and pay-as-you-go pricing (via Globus Provision), and a cloud provisioning tool for auto-scaling (via HTCondor scheduler). Genome sequencing is notoriously data-intensive, and Globus Transfer [59] is designed for fast and secure movement of large amounts of data. Setting up a production instance of Galaxy is a nontrivial task that involves a number of manual installation and configuration steps for both the platform and any dependent software packages—steps that can be both error-prone and time-consuming. Globus Provision addresses the above issues by providing on-demand cluster reconfiguration, user-specific node provisioning, and automatic instance deployment on Amazon EC2.

GenomeCloud (http://www.genome-cloud.com/) is another on-demand Galaxy cloud. It was built upon Galaxy, and is composed of g-Analysis, g-Cluster, g-Storage, and g-Insight services, providing convenient services to the researchers and other users. GenomeCloud is a complete and integrated platform for analyzing genome data to the interpretation of analysis results. It combines the idea of cloud computing with bioinformatics to generate an integrated solution for data storage and sharing, database management, continuously updated computing and analysis tools, and security. GenomeCloud is designed to help researchers perform bioinformatics tasks more easily, as well as to support laboratories without the computational resources to conduct research without hurdles.

## 4.3. Open-Source Tools

The development of tools supporting NGS data analysis with cloud computing has recently become popular in the open-source community [8]. Currently, there are many pipelines and workflows that support cloud computing (**Table 2**). Despite their advantages in cost and flexibility, open-source tools on the cloud also have substantial drawbacks. The users are responsible for designing/setting up the entire analysis pipeline, the data management and hardware configuration, such as CPUs, memory, storage, and security. Quite often, the users have to overcome a laborious series of trial and error before setting up the proper configuration. Although several tools have been developed to date, in most cases, their cloud computing support is incomplete and their functionality is under-developed. Here, we will briefly report some existing bioinformatics tools and then describe Rainbow, a cloud-based tool for large-scale WGS data analysis, in detail in the next section.

CloudAligner [38] and CloudBurst [39] are parallel read mapping algorithms optimized for mapping short reads to human and other reference genomes and can produce alignments for a variety of downstream biological analyses including SNP discovery, genotyping, and personal genomics. Crossbow is a Hadoop- [60] based tool that combines the speed of the short read aligner bowtie [61], with the accuracy of the SNP caller SOAPsnp [62] to perform alignment and SNP detection from WGS data in parallel. Scalable tools for open-source read mapping (STORMseq) [45] is a graphical interface cloud computing solution that performs read mapping, read cleaning, variant calling, and annotation using personal genome data. Variant annotation tool (VAT) [49] has been developed to annotate variants from multiple personal genomes at the transcript level as well as to obtain summary statistics across multiple genes and individuals.

FX [42] is an RNA-seq analysis tool, which runs in parallel on cloud computing infrastructure, for the estimation of gene expression levels and genomic variant calling. Another cloud computing pipeline for calculating differential gene expression in large RNA-seq datasets is Myrna [43]. Myrna uses bowtie [61] for short read alignment and R/bioconductor for quantification, normalization, and statistical testing. These tools are combined in an automatic, parallel pipeline that runs in the cloud, exploiting the availability of multiple computers and processors wherever possible. Stormbow [44] is a scalable, cost-effective, and open-source-based tool for large-scale RNA-seq data analysis. Its performance has been tested by applying it to analyze 178 RNA-seq samples in the cloud. In the test, it took 6–8 h to process each RNA-seq sample with 100 million pair-ended reads in the m1.xlarge instance, and the average cost was only $3.50 per sample. BioVLAB-MMIA-NGS [51, 52] offers the integrated miRNA-mRNA analysis and can be used to identify the "many-to-many" relationship between miRNAs and target genes with high accuracy. PeakRanger [48] is a software package for the analysis of ChIP-seq data. It can be run in a parallel cloud computing environment to obtain extremely high performance on large data sets. Unbiased NGS approaches enable comprehensive pathogen detection in the clinical microbiology laboratory [63] and have numerous applications for public health surveillance, outbreak investigation, and the diagnosis of infectious diseases. Sequence-based ultra rapid pathogen identification (SURPI™) [53] is a computational pipeline for pathogen identification from complex metagenomic NGS data generated.

## 4.4. Rainbow

Crossbow is a software tool that can detect SNPs in WGS data from a single subject; however, it has a number of limitations when applied to large-scale WGS projects. Rainbow [12] is a cloud-based software package that can assist in the automation of large-scale WGS data analyses. Rainbow was built upon Crossbow. By hiding the complexity of the Crossbow command-line options, Rainbow facilitates the application of Crossbow for large-scale WGS analysis in the cloud. Compared with Crossbow, the main improvements incorporated into Rainbow include the ability: (1) to handle BAM as well as FASTQ input files, (2) to split large sequence files for better load balance in downstream clusters, (3) to collect and track the running metrics of data processing and monitoring multiple Amazon EC2 instances, and (4) to merge SOAPsnp outputs from multiple individuals into a single file to facilitate downstream genome-wide association studies.

The workflow of Rainbow is shown in **Figure 3**. Multiple data drives are shipped to Amazon. After the BAM or FASTQ files have been uploaded to S3, large FASTQ files are split into smaller files in parallel. Then multiple clusters are launched in the cloud, with each cluster processing a single sample. Crossbow is responsible for mapping reads to the reference sequence and for SNP calling. The SNPs for all samples are then combined by a Perl script. When the analysis is complete, the results can either be downloaded directly or exported via Amazon Export. We applied Rainbow to analyze the 44 subjects, with 0.55–1 billion pair-ended 100 bp short reads per sample. The running environments were as follows. For step #1 in **Figure 3**, we chose the Amazon m1.large instance, which has two CPUs, 7.5 GB memory, and two 420 GB instance drives. For Crossbow run, each compute cluster has 40 c1.xlarge nodes as recommended by the Crossbow developers. Each c1.xlarge node has 8 CPUs, 7 GB memory, and 1690 GB instance storage.

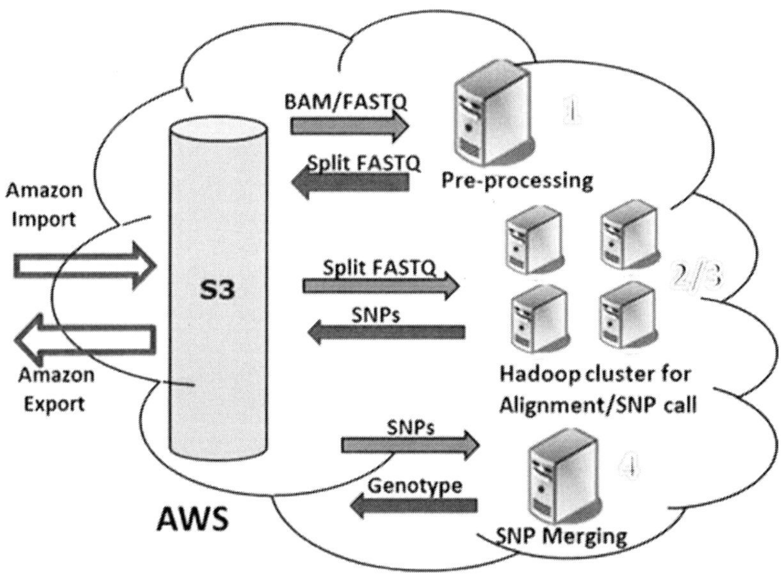


**FIGURE 3.** The Rainbow pipeline. S3 centralizes data storage, including inputs, intermediate results, and outputs. Alignment and SNP call are performed by Crossbow in a cluster with multiple nodes.

The performance of Rainbow is summarized in **Figure 4**. In a 320-CPU (=40 × 8) cluster, the alignment of billions of reads takes between 0.8 and 1.6 h. The linear relationship shown in **Figure 4** indicates that the sequence data blocks in the Hadoop distributed file system (HDFS) are physically local to the nodes that processed them, which reduces virtual I/O delays.

The SOAPsnp running time ranges from 1 to 1.8 h, which takes a little longer than the alignment. All EC2 instances and clusters are terminated immediately after the jobs are finished. On average, it costs less than 120 US dollars to analyze each subject, and the total cost for analyzing those 44 subjects was 5800 US dollars, including data import. More important than the cost is the ability to scale Rainbow up or down, so that the analyses can be accomplished in a reasonably short amount time, regardless of sample size. No upfront investment in infrastructure is required and there is no additional administrative costs involved using Amazon cloud. Rainbow is a scalable, cost-effective, and open-source tool for large-scale WGS data analysis. It is available for third-party implementation and use, and can be downloaded from the Rainbow website.

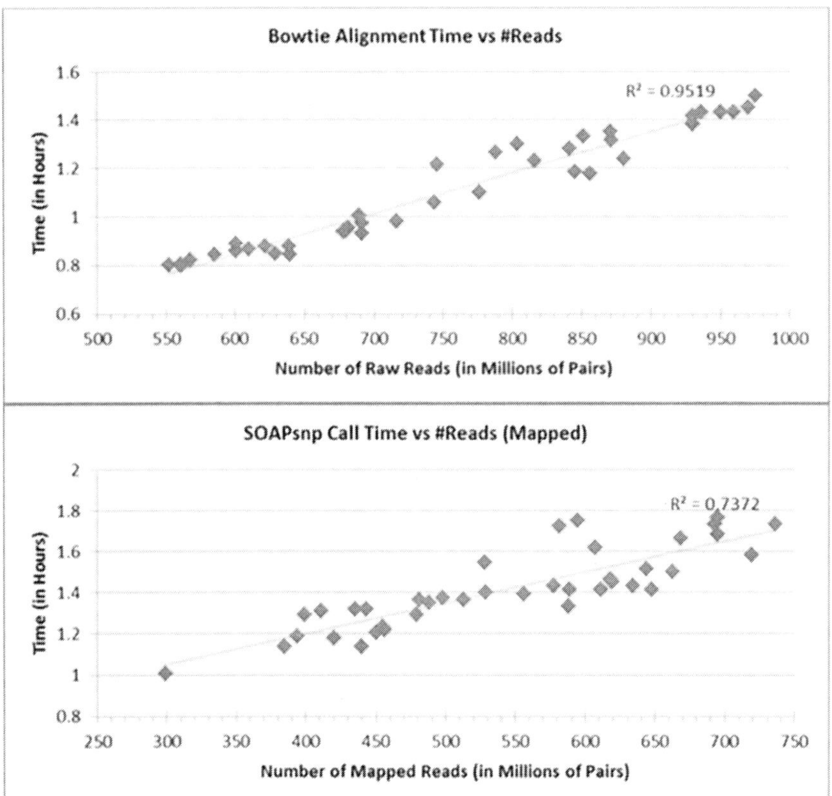


**FIGURE 4.** Top panel: running time of bowtie alignment vs. the number of paired sequence reads. Bottom panel: running time of SOAPsnp vs. the number of paired mapped reads. Note: each cluster consists of 40 c1.xlarge instances (8 CPUs per c1.xlarge instance).

In order to access the Rainbow cloud pipeline, the user must first set up an AWS account (http://aws.amazon.com/). Once registered, the user needs to sign up for Amazon EC2, S3, EMR, and SES services. The user can then start an instance based on the public AMI: ami-0f1f9866 in US-East (N. Virginia); or ami-b6bc89f3 in US-West (N. California). All required software is already preinstalled and configured in the AMI. Then, the user can connect to the instance and configure EC2, EMR, and S3cmd command-line tools. After a successful connection to the instance has been established, the user needs to prepare a sample manifest file in order to run Rainbow. A master manifest file is a plain text file to describe all subjects in a WGS project. Each subject has a corresponding entry in the manifest file and each entry consists of three fields separated by spaces or tabs: (1) a unique identifier; (2) locations of the raw reads in S3; and (3) an output folder in S3. Each individual step in the Rainbow workflow uses this same manifest file as input, thus all output files are named and stored consistently. After the creation of the manifest file, the user just needs to run a couple of command lines and all the analyses will be done automatically in the cloud.

Analyzing large datasets in the cloud is different from performing the same analysis in a local environment. When developing Rainbow, we have learned the following lessons.

- It is not trivial to move large datasets around within the cloud. Users should be prepared to handle network congestion or failures, never assuming data transfer is always successful. If data move fails, it is a good practice to wait a couple of minutes and then try to transfer data again. Repeat the "wait-and-transfer" cycle till data transfer is successful.
- Boot time should be taken into account when new resources are starting up. It is recommended to give cloud providers 10–15 min grace period (waiting time) before attempting to use a newly requested resource, for instance, elastic block store (EBS).
- Cloud providers typically offer a variety of compute instances to choose from. To choose the best option, it is important to understand the bottleneck (CPU, I/O, or network) for the algorithm that is to be run.
- When large amounts of data are moved between cloud resources, it is essential to ensure that they are in the same location or data center.
- It is difficult to debug workflows in the cloud without heavy logging.

# 5. CLOUD COMPUTING HURDLES

Albeit relatively new, cloud computing holds great promise in effectively addressing big data storage and analysis problems in NGS data analysis. Despite the potential gains achieved, there are also several important issues that need to be addressed. Below, we present the main hurdles on the adoption of cloud computing.

## 5.1. Big Data Transfer

To analyze the NGS data in the cloud, data have to be transferred across the wired network and uploaded onto AWS. The volume and complexity of NGS data have exponentially increased, giving rise to issues related to data analysis, management, and transfer to the cloud [64–66]. For example, WGS of 400 subjects at 30× coverage will generate approximately 100 TB raw sequence reads in FASTQ format. In the future, more and more sequencing projects would generate ultra-large volumes of biological data and thus require bioinformatics clouds for big data storage, sharing, and analysis. One of the most challenging issues of cloud computing is data transfer. Transferring vast amounts of biological data to the cloud is a significant bottleneck in cloud computing.

The speed of data transfer is usually slow and at present there are not many solutions available for moving the huge amount of data to cloud. Therefore, we need more efficient data transfer technologies in cloud computing. According to CloudHarmoy's report on download speed relative to the year 2010 (http://blog.cloudharmony.com/2010/02/cloud-speed-test-results.html), the download speed from Amazon AWS EC2 in North Virginia (U.S.) was 2.95 Mb/s, which corresponds to downloading a 10 GB file in 29,116 s (~8 h). Therefore, data transfer is a serious bottleneck in NGS data analysis on cloud service. To deal with the data transfer issue, Aspera (http://www.asperasoft.com/) has developed the fast and secure protocol (FASP) for data transfer with a speed of up to 5 GB/s. Ideally, using FASP, the user can download a 10 GB file in 17.2 s, which is a revolutionary improvement. But still it cannot transfer data at the TB scale. Alternatively, sequencing service providers such as BGI and Illumina offer a service in which they deliver a hard disk drive (HDD) containing the sequencing data. However, the shipping has limitations aside from the time taken up by travel, and once a package (of hard drives) is stamped and sealed, researchers cannot control when (and sometimes if) the parcel arrived or what condition it arrived. This service cannot guarantee safe transfer of data, since the HDD can get lost, stolen, or physical errors can occur.

## 5.2. Most Bioinformatics Tools Are Not Cloud-Aware

Most bioinformatics software tools are written for desktop (rather than cloud) applications and are therefore not provided as cloud-based web services accessible via the Web, making it infeasible to perform complex bioinformatics tasks in the cloud. For instance, bowtie [61] is one of the most popular mapping algorithms, but it requires that input files are stored on local disk when mapping reads and is not compatible with Amazon S3. Even if you run bowtie in an EC2 instance, the raw FASTQ files have to be fetched to an elastic block store (EBS) volume that is attached to the EC2 instance. In other words, bowtie does not have built-in support for S3. Spliced transcripts alignment to a reference (STAR) [67–69] is a popular RNA-seq mapper that performs highly accurate spliced sequence alignment at an ultrafast speed. However, it is not cloud-friendly either. Like bowtie, STAR does not take advantage of AWS cloud services, and cannot work with S3 either. Unfortunately, the majority of bioinformatics tools are developed without native support for cloud computing.

MapReduce [70, 71], developed by Google, is an easy-to-use and general-purpose parallel programming model that is suitable for large data set analysis on a commodity hardware cluster. MapReduce is a software framework, written in Java, designed to run over a cluster of machines in a distributed way. A MapReduce program is composed of a user-defined map function and a reduce function. When a program that is implemented with the map and reduce functions has been launched, the map function processes each key/value pair and produces a list of intermediate key/value pairs, while the reduce function aggregates all the intermediate values with the same keys. MapReduce is an important advancement in cloud computing because it can process huge data sets quickly and safely using commodity hardware.

Hadoop, comprised of MapReduce and the Hadoop distributed file system (HDFS), is based on a strategy of colocating data and processing to significantly accelerate computing performance [60]. Hadoop allows for the distributed processing of large datasets across multiple computer nodes, supports big data scaling, and enables fault-tolerant parallel analysis. The Hadoop framework has been recently deemed as the most suitable method for handling bioinformatics data [70]. Unfortunately, many traditional bioinformatics tools and algorithms have to be redesigned and implemented in order to support and benefit from Hadoop MapReduce infrastructure. Even with the help of the corresponding developers, it will take a while for most bioinformatics tools currently available to add this feature.

Apache Spark™ (https://spark.apache.org/) is a fast and general engine for large-scale data processing, natively supported in Amazon EMR. Apache

Spark supports a variety of languages, including Java, Scala, and Python, for developers to build applications. Hadoop and Apache Spark are both big data frameworks, but they do not really serve the same purposes. Hadoop is essentially a distributed data infrastructure. It distributes massive data collections across multiple nodes within a cluster of commodity servers, Spark, on the other hand, is a data-processing tool that operates on those distributed data collections; it does not do distributed storage. To study the utility of Apache Spark in the genomic context, SparkSeq was created [72]. It is a general-purpose, flexible, and easily extendable library for genomic cloud computing, and can be used to build genomic analysis pipelines in Scala and run them in an interactive way. Recently, SparkBWA [73] was introduced; a new tool that exploits Spark to boost the performance of one of the most widely adopted sequence aligner, the Burrows-Wheeler Aligner (BWA). It is hoped more Apache Spark-based bioinformatics algorithms will be developed for large-scale genomic data analysis in the future.

## 5.3. Open Clouds For Bioinformatics

Currently, the largest cloud computing provider is Amazon, which provides commercial clouds for processing big data. Additionally, Google also provides a cloud platform to allow users to develop and host applications, and to store and analyze data. However, commercial clouds are not yet able to provide ample data and software for bioinformatics analysis. By placing public biological database and software into the cloud and delivering them as services, data and software can be seamlessly and easily integrated into the cloud. AWS hosts a variety of public data sets for free access (https://aws.amazon.com/public-data-sets/). All public datasets in AWS are delivered as services. Previously, large data sets, such as the mapping of the human genome, required hours or days to locate, download, customize, and analyze. Now, anyone can access these data sets via the AWS centralized data repository from any Amazon EC2 instance or Amazon EMR cluster. Google Genomics also helps the life science community organize the world's genomic data and make them accessible and useful.

In the era of big data, however, only a tiny amount of biological data is accessible in the cloud at present (only AWS, including GenBank [35], Ensembl [74], 1000 Genomes [20], etc.) and the vast majority of data are still deposited in conventional biological databases. It is difficult for commercial clouds to keep pace with the emerging needs from academic research, opening up the demand for specific open clouds for bioinformatics studies. Needless to say, open access and public availability of data and software are of great significance to biological science. To satisfy the need for big data storage, sharing, and analysis with lower cost and higher efficiency, it is essential that a large number of biological data as well as a wide variety of bioinformatics tools should be publicly accessible in the cloud and delivered as services. Therefore, future efforts should be devoted to building open bioinformatics clouds for the bioinformatics community. GenomeSpace [75] is a cloud-based, cooperative community resource that currently supports the streamlined interaction of 20 bioinformatics tools and data resources. To facilitate integrative analysis by nonprogrammers, it offers a growing set of 'recipes', short workflows to guide investigators through high-utility analysis tasks. The potential benefits of open bioinformatics clouds include maximizing the scope for data sharing, easing large-scale data integration, and harnessing collective intelligence for knowledge discovery.

## 5.4. Security and Privacy

The many characteristics of cloud computing have made the long-dreamed vision of “computing as a utility” a reality. The cloud computing offers scalable and competitively priced computing resources for the analysis and storage of data from large-scale genomics studies, but it must also ensure that genetic data coming from human subjects are hosted in a context that is both secure and compliant with regulations [76]. When deciding whether to move the analyses into the cloud or not, potential cloud users need to weigh all the factors including system performance, service availability, cost, and most importantly, data security. Genomics data extracted from clinical samples are sensitive data and present unprecedented requirements of privacy and security [11, 77]. In general, there are concerns that genomics and clinical data managed through a cloud are susceptible to loss, leakage, theft, unauthorized access, and attacks. The centralized storage and shared tenancy of physical storage space means the cloud users are at higher risk of disclosure of their sensitive data to unwanted parties. A secure protection scheme will be necessary to protect the sensitive information from medical records. There is considerable amount of work to enforce data protection against security attacks.

However, the question of security in cloud computing is intrinsically complicated. Cloud computing is built on the top of existing architectures and techniques such as SaaS and distributed computing. When combining all the benefits of these architectures and techniques, cloud computing also inherits almost all of their security issues at various levels of the system stack. When cloud users move their applications from within their enterprise/organization boundary into the open cloud, they will lose physical control over their data, and traditional security protection mechanisms such as firewalls are no longer applicable to cloud applications. As a result, cloud users have to heavily rely upon the service providers for data privacy and security protection. In cloud computing, the data and applications from different customers reside on the same physical computing resources. This fact will inevitably bring forth more security risks in the sense that any intentional or inadvertent misbehavior by one cloud user would make other coresidences victims.

## 6. CONCLUSION

Pharmacogenomics is an important branch of genomics that studies the impact of SNP on drug response in patients, the toxicity or efficacy of a drug, and the development of diseases [78, 79]. Pharmacogenomics aims to improve drug therapy with respect to the patients' genotype, to ensure maximum efficacy with minimal adverse effects, and is at the basis of the idea of "precision medicine" where drugs are chosen or optimized to meet the genetic profile of each patient. Thus, the presence (or the absence) of specific SNPs may be used as a clinical marker to predict drug effectiveness, and to foresee the drug responses of individuals with different SNPs. Precision medicine also opens up the possibility to treat diseases based on the genetic makeup of the patient. Identification of the genetic defect underlying early-onset diabetes is important for determining the specific diabetes subtype, providing personalized treatment. The study by Artuso et al. [14] has revealed that NGS provides a highly sensitive method for identification of variants in a new-set of "driver genes" causing diabetes. NGS can be used to analyze the comprehensive landscape of genetic alterations, including known disease-causing gene fusions in transcripts, which brings new insights to study diseases with a highly complex and heterogeneous genetic composition such as cancer [19]. Therefore, NGS facilitates precision medicine and changes the paradigm of cancer therapy, and holds expanded promise for its diagnostic, prognostic, and therapeutic applicability in various diseases.

The substantial decrease in the cost of NGS techniques in the past decade has dramatically reshaped the biomedical research and has led to its rapid adoption in biological research and drug development [3, 4]. Nowadays, massive amount of data, targeting a variety of biological questions, can be generated quickly using NGS platforms. These data range from the function and regulation of genes, the clinical diagnosis and treatment of diseases, to the omics profiling of individual patients for precision medicine. To better understand the association between SNPs and diseases, and to gain deeper insights into the relation between drug response and genetic variations, large-scale sequencing projects are continuously being initiated in research institutes and pharmaceutical companies. The availability of NGS and the genomics studies of large populations are producing an increasing amount of data. However, the storage, preprocessing, and analysis of NGS data are becoming the main bottleneck in the analysis pipeline. With the exponential increase in volume and complexity of NGS data, cluster or high performance computing (HPC) systems are essential for the analysis of large amounts of NGS data. But the associated costs with the infrastructure itself and the maintenance personnel will likely be prohibitive for small institutions or laboratories, and even too much to swallow for big institutions and pharmaceutical companies.

This chapter provides a useful perspective on cloud computing and helps researchers, who plan to analyze their NGS data on cloud services, to gain an understanding of the basic concept. As discussed earlier, cloud computing drives down infrastructure costs both up-front and on an on-going basis. It offers many operational advantages, such as fast completion of massive computational projects and infrastructures can be set up in minutes rather than months. There are growing demands for cloud-based NGS data analysis, which constitutes a good alternative for researchers with little interest in investing in a cluster system. Cloud computing is becoming a technology mature enough for its use in genomic researches. The use of large datasets, the demanding analysis algorithms, and the urgent need for computational resources, make large-scale sequencing projects an attractive test-case for cloud computing. It is likely that in the future, researchers will be able to analyze their NGS data on cloud services for a cost low enough to eliminate the need to introduce clusters into their laboratories. However, we must emphasize that there are a number of open issues and problems associated with the use of cloud, such as privacy and security, especially when managing patients' clinical data. Data transfer of large amounts of NGS data to the cloud remains a challenge and bottleneck in NGS data analysis. Furthermore, many traditional NGS tools are not designed to use in cloud environment, and thus cannot harness the benefits of cloud services. With the ever-increasing demand, commercial companies and bioinformaticians will develop more NGS analysis tools, using APIs offered by service providers, in the foreseeable future, making NGS data analysis in the cloud more efficient, friendly, and secure.

## REFERENCES

1. Bahassi el M, Stambrook PJ. Next-generation sequencing technologies: breaking the sound barrier of human genetics. Mutagenesis. 2014;29(5):303–10.
2. Goodwin S, McPherson JD, McCombie WR. Coming of age: ten years of next-generation sequencing technologies. Nat Rev Genet. 2016;17(6):333–51.
3. Woollard PM, Mehta NA, Vamathevan JJ, Van Horn S, Bonde BK, Dow DJ. The application of next-generation sequencing technologies to drug discovery and development. Drug Discov Today. 2011;16(11–12):512–9.

4. Yadav NK, Shukla P, Omer A, Pareek S, Srivastava AK, Bansode FW, et al. Next generation sequencing: potential and application in drug discovery. Sci World J. 2014;2014:802437.
5. Schatz MC, Langmead B, Salzberg SL. Cloud computing and the DNA data race. Nat Biotechnol. 2010;28(7):691–3.
6. Baker M. Next-generation sequencing: adjusting to data overload. Nat Meth. 2010;7(7):495–9.
7. Calabrese B, Cannataro M. Bioinformatics and microarray data analysis on the cloud. Meth Mol Biol. 2016;1375:25–39.
8. Dai L, Gao X, Guo Y, Xiao J, Zhang Z. Bioinformatics clouds for big data manipulation. Biol Direct. 2012;7:43; discussion
9. O'Driscoll A, Daugelaite J, Sleator RD. 'Big data', Hadoop and cloud computing in genomics. J Biomed Inform. 2013;46(5):774–81.
10. Kwon T, Yoo WG, Lee W-J, Kim W, Kim D-W. Next-generation sequencing data analysis on cloud computing. Genes & Genomics. 2015;37(6):489–501.
11. Datta S, Bettinger K, Snyder M. Secure cloud computing for genomic data. Nat Biotechnol. 2016;34(6):588–91.
12. Zhao S, Prenger K, Smith L, Messina T, Fan H, Jaeger E, et al. Rainbow: a tool for large-scale whole-genome sequencing data analysis using cloud computing. BMC Genomics. 2013;14:425.
13. Reuter JA, Spacek DV, Snyder MP. High-throughput sequencing technologies. Mol Cell. 2015;58(4):586–97.
14. Artuso R, Provenzano A, Mazzinghi B, Giunti L, Palazzo V, Andreucci E, et al. Therapeutic implications of novel mutations of the RFX6 gene associated with early-onset diabetes. Pharmacogenomics J. 2015;15(1):49–54.
15. Allard MW. The future of whole-genome sequencing for public health and the clinic. J Clin Microbiol. 2016;54(8):1946–8.
16. Edwards D, Batley J, Snowdon RJ. Accessing complex crop genomes with next-generation sequencing. Theor Appl Genet. 2013;126(1):1–11.
17. Pareek CS, Smoczynski R, Tretyn A. Sequencing technologies and genome sequencing. J Appl Genet. 2011;52(4):413–35.
18. Abecasis GR, Altshuler D, Auton A, Brooks LD, Durbin RM, Gibbs RA, et al. A map of human genome variation from population-scale sequencing. Nature. 2010;467(7319):1061–73.
19. Xue Y, Wilcox WR. Changing paradigm of cancer therapy: precision medicine by next-generation sequencing. Cancer Biol Med. 2016;13(1):12–8.
20. Zheng-Bradley X, Flicek P. Applications of the 1000 genomes project resources. Brief Funct Genomics. 2016; pii: elw027. [Epub ahead of print]
21. Shringarpure SS, Carroll A, De La Vega FM, Bustamante CD. Inexpensive and highly reproducible cloud-based variant calling of 2,535 human genomes. PLoS One. 2015;10(6):e0129277.
22. Nagalakshmi U, Waern K, Snyder M. RNA-seq: a method for comprehensive transcriptome analysis. Curr Protoc Mol Biol (edited by Frederick M Ausubel [et al]). 2010;Chapter 4:Unit 4.11.1-3.
23. Mutz KO, Heilkenbrinker A, Lonne M, Walter JG, Stahl F. Transcriptome analysis using next-generation sequencing. Curr Opin Biotechnol. 2013;24(1):22–30.
24. Zhao S, Zhang B, Zhang Y, Gordon W, Du S, Paradis T, et al. Bioinformatics for RNA-Seq Data Analysis. In: Abdurakhmonov I, editor. Bioinformatics—Updated Features and Applications: InTech; 2016. pp. 125–49.
25. Picelli S. Single-cell RNA-sequencing: the future of genome biology is now. RNA Biol.2016;21:1–14.
26. Zhao S, Fung-Leung WP, Bittner A, Ngo K, Liu X. Comparison of RNA-seq and microarray in transcriptome profiling of activated T cells. PLoS One. 2014;9(1):e78644.

27. Byron SA, Van Keuren-Jensen KR, Engelthaler DM, Carpten JD, Craig DW. Translating RNA sequencing into clinical diagnostics: opportunities and challenges. Nat Rev Genet. 2016;17(5):257–71.
28. Zhao S, Xi L, Quan J, Xi H, Zhang Y, von Schack D, et al. QuickRNASeq lifts large-scale RNA-seq data analyses to the next level of automation and interactive visualization. BMC Genomics. 2016;17:39.
29. Hoeijmakers WA, Bartfai R, Stunnenberg HG. Transcriptome analysis using RNA-seq. Methods Mol Biol. 2013;923:221–39.
30. Stegle O, Teichmann SA, Marioni JC. Computational and analytical challenges in single-cell transcriptomics. Nat Rev Genet. 2015;16(3):133–45.
31. Jeong HM, Lee S, Chae H, Kim R, Kwon MJ, Oh E, et al. Efficiency of methylated DNA immunoprecipitation bisulphite sequencing for whole-genome DNA methylation analysis. Epigenomics. 2016;8(8):1061–77.
32. Li N, Ye M, Li Y, Yan Z, Butcher LM, Sun J, et al. Whole genome DNA methylation analysis based on high throughput sequencing technology. Methods. 2010;52(3):203–12.
33. Massie CE, Mills IG. Mapping protein-DNA interactions using ChIP-sequencing. Meth Mol Biol. 2012;809:157–73.
34. Nakato R, Shirahige K. Recent advances in ChIP-seq analysis: from quality management to whole-genome annotation. Brief Bioinformatics. 2016; pii: bbw023. [Epub ahead of print]
35. Clark K, Karsch-Mizrachi I, Lipman DJ, Ostell J, Sayers EW. GenBank. Nucleic Acids Res. 2016;44(D1):D67–72.
36. Qu H, Fang X. A brief review on the human encyclopedia of DNA elements (ENCODE) project. Genomics, Proteomics Bioinformatics. 2013;11(3):135–41.
37. Evani US, Challis D, Yu J, Jackson AR, Paithankar S, Bainbridge MN, et al. Atlas2 Cloud: a framework for personal genome analysis in the cloud. BMC Genomics. 2012;13(Suppl 6):S19.
38. Nguyen T, Shi W, Ruden D. CloudAligner: a fast and full-featured MapReduce based tool for sequence mapping. BMC Res Notes. 2011;4:171.
39. Schatz MC. CloudBurst: highly sensitive read mapping with MapReduce. Bioinformatics. 2009;25(11):1363–9.
40. Gurtowski J, Schatz MC, Langmead B. Genotyping in the cloud with crossbow. Genome Biol. 2009;10.
41. Langmead B, Schatz MC, Lin J, Pop M, Salzberg SL. Genotyping in the cloud with crossbow. Curr Protoc Bioinformatics (edited by Andreas D Baxevanis [et al]. 2012;Chapter 15:Unit15.3.
42. Hong D, Rhie A, Park SS, Lee J, Ju YS, Kim S, et al. FX: an RNA-seq analysis tool on the cloud. Bioinformatics. 2012;28(5):721–3.
43. Langmead B, Hansen KD, Leek JT. Cloud-scale RNA-sequencing differential expression analysis with Myrna. Genome Biol. 2010;11(8):R83.
44. Zhao S, Prenger K, Smith L. Stormbow: a cloud-based tool for reads mapping and expression quantification in large-scale RNA-seq studies. ISRN Bioinformatics. 2013;2013:481545.
45. Karczewski KJ, Fernald GH, Martin AR, Snyder M, Tatonetti NP, Dudley JT. STORMSeq: an open-source, user-friendly pipeline for processing personal genomics data in the cloud. PLoS One. 2014;9(1):e84860.
46. Souilmi Y, Lancaster AK, Jung JY, Rizzo E, Hawkins JB, Powles R, et al. Scalable and cost-effective NGS genotyping in the cloud. BMC Med Genomics. 2015;8:64.
47. Reid JG, Carroll A, Veeraraghavan N, Dahdouli M, Sundquist A, English A, et al. Launching genomics into the cloud: deployment of Mercury, a next generation sequence analysis pipeline. BMC Bioinformatics. 2014;15:30.
48. Feng X, Grossman R, Stein L. PeakRanger: a cloud-enabled peak caller for ChIP-seq data. BMC Bioinformatics. 2011;12:139.
49. Habegger L, Balasubramanian S, Chen DZ, Khurana E, Sboner A, Harmanci A, et al. VAT: a computational framework to functionally annotate variants in personal

genomes within a cloud-computing environment. Bioinformatics. 2012;28(17):2267–9.
50. Zhang L, Gu S, Liu Y, Wang B, Azuaje F. Gene set analysis in the cloud. Bioinformatics. 2012;28(2):294–5.
51. Chae H, Rhee S, Nephew KP, Kim S. BioVLAB-MMIA-NGS: microRNA-mRNA integrated analysis using high-throughput sequencing data. Bioinformatics. 2015;31(2):265–7.
52. Lee H, Yang Y, Chae H, Nam S, Choi D, Tangchaisin P, et al. BioVLAB-MMIA: a cloud environment for microRNA and mRNA integrated analysis (MMIA) on Amazon EC2. IEEE Trans Nanobioscience. 2012;11(3):266–72.
53. Naccache SN, Federman S, Veeraraghavan N, Zaharia M, Lee D, Samayoa E, et al. A cloud-compatible bioinformatics pipeline for ultrarapid pathogen identification from next-generation sequencing of clinical samples. Genome Res. 2014;24(7):1180–92.
54. Li H, Durbin R. Fast and accurate long-read alignment with Burrows-Wheeler transform. Bioinformatics. 2010;26(5):589–95.
55. McKenna A, Hanna M, Banks E, Sivachenko A, Cibulskis K, Kernytsky A, et al. The genome analysis toolkit: a MapReduce framework for analyzing next-generation DNA sequencing data. Genome Res. 2010;20(9):1297–303.
56. Krampis K, Booth T, Chapman B, Tiwari B, Bicak M, Field D, et al. CloudBioLinux: pre-configured and on-demand bioinformatics computing for the genomics community. BMC Bioinformatics. 2012;13:42.
57. Afgan E, Baker D, Coraor N, Chapman B, Nekrutenko A, Taylor J. Galaxy CloudMan: delivering cloud compute clusters. BMC Bioinformatics. 2010;11(Suppl 12):S4.
58. Bhuvaneshwar K, Sulakhe D, Gauba R, Rodriguez A, Madduri R, Dave U, et al. A case study for cloud based high throughput analysis of NGS data using the globus genomics system. Comput Struct Biotechnol J. 2015;13:64–74.
59. Madduri RK, Sulakhe D, Lacinski L, Liu B, Rodriguez A, Chard K, et al. Experiences building globus genomics: a next-generation sequencing analysis service using Galaxy, Globus, and Amazon Web Services. Concurr Comput. 2014;26(13):2266–79.
60. Taylor RC. An overview of the Hadoop/MapReduce/HBase framework and its current applications in bioinformatics. BMC Bioinformatics. 2010;11(Suppl 12):S1.
61. Langmead B, Trapnell C, Pop M, Salzberg SL. Ultrafast and memory-efficient alignment of short DNA sequences to the human genome. Genome Biol. 2009;10(3):R25.
62. Li R, Li Y, Fang X, Yang H, Wang J, Kristiansen K, et al. SNP detection for massively parallel whole-genome resequencing. Genome Res. 2009;19(6):1124–32.
63. Bragg L, Tyson GW. Metagenomics using next-generation sequencing. Meth Mol Biol. 2014;1096:183–201.
64. Marx V. Biology: the big challenges of big data. Nature. 2013;498(7453):255–60.
65. Fan J, Han F, Liu H. Challenges of big data analysis. Natl Sci Rev. 2014;1(2):293–314.
66. Mardis ER. The challenges of big data. Dis Models Mech. 2016;9(5):483–5.
67. Dobin A, Davis CA, Schlesinger F, Drenkow J, Zaleski C, Jha S, et al. STAR: ultrafast universal RNA-seq aligner. Bioinformatics. 2013;29(1):15–21.
68. Dobin A, Gingeras TR. Mapping RNA-seq Reads with STAR. Curr Protoc Bioinformatics (edited by Andreas D Baxevanis [et al]). 2015;51:11.4.1-9.
69. Dobin A, Gingeras TR. Optimizing RNA-seq mapping with STAR. Meth Molecular Biol. 2016;1415:245–62.
70. Zou Q, Li XB, Jiang WR, Lin ZY, Li GL, Chen K. Survey of MapReduce frame operation in bioinformatics. Brief Bioinformatics. 2014;15(4):637–47.
71. Mohammed EA, Far BH, Naugler C. Applications of the MapReduce programming framework to clinical big data analysis: current landscape and future trends. BioData Min. 2014;7:22.
72. Wiewiorka MS, Messina A, Pacholewska A, Maffioletti S, Gawrysiak P, Okoniewski MJ. SparkSeq: fast, scalable and cloud-ready tool for the interactive genomic data analysis with nucleotide precision. Bioinformatics. 2014;30(18):2652–3.

73. Abuin JM, Pichel JC, Pena TF, Amigo J. SparkBWA: speeding up the alignment of high-throughput DNA sequencing data. PLoS One. 2016;11(5):e0155461.
74. Yates A, Akanni W, Amode MR, Barrell D, Billis K, Carvalho-Silva D, et al. Ensembl 2016. Nucleic Acids Res. 2016;44(D1):D710-6.
75. Qu K, Garamszegi S, Wu F, Thorvaldsdottir H, Liefeld T, Ocana M, et al. Integrative genomic analysis by interoperation of bioinformatics tools in GenomeSpace. Nat Methods. 2016;13(3):245–7.
76. Aldeen YA, Salleh M, Aljeroudi Y. An innovative privacy preserving technique for incremental datasets on cloud computing. J Biomed Inform. 2016; 62:107–16.
77. Dove ES, Joly Y, Tasse AM, Knoppers BM. Genomic cloud computing: legal and ethical points to consider. Eur J Hum Genetics. 2015;23(10):1271–8.
78. Ortega VE, Meyers DA. Pharmacogenetics: implications of race and ethnicity on defining genetic profiles for personalized medicine. J Allergy Clin Immunol. 2014;133(1):16–26.
79. Rabbani B, Nakaoka H, Akhondzadeh S, Tekin M, Mahdieh N. Next generation sequencing: implications in personalized medicine and pharmacogenomics. Mol Biosyst. 2016;12(6):1818–30.

# CHAPTER 3

# An Automated System for Garment Texture Design Class Identification

**Emon Kumar Dey *, Md. Nurul Ahad Tawhid and Mohammad Shoyaib**

*Institute of Information Technology, University of Dhaka, Dhaka 1000, Bangladesh*

## ABSTRACT

Automatic identification of garment design class might play an important role in the garments and fashion industry. To achieve this, essential initial works are found in the literature. For example, construction of a garment database, automatic segmentation of garments from real life images, categorizing them into the type of garments such as shirts, jackets, tops, skirts, *etc*. It is now essential to find a system such that it will be possible to identify the particular design (printed, striped or single color) of garment product for an automated system to recommend the garment trends. In this paper, we have focused on this specific issue and thus propose two new descriptors namely Completed CENTRIST (cCENTRIST) and Ternary CENTRIST (tCENTRIST). To test these descriptors, we used two different publically available databases. The experimental results of these databases demonstrate that both cCENTRIST and tCENTRIST achieve nearly about 3% more accuracy than the existing state-of-the art methods.

**Keywords:** texture descriptor; garment categories; tCENTRIST; cCENTRIST; garment trend identification

# 1. INTRODUCTION

Garment selling companies as well as fashion industries have created an interesting research area in the field of image processing and pattern recognition. A company always wants to achieve a competitive advantage against its rivals for sustaining itself in the industry. Thus if a company somehow knows the current design trends and choices of people regarding their clothing, the company can adopt proper strategies and produce the clothes based on people choices. Besides this, online shopping is becoming very popular now a days. If a retailer knows which type of design for a particular garment is being bought by the consumers, they can increase their stock for that design. Thus, an automatic identification of design class is necessary. Such an automatic identification of garments trend can help different types of people.

Recently, garment related research has become popular [1,2,3,4,5]. Most of the works focus on the segmentation of garments from real life images. There are also a few works that identify the type of the garments such as which ones are shirts or jackets. Considering all of these are the essential initial works, now it is necessary to develop a system that can also identify the design class of the garments. Thus, all of these as a whole will help the industry or an owner of a retailer of an online shop. The overall flow of this work is shown in Figure 1.

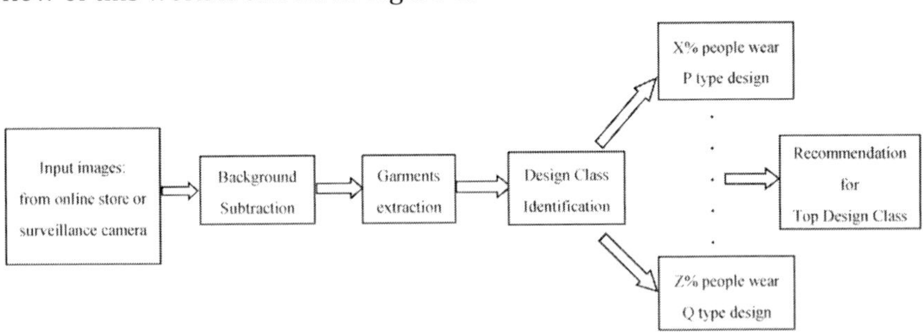


**Figure 1.** Prototype of proposed system.

To identify the design class of a garment product, it is necessary to analyze the texture of the product. For texture classification, there are several existing well known methods such as CENsus Transform hiSTogram (CENTRIST) [6], Local Binary Pattern (LBP) [7], Gabor [8],

Histogram of Oriented Gradient (HOG) [9], GIST [10] *etc*. Among those, LBP and CENTRIST are very similar and gain popularity for their computational simplicities and better accuracies. However, it is well known that LBP and CENTRIST are very sensitive to uniform and near uniform region. Variants of LBP like LTP [11] and Completed Local Binary Pattern (CLBP) [12] can handle this issue to some extent. To capture different orientations of a particular design, the features should be rotation invariant. Thus, CLBP might be a better choice in this regard. However, to categorize the garments product based on design class the global relation among the structural information is necessary. CENTRIST [6] has mostly gained this property by incorporating Spatial Pyramid (SP) structure. Thus, to incorporate the structural information, suppress detail texture information, stability in uniform or near uniform region and to achieve rotation invariance, we have proposed two different descriptors: Completed CENTRIST (cCENTRIST) and Ternary CENTRIST (tCENTRIST) and the major contributions of this paper are as follows:

i. We have introduced an automated system which can categorize garment products into some specific design classes,

ii. For capturing rotation invariant texture properties, we have proposed cCENTRIST and,

iii. Propose tCENTRIST, where there are no rotation invariant textures

The rest of the paper is organized as follows: Section 2 discusses the background studies; Section 3 describes the proposed method of our garments texture classification, Section 4 presents an experimental result of the approach and finally, Section 5 concludes the paper and summarizes the work.

# 2. BACKGROUND STUDIES

In this section, we will discuss the existing garment segmentation and their categorization strategies. We will also describe the existing descriptors that are used for texture based classification which might be used for garment design class identification.

## 2.1. Garment Product Segmentation and Type Identification

Gallagher *et al.* [1] segmented clothing from an image using grab cut algorithm [13] for recognizing a person. This method successfully extracted the region of interest (ROI); however, it is limited to the torso region only. Menfredi *et al.* [14] also proposed an approach for automatic segmentation of garments and classified them into nine different classes (such as shirts, dresses, skirts). For this, they first extracted the shape of a specific garment by using a projection histogram. After that, they divided the whole image into 117 cells (9 × 13 grids) and grouped them into partially overlapped blocks of 3 × 3 cells. The orientations are quantized into nine bins to compute the HOG features [15] in each cell. They used multiclass linear support vector for training by concatenating the projection histogram and HOG features. Similar recent works can be found in [5] where, the authors used conditional random field (CRF) for parsing outfits. Bourdev *et al.* [16] in their research proposed a method for recognizing attributes such as gender, hair style and types of clothes such as t-shirts, pants, jeans shorts *etc.* from an input image. For this, they created a dataset consisting of 8000 people with annotated attributes. Yamaguchi *et al.* [2] proposed a method for parsing clothes from fashion photographs. They introduced a dataset (Fashionista Dataset), which consisted of 158,235 photographs and then selected 685 photos that had good visibility of the whole body and covered a variety of clothing items. For training and testing, they used these 685 images and associated text annotation with the labeling of the images by identifying 14 different parts of a body and different clothing regions. To identify the clothes, they firstly detected the pose of a person from an input image using a method described in [17] and then they detected similar types of clothing from the dataset. Kalantidis *et al.* [3] proposed an approach, which can automatically suggest relevant clothing products. When an input image is given, they estimate the pose of the person using the same method used in [2]. After that, they segment the clothing area, which is followed by the extraction of clothing class (such as shirt, tops *etc.*). Lastly, they apply an image retrieval technique to retrieve the visually similar clothes for each class, which is 50 times faster than [2]. Recently, to find the three different visual trends, namely floral print, pastel color and neon color from runway to street fashion, the authors in [4] used five different features such as color, texture, shape, parse and style descriptor. They produced inspiring results in several areas such as season, year, brand and the influence of runway collection to three potential visual trends—two colors (neon and pastel) and a design class (floral print). However, it would be more beneficial in this field, if more color and design classes could be incorporated.

## 2.2. Texture Based Classification

For texture based classification, there are several existing well known methods such as Wavelets transform [18], Gabor filters [19], Scale-invariant feature transform (SIFT) [20], HOG [9,15], LBP [7] features. Recently, LBP is considered as an effective texture classification methodology which was proposed for describing the local structure of an image. LBP and its variants can be uniform and/or rotation invariant [21] and have been extensively exploited in many applications, for instance, facial image analysis, including face detection [22,23,24,25], face recognition and facial expression analysis [26,27,28,29,30,31,32,33,34]; demographic (gender, race, age, *etc.*) classification [35,36,37,38]; moving object detection [39], *etc.* The major reasons behind the popularity of LBP based methods are their computational simplicity, robustness against monotonic illumination variation and better performance in several areas. However, LBP is very sensitive in uniform and near uniform regions, which makes its code unstable in most of the cases [11]. In the last few years, lots of efforts have been invested in LBP based methodology to improve its performance and fit it with different applications such as derivative-based LBP [40], dominant LBP [41], center-symmetric LBP [42], *etc.* Tan and Triggs proposed Local Ternary Patterns (LTP), which use three-value encoding and shows tolerance to noise up to a certain level [11]. They assumed noises in an image vary within a fixed threshold (±5). With this assumption, the authors in [11] made LTP more discriminant and less sensitive to noise in a uniform region. There exist few other proposals that also handle noises in different application areas, such as the methods described in [43,44,45]. Among them, one of the recent texture based face detection proposal is Local Gradient Pattern (LGP), which is a variant of LBP and uses adaptive threshold for code generation [45]. Apart from sign information (as in LBP), Completed Local Binary Pattern (CLBP) is proposed by Zenhua *et al.* which incorporates sign, magnitude and center pixel information [12]. This is rotation invariant and capable of handling the fluctuation of intensity. Jianxin *et al.* [6] proposed CENsus Transform hiSTogram (CENTRIST) which is very similar to LBP and was proposed mainly as a visual descriptor for recognizing topological places or scene categories. In order to capture the global structure of an image on larger scales, CENTRIST proposes a spatial representation based on a Spatial Pyramid Matching Scheme (SPM) [46], which is a collection of orderless feature histograms computed over cells defined by multi-level recursive image decomposition. CENTRIST uses a total of 31 blocks, which helps to avoid the artifacts created by the non-overlapping blocks in the traditional SP. Among them, 25 blocks come from level 2, five blocks from level 1 and one block from level 0. The SPM construction mechanism is shown in Figure 2.

So far, we have discussed several feature extraction methods, which are proposed to be used with different types of classifiers for solving various types of applications. Among them, different kernels of the Support

Vector Machine (SVM) [47] are popular for their better performances. In recent times, Deep Learning [48,49] has become popular for various classification problems such as speech [48,49], digit [49] and object recognition [50]. Unlike Artificial Neural Networks, it uses many levels to represent highly nonlinear and highly varying functions. Usually, Deep Learning requires a large amount of training data to build the model from scratch and a number of training iterations for better performance [51,52,53].

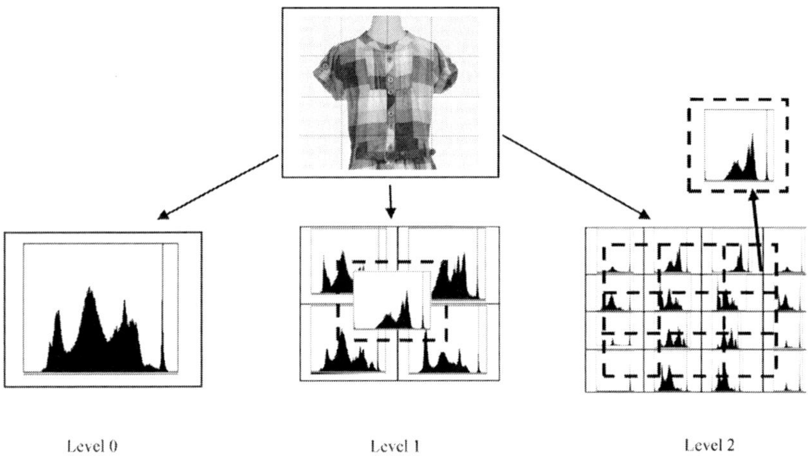


**Figure 2.** An example of Spatial Pyramid Representation.

## 2.3. A Brief Description of Texture Descriptors

Our cCENTRIST and tCENTRIST mainly adopt the idea from CLBP, CENTRIST and LTP. We thus provide a brief description on these three descriptors.

### 2.3.1. CLBP (Completed Local Binary Pattern)

CLBP considers both the signs (CLBP_S) and the magnitude (CLBP_M) information that come from the differences between a pixel and its neighbors. They also generate a binary code (CLBP_C) for the center pixel by global thresholding. Figure 3 shows the framework of CLBP.

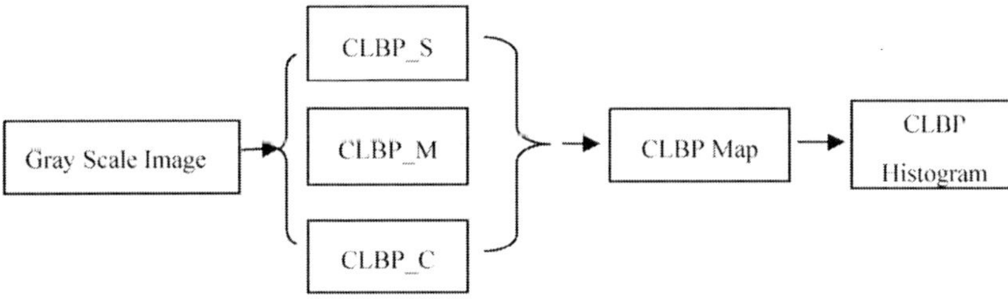


**Figure 3.** CLBP framework.

Figure 4 shows an example for calculating CLBP_S and CLBP_M components. Figure 4a shows the original 3 × 3 image. Figure 4b shows the differences ($d_P$) between each neighboring pixel to the central pixel. This difference is represented by a vector $[d_0,...,d_{P-1}]$. $d_P$ is further decomposed into two components following Equation (1).

| | | |
|---|---|---|
| 19 | 12 | 35 |
| 20 | 25 | 27 |
| 59 | 64 | 56 |

(a)

| | | |
|---|---|---|
| −6 | −13 | 10 |
| −5 | | 2 |
| 34 | 39 | 29 |

(b)

| | | |
|---|---|---|
| −1 | −1 | 1 |
| −1 | | 1 |
| 1 | 1 | 1 |

(c)

| | | |
|---|---|---|
| 6 | 13 | 10 |
| 5 | | 2 |
| 34 | 39 | 29 |

(d)

**Figure 4.** Calculating CLBP_S and CLBP_M; (**a**): 3 × 3 block; (**b**): local difference; (**c**) the sign (CLBP_S); (**d**) magnitude (CLBP_M).

$$d_p = S_P \times m_P \; and \begin{cases} S_P = sign(d_P) \\ m_p = |d_P| \end{cases} \quad (1)$$

Here, $S_P = 1$ when $d_P \geq 0$ otherwise $S_P = -1$. Figure 4c,d shows the result of Equation (1). CLBP_M converted as a binary number format by the

Equation (4) and each −1 is replaced by a 0 in CLBP_S. Equations (2)-(4) shows the calculation of CLBP_C, CLBP_S and CLBP_M.

$$CLBP_{C_{P,R}} = t(g_c, c), t(x,c) = \begin{cases} 1, x \geq c \\ 0, x < c \end{cases} \quad (2)$$

$$CLBP\_S_{P,R} = \sum_{P=0}^{P-1} s(g_p - g_c)2^P, s(x) = \begin{cases} 1, x \geq 0 \\ 0, x < 0 \end{cases} \quad (3)$$

$$CLBP\_M_{P,R} = \sum_{P=0}^{P-1} t(m_p, c)2^P, t(x,c) = \begin{cases} 1, x \geq c \\ 0, x < c \end{cases} \quad (4)$$

Here, $c$ is a threshold, which might be calculated as the average of the whole image. $P$ and $R$ are the number of neighbors and the radius of LBP code. It is noteworthy to mention here that CLBP considers uniform and rotation invariant code. Thus, the size of the histogram of CLBP_S and CLBP_M and CLBP_C are 10, 10 and 2 respectively. To calculate the feature vector using CLBP, a 3D histogram is constructed using CLBP_C, CLBP_S and CLBP_M. If we consider only CLBP_S and construct a histogram, then it will become the original LBP.

### 2.3.2. Centrist

CENTRIST [6] is based on the concept of Census Transform (CT) proposed by R. Zabih *et al.* [54]. It is a non-parametric local transform technique that maps a pixel by comparing intensity value with its eight neighboring pixels and produces an eight bit string (CT values). LBP also use the similar strategy. The only difference is that LBP performs interpolation while considering the corner pixels but CENTRIST considers the corner pixel as is. An example of CT calculation is given in Figure 5.

| | | |
|---|---|---|
| 45 | 46 | 47 |
| 35 | 50 | 1 |
| 70 | 89 | 99 |

⇨

| | | |
|---|---|---|
| 1 | 1 | 1 |
| 1 | | 1 |
| 0 | 0 | 0 |

⇨ $(11111000)_2$ ⇨ CT value ⇨ $(248)_{10}$

**Figure 5.** Example of Census Transform (CT).

CENTRIST uses a histogram of the CT values of image patches for an image to capture both the global and local information. To capture the global structure of an image, they also used spatial representation based on Spatial Pyramid Matching (SPM) scheme, that divides an image into sub regions and integrate correspondence result in those regions, which improves recognition.

### 2.3.3. Local Ternary Pattern (LTP)

Local Ternary Pattern (LTP) [11] follows the same spirit of LBP. LTP introduces a new bit to manage the fluctuations of intensity. Thus, LTP becomes a ternary code at a pixel *c*, which is generated by the following Equation (5):

$$LTP_{n,r}(x_c, y_c) = \sum_{l=0}^{n-1} q(g_l - g_c)3^l \ , q(a) = \begin{cases} 1 \ if \ a \geq \mu \\ -1 \ if \ a < \mu \\ 0 \ otherwise \end{cases} \quad (5)$$

Here, μ is a threshold value which is ±5. An LTP code is usually split into two binary codes (upper pattern and lower pattern) to reduce the size of the feature vector. Two histograms are created separately and then concatenated to represent the feature vector of an image.

## 3. PROPOSED METHOD

An image can be obtained from a camera installed in a public place or from an online shop. These captured images can be segmented to obtain garment information and their type by using the method described in [14]. The proposed descriptors are then applied to classify them into different design classes. Two new descriptors namely, Completed CENTRIST (cCENTRIST) and Ternary CENTRIST (tCENTRIST) are proposed in this regard. These descriptors are a fusion of Completed Local Binary Pattern (CLBP), Local Ternary Pattern (LTP) and CENsus TRanformed hISTogram (CENTRIST). In Section 2, we have described CLBP and CENTRIST and LTP. In this section, we will describe how we have combined them to produce a better result of garment design class categorization. Figure 6 shows the block diagram of our proposed method.

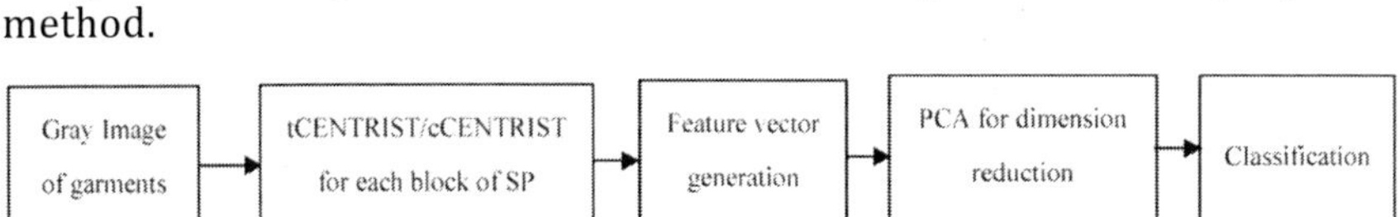


**Figure 6.** Proposed method for garments texture classification.

## 3.1. Completed CENTRIST (cCENTRIST)

cCENTRIST is the combination of CLBP and CENTRIST. For generating features (CT values), unlike LBP, we consider the corner pixel as is. Again, like LBP, we introduce uniform and rotation invariant code of CT considering sign, magnitude and center pixel information. A spatial pyramid (SP) structure is adopted and for each block of SP, a 3D histogram is constructed and the histograms of all these blocks are concatenated. To reduce the dimension of the feature vector, Principle Component Analysis (PCA) is then applied and the final feature vector is constructed, which is then used for garment design class identification. For classification, we have used Support Vector Machine (SVM). Algorithm 1 combines CLBP and CENTRIST to produce the proposed cCENTRIST.

---

**Algorithm1:**

**Input:**Gray scale image $I$

**Output:**Feature vector of $I$

1. For each image $I$, calculate level 2 Spatial Pyramid (SP)
2. **For** each block of SP
    a. Calculate $CLBP\_S_{P,R}$, $CLBP\_M_{P,R}$ and $CLBP\_C_{P,R}$
    b. Construct a 3D histogram (using $CLBP\_S_{P,R}$, $CLBP\_M_{P,R}$ and $CLBP\_C_{P,R}$)

   **End For**
3. Concatenate all histograms and apply PCA to extract M feature points from each block
4. Combine N blocks for constructing a feature vector of length M × N for the input image.

---

## 3.2. Ternary CENTRIST (tCENTRIST)

For generating tCENTRIST, we also adopt SP. For each block of SP, we calculate Local Ternary Pattern (LTP) and construct two histograms—one for upper code and another for lower code of LTP. These two histograms are then concatenated to build a single histogram. Finally, histograms for all blocks are combined and PCA is applied for dimension reduction which gives us the final feature vector for an image. SVM is also used here for classification. Algorithm 2 describes this process.

---

**Algorithm 2:**

**Input:** Gray scale image $I$
**Output:** Feature vectors of $I$

1. For each image $I$, calculate level 2 Spatial Pyramid (SP)
2. **For** each block of SP
   a. calculate LTP
   b. Construct histogram of LTP

   **End For**
3. Concatenate all histograms and apply PCA to extract M feature vector from each block
4. Combine N blocks to construct $M \times N$ feature for each image.

---

# 4. EXPERIMENTS

In this section, we first describe our datasets followed by the training and testing protocol. Finally, experimental results with necessary discussion will be presented.

## 4.1. Dataset

Firstly, we used a publicly available dataset (http://imagelab.ing. unimore.it/ fashion_dataset.asp, Fashion Dataset) which was originally created for Garment Product Recognition [14]. We have manually categorized them into three familiar design classes namely "single color" (2440 images), "Print" (1141 images) and "stripe" (636 images). Figure 7 shows the example dataset. Besides this, we also used the "Clothing Attribute Dataset" [55] for evaluating our proposed method. The original dataset contain 1856 images, and there are different basic design classes such as Floral, Graphics, Plaid, Spotted, Striped and Solid pattern that we have used in our experiments. After that, we manually extracted the garment area of each image and reconstructed the dataset by 1575 images with six different categories of cloth images (69 floral images, 110 graphics images, 105 plaid images, 100 spotted images, 140 striped images and 1051 solid pattern images). Figure 8 shows the example images of "Clothing Attribute Dataset" used in our work.

## 4.2. Training and Testing Protocol

For "Fashion Dataset," we have divided each garment class into training and testing set where100 randomly selected images are taken as training from each of the classes, and rest of the images are considered as testing data. Thus, for training, 300 images are used and the rest of the 3917 images are used for test. This process is repeated five times. For

"Clothing Attribute Dataset" we consider 50 random images from each of the six categories as training and rest are as testing data. For evaluating the performance, we also considered the overall *accuracy, Recall, Precision, F_Measure* which are defined in Equations (6)–(9).

$$accuracy = \frac{number\ correctly\ detected \times 100}{total\ number} \% \quad (6)$$

**Figure 7.** Example dataset: First row is the example of Print category, Second row is for Single color and Third row contains Stripe category.

$$Recall_i = \frac{M_{ii}}{\sum_j M_{ij}} \quad (7)$$

$$Precision_i = \frac{M_{ii}}{\sum_j M_{ji}} \tag{8}$$

$$F_{Measure(i)} = \frac{2 \times Recall_i \times Precision_i}{Recall_i + Precision_i} \tag{9}$$

Here, Mii = Number of correct detection of class *i* as class *i*; Mij = Total number of detection of class *i* as class *i* and *j*; Mji = Number of detection of class *j* detected as class *i* and *j*.

**Figure 8.** Example dataset: Column 1 to 6 represents example of Floral, Graphics, Plaid, Solid Color, Spotted and Striped garments respectively.

## 4.3. Experimental Result and Discussion

We have proposed two different methods, namely cCENTRIST and tCENTRIST for feature extraction. Both of these are compared here to the original CENTRIST, HOG, LGP and GIST feature extraction technique. Table 1 shows the accuracy of experimental results using linear kernel of SVM. We have also calculated the results by taking the square root of the feature vector (Power Kernel) before applying linear kernel. We found the HOG descriptor shows an average of 78.61% accuracy when combining it with SPM structure (we use the default parameter settings of the source code: http://www.mathworks. com/ matlabcentral/fileexchange/28689-hog-descriptor-for-matlab, and as described in [9]). It is noteworthy to mention here that, without using SPM, the accuracy is only 61.22%. We have also compared our results with GIST [10], which is very successful for scene recognition and achieved very competitive results for design class classification.

Table 1 and Figure 9 show the comparison of six different methods and from here it is clear that the proposed tCENTRIST and cCENTRIST perform better than HOG, LGP, GIST and original CENTRIST in Fashion Dataset for most of the categories. Both of the proposed descriptors perform better and the average accuracies are at least 2.5% better than the original proposals.

**Table 1.** Experimental results of different methods for Fashion Dataset.

| | | Print (%) | Single Color (%) | Stripe (%) | Average(%) |
|---|---|---|---|---|---|
| HoG | Linear | 82.32 | 84.44 | 68.09 | 78.28 |
| | Power+Linear | 82.98 | 85.48 | 69.01 | 79.15 |
| GIST | Linear | 81.47 | 92.77 | 67.35 | 80.53 |
| | Power+Linear | 82.20 | 94.34 | 68.48 | 81.67 |
| LGP | Linear | 82.51 | 83.45 | 65.85 | 77.27 |
| | Power+Linear | 77.58 | 85.58 | 76.22 | 79.79 |
| CENTRIST | Linear | 81.51 | 83.50 | 73.72 | 79.58 |
| | Power+Linear | 81.52 | 81.73 | 75.12 | 79.72 |
| tCENTRIST | Linear | 85.95 | 88.44 | 75.90 | 83.43 |
| | Power+Linear | 88.22 | 87.80 | 76.20 | 84.07 |
| cCENTRIST | Linear | 86.82 | 89.62 | 75.96 | 84.13 |
| | Power+Linear | 86.70 | 89.76 | 75.24 | 84.23 |

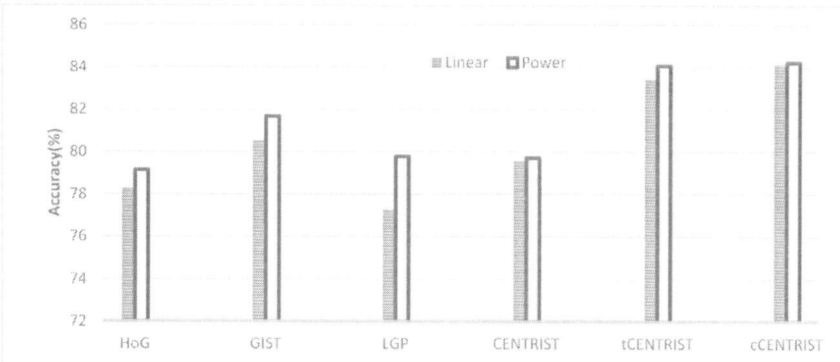


**Figure 9.** Comparison of the existing methods with the proposed methods.

tCENTRIST perform 88.22% accurately for identifying "Print" category which is better than cCENTRIST whereas cCENTRIST performs better for identifying "Single color" category. In every case, the accuracy of "Stripe" category is much less than "Print" and "Single color" category. Again, cCENTRIST performs superior to the tCENTRIST, which is logical. Because the rotation invariance property of CLBP helps to capture differently oriented Print and Stripe design as a same type of Print and Stripe class. In contrast, tCENTRIST do not have any rotation invariant capability. For this reason it might mislead the classification. If we consider more granular division of class such as vertical, horizontal and diagonal orientation of stripe as three different classes of garments then tCENTRIST will perform better.

We have performed five fold cross validations for generating results as we mentioned before. For each round, we calculate the average accuracy of three classes which is shown on Figure 10, where R1, R2, ..., R5 represents results of five different rounds. The most stable output is obtained for cCENTRIST, whereas the most fluctuated result is obtained for LGP, which also advocates the robustness of our proposed method.

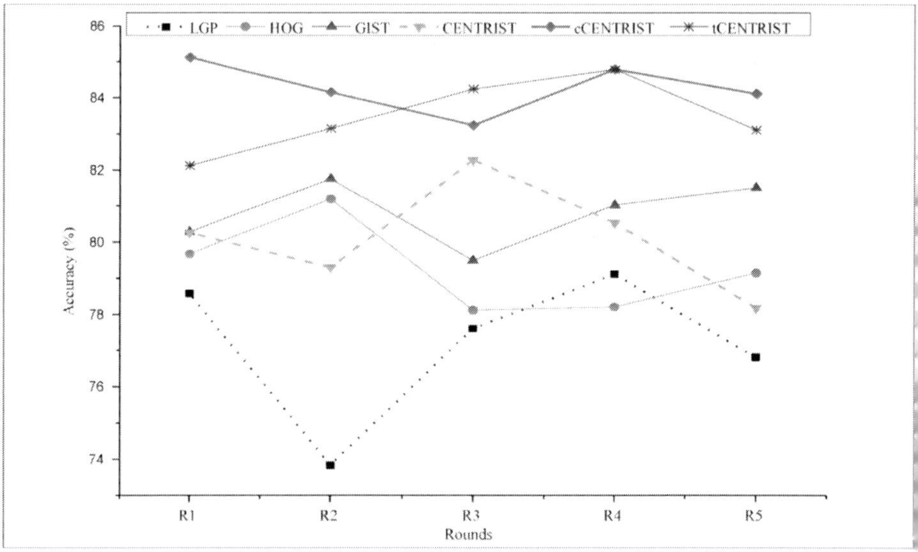


**Figure 10.** Round wise comparison of the existing methods with the proposed methods.

Table 2, Table 3 and Table 4 show the confusion matrix of cCENTRIST and tCENTRIST and CENTRIST using power kernel followed by linear kernel of SVM and using only linear kernel of SVM on Fashion Dataset. Here, each cell represents the number of images. Table 5 and Table 6 shows the result of *Recall, Precision* and *F_Measure* for the same setup; where, Recall, Precision and F_Measure are calculated by Equations (7)–(9).

**Table 2.** Confusion Matrix of cCENTRISTon Fashion Dataset.

| | | Using Power Kernel | | | Using Linear Kernel | | |
|---|---|---|---|---|---|---|---|
| | | Predicted Class | | | Predicted Class | | |
| | | **Print** | **Single** | **Stripe** | **Print** | **Single** | **Stripe** |
| Actual Class | Print | 882 | 106 | 53 | 805 | 159 | 77 |
| | Single | 220 | 2035 | 85 | 197 | 1979 | 164 |
| | Stripe | 62 | 34 | 440 | 62 | 54 | 420 |

**Table 3.** Confusion Matrix of tCENTRIST on Fashion Dataset.

| | | Using Power Kernel Predicted Class | | | Using Linear Kernel Predicted Class | | |
|---|---|---|---|---|---|---|---|
| | | Print | Single | Stripe | Print | Single | Stripe |
| Actual Class | Print | 893 | 72 | 76 | 883 | 103 | 55 |
| | Single | 252 | 1950 | 138 | 218 | 2072 | 50 |
| | Stripe | 40 | 51 | 445 | 51 | 75 | 410 |

**Table 4.** Confusion Matrix of CENTRIST on Fashion Dataset.

| | | Using Power Kernel Predicted Class | | | Using Linear Kernel Predicted Class | | |
|---|---|---|---|---|---|---|---|
| | | Print | Single | Stripe | Print | Single | Stripe |
| Actual Class | Print | 876 | 105 | 60 | 779 | 178 | 84 |
| | Single | 329 | 1915 | 96 | 197 | 1989 | 154 |
| | Stripe | 75 | 81 | 380 | 72 | 65 | 399 |

**Table 5.** Results of three different descriptors using Power Kernel followed by Linear Kernel of SVM on Fashion Dataset.

| | cCENTRIST | | | tCENTRIST | | | CENTRIST | | |
|---|---|---|---|---|---|---|---|---|---|
| | Print | Single | Stripe | Print | Single | Stripe | Print | Single | Stripe |
| **Recall** | 0.85 | 0.87 | 0.75 | 0.86 | 0.84 | 0.80 | 0.84 | 0.81 | 0.70 |
| **Precision** | 0.75 | 0.93 | 0.76 | 0.75 | 0.94 | 0.67 | 0.68 | 0.91 | 0.71 |
| **F_Measure** | 0.80 | 0.90 | 0.78 | 0.80 | 0.88 | 0.73 | 0.75 | 0.86 | 0.70 |

**Table 6.** Result of three different descriptors using only Linear Kernel on Fashion Dataset.

| | cCENTRIST | | | tCENTRIST | | | CENTRIST | | |
|---|---|---|---|---|---|---|---|---|---|
| | Print | Single | Stripe | Print | Single | Stripe | Print | Single | Stripe |
| **Recall** | 0.78 | 0.85 | 0.79 | 0.84 | 0.88 | 0.70 | 0.74 | 0.84 | 0.71 |
| **Precision** | 0.76 | 0.91 | 0.64 | 0.76 | 0.91 | 0.77 | 0.73 | 0.89 | 0.60 |
| **F_Measure** | 0.77 | 0.88 | 0.71 | 0.80 | 0.89 | 0.73 | 0.74 | 0.86 | 0.65 |

Analyzing Table 2, Table 3, Table 4, Table 5 and Table 6, it becomes evident that the proposed descriptors clearly outperform the current state-of-the-art methods, namely CENTRIST on Fashion Dataset. To validate the proposed methods further, we used the "Clothing Attribute Dataset" [55] described on Section 4.1 and Section 4.2. Table 7 shows the experimental results using different feature extraction methods along with our proposed methods in this dataset. It is noteworthy to point out here that we used HOG and LGP features along with SPM structure and used GIST (http://people.csail.mit.edu/torralba/code/spatialenvelope/) as is (without SPM) to meet the spirit of GIST. From Table 7, it is clear that performance of GIST is close to our proposed methods, which is also observed for the previous dataset. Performance of HOG was better in Fashion Dataset, whereas it showed less accuracy in Clothing Attribute Dataset. Again, although LGP used adaptive threshold and showed better performance in face detection, its performance is much lower compared to ours for garment dataset.

**Table 7.** Experimental results using a clothing attribute dataset.

| Methods | Accuracy (%) |
|---|---|
| HOG | 63.76 ±1.20 |
| GIST | 72.31 ±1.59 |
| LGP | 65.55 ± 0.87 |
| CENTRIST | 71.97 ±1.34 |
| tCENTRIST | 74.48 ±2.08 |
| cCENTRIST | 74.97 ± 1.67 |

Instead of handcrafted features like LBP and HOG, deep learning has recently shown inspiring results in many application areas. Even though deep learning requires a large amount of training data to build the model from scratch, it is possible to train with a small amount of data by fine-tuning a pre-trained model (similar to the target application, such as *CaffeNet* [56] for garment texture design class) on the target data, which is demonstrated in the existing literature [53]. Following a straightforward process (https://gist.github.com/jimgoo/ 0179e523 05ca768a601f;http://caffe.berkeleyvision.org/model_zoo.html), we fine tuned the *CaffeNet* for "Clothing Attribute Dataset". In this case, we used 60 images from different classes for training (10 images from each class), 60 images for validation purpose and the remaining 1455 images for testing the dataset. We applied 50,000 iterations with the default settings (e.g., learning rate and batch size) and changed the parameter (num_output: 6) in the layer fc8 and obtained 73.54% accuracy. However, it might be possible to improve the accuracy by changing the layers and other related issues which might be a good research area in this regard.

# 5. CONCLUSIONS

In this paper, we have proposed Completed CENsus Transform hISTogram (cCENTRIST) and Ternary CENsus Transform hISTogram (tCENTRIST) for identifying garment design class. Using two different datasets consisting of three and six classes, we have shown that our proposed tCENTRIST and cCENTRIST perform better than several state-of-the-art methods and cCENTRIST shows slightly better results than tCENTRIST. These descriptors can also be applicable to classify larger categories of design class. Furthermore, these two descriptors can also be used for other vision based classifications such as scene and object recognition.

Like original CENTRIST, our proposed cCENTRIST used gray scale images. We believe that incorporation of color information will increase the overall accuracy, which we will also address in future.

# CONTRIBUTIONS

All authors contributed equally to this work, and have read and approved the final manuscript.

# CONFLICTS OF INTEREST

The authors declare no conflict of interest.

# REFERENCES

1. Gallagher, A.C.; Chen, T. Clothing cosegmentation for recognizing people. In Proceedings of the 2008 IEEE Conference on Computer Vision and Pattern Recognition (CVPR), Anchorage, AK, USA, 23–28 June 2008.
2. Yamaguchi, K.; Kiapour, M.H.; Ortiz, L.E.; Berg, T.L. Parsing clothing in fashion photographs. In Proceedings of the2012 IEEE Conference on Computer Vision and Pattern Recognition (CVPR), Providence, RI, USA, 16–21 June 2012; pp. 3570–3577.
3. Kalantidis, Y.; Kennedy, L.; Li, L.-J. Getting the look: Clothing recognition and segmentation for automatic product suggestions in everyday photos. In Proceedings

of the 3rd ACM Conference on International Conference on Multimedia Retrieval, Dallas, TX, USA, 16–20 April 2013.
4. Vittayakorn, S.; Yamaguchi, K.; Berg, A.C.; Berg, T.L. Runway to realway: Visual analysis of fashion. In Proceedings of the 2015 IEEE Winter Conference on Applications of Computer Vision (WACV), Waikoloa, HI, USA, 5–9 January 2015; pp. 951–958.
5. Edgar, S.-S.; Fidler, S.; Moreno-Noguer, F.; Urtasun, R. A High Performance CRF Model for Clothes Parsing. In Proceedings of the12th Asian Conference on Computer Vision—ACCV 2014, Singapore, Singapore, 1–5 November 2014.
6. Wu, J.; Rehg, J.M. CENTRIST: A visual descriptor for scene categorization. IEEE Trans. Pattern Anal. Mach. Intell. 2011, 33, 1489–1501.
7. Ojala, T.; Pietikainen, M.; Maenpaa, T. Multiresolution gray-scale and rotation invariant texture classification with local binary patterns. IEEE Trans. Pattern Anal. Mach. Intell. 2002, 24, 971–987.
8. Arivazhagan, S.; Ganesan, L.; Priyal, P.S. Texture classification using Gabor wavelets based rotation invariant features. Pattern Recognit. Lett. 2006, 27, 1976–1982.
9. Ludwig, O.; Delgado, D.; Goncalves, V.; Nunes, U. Trainable Classifier-Fusion Schemes: An Application to Pedestrian Detection. In Proceedings of the 12th International IEEE Conference On Intelligent Transportation Systems, St. Louis, MO, USA, 4–7 October 2009; Volume 1, pp. 432–437.
10. Aude, O.; Torralba, A. Modeling the shape of the scene: A holistic representation of the spatial envelope. Int. J. Comput. Vis.2001, 42, 145–175.
11. Tan, X.; Bill, T. Enhanced local texture feature sets for face recognition under difficult lighting conditions. IEEE Trans. Image Process. 2010, 19, 1635–1650.
12. Guo, Z.; Zhang, D. A completed modeling of local binary pattern operator for texture classification. IEEE Trans. Image Process.2010, 19, 1657–1663.
13. Rother, C.; Kolmogorov, V.; Blake, A. Grabcut: Interactive foreground extraction using iterated graph cuts. TOG 2004, 23, 309–314.
14. Manfredi, M.; Grana, C.; Calderara, S.; Cucchiara, R. A complete system for garment segmentation and color classification. Mach. Vis. Appl. 2014, 25, 955–969.
15. Dalal, N.; Triggs, B. Histograms of oriented gradients for human detection. In Proceedings of the 2005 IEEE Conference on Computer Vision and Pattern Recognition (CVPR), San Diego, CA, USA, 25 June 2005; pp. 886–893.
16. Bourdev, L.; Maji, S.; Malik, J. Describing people: A poselet-based approach to attribute classification. In Proceedings of the 2011 IEEE International Conference on Computer Vision (ICCV), Barcelona, Spain, 6–13 November 2011.
17. Yi, Y.; Ramanan, D. Articulated pose estimation with flexible mixtures-of-parts. In Proceedings of the 2011 IEEE Conference on Computer Vision and Pattern Recognition (CVPR), Colorado Springs, CO, USA, 20–25 June 2011; pp. 1385–1392.
18. Arivazhagan, S.; Ganesan, L. Texture classification using wavelet transform. Pattern Recognit. Lett. 2003, 24, 1513–1521.
19. Arivazhagan, S.; Ganesan, L.; Padam, P.S. Texture classification using Gabor wavelets based rotation invariant features. Pattern Recognit. Lett. 2006, 27, 1976–1982.
20. Warren, C.; Hamarneh, G. SIFT—Scale Invariant Feature Transform. IEEE Trans. Image Process. 2009, 18, 2012–2021.
21. Guo, Z.; Zhang, L.; Zhang, D. Rotation invariant texture classification using LBP variance (LBPV) with global matching. Pattern Recognit. 2010, 43, 706–719.
22. Hadid, A.; Pietikainen, M.; Ahonen, T. A discriminative feature space for detecting and recognizing faces. In Proceedings of the 2004 IEEE Conference on Computer Vision and Pattern Recognition (CVPR), Washington, DC, USA, 27 June–2 July 2004; pp. 797–804.
23. Jin, H.; Liu, Q.; Lu, H.; Tong, X. Face detection using improved LBP under Bayesian framework. In Proceedings of the Third International Conference on Image and Graphics (ICIG), Hong Kong, China, 18–20 December 2004; pp. 306–309.

24. Zhang, L.; Chu, R.; Xiang, S.; Li, S.Z. Face detection based on Multi-Block LBP representation. In Proceedings of the International Conference on Advances in Biometrics (ICB), Seoul, Korea, 27–29 August 2007; pp. 11–18.
25. Zhang, H.; Zhao, D. Spatial histogram features for face detection in color images. In Proceedings of the Advances in Multimedia Information Processing: Pacific Rim Conference on Multimedia, Tokyo, Japan, 30 November–3 December 2004; pp. 377–384.
26. Li, S.Z.; Zhao, C.; Ao, M.; Lei, Z. Learning to fuse 3D+2D based face recognition at both feature and decision levels. In Proceedings of the Second International Workshop on Analysis and Modeling of Faces and Gestures (AMFG), Beijing, China, 16 October 2005; pp. 44–54.
27. Zhao, J.; Wang, H.; Ren, H.; Kee, S.-C. LBP discriminant analysis for face verification. In Proceedings of the 2005 IEEE Conference on Computer Vision and Pattern Recognition (CVPR), San Diego, CA, USA, 25 June 2005; p. 167.
28. Shan, C.; Gong, S.; McOwan, P.W. Facial expression recognition based on local binary patterns: A comprehensive study. Image Vis. Comput. 2009, 27, 803–816.
29. Feng, X.; Hadid, A.; Pietikainen, M. A coarse-to-fine classification scheme for facial expression recognition. In Proceedings of the International Conference on Image Analysis and Recognition (ICIAR), Porto, Portugal, 29 September–1 October 2004; pp. 668–675.
30. Liao, S.; Fan, W.; Chung, A.C.S.; Yeung, D.Y. Facial expression recognition using advanced local binary patterns, Tsallis entropies and global appearance features. In Proceedings of the IEEE International Conference on Image Processing (ICIP), Atlanta, GA, USA, 8–11 October 2006; pp. 665–668.
31. Zhao, G.; Pietikainen, M. Experiments with facial expression recognition using spatiotemporal local binary patterns. In Proceedings of the 2007 IEEE International Conference on Multimedia and Expo (ICME), Beijing, China, 2–5July 2007; pp. 1091–1094.
32. Shoyaib, M.; Youl, J.M.; Alam, M.M.; Chae, O. Facial expression recognition based on a weighted local binary pattern. In Proceedings of the 2010 13th International Conference on Computer and Information Technology (ICCIT), Dhaka, Bangladesh, 23–25 December 2010; pp. 321–324.
33. Ibrahim, M.; Alam Efat, M.I.; Khaled, S.M.; Shoyaib, M. Face verification with fully dynamic size blocks based on landmark detection. In Proceedings of the 2014 International Conference on Informatics, Electronics & Vision (ICIEV), Dhaka, Bangladesh, 23–24 May 2014; pp. 1–5.
34. Ibrahim, M.; Alam Efat, M.I.; Kayesh, S.H.; Khaled, S.M.; Shoyaib, M.; Abdullah-Al-Wadud, M. Dynamic Local Ternary Pattern for Face Recognition and Verification. In Proceedings of the International Conference on Computer Engineering and Applications, Tenerife, Spain, 10–12 January 2014.
35. Sun, N.; Zheng, W.; Sun, C.; Zou, C.; Zhao, L. Gender classification based on boosting local binary pattern. In Proceedings of the Third International Symposium on Neural Networks (ISNN), Chengdu, China, 28 May–1 June 2006; pp. 194–201.
36. Yang, Z.; Ai, H. Demographic classification with local binary patterns. In Proceedings of the international Conference on Advances in Biometrics (ICB), Seoul, Korea, 27–29 August 2007; pp. 464–473.
37. Rahman, M.M.; Rahman, S.; Dey, E.K.; Shoyaib, M. A Gender Recognition Approach with an Embedded Preprocessing. Int. J. Inf. Technol. Comput. Sci. 2015, 7, 19–27.
38. Dey, E.K.; Khan, M.; Ali, M.H. Computer Vision-Based Gender Detection from Facial Image. Int. J. Adv. Comput. Sci. 2013, 3, 428–433.
39. Heikkila, M.; Pietikainen, M.; Heikkila, J. A Texture-Based Method for Detecting Moving Objects. In Proceedings of the British Machine Vision Conference, London, UK, 7–9 September 2004.
40. Huang, X.; Li, S.Z.; Wang, Y. Shape localization based on statistical method using extended local binary pattern. In Proceedings of the Third International Conference

on Image and Graphics (ICIG), Hong Kong, China, 18–20 December 2004; pp. 184–187.
41. Liao, S.; Law, M.W.K.; Chung, A.C.S. Dominant local binary patterns for texture classification. IEEE Trans. Image Process.2009, 18, 1107–1118.
42. Heikkilä, M.; Pietikäinen, M.; Schmid, C. Description of interest regions with local binary patterns. Pattern Recognit. 2009, 42, 425–436.
43. Shoyaib, M.; Abdullah-Al-Wadud, M.; Chae, O. A Noise-Aware Coding Scheme for Texture Classification. Sensors 2011, 11, 8028–8044.
44. Zahid Ishraque, S.M.; Shoyaib, M.; Abdullah-Al-Wadud, M.; Monirul Hoque, Md.; Chae, O. A local adaptive image descriptor. New Rev. Hypermedia Multimed. 2013, 19, 286–298.
45. Jun, B.; Choi, I.; Kim, D. Local transform features and hybridization for accurate face and human detection. IEEE Trans Pattern Anal. Mach. Intell. 2013, 35, 1423–1436.
46. Lazebnik, S.; Schmid, C.; Ponce, J. Beyond bags of features: Spatial pyramid matching for recognizing natural scene categories. In Proceedings of the 2006 IEEE Conference on Computer Vision and Pattern Recognition (CVPR), New York, NY, USA, 17–22 June 2006; pp. 2169–2178.
47. Chang, C.-C.; Lin, C.J. LIBSVM: A library for support vector machines. ACM Trans. Intell. Syst. Technol. (TIST) 2011, 2.
48. Dahl, G.E.; Yu, D.; Deng, L.; Acero, A. Context-dependent pre-trained deep neural networks for large-vocabulary speech recognition. IEEE Trans Audio Speech Lang. Process. 2012, 20, 30–42.
49. LeCun, Y.; Bengio, Y.; Hinton, G. Deep learning. Nature 2015, 521, 436–444.
50. Nair, V.; Hinton, G.E. 3D object recognition with deep belief nets. In Proceedings of the Advances in Neural Information Processing Systems 22, Vancouver, BC, Canada, 7–10 December 2009; pp. 1339–1347.
51. Shoyaib, M.; Abdullah-Al-Wadud, M.; Chae, O. A skin detection approach based on the Dempster–Shafer theory of evidence. Int. J. Approx. Reason. 2012, 53, 636–659.
52. Chilimbi, T.; Suzue, Y.; Apacible, J.; Kalyanaraman, K. Project adam: Building an efficient and scalable deep learning training system. In Proceedings of the 11th USENIX Symposium on Operating Systems Design and Implementation (OSDI 14), Broomfield, CO, USA, 6–8 October 2014; pp. 571–582.
53. Girshick, R.; Donahue, J.; Darrell, T.; Malik, J. Rich feature hierarchies for accurate object detection and semantic segmentation. In Proceedings of the 2014 IEEE Conference on Computer Vision and Pattern Recognition (CVPR), Columbus, OH, USA, 23–28 June 2014; pp. 580–587.
54. Zabih, R.; Woodfill, J. Non-parametric local transforms for computing visual correspondence. In Proceedings of the Third European Conference on Computer Vision, Stockholm, Sweden, 2–6 May 1994; Volume 2, pp. 151–158.
55. Chen, H.; Gallagher, A.; Girod, B. Describing Clothing by Semantic Attributes. In Proceedings of the 12th European Conference on Computer Vision (ECCV), Florence, Italy, 7–13 October 2012.
56. Jia, Y.; Shelhamer, E.; Donahue, J.; Karayev, S.; Long, J.; Girshick, R.; Guadarrama, S.; Darrell, T. Caffe: Convolutional architecture for fast feature embedding. In Proceedings of the ACM International Conference on Multimedia, Orlando, FL, USA, 3–7 November 2014; pp. 675–678.

# CHAPTER 4

# Towards Trustworthy Collaborative Editing

**Mamdouh Babi** † **and Wenbing Zhao** *,†

*Department of Electrical Engineering and Computer Science, Cleveland State University, 2121 Euclid Ave, Cleveland, OH 44115, USA*

## ABSTRACT

Real-time collaborative editing applications are drastically different from typical client–server applications in that every participant has a copy of the shared document. In this type of environment, each participant acts as both a client and a server replica. In this article, we elaborate on how to adapt Byzantine fault tolerance (BFT) mechanisms to enhance the trustworthiness of such applications. It is apparent that traditional BFT algorithms cannot be used directly because it would dictate that all updates submitted by participants be applied sequentially, which would defeat the purpose of collaborative editing. The goal of this study is to design and implement an efficient BFT solution by exploiting the application semantics and by doing a threat analysis of these types of applications. Our solution can be considered as a form of optimistic BFT in that local states maintained by each participant may diverge temporarily. The states of the participants are made consistent with each other by a periodic synchronization mechanism.

**Keywords:** Byzantine fault tolerant; collaborative editing; Byzantine agreement; operational transformation

# 1. INTRODUCTION

By collaborative editing, we mean that two or more participants work on a shared document concurrently via a network. Collaborative editing has been an active research area since the 1980s [1,2,3]. Collaborative editing systems are desirable because they help increase the productivity for organizations and increase the convenience for employees. The increased popularity of real-time collaborative editing systems in recent years has inevitably elevated the trustworthiness expectation from their users. Considering the untrusted nature of the Internet, there is a strong need to make such applications more robust against various malicious attacks. Byzantine fault tolerance (BFT) appears to be an excellent means to achieve the goal [4]. However, BFT algorithms are designed for client–server applications and they typically require all requests to be executed sequentially to ensure replica consistency. Hence, these algorithms cannot be directly employed for collaborative editing systems.

In designing BFT mechanisms for real-time collaborative editing systems, we must consider the following aspects:

- Replication: With replication, each participant has a copy of the shared document. In this configuration, each participant acts as both a client and a server replica because anyone could make changes to the shared document. Changes made would be propagated to all other participants. In essence, a collaborative editing application is a form of fault tolerance system with active replication [5] and every participant constitutes as a replica. On the other hand, a client–server application configuration by itself does not have built-in replication feature. If fault tolerance is necessary, the server must be explicitly replicated in client–server applications. The intrinsic replication design in collaborative editing systems makes it very attractive to employ replication-based fault tolerance solutions to increase the trustworthiness. Since the redundancy has already been built into the application, both the hardware cost (i.e., no need to purchase more computers) and runtime overhead are reduced (i.e., the application itself must have incorporated some replica coordination mechanisms).
- Concurrency: Real-time collaborative editing systems are designed to allow concurrent updates to a shared document [6]. Therefore, it is not acceptable to impose any sequential order on the updates to the

shared document among all participants because this would be completely against the design purpose of the collaborative editing applications. For typical client–server applications, however, losing concurrency constitutes only a performance issue. For collaborative editing, we will adopt the optimistic replication strategy [7], which means that the states of the replicas could diverge temporarily and it is inevitable for us to use the eventual replica consistency model.

- Role: In collaborative editing applications, each participant acts both as a client and a server. As the client, it may introduce state changes to the shared document. As a server, it will receive and incorporate changes made by other participants. In typical client–server applications, a client only issues requests to the server and anticipates the corresponding replies from the server, and the server passively waits for requests issued by clients and processes the requests and generates replies. Basically, the server provides a function to serve its clients. The server state will not change unless it has processed a request. With the adoption of the optimistic replication strategy, the dual-role of each participant in collaborative editing is no longer an issue.
- Membership: In general, a real-time collaborative editing application only allows a finite set of participants to modify a shared document. For a user to participate, he/she would have to register with the application prior to being granted the privilege to change the shared document. However, client–server applications typically are designed to serve many clients concurrently. Hence, we normally do not need to worry about the scalability issues for collaborative editing applications.

The goal of this study is to design and implement an efficient BFT solution by exploiting the application semantics and by doing a threat analysis of these types of applications. In our solution, each participant is free to introduce changes to the shared document and the propagation of the changes to other participants is done as usual. Our mechanisms ensure eventual replica consistency by synchronizing the states of the replicas periodically.

The remaining of the article is organized as follows. Section 2 presents background information and related work. Section 3 elaborates on the methods used in this research, which includes a threat analysis, system model, membership, and state synchronization. Section 4 provides experimental results. Section 5 concludes this article.

# 2. BACKGROUND

## 2.1. Collaborative Editing

Real-time collaborative editors facilitate multiple participants to work on a shared document concurrently [8,9]. Typically, one user initiates the collaboration by creating a document and making it available (i.e., publish it) to other users. In order to achieve consistency and good response, the shared document and related data (such as membership) are replicated on all sites allowing any participant to edit the document at any time. When two participants generate concurrent operations (O1, O2), the system has to ensure convergence to the best possible state.

Most common mechanisms for collaborative editing applications are based on Operational Transformation (OT). OT was introduced to reconcile conflicting operations [1,10,11]. OT algorithms should ensure causality, convergence and intention preservation for real-time collaborative editing systems. As shown in Figure 1, an operation O1 generated at site S1 by participant 1 is executed locally immediately and broadcasted to all other sites to be re-executed (e.g., at site S2 for participant 2). Without a proper mechanism to resolve conflicts, the state at different sites would diverge. For example, the delete operation issued by site S2 would result in the deletion of "a" instead of "b" without transformation. OT allows the execution of operations (O1, O2) immediately after both have been generated locally, and then transforms concurrent operations (if necessary) to ensure state converges at both sites S1 and S2 [9]. Using the same example as shown in Figure 1, the operation O2 is transformed at site S1 so that character "b" is deleted.

## 2.2. The ACE Collaborative Editor

The ACE real-time collaborative editor is the only well-documented, open source project that we could find (http://sourcefrog.net/project/ace/). Note that the term ACE is simply the name for the editor instead of an acronym. The editor is written in Java and it implements the Jupiter algorithm [12]. The Jupiter algorithm is a centralized algorithm for participant coordination and operational transformation. The ACE collaborative editor architecture is shown in Figure 2. The session server component is created when a user first publishes a document. At this point, this user becomes the publisher for the document. The session server manages all interactions between the publisher and participants for the same shared document.

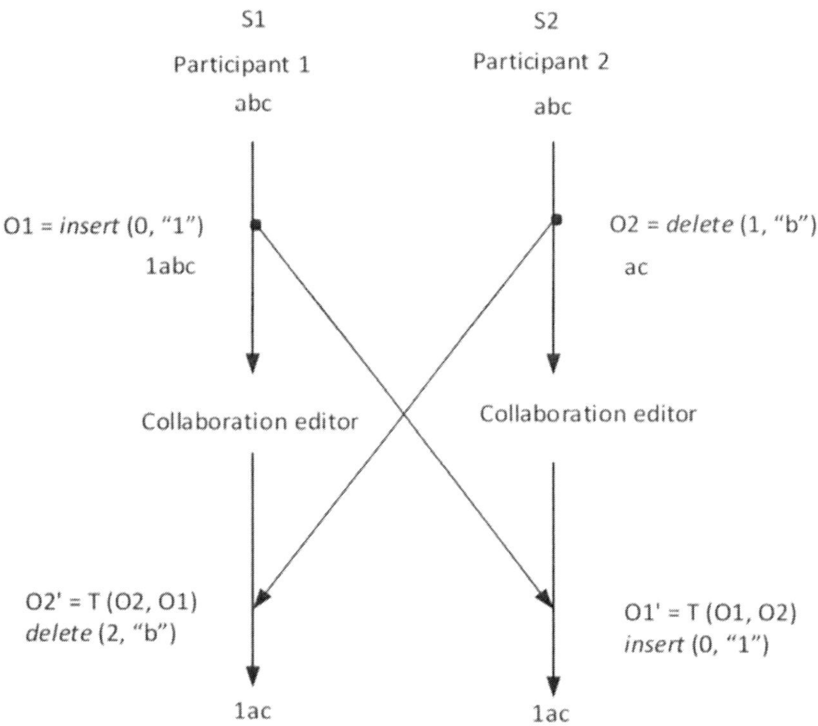


**Figure 1.** An example scenario for two participants using Operational Transformation.

A user can join an editing session by sending the publisher a join request. If the publisher accepts the join request, it notifies all existing participants of the session for the shared document. Similarly, a participant could leave a session by sending a leave request, and all existing participants will be notified for the membership change as well. The publisher can also remove a misbehaving participant from the session and blacklist the faulty participant to prevent it from ever joining again. In addition to managing the membership of the system, the publisher handles update operations submitted by all participants.

The interaction between a participant and the publisher is shown in Figure 3. As shown in Figure 3, the user requests to join a session (step 1) and then the publisher will accept or deny the request (step 2). Upon acceptance, the user requests creating a session (step 3) to participate in the editing of the shared document. The publisher provides the user with a session ID (step 4) and issues a nested invocation to create a

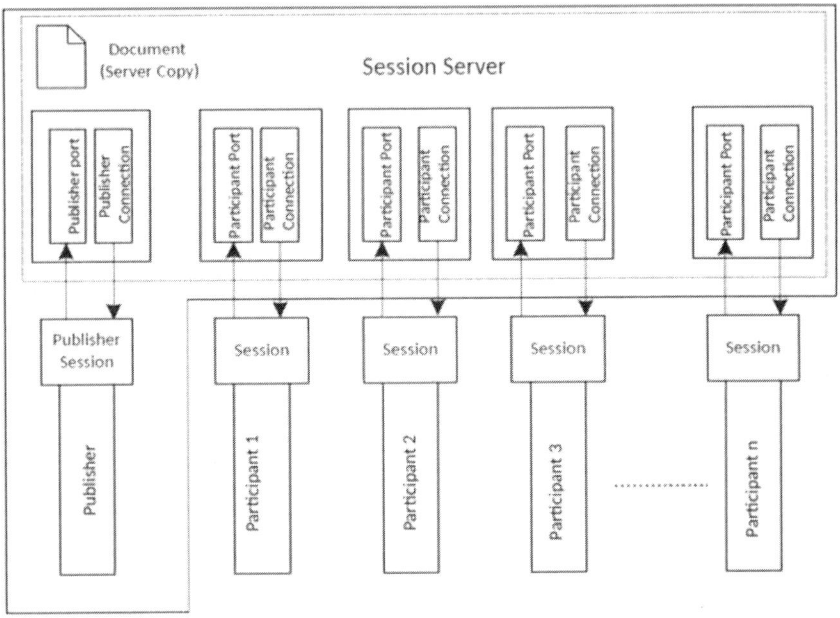


**Figure 2.** The architecture of the ACE editor with one publisher and multiple participants.

document's replica (step 5 and step 6) and sends the replica to the participant (step 7). The participant can then edit the shared document (Step 8). The server copy of the shared document is updated (step 9 and step 10) and the updated document is also exchanged with the participant (step 11). The session can be terminated at any time between the participant and the publisher (step 12 and step 13).

## 2.3. Related Work

Compared with the traditional way of ensuring replica consistency in a replicated system, which is typically based on totally ordering all updates and applying them sequentially, OT algorithms [1,10,11,13] provide a powerful alternative while facilitating concurrent execution of updates. However, they are not designed with fault tolerance in mind.

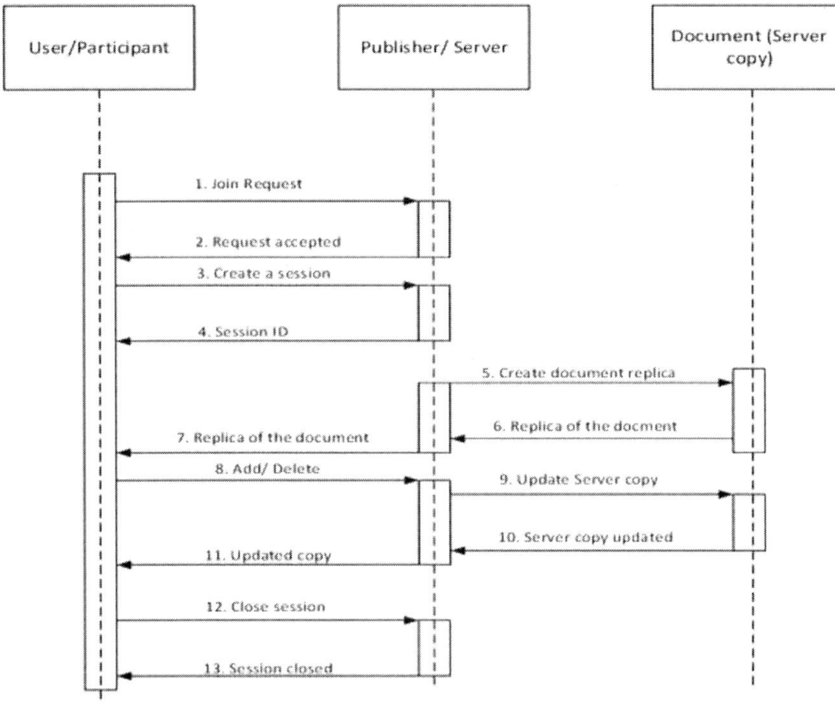


**Figure 3.** An example editing session with ACE.

Besides our own research on this topic [14,15], the limited number of publications on improving fault tolerance for collaborative editing systems all require the use of the crash–fault model [16,17,18]. Qin and Sun proposed using a primary-backup scheme to tolerate a single crash fault at the server [16,17], where the shared document is maintained only at the server and it is replicated for fault tolerance. Another contribution from [16,17] is the use of periodic checkpointing to reduce the recovery time for a failed client. The state synchronization mechanism in our work also depends on the checkpointing of the shared document. Shim and Prakash [18] proposed to use a stateful group communication system to build fault tolerant groupware applications. The application programming interfaces provided by the group communication system are used to make it easier to manage the shared document and the membership changes at such applications. As a tradeoff, using a proprietary group communication system would make it difficult to deploy the system over the Web. The mechanisms introduced in this paper not only protect the system from both crash and malicious faults, they do so by utilizing the built-in redundancy of collaborative editing systems.

Byzantine fault tolerance has been a hot research area since Castro and Liskov revitalized this field with their seminal work [4]. Numerous BFT algorithms have been proposed [19,20,21,22,23,24,25,26,27,28,29]. Many of these algorithms are designed to protect generic stateful servers against Byzantine faulty server replicas and faulty clients. It is not our goal to develop a competing algorithm to traditional BFT algorithms. Rather, our objective is to develop efficient BFT solutions for collaborative editing systems by using a combination of lightweight mechanisms and by employing traditional BFT algorithms only when they are needed. This is inline with our previous research on other types of systems [7,20,24,25,30].

This article is an extension of our conference paper [14]. Even though we followed the approach as in [14], we have made a number of extensions, including correcting a technical error related to state synchronization, providing a more detailed state synchronization algorithm, defining the correctness properties of the mechanisms with proof, implementing the proposed mechanisms, and reporting the performance evaluation results of the mechanisms. The state synchronization mechanism in our work is in a way similar to the deferred updates idea proposed by Luiz et al. [31]. Both mechanisms require a primary replica to disseminate information to other replicas, and both require a round of a Byzantine agreement (for each transaction in [31], and for each round of state synchronization in our work). However, our mechanism differs from that in [31] in that our mechanism is an optimistic replication mechanism where updates are applied to a local replica immediately and the state synchronization is used to achieve the eventual consistency of different replicas. The deferred updates mechanism in [31] operates within the boundary of a transaction, where updates are not visible to other transactions or clients until the transaction has been committed. Furthermore, our mechanism allows for the flexibility of applying state synchronization for a different number of updates. The number of deferred updates in each transaction in [31] cannot be changed arbitrarily because it is determined by the application semantics. Typically, the number of updates used in our state synchronization mechanism is much larger than that in each transaction.

# 3. METHODS

We first conduct a threat analysis on the real-time collaborative editing system. Based on the threats, we then propose a set of BFT mechanisms to control these threats. The correctness properties and the proof of correctness of our mechanisms are provided in Appendix A.

## 3.1. Threat Analysis

In this section, we analyze potential threats that could compromise the integrity of a collaborative editing system. We limit our analysis to systems that use centralized coordination such as ACE. As argued in the ACE documentation, centralized coordination is the only way to facilitate operational transformation that is provably correct. Centralized coordination requires the existence of a publisher that carries more responsibility than regular participants (such as user registration and mediation of updates), as we have outlined in the previous section. As a tradeoff, a compromised publisher could impose greater threat to the integrity of the collaborating editing application. Note that the use of a publisher does not necessarily mean that there is a single point of failure in the system. A regular participant could assume the role of the publisher if the current publisher has been found to have been compromised. On the other hand, centralized coordination brings benefits as well. It insulates participants from each other so that a faulty participant cannot directly affect another participant.

In this study, we only consider insider threats, such as threats from compromised participants or the publisher. We do not consider threats launched by external adversaries. Such threats could be launched against any system. Hence, they are out of the scope of this article.

### 3.1.1. Threats From A Faulty Publisher

The following threats can be imposed by a faulty publisher:

1. Malicious updates: A faulty publisher might introduce malicious updates on the shared document.
2. Partition attack: A faulty publisher may selectively pass on a membership change to a portion of participants with the intention of creating artificial partitions among the participants. The consequence of this attack is that participants in different partitions would have different versions of the shared document.
3. Inconsistent updates: A faulty publisher may selectively relay an update submitted by a participant to a subset of the participants. Again, this attack would cause participants to have different versions of the shared document.

4. Denial-of-service attack: A faulty publisher might launch a denial-of-service attack on any of the participants by refusing to accept a join request.

In all these cases, the integrity of the services is compromised. These types of threats except case 4 can be controlled by our lightweight BFT algorithms. For case 4, the user could notify the system administrator for being refused service by the publisher.

### 3.1.2. Threats From A Faulty Participant

The following threats may be imposed by a faulty participant:

1. Malicious updates: A faulty participant can inject malicious updates to the shared document. For example, a faculty participant can introduce inappropriate texts or delete texts that should not be deleted from the shared document.
2. Denial-of-service attack: A faulty participant can repeatedly join and leave an editing session with the intention to increase the load on the publisher (the session server to be specific). Handling the join request is an expensive operation for the publisher because the publisher would have to send the current shared document to the new participant on each join. This constitutes a form a denial-of-service attack on the publisher (and hence on the entire application).

Case 1 can be controlled by the proposed BFT mechanisms by detecting malicious updates and by rolling back detected malicious updates. Case 2 can be controlled relatively trivially by implementing some heuristic decision at the publisher. If within a short period of time, a user repeatedly joins and leaves, the user is blacklisted and banned from joining in the future.

## 3.2. The Lightweight BFT Mechanisms

In this section, we present the system model and the main lightweight BFT mechanisms. Our mechanisms accomplish two objectives: (1) ensure a consistent membership; and (2) achieve eventual replica consistency. From the threat analysis, we can see that a faulty publisher could partition the system, hence creating serious problems. To control such threats, we ensure that all membership related operations, such as join and leave, reach a Byzantine agreement before they are executed. This conservative approach is acceptable because such operations must be done sequentially anyway. For normal updates issued by a participant of the system, on the other hand, they must be allowed to proceed concurrently and immediately. Hence, optimistic Byzantine fault tolerance must be used. For this, we follow the "trust, but verify" principle in that we allow the users to proceed as usual most of the time, but periodically synchronize their state.

### 3.2.1. System Model

We assume that the system is centralized where a centralized algorithm is used to coordinate all participants of a shared document. If the system is deployed in a local area network, users can learn the existing published documents and the participants of each published document automatically via a zero-configuration networking mechanism [32] called Bonjour [33]. Bonjour uses multicast Domain Name System (DNS) and DNS service discovery. On the other hand, if the system is deployed on the Internet, either the publisher posts its contact information (IP address, port, public key, etc.) so that others may request to join an editing session, or the publisher explicitly invites perspective users to join the session. We do not assume that the users know each other's contact information unless they have joined the same session.

We further assume that each user has a public/private key pair. The public key is known to all potential users and participants in the same session, while the private key is kept secret to its owner. All messages exchanged in the system are digitally signed to ensure accountability and to prevent spoofing. Furthermore, adversaries have limited computing power so that they cannot break the digital signatures created by nonfaulty users. We assume that the messages can be reliably exchanged between different entities in a session-oriented application, which can be satisfied by using the Transmission Control Protocol (TCP) and by protecting messages sent via TCP with digital signatures.

Finally, we assume that there is sufficient number of users (publisher and participants combined). Given $N$ numbers of users, the system could tolerate up to $f = (N-1)/3$ compromised users. Obviously, $N$ must be greater or equal to 4. This large total number of users is necessary to achieve Byzantine agreement among nonfaulty users.

### 3.2.2. Consistent Membership

The foundation for correct operation in any distributed system is the agreement on who is part of the system, i.e., every participant of the system should have a consistent view of the current membership. When the publisher receives a join request from a new user, it adds the user to the current membership and initiates a Byzantine agreement on the new membership with all current participants. To reach a Byzantine agreement, the publisher and the existing participants follow the three-phase commit algorithm (referred to as the PBFT algorithm) introduced by Castro and Liskov in [6], as shown in Figure 4. Compared with the PBFT algorithm, there are several differences in our membership algorithm:

- The PBFT algorithm only ensures the agreement on one thing: the binding between a particular sequence number (representing the total order) and an incoming request. In our case, we want to reach an agreement on the new membership. Hence, the sequence number is replaced by a membership operation sequence number, and the message digest of the request is replaced by the full membership set.
- If the publisher could complete the Byzantine agreement step, it approves the membership and notifies the new user about the membership. In the notification message, the full membership information signed by all voting participants is included so that the new participant could participate future group-wise activities, such as new membership changes and state synchronizations. It is important that the membership is signed by every voting participant so that a faulty publisher cannot send a fake membership to the new participant.

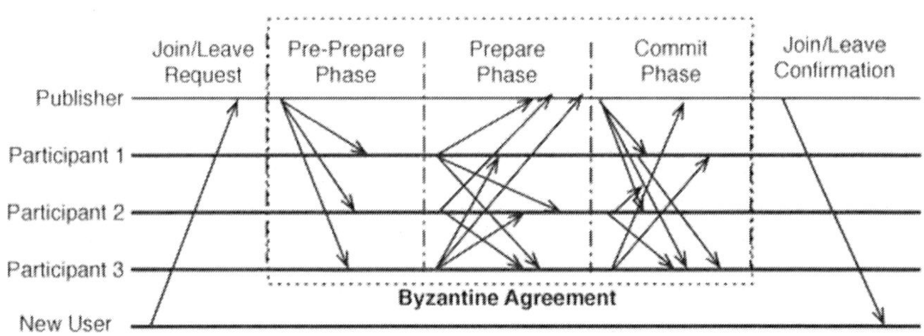


**Figure 4.** Byzantine agreement on membership changes.

We should note that a membership service is essential to traditional group communication systems [34,35]. The membership mechanism described here is different from these traditional approaches because it is built on top of Byzantine agreement algorithms.

If the publisher is faulty and intentionally disrupts the agreement on the membership operation by sending different memberships to different participants, the agreement may not be completed at some or all participants. These kind of attacks can be easily detected during the prepare phase of the Byzantine agreement because all nonfaulty participants broadcast the membership that have received from the publisher to all others. On receiving a conflicting signed membership, a participant suspects the publisher and initiates a view change to elect a new publisher.

### 3.2.3. State Synchronization

The state synchronization is the key mechanism to achieve eventual consistency among the participants. The main steps for the mechanism are illustrated in Figure 5. The first step is to determine a synchronization point. Because we assume that centralized coordination is used, the publisher is in the best position to decide when it is time to perform a new round of state synchronization. For example, the publisher could be configured to perform a new round of synchronization for every *n* updates (e.g., 100 updates) processed. Right after the publisher processed the *n*-th update since the last synchronization, it issues a state synchronization request to all participants. Because each participant is performing updates on the shared document independently until receiving the synchronization request, it may happen that a participant has already applied one or more local updates by the time the sync request arrives. In this case, the local updates at the participant must be rolled back. This is inevitable.

There are two modes of operations for state synchronization: (1) normal operation; (2) recovery. All state synchronization starts with the normal operation. If the publisher is not faulty, state synchronization would run successfully in the normal operation mode. If the normal operation could complete successfully, then a stable checkpoint of the current version of the shared document would be produced for this round of state synchronization and saved on stable storage. This stable checkpoint will be used if recovery is needed in the next round of state synchronization.

Note that, even for the normal operation, a Byzantine agreement is needed to ensure that all nonfaulty participates agree on both the synchronization point and the checkpoint produced in the current round of state synchronization. When the publisher decides that it is time to do a new round of state synchronization, it multicasts a sync-init message to all participants. The message has the form <SYNC-INIT, v,r,S,d,i>σi, where *v* is the current view number, *r* is the round number, which is increased by one for every new round of state synchronization, *S* is the set of two-dimensional vectors, one per participant, that indicate the last update that should have been applied at each participant, *d* is the digest of the shared document, *i* is the site id, and σi is the digital signature signed by sender *i*.

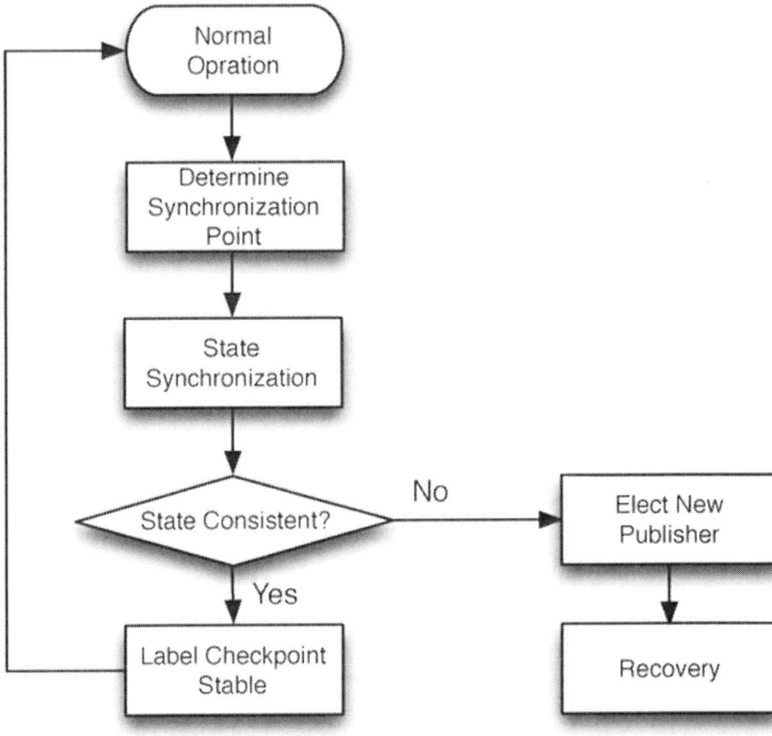


**Figure 5.** Main steps in state synchronization.

On receiving the sync-init message from the publisher, the participant validates the signature, and checks the validity of the request regarding issues such as whether or not the synchronization point is correct. If the request passes this validation test, the participant checks to see if it has applied any local updates that are logically later than the synchronization point. If so, such local updates are undone first. Then, the participant compares the received digest *d* with the digest of its local copy of the shared document. If two digests are identical, the participant produces a local checkpoint of the shared document at this synchronization point, saves the checkpoint to the stable storage, and multicasts a sync-prepare message, which takes the form <SYNC-PREPARE, v,r,d,R,j>σj, where *j* is the site id of the participant, and *R* is the sync-init message received by the sending participant. *R* is necessary for a nonfaulty participant to tell who is at fault in cases when the digest *d* in the sync-prepare message is different from that of its own.

On receiving the sync-init message together with 2f matching sync-prepare messages from different participants (including the one it has sent), the participant multicasts a sync-commit message, which takes the form <SYNC-COMMIT, v,r,d,j>σj. The publisher also multicasts the sync-commit message once it has collected 2f matching sync-prepare messages from different participants. On receiving 2f matching sync-commit messages from other participants and the publisher, the participant or the publisher concludes the Byzantine agreement for state synchronization, and label the local checkpoint stable. This concludes the round of state synchronization.

When a participant detects that the digest *d* included in the sync-init message from the publisher is different from that of its own, it suspects the publisher and initiates a round of view change. Similarly, a participant may find that the digest included in the sync-prepare message sent by some another participant is different from that of its own. This might happen if the any of the following is the case:

- A faulty publisher could send different sync-init messages (for the same round of state synchronization) to different participants with the malicious intent of getting nonfaulty participants to commit to different states;
- A faulty participant sends a sync-prepare message with a different digest from that of the nonfaulty publisher.

It is important for a nonfaulty participant to differentiate the two cases because the publisher should be suspected in the former case, while the publisher should not be suspected in the latter case. The piggybacking of the sync-init message *R* in the sync-prepare message serves the purpose. If the digest included in *R* is different from the digest included in the sync-prepare message, then the sending participant is apparently faulty. On the other hand, if the digest in *R* is identical to the digest in the sync-prepare message, and the digest is different from participant's own digest for the shared document, then the publisher is faulty. The piggybacking of *R* in the sync-prepare message is an important mechanism to prevent a faulty participant from lying without being detected. Previously, we applied a similar mechanism in the context of distributed transaction commitment [24].

There is yet another scenario that will lead to the suspicion of the publisher. A publisher might attempt to delay the start of a new round of state synchronization, i.e., it fails to launch a new round of state synchronization when it should. A participant could detect this attack easily by summing up the local and remote timestamps in the vector timestamp included in the update message sent by the publisher. If the sum reaches the multiple of the predefined period for state synchronization, the next message coming from the publisher must be the sync-init message. Note that the participant that made the last update before the state synchronization will not have the opportunity to receive this message, but this will not be a problem because it could detect this attack on receiving the next update message sent by the publisher.

On detection of the faulty publisher or a faulty participant, the operation switches to the recovery mode. If the publisher is suspected, participants will elect a new publisher by initiating a view change, as shown in Figure 6. When a participant suspects the publisher, it multicasts a view-change message to all other participants. The message takes the form <VIEW-CHANGE, v+1,r,A,P,i>σi, where v+1 is the next view number, *r* refers to the current round of state synchronization, *i* is the sender id, *A* is the set of updates submitted by participant *i* together with their respective timestamps, and *P* is the evidence that the publisher misbehaved, if any.

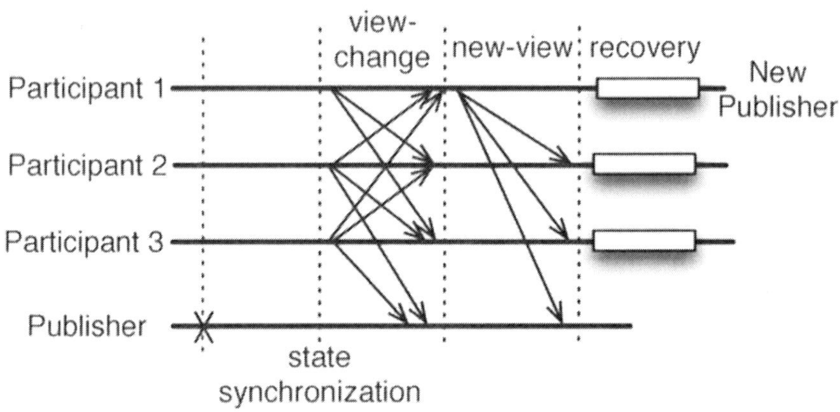


**Figure 6.** Steps in recovering from a faulty publisher.

On receiving a view-change message, a participant accepts the message and temporarily buffers the message if the message is valid. If the message contains a valid *P* component, or the participant has received f+1 valid view-change messages from other participants, then the participant also multicasts a view-change message. If the publisher in view v+1could receive 2f+1 valid view-change messages from different participants (including its own), it assumes the leadership and multicasts a new-view message, which takes the form <NEW-VIEW, v+1,r,AS,i>σi, where AS is the collection of the *A* sets submitted by the 2f+1 participants.

When a participant receives a valid new-view message, the leader election is concluded. Before a participant switches to the normal operation mode, however, it has to go through a recovery stage. Unlike other systems where the information included in the 2f+1 view-change messages is sufficient for recovery, in a collaborative editing system, the updates submitted by all nonfaulty participants are needed for a full recovery. To facilitate recovery, the new publisher will continue collecting the view-change messages until all participants have responded. If a participant fails to send their view-change messages within a predefined period, the new publisher removes that participant from the membership to ensure the liveness of the system. On receiving any of these additional view-change messages that are not part of the 2f+1 view-change messages, the new publisher extracts the *A* component and forwards it to all participants.

On receiving the set of updates from every participant in the membership, both the publisher and the participants follow a deterministic algorithm to build the full set of updates. A participant first rolls back its local copy of the shared document to the last stable checkpoint, and then applies this set of updates on the local copy of the shared document.

On detection of a faulty participant, all updates submitted by this participant are to be removed. Since they have already been applied to the shared copy, it is not trivial to cancel their effect. One possible way to achieve this purpose is to first rollback to the last stable checkpoint, and re-apply the updates submitted by nonfaulty participants that are causally preceding to the first operation submitted by the faulty participant since the last state synchronization. Updates that are causally depending on any of the updates submitted by the faulty participant must also be discarded.

### 3.2.4. Discussion

So far, we have assumed that there is a sufficient number of participants to complete a Byzantine agreement. If this is not the case, then we will have to let the publisher make the sole decision on routine membership changes such as the joining and leaving of a participant. However, periodic state synchronization can be formed even if there is not a sufficient number of participants with some changes to the mechanisms described previously, as explained below.

When it is time to perform a round of state synchronization, the publisher would multicast a sync-init message as usual. A participant would then multicast a sync-prepare message in response if the sync-init is valid. Instead of collecting 2fmatching sync-prepare messages, a publisher/participant would attempt to collect sync-prepare messages from all participants currently in the membership. In the absence of failure, everyone would be able to collect all the required set of messages, which would conclude the round of state synchronization.

Obviously, if a participant fails, the publisher must remove the failed participant(s) before the state synchronization can be completed.

If a state discrepancy is detected, and there is solid evidence that the publisher misbehaved, a view change would take place. The view change algorithm is modified in a similar fashion as that for the state synchronization in that the input from all participants would be required. If a participant is found to have misbehaved, it will be removed from the membership.

Finally, we note that our state synchronization mechanisms incurs minimum blocking in the absence of failures because a local checkpoint is taken as soon as a participant has validated the sync-init message. The participant is free to submit updates immediately after the checkpoint is taken.

# 4. RESULTS

The proposed mechanisms have been incorporated into the ACE editor. The digital signature and message digest computation are implemented using Java Cryptography Extension. Communication between the publisher and the participants is done via TCP/IP. For Byzantine agreement, we employ the PBFT algorithm [4]. In previous works [20,24,30,36], we have implemented the PBFT algorithms in Java for multiple systems. The implementation was adapted for the ACE editor.

The evaluation is carried out using a testbed consisting of four nodes connected via a Gigabit Ethernet. Each node is equipped with a Core i5-4250U CPU and 4GB of RAM, and runs the Ubuntu 14.04 Linux. One of them initially runs as the publisher and the remaining ones run as the participants. The system is set up to tolerate a single Byzantine faulty node.

Because of the nature of collaborative editing, we are not concerned about scalability and system throughput. Furthermore, we do not evaluate the runtime overhead of the join/leave operations because the latency of such operations would only impact that user that wishes to join and leave without affecting those who are editing the shared document. We report two performance characteristics of our mechanisms: (1) the latency of a round of state synchronization in the absence of faults; and (2) the latency of view change in the presence of a faulty publisher. We experimented with eight different state synchronization period, ranging from 100 to 800 updates per synchronization with 100 increment. Each update is encoded as a tuple of four elements: (1) the character inserted or deleted; (2) the operation type, such as deletion or insertion; (3) the position of the operation in the shared document (which is modeled as an array of characters), and a two-dimensional vector timestamp of the update (one dimension for the local timestamp, and the other for the remote timestamp, indicating how many updates have been submitted by the local and remote sites, respectively). For each configuration, we run 100 times and take the average latency. The ACE editor is modified so that updates are submitted programmatically in a loop instead of manually by a user.

Figure 7 shows the experimental results. In Figure 7a, we show both the blocking time that a user would experience during each round of state synchronization, and the total latency of the entire round of state synchronization. As can be seen, the blocking time is below 10 ms, which shouldn't be noticeable by a user of the system. The total state synchronization latency is about only 20 ms. It may be surprising that there is no apparent dependency between the latency and the synchronization period. However, the lack of dependency is expected because the state synchronization messages only include the digest of the shared document instead of the actual updates submitted by participants. This implies that in the local area network context, we can aggressively perform state synchronization more frequently without incurring excessive runtime overhead while enjoying the benefit of catching a faulty publisher quickly. On the other hand, if the system is deployed on the Internet where users are geographically distributed, the additional delay introduced by the Internet (which is typically around 100 ms) would make it impractical to have frequent state synchronization.

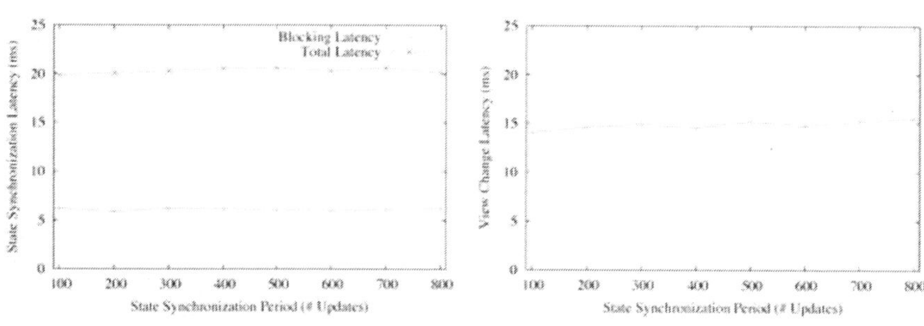


**Figure 7.** Experimental results. (**a**) state synchronization latency; (**b**) view change latency.

As can be seen in Figure 7b, the view change latency is only about 15 ms and it has very weak dependency on the synchronization period. Even though the message size increases with larger synchronization period, the total length is still small because each update-record is only 16 bytes long. The use of a Gigabit Ethernet ensures that the transmission latency of the messages is below 1 ms even when the synchronization period is 800 updates. This would change if the system is deployed on the Internet, where the upload bandwidth is very limited (in the United States, it is common to have an upload bandwidth as low as 1 Mbps for residential Internet services). For example, if the upload bandwidth is 1 Mbps, the transmission latency for view change messages would range from about 13 ms for 100-update-per-state-synchronization, to about 103 ms for 800-update-per-state-synchronization.

## 5. CONCLUSIONS

In this article, we presented how to enhance the trustworthiness of a real-time collaborative editing application with a set of lightweight Byzantine fault tolerance mechanisms. We followed the principle of optimistic replication [7] by allowing each participant to apply its updates immediately to its local copy and to all remote copies of the shared document. Periodically, a round of state synchronization is conducted to ensure that the states of the participants become consistent. Byzantine agreement is used only to achieve consistent membership and during the state synchronization. We have implemented the proposed mechanisms and integrated them into the ACE real-time collaborative editor. We further characterized the cost of state synchronization and view change of the implemented system with respect to different state synchronization periods. We found that the latency overhead caused by our mechanisms normally does not have negative impact to users.

## ACKNOWLEDGMENTS

This study is supported by the Graduate Faculty Research Support Program at Cleveland State University. We did not receive funds for covering the costs to publish in open access. We would like to sincerely thank the anonymous reviewers for their insight comments and suggestions on an early version of the manuscript.

## AUTHOR CONTRIBUTIONS

Mamdouh Babi and Wenbing Zhao conceived and designed the experiments; Mamdouh Babi performed the experiments; Mamdouh Babi and Wenbing Zhao analyzed the data; Mamdouh Babi and Wenbing Zhao wrote the paper. Both authors have read and approved the final manuscript.

## CONFLICTS OF INTEREST

The authors declare no conflict of interest. The funding sponsors had no role in the design of the study; in the collection, analyses, or interpretation of data; in the writing of the manuscript, and in the decision to publish the results.

## REFERENCES

1. Ellis, C.A.; Gibbs, S.J. Concurrency control in groupware systems. In Proceedings of the 1989 ACM SIGMOD International Conference on Management of Data (SIGMOD '89), Portland, OR, USA, 31 May–2 June 1989; ACM: New York, NY, USA, 1989; pp. 399–407.
2. Li, D.; Li, R. An Admissibility-Based Operational Transformation Framework for Collaborative Editing Systems. Comput. Support. Coop. Work 2010, 19, 1–43.
3. Sun, C.; Jia, X.; Zhang, Y.; Yang, Y.; Chen, D. Achieving convergence, causality preservation, and intention preservation in real-time cooperative editing systems. ACM Trans. Comput. Hum. Interact. 1998, 5, 63–108.
4. Castro, M.; Liskov, B. Practical Byzantine fault tolerance and proactive recovery. ACM Trans. Comput. Syst. 2002, 20, 398–461.
5. Zhao, W. Building Dependable Distributed Systems; Wiley-Scrivener: Beverly, MA, USA, 2014.
6. Zhao, W. Concurrency Control in Real-Time E-Collaboration Systems. In Encyclopedia of E-Collaboration; Kock, N., Ed.; Idea Group Publishing: Hershey, PA, USA, 2008; pp. 95–101.
7. Zhao, W. Optimistic Byzantine fault tolerance. Int. J. Parallel Emerg. Distrib. Syst. 2016, 31, 254–267.
8. Babi, M.; Zhao, W. Conflicts and Resolutions in Computer Supported Collaborative Work Applications. In Encyclopedia of Information Science and Technology, 3rd ed.; Khosrow-Pour, M., Ed.; IGI Global: Hershey, PA, USA, 2015; pp. 567–575.
9. Babi, M.; Zhao, W. Increasing the Trustworthiness of Collaborative Applications. In Encyclopedia of Information Science and Technology, 3rd ed.; Khosrow-Pour, M., Ed.; IGI Global: Hershey, PA, USA, 2015; pp. 4317–4324.
10. Sun, C.; Ellis, C. Operational transformation in real-time group editors: Issues, algorithms, and achievements. In Proceedings of the 1998 ACM Conference on Computer Supported Cooperative Work, Seattle, WA, USA, 14–18 November 1998; pp. 59–68.

11. Li, R.; Li, D. A new operational transformation framework for real-time group editors. IEEE Trans. Parallel Distrib. Syst. 2007, 18, 307–319.
12. Nichols, D.A.; Curtis, P.; Dixon, M.; Lamping, J. High-latency, low-bandwidth windowing in the Jupiter collaboration system. In Proceedings of the 8th Annual ACM Symposium on User Interface and Software Technology (UIST '95), Pittsburgh, PA, USA, 15–17 November 1995; ACM: New York, NY, USA, 1995; pp. 111–120.
13. Sun, D.; Xia, S.; Sun, C.; Chen, D. Operational transformation for collaborative word processing. In Proceedings of the 2004 ACM Conference on Computer Supported Cooperative Work, Chicago, IL, USA, 6–10 November 2004; pp. 437–446.
14. Zhao, W.; Babi, M. Byzantine fault tolerant collaborative editing. In Proceedings of the IET International Conference on Information and Communications Technologies, Beijing, China, 27–29 April 2013; pp. 233–240.
15. Zhao, W.; Babi, M.; Yang, W.; Luo, X.; Zhu, Y.; Yang, J.; Luo, C.; Yang, M. Byzantine fault tolerance for collaborative editing with commutative operations. In Proceedings of the IEEE International Conference on Electro Information Technology, Grand Forks, ND, USA, 19–21 May 2016; pp. 246–251.
16. Qin, X.; Sun, C. Efficient Recovery Algorithm in Real-Time and Fault-TolerantCollaborative Editing Systems. In Proceedings of the ACM Workshop on Collaborative Editing Systems, Philadelphia, PA, USA, 2–6 December 2000.
17. Qin, X.; Sun, C. Recovery Support for Internet-Based Real-Time Collaborative Editing Systems. In Proceedings of the International Conference on Computer Networks and Mobile Computing (ICCNMC '01), Beijing China, 16–19 October 2001; IEEE Computer Society: Washington, DC, USA, 2001; p. 181.
18. Shim, H.S.; Prakash, A. Tolerating Client and Communication Failures in Distributed Groupware Systems. In Proceedings of the 17th IEEE Symposium on Reliable Distributed Systems, Madrid, Spain, 2–4 December 1998; IEEE Computer Society: Washington, DC, USA, 1998; p. 221.
19. Amir, Y.; Danilov, C.; Kirsch, J.; Lane, J.; Dolev, D.; Nita-Rotaru, C.; Olsen, J.; Zage, D. Scaling Byzantine fault-tolerant replication to wide area networks. In Proceedings of the International Conference on Dependable Systems and Networks, Philadelphia, PA, USA, 25–28 June 2006; pp. 105–114.
20. Chai, H.; Zhang, H.; Zhao, W.; Melliar-Smith, P.M.; Moser, L.E. Toward trustworthy coordination of Web services business activities. IEEE Trans. Serv. Comput. 2013, 6, 276–288.
21. Cowling, J.; Myers, D.; Liskov, B.; Rodrigues, R.; Shrira, L. HQ Replication: A Hybrid quorum protocol for Byzantine fault tolerance. In Proceedings of the Seventh Symposium on Operating Systems Design and Implementations, Seattle, WA, USA, 6–8 November 2006.
22. Kotla, R.; Alvisi, L.; Dahlin, M.; Clement, A.; Wong, E. Zyzzyva: Speculative Byzantine fault tolerance. In Proceedings of the 21st ACM Symposium on Operating Systems Principles, Stevenson, WA, USA, 14–17 October 2007.
23. Zhang, H.; Zhao, W.; Moser, L.E.; Melliar-Smith, P.M. Design and implementation of a Byzantine fault tolerance framework for non-deterministic applications. IET Softw. 2011, 5, 342–356.
24. Zhang, H.; Chai, H.; Zhao, W.; Melliar-Smith, P.M.; Moser, L.E. Trustworthy coordination for Web service atomic transactions. IEEE Trans. Parallel Distrib. Syst. 2012, 23, 1551–1565.
25. Zhao, W. Performance optimization for state machine replication based on application semantics: A review. J. Syst. Softw. 2016, 112, 96–109.
26. Veronese, G.S.; Correia, M.; Bessani, A.N.; Lung, L.C.; Verissimo, P. Efficient byzantine fault-tolerance. IEEE Trans. Comput. 2013, 62, 16–30.
27. Behl, J.; Distler, T.; Kapitza, R. Consensus-oriented parallelization: How to earn your first million. In Proceedings of the 16th Annual Middleware Conference, Vancouver, BC, Canada, 7–11 December 2015; pp. 173–184.
28. Duan, S.; Peisert, S.; Levitt, K.N. hBFT: Speculative Byzantine fault tolerance with minimum cost. IEEE Trans. Dependable Secur. Comput. 2015, 12, 58–70.

29. Sousa, J.; Bessani, A. Separating the wheat from the chaff: An empirical design for geo-replicated state machines. Proceedigns of the IEEE 34th Symposium on Reliable Distributed Systems IEEE, Montreal, QC, Canada, 28 September–1 October 2015; pp. 146–155.
30. Chai, H.; Zhao, W. Byzantine fault tolerant event stream processing for autonomic computing. In Proceedings of the IEEE 12th International Conference on Dependable, Autonomic and Secure Computing, Dalian, China, 24–27 August 2014; pp. 109–114.
31. Luiz, A.F.; Lung, L.C.; Correia, M. Byzantine fault-tolerant transaction processing for replicated databases. In Proceedings of the 10th IEEE International Symposium on Network Computing and Applications, Cambridge, MA, USA, 25–27 August 2011; pp. 83–90.
32. Zero Configuration Networking (Zeroconf). Available online: http://www.zeroconf.org/ (accessed on 23 March 2017).
33. Krochmal, M. Rendezvous Is Changing to ... Available online: https://lists.apple.com/archives/rendezvous-dev/2005/Apr/msg00001.html (accessed on 23 March 2017).
34. Reiter, M.K. A secure group membership protocol. IEEE Trans. Softw. Eng. 1996, 22, 31–42.
35. Correia, M.; Neves, N.F.; Lung, L.C.; Veríssimo, P. Worm-IT—A wormhole-based intrusion-tolerant group communication system. J. Syst. Softw. 2007, 80, 178–197.
36. Zhao, W. Design and implementation of a Byzantine fault tolerance framework for Web services. J. Syst. Softw. 2009, 82, 1004–1015.

# CHAPTER 5

# Designing the Digital Organization

**Charles C. Snow[1], Øystein Devik Fjeldstad[2]* and Arthur M. Langer[3]**

[1] *Department of Management and Organization, Smeal College of Business, Pennsylvania State University, University Park, Pennsylvania PA 16802, USA.*

[2] *BI Norwegian Business School, Oslo, Norway.*

[3] *Department of Decision, Risk, and Operations Management, School of Business, Columbia University, New York NY 10027, USA.*

## ABSTRACT

Increasingly, organizations are assessing their opportunities, developing and delivering products and services, and interacting with customers and other stakeholders digitally. Mobile computing, social media, and big data are the drivers of the future workplace, and these and other digitally based technologies are having large economic and social impacts, including increased competition and collaboration, the disruption of many industries, and pressure being put on organizations to develop new capabilities and transform their cultures. In this article, we provide a conceptual framework for the design of effective digital organizations. Our framework is predicated on the current state of digitization across diverse sectors of the global economy. In the digital world, all activities and transactions leave digital marks, and all actors, things, and places can be reached and affected digitally. As a result, we can design for self-organization rather than using hierarchical mechanisms for control and coordination. Such designs require the strategic and cultural alignment of digital technologies within the organization and externally with stakeholders. We propose that "actor-oriented" principles are at the heart of designing digital organizations and that, if properly applied, can result in a workplace where organization members are highly engaged and productive.

**Keywords:** Digital technology Digital organization Digital disruption New organizational forms Organizational architecture Workplace of the future Collaboration tools

Digital technologies are transforming the global economy. In his pioneering book *Being Digital* (1995), technology futurist Nicholas Negroponte (1995), described how the old industrial economy would be eaten away by a new digital economy. Moreover, digital technology makes it possible for members of an organization to self-organize and thereby avoid the delays, distortions, and other damaging effects of hierarchically organized systems (Benkler, 2002). Established companies recognize that digital technologies can help them operate their businesses with greater speed and lower costs and, in many cases, offer their customers opportunities to co-design and co-produce products and services (Sambamurthy et al. 2003). Many start-up companies use digital technologies to develop new products and business models that disrupt the present way of doing business and take customers away from firms that cannot change and adapt.

Software tools and applications, robots, and a host of other digital technologies "... are doing for mental power – the ability to use our brains to understand and shape our environments – what the steam engine and its descendants did for muscle power" (Brynjolfsson & McAfee, 2014: 7–8). Properly harnessed, digital technology can enable individuals, firms, cities, and governments to become smarter – to expand their capabilities and to adapt to new and changing conditions. As an agile organizational form (Alberts, 2007), the digital organization will be populated with individuals and teams who are facile with technology and who can collaborate both inside and outside the organization to make process improvements and develop new solutions.

In our article, we offer organizational designers, change agents, and managers a conceptual framework for the design of a digital organization – identifying its major components and showing how they should be put together. A fully digital enterprise is a powerful combination of people, technology, and organizing ability that is well suited to today's economic and social environment. In the first section, we discuss how digital technologies are used by organizations to increase their efficiency and effectiveness. Digital technologies augment and support work activities and decision-making, connect members of the organization, and aid in managing relationships with customers, suppliers, and other stakeholders. In the second section, we describe the organizational architecture that is appropriate for a knowledge-intensive, highly collaborative digital organization. This architecture is "actor" oriented – that is, it places a premium on the ability of organization members to self-organize while performing their work tasks. Actor-oriented organizations mostly rely on protocols, commons, and infrastructures to maintain control and coordination instead of hierarchical mechanisms. In the final section, we discuss how to apply the actor-oriented architecture for those organizations wanting to develop their digitally based capabilities. Here we address the skills and motivation of actors, the creation of commons that support their work activities, and the protocols and infrastructures that connect actors and facilitate their interactions.

## DIGITAL TECHNOLOGY

Technology is a way of getting work done (Perrow, 1967). New technologies are seldom "invented" but rather are developed by combining technologies that already exist. Unlike older technologies, which mostly produce fixed physical outputs, digital technologies are generative (Zittrain, 2006) -- they can be combined and recombined endlessly for fresh purposes (Arthur, 2009). In many cases, digital technologies also can enable replication and distribution of products and services at close to zero marginal cost (Shapiro and Varian, 1999; Varian, 2000). The domain of digital technology includes computer hardware, software, transmission networks, protocols, programming languages, very large-scale integrated circuits, algorithms, and all the components and practices that belong to these various technologies. Digital technology enables immense amounts of information to be easily compressed, preserved, and transmitted. In recent years, digital technology has disrupted one industry after another (Christensen, 1997), and it is rapidly transforming how people communicate, learn, and work. Many products and services are fully or partially digital, such as news and entertainment, and increasingly work is being done digitally.

The essence of the digital revolution has been concisely described by Brynjolfsson and McAfee (2014). They explain that technological progress in the digital era is due to three characteristics of technology: it is *exponential, digital,* and *combinatorial* (p. 37). The exponential aspect of technology means that its power and usefulness are getting better and better all the time and that "... what's come before is no longer a particularly reliable guide to what will happen next" (p. 55). Digitization turns various kinds of data and information into bits – the ones and zeroes that are the language of computers. Advances in digitization have resulted in "... new ways of acquiring knowledge...and higher rates of innovation" (p. 62). Lastly, digital innovation is combinatorial: "Each development becomes a building block for future innovations" (p. 81). Coupled with human ingenuity, these three characteristics allow digital technologies to be developed and applied at a rapid rate.

## Adaptation and disruption

Organizations adapt to the needs of the market; to the technologies available for the design, production, and delivery of products and services; and in their means of organizing (Miles and Snow, 1978). The digitization of society is affecting customer needs, product and service properties and delivery mechanisms, and organization design (Langer, 2017). Changes across these areas are coalescing. For example, music has changed from a product to a service industry wherein consumer demand has evolved from purchasing packaged CDs to accessing customized, streamed playlists which are organized by aggregators such as iTunes, Tidal, Spotify, and Pandora, with distribution driven by artists instead of studios. "Products as services" is a business model that is growing in many arenas (Porter and Hempelmann, 2014).

Technological innovations can be incremental or disruptive. Incremental innovations are characterized by small improvements to existing products, services, and processes. Disruptive innovations, on the other hand, may create new markets and business models, and often may displace market leaders (Christensen, 1997; Christensen and Bower, 1996). In past decades, organizational responses to technological changes were mostly incremental and, in part, enabled by IT improvements that allowed greater scope and dimensionality of organizational control and coordination. Most of those adaptive responses were made within existing hierarchical forms of organizing (Altman et al. 2015). Digital technologies, however, often disrupt established ways of organizing and require adaptation through collaboration as well as self-organization around situation awareness (Endsley, 2000) and knowledge commons (Hess and Ostrom, 2006; Ostrom, 1990, 2010). Self-organization and collaboration, as an adaptive response, is faster and more effective than a hierarchical response.

The technological manifestations of disruption in organization design are clearly visible, as are workplace changes and changes in inter-organizational relationships. What is less visible are changes in the associated design paradigm, which enable organizations to obtain efficiency and effectiveness improvements by investing in digital technology. The new organization design principles are similar to those used in designing digital technologies themselves. Their roots are found in object-oriented systems design (Dahl and Nygaard, 1966) and in the architecture of the Internet (Krol, 1993). In organizational terms, these principles are embodied in actor-oriented architectures (Fjeldstad et al. 2012).

## Working and organizing digitally

Digital technologies play a role in all aspects of operating, controlling, and coordinating the activities of organizations (Setia et al. 2013). Broadly speaking, they are used for automating and augmenting tasks, communicating internally among organization members and externally with customers and partners, and in collaborative decision-making among digital and human agents (Davenport and Kirby, 2015; Engelbart 1962; Huber, 1990; Licklider, 1960; Simon, 1973). At Tesla's manufacturing facility in Fremont, California, technicians work alongside 185 robots made by the German firm Kuka Robotics to assemble the electric cars. By using artificial intelligence "reinforcement learning algorithms," the robots are able to switch tools and perform certain tasks far better and faster than their human co-workers (Gershgorn, 2016). Surgeons at the Mayo Clinic use robots to augment a variety of surgical procedures in heart, head, and neck operations. The surgeons perform those operations by controlling surgical micro-instruments attached to robotic arms (Mayo Clinic, 2016).

Both intra- and inter-organizational transactions and communications have been performed digitally for a long time (Fedorowicz and Konsynski, 1992). Walmart exemplifies a highly digitized supply chain connecting its stores, distribution centers, and suppliers (Mata et al. 1995). Currently, social media such as Facebook and Twitter are used by companies to communicate with their customers and other stakeholders, and digital platforms such as Facebook at Work and Microsoft's SharePoint allow for internal communication and for collaboration with partners.

Digital technologies are also used for learning, decision-making, and design. E-commerce companies such as Amazon, Google, Airbnb, and Uber study the data trails of consumer behavior to design markets for greater efficiency and build new markets (Lohr, 2016). Intelligent digital design tools are used in engineering and creative industries. Those tools typically offer 3D representation of the objects under design, and they allow designers to simulate the operations and performance of alternative design choices (Fujitsu, 2016). In semiconductor manufacturing, the designs are digitally transmitted to equipment that manufactures the product. With continuing development and wider adoption of 3D printing technologies, the design-to-manufacturing process will become fully digital across many more industries (Sasson and Johnson, 2016). MTR Corporation, which owns and operates the Hong Kong subway system, uses artificial intelligence to schedule maintenance tasks. In a typical week, more than 10,000 people carry out 2,600 work orders. The system was "trained" by using expertise extracted from human experts and then transformed into work rules. The main difference between normal software and MTR's artificial intelligence is that it contains human knowledge that takes years to acquire through experience (Hodson, 2014). Some companies employ digital design tools in collaborating with their customers and partners. Lego provides toolkits on its website that enable entrepreneurs and customers to submit product ideas and start new Lego brick-based businesses (Heinerth et al. 2014). (See Table 1 for a summary of digital applications and leading digital firms and organizations.)

**Table 1.** Digital applications used in leading digital firms

| Target area | Goal | Leading digital firms and their industries |
|---|---|---|
| Customer experiences | Customer co-creation of products and services<br>Customer engagement and loyalty<br>Customized offerings | Burberry (clothing)<br>Starbucks (specialty retailing)<br>Caesars (gambling and entertainment) |
| Internal operations | Increased efficiency<br>Lower costs<br>Greater speed<br>Higher quality | Asian Paints (paint and adhesives)<br>Codelco (mining) |
| Business models | Reinventing industries<br>Substituting products or services<br>Creating new digital businesses<br>Reconfiguring value delivery models<br>Rethinking value propositions<br>Market design | Airbnb (private lodging)<br>Uber (taxi services)<br>Amazon (online retailing)<br>UPS (logistics services) |
| Product design and development | Intelligent product design<br>User-driven innovation | Fujitsu (electronics)<br>Nike (athletic shoes and apparel)<br>Lego (toys) |
| Organizing | Agile organizations<br>Collaborative processes<br>Non-hierarchical means of control and coordination | IBM (technology and consulting)<br>Accenture (professional services)<br>NATO military forces (national defense) |

Source: Adapted from Westerman et al. (2014)

An organization is a goal-directed, boundary-maintaining activity system (Aldrich and Ruef, 2006). In traditional organizations, technological artifacts such as manufacturing equipment and computers are controlled by human operators. With the declining costs of global communication and information processing, hierarchy is being replaced by radically different ways of organizing (Fjeldstad et al., 2012), the digital elements of which include cloud computing, big data analytics, cognitive computing, and collaboration platforms. Artificial intelligence embedded in machinery and tools, as exemplified above, plays an ever-larger role in emerging digital organizations (for a survey see Kolbjørnsrud et al. 2016). As a result, employees collaborate with, rather than merely control, the technology in use, and organizational designs have to encompass both human and digital agents. Organizing digitally means collaboration with more entities and less reliance on hierarchy for control and coordination. It also entails empowering employees, partners, and customers who use digital tools for the co-creation and co-production of products and services as well as providing digital platforms for self-organized collaboration (Boudreau et al. 2011).

## ACTOR-ORIENTED ORGANIZATIONAL ARCHITECTURE[1]

Digital technology is not only changing how organizations operate but also the way we think about organizing. Organizations increasingly include digital and human agents who share means of communication, control, and coordination. A traditional organization is arranged hierarchically – that is, control and coordination are achieved through an authority (reporting) structure in which superiors plan and coordinate the activities of subordinates, allocate resources, and resolve problems and conflicts (Simon, 1962). A hierarchical organization can be effective in stable and predictable environments because the organization does not have to regularly innovate or adapt to change. Many of today's environments, however, are not stable and predictable; they are volatile, uncertain, complex, and even ambiguous (Johansen, 2007; Suhayl & Joshi, 2015). Such environments are characteristic of knowledge-intensive industries like biotechnology, computers, healthcare, professional services, and national defense. Organizations operating in these types of environments rely heavily on the agency of their members. A hierarchical organization inevitably instills a hierarchical mindset among its members. Members understand that they are being paid to do a particular job, and they look to their managers to set goals, develop plans, and approve the quality of their work. As a result, organization members become psychologically as well as economically dependent on the hierarchy. In addition to the friction created by "relay managers" (Drucker, 1988) who merely pass along information, hierarchical management styles tend to reduce intrinsic employee motivation to take initiative.

Prior research has proposed an actor-oriented organizational architecture that is appropriate for knowledge-intensive sectors where organizations must continuously learn and adapt (Fjeldstad et al. 2012). Actor-oriented organizations rely on self-organizing, with only minimal use of hierarchical mechanisms to achieve control and coordination. Such organizations are particularly useful for large-scale, multi-party collaboration – a required capability in knowledge-intensive industries (Benkler, 2002; Powell et al. 1996). Collaboration has been shown to reduce risk, speed products to market, decrease the costs of solution development and process improvement, and enable access to new knowledge, technologies, and markets (Eisenhardt and Schoonhoven, 1996; Hagedorn, 1993; Kogut, 1988; Wheelwright and Clark, 1992).

The actor-oriented architecture is composed of three elements: (1) *actors* who have the capabilities and values to self-organize; (2) *commons* where the actors accumulate and share resources; and (3) *protocols, processes,* and *infrastructures* that enable multi-actor collaboration (see Table 2). In actor-oriented organizations, control and coordination are based on direct exchanges among the actors themselves rather than on hierarchical planning, delegation, and integration. Although hierarchy is present in actor-oriented organizations, these designs mainly rely on lateral, reciprocal relationships among actors for control and coordination. As an illustration of how an actor-oriented organization works in an easy-to-grasp context, see Table 3, which describes the organization of ants foraging for food.

**Table 2.** Elements of an actor-oriented organization

| Element | Function | Examples |
|---|---|---|
| Actors | Perform work activities by self-organizing and collaborating | Individuals or teams in an organization<br>Firms in a collaborative community<br>Citizens, firms, and municipal agencies in a smart city |
| Commons | Shared resources made available to actors to support their work | Shared knowledge<br>Shared databases<br>Shared situation awareness |
| Protocols, processes, and infrastructures | Infrastructures connect actors with one another<br>Protocols guide actor behavior<br>Processes that combine to create an agile organization | Software apps that announce projects as well as the availability and expertise of actors<br>Shared norms and values concerning how actors should behave<br>Intra- and inter-organizational collaboration |

**Table 3**. Ants foraging for food

| |
|---|
| A queen ant lays the eggs that establishes the colony. She gives the ants their innate characteristics but does not directly control and coordinate what they do. Worker ants operate according to a set of processes and communication protocols that enable them to self-organize their work. For instance, when an ant finds food, it releases pheromones on the way back to the nest. The scent is a signal that mobilizes other worker ants to follow the chemical traces to the food source. They then collect and transport food in efficient columns back to the nest until the food source is empty. When there is no more food to collect, the ants stop releasing pheromones as they return to the nest. The scent weakens, and the ants start exploring new terrain to find more food. |
| This example includes the core elements of the actor-oriented architecture. The *actors* in the ant organization are the queen, workers, drones, and soldiers (Buckingham, 1911; Gordon, 2014), all of whom have different *capabilities*. The queen is the one who starts the colony and lays all the eggs. Drones are male ants who do not perform any work in the colony; their sole function is to fertilize a new queen. Soldier ants defend the nest. Worker ants perform a variety of tasks including nest building and maintenance as well as food foraging, and they coordinate by using pheromones as communication *protocols*. In food foraging, the worker ants search randomly for food in the absence of a nearby pheromone trail, drop pheromones on the way back to the nest while carrying food, and follow a pheromone trail to a food source. Thus, pheromone trails provide the ants with a *shared situation awareness* of food sources. The worker ants each contribute to updating the situation awareness, and they all use this *commons* to determine their own behavior. Updating and using the pheromone trail for navigation is part of the ants' collaborative capabilities. |

## Actors

Actors – whether they are individuals, teams, or firms – must possess the capabilities and values to self-organize. They engage in self-management rather than wait to respond to directions received from the hierarchy. They also act with integrity, developing a reputation for consistent, competent behavior – social capital that can be used at other times and in other arenas to develop new relationships and business opportunities. The trust that is built up between actors saves the costs of designing and using elaborate control mechanisms that monitor and ensure proper actor behavior. In an actor-oriented organization, actors understand the overall structure and processes of the organization, and their decisions and actions are taken in pursuit of the organization's common good. By focusing on the common good, actors can take advantage of shared values, norms of reciprocity, and trust in the self-governance process (Hess and Ostrom, 2006; Ostrom, 1990, 2010).

## Commons

Commons refers to resources that are collectively owned and available to actors (members of the organization). One type of commons is a knowledge commons, a repository of knowledge that organization members can both contribute to and use. For example, Blade.org, a collaborative community of more than 70 firms in the computer server industry, posted all of the solutions developed by member firms on the organization's website. Any Blade.org member firm could access the website and examine the solutions for ideas that might apply to its particular market or customer base (Snow et al. 2011). Smart Aarhus, the smart-city initiative of Aarhus, Denmark, has a database called Open Data Aarhus whose purpose is to make relevant data and information accessible to Aarhus citizens and organizations. These datasets can be used to develop new products, services, and digital applications. Any firm or individual citizen can access the more than 75 datasets in Open Data Aarhus and use the data for collective purposes (Snow et al. 2016).

Shared situation awareness is a commons that facilitates self-organization. Situation awareness refers to knowing what is going on in the organization (Endsley, 2000). Digitally shared situation awareness provides an up-to-date portrait of problems and opportunities in the organization's environment as well as the current availability of resources to address those problems and opportunities. Through digitally shared situation awareness, valuable information is widely available to organization members in their decision-making. Originally developed as an operational tool for fighter pilots in World War I, situation awareness is used today in air traffic control, power plants, and advanced manufacturing systems (Endsley, 2000), and its use is growing in healthcare and other sectors. When actors share an up-to-date awareness of the organization's situation, everybody in the organization can make the right decision or take the correct action without seeking direction or authorization from the hierarchy.

### Infrastructures, processes, and protocols

Infrastructures connect actors and allow access to the same information, knowledge, and other resources. Actors who have the knowledge, information, tools, and values needed to set goals, and who can assess the consequences of potential actions for the achievement of those goals, can self-organize. Self-organizing actors use protocols to guide their collaborative interactions. Protocols are "codes of conduct" used by organizational actors in their exchanges and collaboration activities. An important category of protocols deals with the division of labor, the mobilization and linking of actors for a particular project or task. Examples are protocols by which actors advertise problems or opportunities as well as their own capabilities and availability, and protocols by which actors search for potential collaborators.

In summary, actor-oriented organizational architecture is focused on the organization's actors: the work that they do, and the principles and processes by which they relate to one another. Competent actors working for the common good of the organization can self-organize and self-manage with only minimal need for hierarchical control and coordination. Commons, infrastructures, and protocols are used to guide and support actor behavior, connecting organization members with one another and facilitating their work activities.

## APPLYING THE ACTOR-ORIENTED SCHEME TO THE DESIGN OF THE DIGITAL ORGANIZATION

Traditional organization design is centered on structural relationships – the boxes on the organization chart and the reporting lines that connect them. Actor-oriented design, by contrast, is centered on shared access to information and other resources as well as the protocols and infrastructures by which actors connect and collaborate. Born-digital companies can apply an actor-oriented design at their inception. Established firms, however, typically must be *re*designed. Redesign involves changing a predominantly hierarchical system supported by legacy technologies to an actor-oriented system (Langer, 2017). Having targeted a particular area for redesign, designers and decision-makers need to address each of the components of the actor-oriented scheme.

## Collaborating, self-organizing actors

A competent actor is one who possesses the knowledge, skills, and values suited to an actor-oriented system. In building a digital organization, the effective composition and mobilization of a set of competent actors may require a combination of selection, training, mentoring, and replacement of personnel. An actor-oriented digital organization is especially conducive to use by millennials (people born after 1980) who have acquired knowledge and expertise from their Internet activities (Langer, 2017: Ch. 10), and it may be difficult to use by employees who lack social media skills and who have been ingrained with hierarchical approaches to organizing and managing (Espinoza and Ukleja, 2016; Saxena and Jain, 2012).

In 2015, millenials became the largest generation in the U.S. workforce, and by 2025 they will constitute 75% of that workforce (Meister and Willyerd, 2010). A forecasted skill set for the digital-age workforce is shown in Table 4. As shown, the digital organization will require its members to have a demanding set of both hard and soft skills. Hard skills include computational thinking and trans-disciplinarity. Soft skills include social intelligence, cross-cultural competency, and the ability to collaborate. To capitalize on these skills, the digital organization must provide flexible workspaces and policies that motivate millennials and enable them to be productive. Such workspaces will include appropriate collaboration tools and be designed according to sound psychological theories and principles. It is well established that people are extrinsically motivated by reward systems, evaluations, and the opinions others have of them (Herzberg, 1966). Self-determination theory (Ryan and Deci, 2017) holds that just as frequently people are motivated from within – by their interests, curiosity, concern for others, and abiding values. Following self-determination theory, jobs must be designed so that they meet the core psychological needs of *competence, relatedness,* and *autonomy.* Such designs foster the most volitional and high-quality forms of motivation and positive work outcomes, including enhanced performance, persistence, and creativity. Conversely, the degree to which any of these basic psychological needs is unsupported or thwarted in an organizational context will have a detrimental impact on people's well-being and performance in that setting.

**Table 4.** Work skills required by an actor-oriented digital organization

| |
|---|
| Sense-making |
| Ability to determine the deeper meaning or significance of what is being expressed |
| Social Intelligence |
| Ability to connect to others in a deep and direct way, to sense and stimulate reactions and desired interactions |
| Cross-cultural Competency |
| Ability to operate in different cultural settings |
| Computational Thinking |
| Ability to translate large amounts of data into abstract concepts and to understand data-based reasoning |
| Media Literacy |
| Ability to critically assess and develop content that uses new media forms and to leverage these media for persuasive communication |
| Trans-disciplinarity |
| Literacy in and ability to understand concepts across multiple disciplines |
| Design Mindset |
| Ability to represent and develop tasks and work processes for desired outcomes |
| Cognitive Load Management |
| Ability to discriminate and filter information for importance, and to understand how to maximize cognitive functioning using a variety of tools and techniques |
| Virtual Collaboration |
| Ability to work productively, drive engagement, and contribute as a member of a virtual team |
| Source: https://www.sfu.ca/career/WCID/iftf_futureworkskills.html |

The individual capabilities of actors must be turned into collective capabilities in order for the organization to operate at its desired scale and speed. The development of organizational capabilities occurs through a managed learning process in which individuals, technology, and organizational culture evolve together (Langer, 2017). At Valve Corporation, a digital distribution platform that operates with few hierarchical mechanisms, organizational capabilities are developed along actor-oriented lines (Felin and Powell, 2016). First, Valve recruits individuals who, in their estimation, have the capacity to create value in a marketplace of ideas. Second, those actors are allowed to self-select the projects on which they want to work. Third, a new project can be started if at least three peers agree that it is worthwhile (the "rule of three"). Fourth, project teams are empowered to sense, shape, and seize their own market opportunities. It is expected that teams will engage with external stakeholders via open innovation methods such as crowdsourcing, user communities, innovation contests, and so on.

Historically, organizations have been populated by humans using tools and equipment to accomplish their tasks. Increasingly, human actors work collaboratively with digital agents such as robots, adding a digital actor to the organization. Newer robots with abilities in social interaction are able to learn from their human counterparts through cooperation and tutelage (Green et al. 2008). Effective collaboration requires human and digital agents to share goals and situation awareness as well as the capability to communicate directly with one another.

## Commons that support collaboration

Designing commons for a digital organization will be specific to each organization and its needs, but two commons in particular deserve attention: situation awareness and knowledge. To be effective, actors need a shared awareness of the resources and activities in their environment. For example, in the self-dialysis clinic at the Ryhov Hospital in Sweden, all dialysis patients share a common electronic calendar that allows them to schedule their own treatment sessions. In addition, the equipment of the center is designed in a way that allows patients to perform their own treatment. The roles of the actors in this example are different from those of a hierarchically organized treatment center. Here patients self-organize their treatment while doctors and nurses use shared information about the patient's condition to intervene only if necessary (IHI Annual Report, 2012). Functionality that supports shared situation awareness is emerging across a wide variety of software platforms. Such platforms are extensively used by military organizations and advanced technology firms for collaborative problem solving and decision-making (Kolfschoten and Briggs, 2015; Nunamaker et al. 2009). Several recent software platforms support project management, and office productivity tools increasingly support real-time collaboration around documents and spreadsheets. Galbraith (2010) provides an account of how Procter & Gamble uses a collaborative spreadsheet program to speed up the reconciliation of corporate plans and budgets.

A knowledge commons is information and data that is shared by the actors who make up the organization. It is typical to distinguish between declarative and procedural knowledge (Kogut and Zander, 1992). Declarative knowledge is factual whereas procedural knowledge is know-how. For example, the Open Source Drug Discovery community maintains declarative knowledge in a repository of all scientific discoveries made by its members (Kolbjørnsrud, 2017). This allows all contributors to have a real-time awareness of the problem state (Newell and Simon, 1972) – how far the members of the community have come toward a solution and the knowledge gaps that still need to be closed. Many consulting firms, such as

Accenture, maintain procedural knowledge of the best practices used by their consultant teams (Langer and Yorks, 2013). The overall purpose of a procedural commons is to provide a set of shared resources that helps an organization learn and adapt.

In a given digital organization, all actors may not use the entire commons. Some software platforms allow the commons to be subdivided such that actors can collaborate around selected subsets. Subdivision of the commons permits actors to use only those resources relevant to their task and situation.

## Protocols, processes, and infrastructures that connect and guide actors

Guiding interactions among actors and accessing commons require protocols that reduce ambiguity and increase the effectiveness and efficiency of interaction. There are self-organizing processes associated with each protocol that actors follow in order to achieve control and coordination. In a digital organization, actors use their collaborative tools to signal both the tasks to be done and the availability of resources to perform them. Although protocols are specific to the type of collaboration, there are commonalities. Military and emergency response platforms, for example, have protocols and processes for publishing updates to the situation awareness database and subscribing to particular types of information, such as new events occurring in a geographic area (DeMarco, 2016; Liang and Gao, 2010). Similarly, platforms for collaborative project management (Chen et al. 2003) have protocols for inviting collaborators, sharing information about the whole project or particular tasks, and alerting collaborators to changes affecting their portion of the project (c.f. www.smartsheet.com). The infrastructure that allows the actors to connect with one another consists of communication networks and computer servers.

# CONCLUSION

Digital organizations are increasing in both numbers and sophistication. We have described how digital technologies can be integrated into organizations and have shown how actor-oriented principles and designs can be used to organize and perform activities. Actor-oriented digital organizations are collaborative, agile, and minimally hierarchical. In many industries, they are populated by human and digital agents who work together collaboratively. Digital organizations need technologically aware and adept leaders who can set the digital agenda and create the context for the digitization of every relevant aspect of their organizations. Digitization is occurring at an accelerating pace; successful leaders need to synchronize their organizations to digital clock speed.

## FOOTNOTES

*1* This section draws extensively on an article that introduced the actor-oriented framework (Fjeldstad et al. 2012).

## ACKNOWLEDGEMENTS

The authors thank John Colman for helpful comments to the "Ants Foraging for Food" example.

## AUTHORS' CONTRIBUTIONS

ODD and CCS developed the actor-oriented framework discussed in the article. AML has written books and articles on digital technologies and how to incorporate them into companies and other types of organizations. All three authors read and approved the final manuscript.

## COMPETING INTERESTS

The authors declare that they have no competing interests.

## PUBLISHER'S NOTE

Springer Nature remains neutral with regard to jurisdictional claims in published maps and institutional affiliations.

## REFERENCES

1. Alberts DS (2007) Agility, focus, and convergence: the future of command and control. Int C2 J 1(1):1–30
2. Aldrich HE, Ruef M (2006) Organizations Evolving, 2nd edn. Sage, Thousand Oaks
3. Altman EJ, Nagle F, Tushman M (2015) Innovating without information constraints: organization, communities, and innovation when information costs approach zero. In: Hitt MA, Jing Z (eds) The Oxford Handbook of Creativity, Innovation, and Entrepreneurship. Oxford University Press, New York, pp 353–379
4. Arthur WB (2009) The Nature of Technology: What It Is and How It Evolves. Free Press, New York
5. Benkler Y (2002) Coases's penguin, or, Linux and the nature of the firm. Yale Law J 112:369–446
6. Boudreau KJ, Lacetera N, Lakhani KR (2011) Incentives and problem uncertainty in innovation contests: an empirical analysis. Manag Sci 57(5):843–863
7. Brynjolfsson E, McAfee A (2014) The Second Machine Age: Work, Progress, and Prosperity in a Time of Brilliant Technologies. W.W. Norton, New York
8. Buckingham E (1911) Division of labor among ants. Proc Am Acad Arts Sci 46(18):425–508
9. Chen F, Nunamaker JF, Roman N, Briggs RO (2003) A collaborative project management architecture. Proceedings of the 36th IEEE Annual Hawaii International Conference on System Sciences, pp 233–242.
10. Christensen CM (1997) The Innovator's Dilemma: When New Technologies Cause Great Firms to Fail. Harvard Business School Press, Boston
11. Christensen CM, Bower JL (1996) Customer power, strategic investment, and the failure of leading firms. Strateg Manage J. 17(3):197–218.
12. Dahl OJ, Nygaard K (1966) SIMULA – an ALGOL-based simulation language. Commun ACM 9(9):671–678
13. Davenport TH, Kirby J (2015) Beyond automation. Harv Bus Rev 94(6):59–65
14. DeMarco DL (2016) A visual language for situational awareness. Doctoral dissertation. Naval Postgraduate School, Monterey

15. Drucker PF (1988) The coming of the new organization. Harv Bus Rev 66(1):45–53
16. Eisenhardt KM, Schoonhoven CB (1996) Resource-based view of strategic alliance formation: strategic and social effects in entrepreneurial firms. Organ Sci 7(2):136–150
17. Endsley MR (2000) Theoretical underpinnings of situation awareness: a critical review. In: Endsley MR, Garland DJ (eds) Situation Awareness Analysis and Measurement. Lawrence Erlbaum Associates, Mahwah
18. Engelbart, DC (1962). Augmenting human intellect: a conceptual framework. Summary Report AFOSR-3223 under Contract AF 49 (638)-1024, SRI Project 3578 for Air Force Office of Scientific Research. Stanford Research Institute, California. Retrieved on March 1, 2007
19. Espinoza C, Ukleja M (2016) Managing the Millennials: Discover the Core Competencies for Managing Today's Workforce, 2nd edn. Wiley, New York
20. Fedorowicz J, Konsynski B (1992) Organization support systems: bridging business and decision processes. J Manag Inf Syst 8(4):5–25
21. Felin T, Powell TC (2016) Designing organizations for dynamic capabilities. Calif Manag Rev 58(4):78–96
22. Fjeldstad ØD, Snow CC, Miles RE, Lettl C (2012) The architecture of collaboration. Strateg Manag J 33(6):734–750
23. Fujitsu (2016). http://www.fujitsu.com/global/about/resources/news/press-releases/2016/0609-01.html. Retrieved on July 7, 2016.
24. Galbraith JR (2010) The multi-dimensional and reconfigurable organization. Organ Dyn 39(2):115–125
25. Gershgorn D (2016). Elon Musk's artificial intelligence group opens a 'gym' to train A.I. Popular Science (http://www.popsci.com/elon-musks-artificial-intelligence-group-opens-gym-to-train-ai). April 27, 2016.
26. Gordon (2014). What ants teach us about the brain, cancer and the Internet? https://www.ted.com/talks/deborah_gordon_what_ants_teach_us_about_the_brain_cancer_and_the_internet. Retrieved on November 18, 2016.
27. Green SA, Billinghurst M, Chen X, Chase G (2008) Human-robot collaboration: a literature review and augmented reality approach in design. Int J Adv Robot Syst 5(1):1–18
28. Hagedorn J (1993) Understanding the rationale of strategic technology partnering: interorganizational modes of cooperation and sectoral differences. Strateg Manag J 14(5):371–385

29. Heinerth C, Lettl C, Keinz P (2014) Synergies among producer firms, lead users, and user communities: the case of the LEGO producer-user ecosystem. J Prod Innov Manag 31(4):848–866
30. Herzberg F (1966) Work and the Nature of Man. World Publishing, Cleveland
31. Hess C, Ostrom E (eds) (2006) Understanding Knowledge as a Commons: From Theory to Practice. The MIT Press, Cambridge
32. Hodson H (2014) The AI boss that deploys Hong Kong's subway engineers. New Scientist July 7. https://www.newscientist.com/article/mg22329764-000-the-ai-boss-that-deploys-hong-kongs-subway-engineers/. Retrieved on November 18, 2016.
33. Huber GP (1990) A theory of the effects of advanced information technologies on organizational design, intelligence, and decision making. Acad Manag Rev 15(1):47–71
34. IHI Annual Report (2012) http://www.ihi.org/about/Documents/IHI_AnnualReport_2012.pdf. Retrieved on April 11, 2017
35. Johansen B (2007) Get There Early: Sensing the Future to Compete in the Present. Berrett-Koehler, San Francisco
36. Kogut B (1988) Joint ventures: theoretical and empirical perspectives. Strateg Manag J 9(4):319–332
37. Kogut B, Zander U (1992) Knowledge of the firm, combinative capabilities, and the replication of technology. Organ Sci 3(3):383–397
38. Kolbjørnsrud V (2017) Agency problems and governance mechanisms in collaborative communities. Strat Organ 15(2):141–173
39. Kolbjørnsrud V, Amico R, Thomas RJ (2016). The promise of artificial intelligence: redefining management in the workforce of the future. Accenture Institute for High Performance Business. https://www.accenture.com/_acnmedia/PDF-19/AI_in_Management_Report.pdf. Retrieved on September 19, 2016.
40. Kolfschoten GL, Briggs RO (2015) Organizing the theoretical foundation of collaboration engineering. In: Kolfschoten GL, Nunamaker JF (eds) Collaboration Systems: Concept, Value, and Use. Routledge, Taylor and Francis Group, London, pp 27–41
41. Krol E (1993) FYI on 'what is the internet?' Available at: http://www.rfc-editor.org/rfc/rfc1462.txt. Retrieved on November 18, 2016.
42. Langer AM (2017) Information Technology and Organizational Learning: Managing Behavioral Change through Technology and Education, 3rd edn. CRC Press, New York
43. Langer AM, Yorks L (2013) Strategic IT: Best Practices for Managers and Executives. Wiley, New York

44. Liang S, Gao Y (2010) Real-time notification and improved situational awareness in fire emergencies using geospatial-based publish/subscribe. International Journal of Applied Earth Observation and Geoinformation 12(6):431–438
45. Licklider JCR (1960) Man-computer symbiosis. IRE Transac Hum Factors Electron 1:4–11
46. Lohr S (2016). Goodbye, ivory tower. Hello, candy store. The New York Times Sunday Business (September 4):1–4.
47. Mata FJ, Fuerst WL, Barney JB (1995) Information technology and sustained competitive advantage: a resource-based analysis. MIS Q 19(4):487–505
48. Mayo Clinic (2016) Robotic surgery: treatment at Mayo. http://www.mayoclinic.org/tests-procedures/robotic-surgery/care-at-mayo-clinic/treatment/prc-20013988. Retrieved on July 22, 2016
49. Meister JC, Willyerd K (2010) The 2020 Workplace: How Innovative Companies Attract, Develop, and Keep Tomorrow's Employees Today. HarperCollins, New York
50. Miles RE, Snow CC (1978) Organizational Strategy, Structure, and Process. McGraw-Hill, New York
51. Negroponte N (1995) Being Digital. Knopf, New York
52. Newell A, Simon HA (1972) Human problem solving (Vol. 104, No. 9). Prentice-Hall, Englewood Cliffs
53. Nunamaker JF, Reinig BA, Briggs RO (2009) Principles for effective virtual teamwork. Commun ACM 52(4):113–117
54. Ostrom E (1990) Governing the Commons: The Evolution of Institutions for Collective Action. Cambridge University Press, Cambridge
55. Ostrom E (2010) Beyond markets and states: polycentric governance of complex economic systems. Am Econ Rev 100(3):641–672
56. Perrow C (1967) A framework for the comparative analysis of organizations. Am Sociol Rev 32(2):194–208
57. Porter ME, Hempelmann JE (2014) How smart, connected products are transforming competition. Harvard Busi Rev 92(11):1–23.
58. Powell WW, Koput KW, Smith-Doerr L (1996) Interorganizational collaboration and the locus of innovation: networks of learning in biotechnology. Adm Sci Q 41(1):116–145
59. Ryan RM, Deci EL (2017) Self-Determination Theory: Basic Psychological Needs in Motivation, Development, and Wellness. Guilford, New York
60. Sambamurthy V, Bharadwaj A, Grover V (2003) Shaping agility through digital options: reconceptualizing the role of information technology in contemporary firms. MIS Q 27(2):237–263

61. Sasson A, Johnson JC (2016) The 3D printing order: variability, supercenters and supply chain reconfigurations. Int J Phys Distribut Logistics Manage 46(1):82–94
62. Saxena P, Jain R (2012) Managing career aspirations of Generation Y at work place. Int J Adv Res Comput Sci Softw Eng 2(7):114–118
63. Setia P, Venkatesh V, Joglekar S (2013) Leveraging digital technologies: how information quality leads to localized capabilities and customer service performance. MIS Q 37(2):565–590
64. Shapiro C, Varian HR (1999) Information Rules: A Strategic Guide to the Network Economy. Harvard Business School Press, Boston
65. Simon HA (1962) The architecture of complexity. Proc Am Philos Soc 106(6):466–482
66. Simon HA (1973) Applying information technology to organization design. Public Adm Rev 33(3):268–278
67. Snow CC, Fjeldstad ØD, Lettl C, Miles RE (2011) Organizing continuous product development and commercialization: the collaborative community of firms model. J Prod Innov Manag 28:3–16
68. Snow CC, Håkonsson DD, Obel B (2016) A smart city is a collaborative community: lessons from Smart Aarhus. Calif Manag Rev 59(3):92–108
69. Suhayl A, Joshi M (2015) The VUCA Company. Jaico Publishing House, Mumbai
70. Varian HR (2000) Buying, sharing and renting information goods. J Ind Econ 48(4):473–488
71. Westerman G, Bonnet D, McAfee A (2014) Leading Digital: Turning Technology into Business Transformation. Harvard Business Review Press, Boston
72. Wheelwright SC, Clark K (1992) Revolutionizing Product Development. Free Press, New York
73. Zittrain JL (2006) The generative Internet. Harvard Law Rev 119(7):1974–2040

# CHAPTER 6

# Ergonomic Challenges of Employees Using Computers at Work in a Tertiary Institution in Ghana

**Kumah DB*, Akuffo KO, Affram DE, Ankamah E and Osae EA**

*Department of Optometry, Kwame Nkrumah University of Science and Technology, Kumasi, Ghana*

## ABSTRACT

**OBJECTIVE:** Ergonomically designed workstations have direct bearing on the comfort and safety of office computer users. Tremendous usage of computers in most offices of emerging economies have however, not seen accompanying applications of ergonomics in the design of computer workstations despite the numerous benefits. Injuries and discomforts therefore have higher propensity to occur since most offices formally designed for paperbased work now accommodate computer workstations, without corresponding redesigning. The study therefore sought to assess computer workstation designs in administrative offices at Kwame Nkrumah University of Science and Technology, with the aim of creating awareness of ergonomics and its application among administrative office computer users.

**METHOD:** A total of 150 office employees purposively sampled participated in this study. Respondents selected included secretaries, research assistants and data and account processors. This cross-sectional study consisted of a checklist (computer workstation components, visual complaints and ergonomics knowledge), work posture observations and measurements of workstation linear distances and monitor tilt angle. Descriptive statistics using Statistical Package for Social Sciences (SPSS) Version 20.0 was used for data analysis.

**RESULTS:** Almost half (50%) of respondents had monitors facing windows without appropriate blinds, 42% with monitor tilt angle less than 10 degrees and majority (76%) observed monitors either at or above horizontal eye level. Most (70%) of the workers acknowledged not having knowledge of ergonomics whiles 100% noted that they did not have any ergonomic assessment of their workstations. Neck, back and shoulder pains were reported by 85% of respondents while 73% complained of eyestrain.

**CONCLUSION:** The study revealed lack of information and skills in ergonomics contributing to poor ergonomic conditions and consequent visual discomforts among computer users in the work place.

**Keywords:** Computer; Workstation; Ergonomics; Administrative; Tilt angle; Musculoskeletal disorders

## INTRODUCTION

Office work is rapidly changing, as new developments in computer technology which make jobs easier are emerging. This emergence presents occupational health and safety problems for both management and employees [1]. While the first few decades of the development of the computer for business focused mainly on automating a wide range of industrial processes, the next step brought personal computers as productivity tools and entertainment devices to homes and workplaces everywhere. More recent refinements in computers and information technology such as mobile devices have led to a host of business and consumer-focused "apps" designed to help people to be more organized, efficient and productive [2].

Sitting at a desk and conducting daily routines on the computer for hours on end demands a computer workstation setup. Considering the long working hours and demands on a modern office worker, the nature and design of such workstation should be proper to ensure the comfort, safety and the total well-being of the worker. The application of the scientific discipline of ergonomics, defined as the "the science of fitting workplace conditions and job demands to the capabilities and inabilities of the individual worker" [3], is a vital element in the crafting of properly designed workstation. The concept of an ergonomically designed workstation is complex and depends on a myriad of elements. However, this simply should consist of a proper seating, adequate desk height, and proper distance of computer from the users' eyes as well as environmental issues such as proper lighting, noise levels among others [4].

The problem of an improper workstation design may be due to lack of knowledge or inappropriate application of ergonomic principles. Workstation designs significantly affect working posture, which in turn, contributes to physical symptoms experienced by Visual Display Unit (VDU) operators [5,6]. The adverse health consequences of this discrepancy mostly include musculoskeletal disorders and visual discomforts. For instance, ergonomic workstation deficiency hazards in a report presented to the United States Bureau of Labor Statistics has been noted as the fastest growing category of work-related illnesses [7] and worker compensation claims as well as absenteeism are drastically soaring due to same [8].

In most cases, symptoms of computer vision syndrome or digital eye strain occur because the visual demands of the task exceed the visual abilities of the individual to comfortably perform them. These symptoms may be caused by ergonomic workstation failures such as poor lighting, glare on digital screens, improper viewing distances, poor seating procedure, uncorrected vision problems and a combination of these factors [9].

Proper ergonomic design and adjustment of the computer and the work environment therefore play an important role in every office setting as it can increase productivity and worker comfort by decreasing the visual demands of the task.

Literature review on this subject revealed little information on ergonomic assessment in Ghana. Furthermore, very little is known amongst professionals regarding conducive workstation and the health consequences associated with prolonged computer use as well as improper workstation design.

This study was therefore carried out to assess computer workstations setup in administrative offices and the challenges workers face at the work place in the tertiary institution, with the aim of creating awareness of ergonomics and its application among administrative office computer users and by extension the larger university community.

## Methods

This descriptive cross-sectional study was undertaken at administrative offices of the Kwame Nkrumah University of Science and Technology (KNUST), Kumasi. The University is situated approximately on a 16 $km^2$ facility, about 7 km away from the central business district of the city of Kumasi. The staff strength of the University as at 2012 was 3,698 comprising of 1,010 senior members (senior lecturers, junior lecturers and senior administrators), 992 senior staff (non-teaching support staff with first degree) and 1,696 junior staff (support staff with less than first degree) [10]. The participants recruited for the study were administrative workers (secretaries, research assistants and data and account processors) who routinely work at a computer for a total of 4 hours or more during an 8-hour period of work, a close definition based on generally accepted ergonomic guidelines [11].

The study area was divided into seven clusters, comprising the University's six colleges and the school administration. Out of these, four clusters were randomly selected using a simple random sampling technique. One hundred and fifty (150) respondents present on the days of the visits who consented to participate in the study were sampled from these clusters for the study.

### DATA COLLECTION TECHNIQUE

The major instrument used for the study was a structured questionnaire (Supplementary 1). The questionnaire was designed with Likert scale questions based on ergonomic guidelines at computer workstation designs found in literature [12]. The questionnaires were self-administered and certain physical measurements of workstations were taken. The questionnaire consisted of four sections: Questions on demographics, physical workstation characteristics, visual strain symptoms as related to computer usage and ergonomics knowledge.

Instruments

Tape measure was used to measure linear distances and protractor used to measure angle of tilt of the monitor.

### MEASUREMENTS OF LINEAR DISTANCES AND ANGLES

The measurements were designed to quantify the actual working posture of each individual employee while at his/her computer workstation. The employee was asked to maintain his/her usual working postures while measurements were taken using measuring tape. This also helped in the determination of the sitting postures adopted as well as the relative position of top of monitor to horizontal eye level. The linear measurement indicators included: current seat height from the floor, monitor height from the floor, and distance between the eyes and the computer monitor.

The linear measurements of the following variables were measured as follows:

**SEAT HEIGHT:** This was measured as the distance from the floor to the top surface of the seat using the tape measure. Ideal seat height is between 38 cm-52 cm [13].

**MONITOR HEIGHT:** This was measured as the distance from the floor to the middle of the monitor using the tape measure. Ideal monitor height is between 90 cm-115 cm [13].

**EYE-TO-MONITOR DISTANCE:** This was measured as the distance from the eye to the top of the monitor using the tape measure. Ideal eye-tomonitor distance is between 60 cm-90 cm [13].

## POSTURAL POSITIONS

Gaze angle and sitting posture were evaluated by observation. These were noted by asking each participant to perform his or her usual keyentry task in his or her usual keying position. Gaze angle was taken based on the relative eye position to the middle of the monitor whilst the sitting posture took cognizance of the bend of the head from the "neutral" straight-up position.

## ETHICAL CONSIDERATION

Permission to carry out the study was obtained from the relevant heads of the various administrative units prior to the initiation of the project. Informed consent was obtained from the participants. The purpose of the study was explained to the study subjects and they were assured about the confidentiality and anonymity of the information so obtained.

## DATA ANALYSIS

The collected data was coded and entered in the Statistical Package for Social Sciences (SPSS) version 20.0 compatible with Windows. Descriptive and frequency analysis were used to summarize the data distribution, including demographic information, work practices, physical workstation characteristics and work posture.

# RESULTS

## DEMOGRAPHIC INFORMATION OF RESPONDENTS

**TABLE 1** below presents the demographic profile of study respondents. The respondents comprised 62.7% males and had a mean age of 37.4 ± 11.5 years.

**TABLE 1:** Demographic profile of study participants.

| | |
|---|---|
| **Gender Distribution Of Respondents** | |
| Male | 94(62.7%) |
| Female | 56(37.3%) |
| Total | 150 (100%) |
| **Age of Respondents** | |
| Age Range (years) | Mean Age (Mean ± SD) in years |
| 20 to 59 | 37.4 ±11.5 |
| **Nature of job undertaken by respondents** | |
| Administrative assistants | 96(64.0%) |
| Data and account processors | 42(28.0%) |
| Research assistants | 12(8.0%) |
| Total | 150 (100%) |
| **Hours spent in front of a computer** | |
| 1-4 h/day | 15 (10.0%) |
| 5-8 h/day | 94 (62.7%) |
| 8 h/day | 41 (27.3%) |
| Total | 150 (100%) |

Physical attributes of the workstations are reported in **TABLE 2**. Of the 150 workstations assessed, 85.0% had the monitor placed on the table or desk surface and 12.0% had the monitor placed on the processor, which in turn was placed on the desk surface.

**TABLE 2:** Measured workstation attributes among study respondents.

| Eye to monitor distance (cm) | n (%) |
|---|---|
| < 60 | 22 (14.7) |
| 60-90 | 91 (60.7) |
| > 90 | 37 (24.6) |
| **Tilt angle (degree)** | |
| < 10 | 63 (42.0) |
| 10-20 | 68 (45.3) |
| >20 | 19 (12.7) |
| **Height of monitor (cm)** | |
| < 90 | 1 (0.7) |
| 90-115 | 135 (90.0) |
| >115 | 14 (9.3) |
| **Height of chair (cm)** | |
| 38-52 | 92 (61.3) |
| >52 | 58 (38.7) |

## FURNITURE

Nearly all, (85.0%) of the workstations evaluated used office tables, 104 (69.3%) respondents used semi adjustable chairs (only the height could be adjusted) and the remaining 46 (30.7%) used non-adjustable office chairs.

In **TABLE 3**, the worker's eye level at the monitor measurements are displayed. It shows that only 24.0% of the respondents had their eye level below the horizontal.

**TABLE 3:** Worker Eye Level at Monitor.

| Horizontal eye level to monitor | n (%) |
|---|---|
| Upward (Above User's eye level) | 53 (35.3) |
| Horizontal (At User's eye level) | 61 (40.7) |
| Downward (Below User's eye level) | 36 (24.0 ) |

## COMPUTER VISION SYNDROME (CVS) SYMPTOMS

In **TABLE 4A** the symptoms associated with computer vision syndrome are displayed. Musculoskeletal symptoms (neck, back and shoulder pains) have the highest prevalence among the respondents (85%) followed by eyestrain (74%).

**TABLE 4A:** Computer vision syndrome symptom distribution among respondents.

| S/N | Symptoms | n (%) |
|---|---|---|
| 1 | Eyestrain | 111 (74.0) |
| 2 | Blurred near vision | 35 (23.3) |
| 3 | Glare | 30 (20.0) |
| 4 | Difficulty focusing | 32 (21.3) |
| 5 | Blurred distance vision | 30 (20.0) |
| 6 | Burning, itching | 87 (58.0) |
| 7 | Dry eye | 67 (44.7) |
| 8 | Headaches | 72 (48.0) |
| 9 | Neck, back, shoulder pain | 128 (85.3) |
| 10 | Double vision | 21 (14.0) |

**TABLES 4B** and **4C** illustrate the degree of discomfort and the frequency with which the various symptoms of Computer Vision Syndrome occurred among users while working on the computer respectively. The highest degree of discomfort was reported as those of neck, back and shoulder pains with a total of 55.0% describing the symptom as either severe or moderate. Other details are displayed in **TABLE 4B**.

**TABLE 4B:** Symptoms Severity and Number of Respondents (%).

| S/N | Symptoms | Severe | Moderate | Mild | Never |
|---|---|---|---|---|---|
| 1 | Eyestrain | 8.0 | 24.0 | 42.0 | 26.0 |
| 2 | Blurred near vision | 5.3 | 2.0 | 16.0 | 76.7 |
| 3 | Glare | 2.0 | 5.0 | 13.0 | 80.0 |
| 4 | Difficulty focusing | 0.0 | 8.0 | 13.3 | 78.7 |
| 5 | Blurred distance vision | 3.0 | 4.0 | 13.0 | 80.0 |
| 6 | Burning, itching | 6.0 | 14.0 | 38.0 | 42.0 |
| 7 | Dry eye | 8.7 | 10.0 | 26.0 | 55.3 |
| 8 | Headaches | 7.0 | 9.0 | 32.0 | 52.0 |
| 9 | Neck, back, shoulder pain | 17.3 | 38.0 | 30.0 | 14.7 |
| 10 | Double vision | 2.0 | 3.0 | 9.0 | 86.0 |

**TABLE 4C:** Symptoms Frequency and Number of Respondents (%).

| S/N | Symptoms | Never | Occasionally | Frequently |
|---|---|---|---|---|
| 1 | Eyestrain | 26.0 | 66.0 | 8.0 |
| 2 | Blurred near vision | 76.7 | 17.3 | 6.0 |
| 3 | Glare | 80.0 | 16.0 | 4.0 |
| 4 | Difficulty focusing | 78.7 | 18.0 | 3.3 |
| 5 | Blurred distance vision | 80.0 | 14.0 | 6.0 |
| 6 | Burning, itching | 42.0 | 50.0 | 8.0 |
| 7 | Dry eye | 55.3 | 38.0 | 6.7 |
| 8 | Headaches | 52.0 | 41.0 | 7.0 |
| 9 | Neck, back, shoulder pain | 14.7 | 58.0 | 27.3 |
| 10 | Double vision | 86.0 | 12.0 | 2.0 |

### KNOWLEDGE OF ERGONOMICS

Most (70%) of the workers acknowledged not having knowledge of ergonomics whiles all the respondents (100%) noted that they did not have any ergonomic assessment of their workstations. An individual's knowledge base plays a crucial role in the behavioral patterns he or she adopts. Thus, the low knowledge base of the respondents in this survey regarding ergonomics could affect their work habits, postures adopted and their perceptions towards the discomforts they were experiencing.

## DISCUSSION

According to this study, deviations in the physical layout and measurement of certain key dimensions of a safe and adequate workstation from recommended designs and parameters were observed. Most of the workstations surveyed in the present study had the normal office tables and chairs (with no ergonomic features), some semi-adjustable chairs, poor lighting condition and computer monitors facing windows. These deviations from recommendations greatly contribute to ergonomic problems.

Our results were similar to and consistent with a study conducted by Shikdar and Al-Kindi among forty employees and forty workstations in an oil company in Sultanate of Oman. In that study, 45% of the employees used nonadjustable chairs, 48% of computers faced windows, 45% of the employees adopted bent and unsupported back postures, and 20% used office tables for computers [14]. These results lead credence to the sort of workstations used in the developing world. Thus most workstations being used by prolonged VDU users in developing countries still lack ergonomically designed furniture for comfortable computer work. In addition, the research shows significant level of neck, back and shoulder pain, which could be attributed to the ergonomic deficiencies at the workstations surveyed. This observation is consistent with research studies that indicate that many cases of shoulder and neck pain were caused by inappropriate design or use of furniture [14,15].

The findings from this study also revealed that all respondents suffer one form or another of visual discomfort as a result of prolonged computer usage. Prominent amongst these discomforts were neck, back and shoulder pains, eyestrain, burning and itchy, headache and red eyes. A study by Sheedy [16], also showed the five most common symptoms of CVS as eyestrain, headache, blurred vision, dry eyes, and neck/back pain. These symptoms could be attributed to poor workstation ergonomics ranging from bad lighting conditions, bad ventilation, and monitor placement [17] amongst others.

Our study, however, revealed a relatively low prevalence of the symptoms of CVS as compared with other studies. For instance, a research work conducted among clerical VDT workers by Smith et al., revealed burning eyes (80%), irritated eyes (74%) and blurred vision (71%) as the most frequent complaints [18]. This difference could be attributed to several reasons, notable among them are the low level of knowledge of CVS among study population, differences in pain threshold, differences in sampling technique and sample size as well as the methodologies adopted. According to Anshel and Sheedy, though the problem of CVS is very prevalent, CVS still remains unknown to a lot of computer users including professional computer users [16,19]. Thus a lot of the respondents in this present survey might have been experiencing these symptoms, but very few of them were well informed enough to be able to attribute these symptoms to prolonged computer work.

# CONCLUSION AND RECOMMENDATION

Workstations employed for computer work at the university deviate considerably from the ergonomic workstation design per standards and recommendations from industrialized world. Respondents lacked knowledge regarding ergonomic principles and their applications within a Visual Display Unit (VDU) office environment. Therefore, the workstations surveyed were not ergonomically safe and comfortable for prolonged computer use.

We recommend that:

1. Computer workstations in offices should be laid out following ergonomics standards, guidelines, and recommendations.
2. Ergonomically designed facilities (workstation components) should be provided in order to better maintain and follow ergonomics standards.

## Limitation of Study

As a cross-sectional study, comprehensive ocular and general health assessment were not carried out for any respondent. The authors acknowledge this as a limitation as musculoskeletal disorders could arise also as a result of medical complications and not from ergonomic deficiencies in workstations only. The study did not look at the causal relationship between the postures as adopted by respondents in the study with the ocular symptoms they experience. We could thus not tell the extent to which the "supposed" poor postures contributed to the development of these symptoms.

## ACKNOWLEDGEMENTS

We thank so much Whitney Owusu -Ansah and Abigail Darkwa for their commitment in the preparation of the final draft of the manuscript. We also thank the respondents for volunteering for this study.

## REFERENCES

1. WISHA Service Division, Washington State Department of Labor and Industries (2002) Office ergonomics, Practical Solutions for a safer work place.
2. Browne C (2014) How have computers changed the workplace?
3. Salvendy G (2001) Handbook of industrial engineering: technology and operations management 3rd edition. John Wiley & Sons, Inc. New York, pp. 1112-1127.
4. Erstad S (2007) Office Ergonomics.
5. Lu H, Aghazadeh A (1996) Risk factors and their interactions in VDT workstation systems. In: Proceedings of the Human Factors and Ergonomics Society 40th Annual Meeting. Santa Monica, CA, USA: Human Factors and Ergonomics Society; 1996. 637-641.
6. Thomson WD (1998) Eye problems and visual display terminals--the facts and the fallacies. Ophthalmic Physiol Opt 18: 111-119.
7. Roth C (2011) The Importance of Ergonomics for the Safety Professional-It is a new year and as a safety professional, you already have a full plate. Dealing with identifying risk, maintaining compliance and regulatory standards, developing training, keeping budgets and ergonomics too? EHS Today, 4: 45.
8. Shikdar AA, Sawaqed NM (2003) Worker productivity, and occupational health and safety issues in selected industries. Computers & Industrial Engineering, 45: 563-572.
9. http://www.aoa.org/patients-and-public/caring-for-your-vision/protecting-your-vision/computer-vision-syndrome?sso=y
10. https://www.knust.edu.gh/staff
11. Rizzo T (1995) The Stanford Computer Injury Prevention Educational Intervention (SCIPEI) ergonomic bibliography: 205 Citation. Palo Alto California: Stanford University Health Improvement Program.
12. Cook C, Burgess-Limerick R (2003) Guidelines for computer workstations. Ergonomics Australia 17, 19-33.
13. Jackson D (1999) CUASA Ergonomics booklets, make your work area work for you.
14. Shikdar AA, Al-Kindi MA (2007) Office ergonomics: deficiencies in computer workstation design. Int J OccupSaf Ergon 13: 215-223.
15. Wall MDE, Van Riel MPJM, Aghina JCFM, Burdorf A, Snijders CJ (1992) Improving the sitting posture of CAD/CAM workers by increasing VDU monitor working height. Ergonomics 35: 427-436.
16. Sheedy JE (1992) Vision problems at video display terminals: a survey of optometrists. J Am OptomAssoc 63: 687-692.

17. Ankrum DR, Nemeth KJ (1995) Posture, comfort, and monitor placement. Ergonomics in Design: The Quarterly of Human Factors Applications 3: 7-9.
18. Smith MJ, Cohen BG, Stammerjohn LW Jr (1981) An investigation of health complaints and job stress in video display operations. Hum Factors 23: 387-400.
19. Anshel J (2005) Visual ergonomics handbook. Taylor & Francis Group, California, USA, pp. 45-50.

# CHAPTER 7

# Emotion Elicitation in a Socially Intelligent Service: The Typing Tutor

**Andrej Košir [1,†,*] and Gregor Strle [2,†]**

[1]*Faculty of Electrical Engineering, University of Ljubljana, Tržaška cesta 25, 1000 Ljubljana, Slovenia*

[2]*Institute of Ethnomusicology, Research Centre of the Slovenian Academy of Sciences and Arts, Novi trg 2, 1000 Ljubljana, Slovenia*

## ABSTRACT

This paper presents an experimental study on modeling machine emotion elicitation in a socially intelligent service, the typing tutor. The aim of the study is to evaluate the extent to which the machine emotion elicitation can influence the affective state (valence and arousal) of the learner during a tutoring session. The tutor provides continuous real-time emotion elicitation via graphically rendered emoticons, as an emotional feedback to learner's performance. Good performance is rewarded by the positive emoticon, based on the notion of positive reinforcement. Facial emotion recognition software is used to analyze the affective state of the learner for later evaluation. Experimental results show the correlation between the positive emoticon and the learner's affective state is significant for all 13 (100%) test participants on the arousal dimension and for 9 (69%) test participants on both affective dimensions. The results also confirm our hypothesis and show that the machine emotion elicitation is significant for 11 (85%) of 13 test participants. We conclude that the machine emotion elicitation with simple graphical emoticons has a promising potential for the future development of the tutor.

**Keywords:** affective computing; emotion elicitation; social intelligence; human-machine communication; intelligent tutoring systems

# 1. INTRODUCTION

Human communication requires a certain level of social and emotional intelligence, including the ability to detect and express non-verbal communication cues (e.g., facial expressions, gestures, body posture, movement), which in turn provide sustenance for verbal communication in given context. Individual's emotional involvement through expressions of affect and emotions is an essential indicator of their attention and overall engagement in communication and provides further clues about their affective state, intentions, and attitudes [1,2,3,4].

For humans, the ability to sustain communication in real-time, and recognize, respond to, and elicit affective states, seems almost effortless. For machines, on the other hand, even a minimal level of social intelligence is much harder, if not impossible, to replicate [5]. The computational modeling of affective processes is extremely difficult—not only because of the procedural aspects related that also need to run in real-time (e.g., recognition, detection, processing, modeling, and generation of affect), but primarily due to the complexity of human behavior and multimodality of human interaction [6]. The interplay between behavioral and psychological aspects of human behavior and the idiosyncratic nature and variable expressions of human affect and emotions pose further challenges for the affective computing [7]. Any advances in these areas can improve human-machine interaction (HCI). From the applied perspective the core research challenges are to produce for humans meaningful output [8,9,10] and more generally to "enable computers to better serve people's needs" [7].

Being able to recognize, measure, model human affect, and generate appropriate affective feedback to establish a more naturalistic human-machine-communication (HMC) is key to the design of intelligent services. As in human communication, the use of affect and emotions in HMC is necessary for measuring and improving user experience and overall engagement [11,12,13,14]. Naturalistic HMC can also minimize user-service adaptation procedures and maximize the engagement and the intended use of a service [15,16,17]. For a socially intelligent service to be successful, it should be capable of expressing some level of social and emotional intelligence. Such service is socially intelligent when it is capable of reading, detecting, measuring and estimating user's verbal and/or non-verbal social signals, producing machine-generated reasoning and emotional feedback, and sustaining HMC in real-time [18].

The paper presents an experimental study on machine emotion elicitation in a socially intelligent service, the touch-typing tutor. The main hypothesis is that learner's affective state can be influenced by the machine-generated emotion expressions. The underlying assumption, not addressed in this paper, is that machine emotion elicitation can contribute to the learner's increased performance, attention, motivation, and overall engagement with a system [19]. In this paper, we evaluate the effect of machine emotion elicitation on the learner's affective state during a touch-typing session. For this purpose, two emotion models are integrated into the tutor. The machine emotion model of the tutor provides continuous real-time machine emotion elicitation via graphically rendered emoticons, as an emotional feedback to the learner's performance during the session. Simultaneously, the user emotion model of the tutor captures and maps learner's facial emotion expressions onto a 2-dimensional affective space of valence and arousal, for the evaluation of emotion elicitation effect.

The paper is structured as follows. After the general overview of related work in Section 2, Section 3 presents the architecture and the emotion models of the intelligent typing tutor. Section 4 presents the design of the experimental study. The experimental results are presented in Section 5, focusing on the evaluation of the machine emotion model, the correlation between the machine generated emoticon and learner's valence-arousal space, and the influence of the machine emotion elicitation on the learner's affective state. The paper ends with general conclusions and future work in Section 6.

# 2. RELATED WORK

Research and development of a fully functioning socially intelligent service are still at a very early stage. However, various components that can ultimately lead to such a service have been under intensive development for several decades. We briefly present them below.

## 2.1. Social Intelligence, Social Signals, and Nonverbal Communication Cues

Various definitions of social intelligence exist, including skills in social interactions, ability to decode social information, exhibiting behavioral flexibility and adaptivity in different social contexts, among others. Thorndike coined the phrase "social intelligence" and defined it as the ability to "to act wisely in human relations" [20]. Gardner later argued for a theory of multiple intelligence, a more nuanced view of social intelligence which requires multiple cognitive abilities to adapt and respond to a particular social situation [21]. For Cantor and Kihlstrom, social intelligence is an "organizing principle", "a fund of knowledge about the social world", where differences in social knowledge cause differences in social behavior [22,23]. A broader definition, also used in this paper, is given by Vernon [24], who defines social intelligence as person's "ability to get along with people in general, social technique or ease in society, knowledge of social matters, susceptibility to stimuli from other members of a group, as well as insight into the temporary moods or underlying personality traits of strangers". Social intelligence is also viewed as an ability to express and recognize social cues and behaviors [25,26], including various non-verbal cues, such as gestures, postures and face expressions, exchanged during social interactions [27].

Social signals (cues) are extensively being analyzed in the field of HCI [27,28,29], often under different terminology. For example, [30] use the term "social signals" to define a continuously available information required to estimate emotions, mood, personality, and other traits that are used in human communication. Others [31] define such information as "honest signals", as they allow to accurately predict the non-verbal cues and, on the other hand, one is not able to control the non-verbal cues to the extent one can control the verbal form. In this paper, we will use the term "social signal".

**Behavioral Measurements**

The development of wearable sensors has enabled acquisition of user data in near real-time. As a result, notable advances can today be found in research on multimodal expressions of human behavior, especially in the fields of social computing, affective computing, and HCI, with the development of several novel measurement related procedures and techniques. For example, behavioral measurements are used to extend communication bandwidth and develop smart technologies [32], conversational intelligence based on the environmental sensors [33], and estimation of user behavior (e.g., emotion estimation) [34,35]. Several research works use behavioral measurements to study human behavior and usability aspects in regard to technology use, analyzing stress estimation [36], workload estimation [37], cognitive load estimation [38,39,40], and classification [41], among many others. A good example where aforementioned measurements all come into play is in intelligent tutoring systems [42], which are also relevant to the topic of this paper.

## 2.2. Intelligent Tutoring Systems

Intelligent tutoring systems (ITS) use technology to enable meaningful and effective learning. Research has shown that ITSs are nearly as effective as human tutoring [43]. ITSs often use affective computing and emotion mediation to improve user experience and performance of learning [44,45,46,47]. Moreover, several ITSs exist that support some level of social intelligence, ranging from emotion-aware to meta-cognitive. One of the more relevant examples is the intelligent tutoring system AutoTutor/Affective AutoTutor [47]. AutoTutor/Affective AutoTutor employs both affective and cognitive modeling to support learning and engagement, tailored to the individual user [47]. Some other examples include: Cognitive Tutor [48]—an instruction based system for mathematics and computer science, Help Tutor [49]—a meta-cognitive variation of AutoTutor that aims to develop better general help-seeking strategies for students, MetaTutor [50]—which aims to model the complex nature of self-regulated learning, and various constraint-based intelligent tutoring systems that model instructional domains at an abstract level [51], among many others. Studies on affective learning indicate the superiority of emotion-aware over non-emotion-aware services, with the former offering significant performance increase in learning [52,53,54] and release of stress and frustration [55,56].

## 2.3. Computational Models of Emotion

One of the core requirements for a service to be socially intelligent is the ability to detect and recognize emotions and exhibit the capacity for expressing and eliciting basic affective (emotional) states. Most of the literature in this area is dedicated to the affective computing and computational models of emotion [10,57,58], which are mainly based on the appraisal theories of emotion [8].

The field of affective computing has developed several approaches to modeling, analysis, and interpretation of human emotions [5]. One of the most known and widely used emotion annotation and representation models is the valence-arousal emotion space, based on Russell's valence-arousal model of affect [59]. The valence-arousal space is used in many human to machine interaction settings [60,61,62], and was also adopted in the socially intelligent typing tutor (see Section 3.3.2). There are other attempts to define models of human emotions, such as specific emotion spaces for human-computer interaction [63], or more recently, models for the automatic and continuous analysis of human emotional behavior [5].

Several challenges remain, most notably in design, training, and evaluation of computational models of emotion [64], critical analysis and comparison, and their relevance for other research fields (e.g., cognitive science, human emotion psychology) [10]. Recent research on emotions argues that traditional emotion models might be overly simplistic [9], pointing out the notion of emotion is multi-componential and includes "appraisals, behavioral activation, action tendencies, and motor expressions" [65]. There is a need for the "multifaceted conceptualization" in the modeling of emotions that can be linked to "qualitatively different types of evaluations" used in the appraisal theories [66].

### 2.3.1. Emotion Recognition From Facial Expressions

Research on emotions has demonstrated the central importance of facial expressions in recognition of emotions [1]. As a result, various classification systems for mapping facial expressions and emotions had been developed [6], most of them based on emotions studied by [67]. For example, Ekman and Friesen had developed the Facial Action Coding System (FACS), where observable components of facial movements are encoded in 44 different Action Units (AUs)—various combinations of AUs represent various facial expressions of emotion [68]. Several other alternatives exist, such as the MPEG-4 Facial Animation Parameters (FAP) standard for virtually representing humans and humanoids [69] and the FACS+, which is based on computer vision system for observing facial motion [70].

### 2.3.2. Emotion Elicitation Using Graphical Elements

Research on emotion elicitation using simple graphical elements (such as emoticons and smilies) is far less common than research on emotion elicitation with affective agents such as facial expressions, humanoid faces, or emotional avatars [71,72,73,74,75,76]. Whereas several studies on emotion elicitation use different stimuli (e.g., pictures, movies, music) [77,78] and behavioral cues [72], only a few tackle the challenges of affective graphical emoticons for purpose of emotion elicitation [74]. In the intelligent typing tutor, the learner's emotions are elicited by the graphical emoticons (smilies) via tutor's dynamic graphical user interface. The choice of smilies was due to their semantic simplicity, unobtrusiveness, and ease of continuous adaptation (various degrees of a smile) and measurement. Using pictures as emotional stimuli would add additional cognitive load, possibly elicit multiple emotions, and distract the learner from a task at hand. The presented approach also builds upon the findings of the existing research in affective computing and emotion elicitation, which shows that the recognition of emotions represented by affective agents is intuitive for humans [79], that human face-like graphics increase user engagement [80,81], and that emotion elicitation with simple emoticons can be significant [56,76]. The latter is discussed in Section 5.

# 3. EMOTION ELICITATION IN A SOCIALLY INTELLIGENT SERVICE: THE INTELLIGENT TYPING TUTOR

The following sections discuss general requirements of a socially intelligent service, the architecture of the intelligent typing tutor, and the models used for emotion elicitation in our experimental study.

## 3.1. General Requirements for Emotion Elicitation in a Socially Intelligent Service

A socially intelligent service should be capable of performing the following elements of social intelligence in regard to emotion elicitation:

1. Conduct behavioral measurements and gather data for relevant user behavior. Human emotions are conveyed via behavior and non-verbal communication cues, such as face expression, gestures, body posture, voice color, among others. Selected behavioral measurements (pupil size, acceleration of the wrist, etc.) are believed to be correlated with user's affective state and other non-verbal communication cues.

2. Analyze, estimate, and model user emotions and non-verbal (social) communication cues via computational models. Selected behavioral measurements are used as an input to the computational model of user emotions and for modeling machine emotion feedback.

3. Use emotion elicitation to reward performance and improve user engagement. For example, the notion of positive reinforcement could be integrated into a service to reward and improve performance and user engagement, taking into account user's temporary affective state and other non-verbal communication cues.

4. Naturalistic affective interaction. A continuous feedback loop between a user and a service, based on non-verbal communication cues.

5. Context and task-dependent adaptation: adapt a service according to the design goals. For example, in the intelligent typing tutor case study, the intended goal is to reward learner's performance and progress. The touch-typing lessons are carefully designed and adapt in regard to the typing speed and difficulty to meet user's capabilities, temporary affective state, and other non-verbal communication cues.

Such service is capable of sustaining efficient, continuous, and engaging HMC. It also minimizes user-service adaptation procedures. An early-stage example of a socially intelligent service that uses emotion elicitation to reward learner's performance is provided below.

## 3.2. The Architecture of the Intelligent Typing Tutor

The overall goal of the typing tutor is to reward learner's performance and thus improve the process of learning touch-typing. For this purpose, machine generated emotion elicitation is used together with the notion of positive reinforcement to respond to and reward learner's performance. In its current version, the tutor employs simple emoticon-like graphics for the machine emotion elicitation and state-of-the-art sensor technology to continuously measure and analyze learner's behavior.

Typing tutor's main building blocks consist of:

1. Web GUI: to support typing lessons and machine-generated graphical emoticons (see Figure 1). Data is stored on the server for later analysis and human annotation procedures. Such architecture allows for crowd-sourced testing and efficient remote maintenance.

2. Sensors: to gather behavioral data and monitor learner's status in real-time. The recorded data is later used to evaluate the effectiveness of the machine generated emotion elicitation. The list of sensors integrated into the typing tutor environment includes:

    - Keyboard input recorder: to monitor cognitive and locomotor errors that occur while typing;
    - Wrist accelerometer and gyroscope: to trace hand movement;
    - Emotion recognition software: to extract learner's facial emotion expressions in real-time;

- Eye tracking software: to measure eye gaze and pupil size, and estimate learner's attention and possible correlates to typing performance.

1. Machine emotion model: for modeling machine-generated emotion expressions (through graphical emoticons; see Section 3.3.1).
2. User emotion model: for measuring learner's emotion expressions (and performance) during a tutoring session (see Section 3.3.2).
3. Typing content generator: which uses learner's performance to recommend the appropriate level of typing lectures.

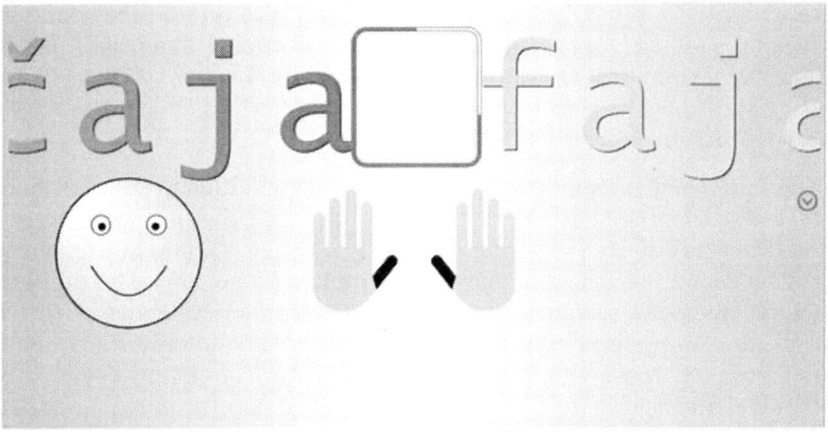

**Figure 1.** Socially intelligent typing tutor integrates touch-typing tutoring and machine-generated graphical emoticons (for emotion elicitation) via the graphical user interface.

The intelligent typing tutor is publicly available as a client-server service running in a web browser [82].

## 3.3. Modeling Emotions in the Intelligent Typing Tutor

The typing tutor employs two emotion models: (a) the machine emotion elicitation model based on the graphical emoticons and (b) the user emotion model that maps learner's emotions onto a valence-arousal space. The role of emotion elicitation in the intelligent typing tutor is that of basic HMC and reward system. The underlying argument for the emotion elicitation is that by employing machine-generated emotion elicitation we can to some extent influence learner's affective state and thus reward their performance. The notion of positive reinforcement [83] was used in the design of the machine emotion model. According to the positive reinforcement theory, the rewarded behaviors will appear more frequently in future, and also improve learner's motivation and engagement [83,84,85,86]. In the tutor, the machine-generated positive emotion expressions (smilies) act as rewards for the learner's performance in the touch-typing practice. Learners are rewarded by the positive emotional response when they successfully complete a series of sub-tasks within a limited time (e.g., use correct fingering and keyboard input per letter). Negative reinforcement, where learners would be penalized for their mistakes, is not supported for two reasons. First, there is no clear indication that negative reinforcement would positively contribute to the learning experience and overall engagement, and second, such an approach would require additional dimension, adding additional complexity to the experimental study.

### 3.3.1. Machine Emotion Elicitation Model

The intelligent typing tutor uses the machine emotion elicitation model to reward learner's performance. It is based on the notion of positive reinforcement—the rewards come as positive emotional responses conveyed by the machine-generated graphical emoticon. The graphical emoticons were selected from the subset of the emoticons in Official Unicode Consortium code chart [87], via tutor's interface (as shown in Figure 1). These emotional responses range from neutral to positive (smiley) and act as stimuli to boost learner's performance.

The intensity of the emoticon $\Phi m$ is defined by the interval [0,1], ranging from neutral to positive. The neutral emoticon is defined by the threshold eT that covers the lower 15% of the total emoticon intensity interval. This threshold eTrepresents the intensity of the neutral emoticon where the changes in its mouth curvature are visually still perceived as neutral. The threshold for the neutral emoticon was defined by the human observation of the $\Phi m$ levels.

The machine emotion model was designed following the recommendations of the typing expert. The typing session starts with a neutral emoticon. As the session progresses, the emoticon intensity $\Phi m$ updates gradually based on the performance values from the past time windows and the number of samples (see also Section 5). The performance is estimated as good or bad by the learner's typing errors and input delays (e.g., incorrect key input for the character presented on screen, the delay between the character presented and the key pressed, etc.). Note that the positive reinforcement (i.e. for the positive emoticon to come into effect and reward good performance) is not immediate and requires the learner to show good performance over time. Such approach also avoids rapid switching between the different intensity levels. Consequently, there are short time intervals of good performances represented by the neutral emoticon, before the positive reinforcement starts.

To reward and improve learner's performance, as well as attention, motivation, and overall engagement, the machine-generated emotional feedback needs to function in real-time. To implement it successfully the designer needs to decide which behaviors need reinforcement and how often. However, in this early version, the positive reinforcement of the machine emotion model is linked exclusively to the learner's performance, with the aim to reward it. More realistic applications of the machine emotion elicitation model are planned to align the notion of positive reinforcement with other aspects, such as learner's affective state, attention, motivation, frustration level, and task-load, among others. Such an approach would also enable dynamic personalization, similar to the conversational RecSys [88].

### 3.3.2. User Emotion Model

The underlying argument for the emotion elicitation presented in this paper is that learner's affective state can be to some extent elicited by the machine-generated graphical emoticons.

The learner's affective state is measured with the valence-arousal model [59]. The user emotion model automatically measures learner's facial emotion expressions and maps them onto the valence-arousal space in real-time, using emotion recognition software Noldus FaceReader Version 6.1. [89].

Two independent linear regression models were used to analyze the emotion elicitation in the typing tutor, and to obtain the models' quality of fit and the proportion of the explained variance. The valence and arousal data gathered from learner's emotion expressions were fitted as dependent variables, whereas the machine-generated emoticon was fitted as an independent variable (Equation (1)). Analysis of the data showed the variation of the independent variable was sufficiently high to reliably estimate the goodness-of-fit measure R2 (R2 represents the coefficient of determination).

$$\Phi_{uV} = \beta_{1V}\Phi_m + \beta_{0V} + \varepsilon_V, \quad \Phi_{uA} = \beta_{1A}\Phi_m + \beta_{0A} + \varepsilon_A, \tag{1}$$

where $\Phi m$ stands for the one dimensional parametrization of the intensity of the emoticon, for the interval [0,1]. Notations $\beta 1V$ and $\beta 1A$ are the emotion elicitation linear model coefficients for the dimensions of valence and arousal, $\beta 0V$and $\beta 0A$ are the averaged effects of other influences on the dimensions of valence and arousal, and $\varepsilon V$ and $\varepsilon A$ are the independent variables of white noise.

There is no indication that emotion elicitation should be modeled as linear. Non-linear models might be more efficient at modeling emotion elicitation. However, the linear regression model was selected due to its efficient fitting procedure. Results show that the linear model can adequately capture the emotion elicitation process (see Section 5). Additionally, the residual plots (not reported here) showed that linear regression assumptions (homoscedasticity, the normality of residuals) are not violated.

# 4. EXPERIMENTAL STUDY

The experimental study consisted of 32 participants that completed the typing session, with the average duration approx. 17 min (1020 s) per session. The participants that did not complete the session, or the pre- and post- questionnaires, were excluded from the study. The participants were a homogeneous of the 4th year university female students (from the Faculty of Education, University of Ljubljana), with a similar level of typing expertise. The participants signed the experiment consent form and completed a short test with the pre-questionnaire inquiring about their typing technique and experience. The results showed none of the participants was skilled in touch-typing—they used different typing patterns, required frequent visual (keyboard-to-screen) reference while typing, and engaged max. 3–4 fingers on each hand while typing. None of the participants had had previous experiences with a structured touch-typing practice.

For the typing session, the same set of expertly designed touch-typing lessons was given to all the participants. Additionally, the participants were required to complete four self-reports. Two self-reports were required from the participants before and after the experiment, inquiring about their attention, enthusiasm, tiredness, stress and task-load. Two identical in-session self-reports were given to the participants during the experiment, with three questions for rating their attention, task difficulty, and performance.

Additionally, the automatic interruptions (distractors) were integrated into the experiment to observe the participant's behavior during the touch-typing session in different attentional conditions (in line with the divided attention theory [90,91]). Three different experimental conditions were created: the primary task of touch-typing, the secondary task (given the distractor to the primary task), and switching from the primary to the secondary task and back. These experimental conditions were used to simulate the demanding modern working/learning environment where multitasking and interruptions (distractions) are very common.

The data was acquired in real-time using sensors and Noldus FaceReader emotion recognition software (as described in Section 3.2). For the analysis of results presented in the Section 5, 13 randomly selected participants were analyzed on the test segment of the overall experiment. The number of test participants is sufficient (comprising 40% of the participants) given the homogeneous study group. The main reason for not analyzing all 32 participants was due to the synchronization issues with our measuring system, which initially required manual synchronization of the data time stamps for each of the participants. Thus, the participants were first randomly selected and subsequently their data double-checked by manually. The duration of the test segment was 380 s, taken from the 6 to 12.2 min interval of the overall duration of the experiment (1020 s).

The test segment includes one in-session self-report and both interruptions, and is composed of the following steps:

1. Before the experiment: the instructions are given to the test users, who are informed by the personnel about the goal and the procedure of the experiment. Setting up sensory equipment;
2. At 00 s: the start of the experiment: the wrist accelerometer and the video camera are set on, and the experimental session starts;
3. At 30 s: the self-report with three questions, inquiring about the participant's attention, task difficulty, and performance. (The results of the self-reports are not presented in this paper.);
4. At 60 s: the machine-generated sound disruption of the primary task: "Name the first and the last letter of the word: mouse, letter, backpack, clock";
5. At 240 s: the machine-generated sound disruption of the primary task: "Name the color of the smallest circle" on the image provided in the tutor's graphical user interface. This cognitive task is expected to significantly disrupt the learner's attention away from the typing exercise;
6. The test segment ends at 380 s.

The following section presents the results of the experimental study and the evaluation of the emotion elicitation in the intelligent typing tutor.

# 5. RESULTS OF THE EXPERIMENTAL STUDY

The analysis of the experimental data was conducted to measure the effect of emotion elicitation in the tutor. The estimation is based on the emotion elicitation model (1) fitting. The model (1) is fitted using linear regression on the measured data for the duration of the test segment. R2s are computed for each discrete time instant of the test segment, using the window reaching 4 s (40 samples) in the past. Valence and arousal dimensions are treated as dependent variables, whereas the machine emotion elicitation expressed through the graphical emoticon is treated as the independent variable ranging from 0 (neutral elicitation) to 1 (maximum positive elicitation). R2s for the two modes of emotion elicitation are obtained—R2 for the neutral elicitation with the emoticon threshold eT close to 0 (see Section 3.3.1), and R2 for the positive elicitation in all other cases.

The data is sampled in a non-uniform manner due to the technical properties of the sensors (internal clocks of sensors are not sufficiently accurate, etc.). The data is approximated by continuous smooth B-splines of order 3, according to the upper-frequency limit of measured phenomena, and uniformly sampled to time-align data (for brevity, we skip resampling details). Mann-Whitney U test was used for the statistical hypothesis testing, for the analysis of valence and arousal, and for the comparison of mean R2s. The significance level used in all tests was $\alpha=0.05$.

The results of the experimental study are presented in the following sections. The results in Section 5.1 are presented in the context of the "positive reinforcement", the term we use throughout this paper to define the connection between the emoticon and the performance. We present the dynamics of the learner's affective state throughout the test segment. The supporting tables and figures show differences in R2s and significance levels for the valence and arousal dimensions, and error rates and time interval durations, given the positive reinforcement. Section 5.2 tests our main hypothesis. It introduces additional criteria to conduct the measurement of the machine emotion elicitation and evaluate its influence on the affective state of the learner.

## 5.1. Measuring Learner's Affective State

The machine emotion elicitation model is based on the notion of positive reinforcement, defined by the learner's typing performance. The performance is estimated as good or bad based on the learner's typing errors and input delays and analyzed within a predefined time window (see Section 3.3.1).

To fit the regression models the 40 past samples from the time window of 4 s of real-time were used (see the previous section). These two values were selected as an optimum to the competitive arguments for more statistical power (requires more samples) and for enabling the detection of the time-dynamic changes in the effectiveness of emotion elicitation (requiring shorter time intervals, leading to fewer samples). Note that changing this interval from 3 to 5 s did not significantly affect the fitting results. Results are given in terms of R2V, R2A representing the part of the explained variance for valence and arousal, and in terms of the pV, pA-values testing the null hypothesis regression models H0V=[R2V=0], H0A=[R2A=0], given the emoticon. To detect the time intervals when the affective state of the learner changes due to the positive reinforcement, we conducted the null hypothesis testing H0=[R2=0]. The influence of the positive reinforcement is determined as the present where the null hypothesis is rejected.

Figure 2 and Table 1 show the valence-arousal ratings for five test participants. Note that, due to space constraints of this paper, the results presented in the figures are limited to five test participants. The X-axis times for all the figures are relative in seconds [s] and show the overall duration of the test segment. The figure shows the variations in the learner's affective state through time, with the higher values for the arousal dimension for the presented test participants.

Table 1 shows the average values of R2s for the test participants—these values are part of the explained variance for the learner's affective state during the tutoring session. The average R2s vary across test participants from 18.3% to 24.5% for valence and 19.7% to 31.4% for arousal, for all time intervals. If we average only over the time intervals when the positive reinforcement is active, the average value of R2s varies across the participants from 32.5% to 39.3% for valence and 36.3%to 44.9% for arousal.

The learner's affective state given the positive reinforcement is represented by the *p*-values pA and pV in Figure 3.

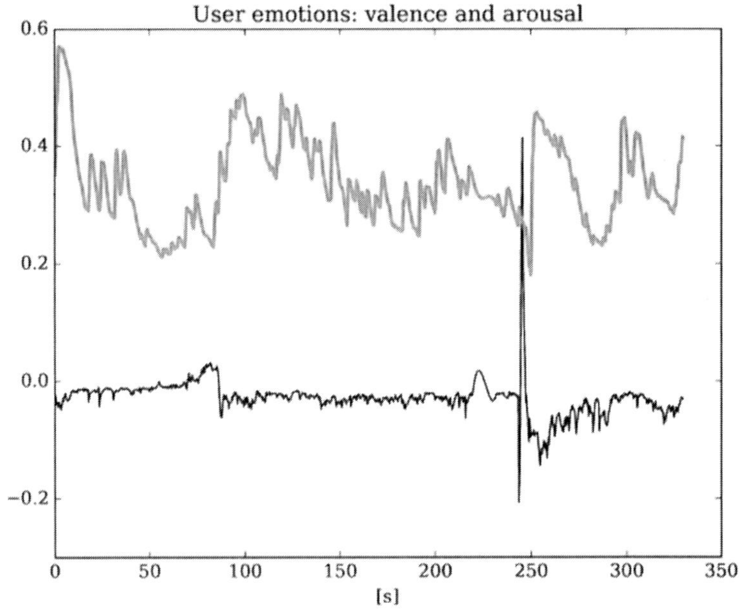


**Figure 2.** Learner's affective state: valence (black line) and arousal (magenta, light line) ratings for five test participants throughout the test segment.

**Table 1.** Average values of the explained variance for valence and arousal in % for all test participants. The table compares values for all the intervals vs. the time intervals when the positive reinforcement is active.

| | Valence | | Arousal | |
|---|---|---|---|---|
| uID | All int | Pos. reinf. | All int | Pos. reinf. |
| 3 | 20.8 | 34.6 | 28.1 | 39.9 |
| 8 | 24.1 | 38.2 | 30.9 | 43.4 |
| 10 | 18.3 | 32.5 | 19.7 | 36.3 |
| 15 | 15.7 | 29.7 | 17.9 | 33.1 |
| 16 | 20.4 | 33.2 | 26.9 | 38.7 |
| 18 | 21.8 | 35.8 | 34.6 | 47.8 |
| 19 | 19.4 | 33.8 | 27.4 | 39.2 |
| 20 | 24.5 | 39.3 | 31.4 | 44.9 |
| 22 | 17.4 | 32.6 | 18.9 | 35.0 |
| 26 | 23.6 | 38.5 | 29.2 | 42.2 |
| 27 | 19.8 | 33.3 | 23.9 | 39.9 |
| 30 | 25.1 | 40.1 | 31.9 | 45.1 |
| 34 | 21.7 | 35.4 | 26.8 | 40.2 |

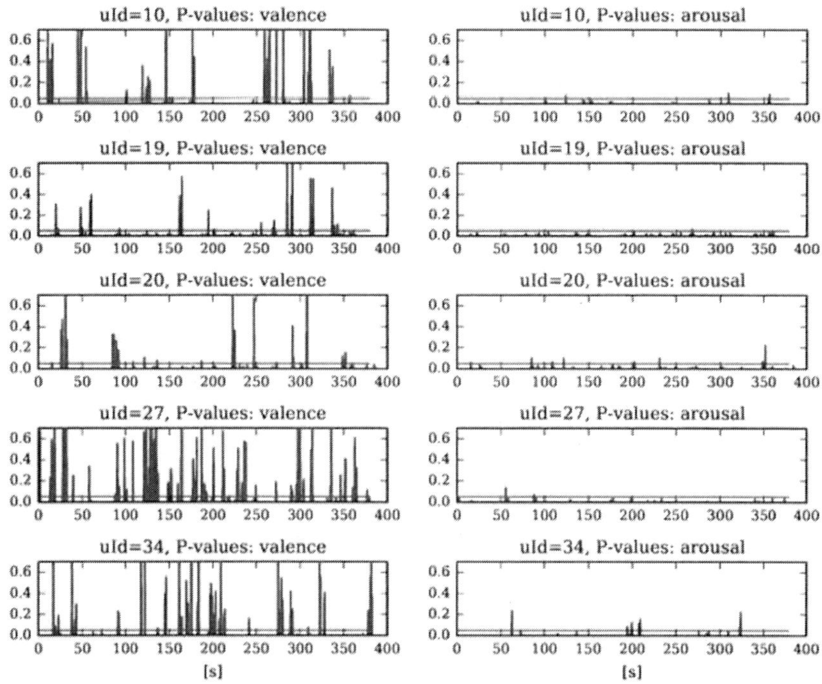


**Figure 3.** *P*-values for the null hypothesis testing H0=[R2=0] showing the effect of the positive reinforcement for five test participants, separately for valence (left) and arousal (right). The horizontal red line marks the significance level α=0.05, with *p*-values below the line indicating significant effect.

The linear regression model (R2) as a function of time for the valence and arousal dimensions is presented in Figure 4. The figure shows that the effect of positive reinforcement varies highly. Similar results were detected among all participants. The variations on the valence and arousal dimensions are probably due to general difficulties of capturing unstructured and noisy behavioral data, especially when using automatic emotion recognition from facial expressions in a real-world scenario. However, it is too early to draw any meaningful conclusion on the reasons for the high variations at this stage, as other potential factors influencing the measurement of learner's affective state (such as their emotion expressivity, task load, stress level, etc.) need to be evaluated.

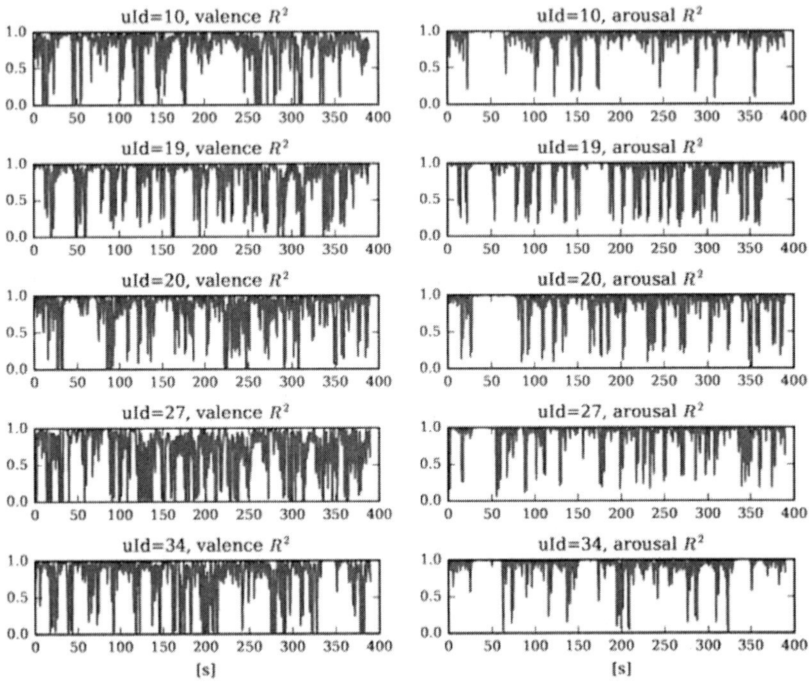


**Figure 4.** Linear regression model R2 as a function of time for valence (left) and arousal (right), given the positive reinforcement, for five test participants.

Histograms (Figure 5 and Figure 6) show the durations for the time intervals when the positive reinforcement is active vs. inactive, for the valence and arousal dimensions respectively. The results show longer time intervals (longer duration) for instances where the reinforcement is active: on average 18.34 s for valence and 25.64 s for arousal, compared to the average durations of 2.54 s for valence and 2.09 s for arousal when reinforcement is inactive. Such large differences in the average durations are due to the design of the positive reinforcement in the machine emotion model, which is based exclusively on the learner's performance.

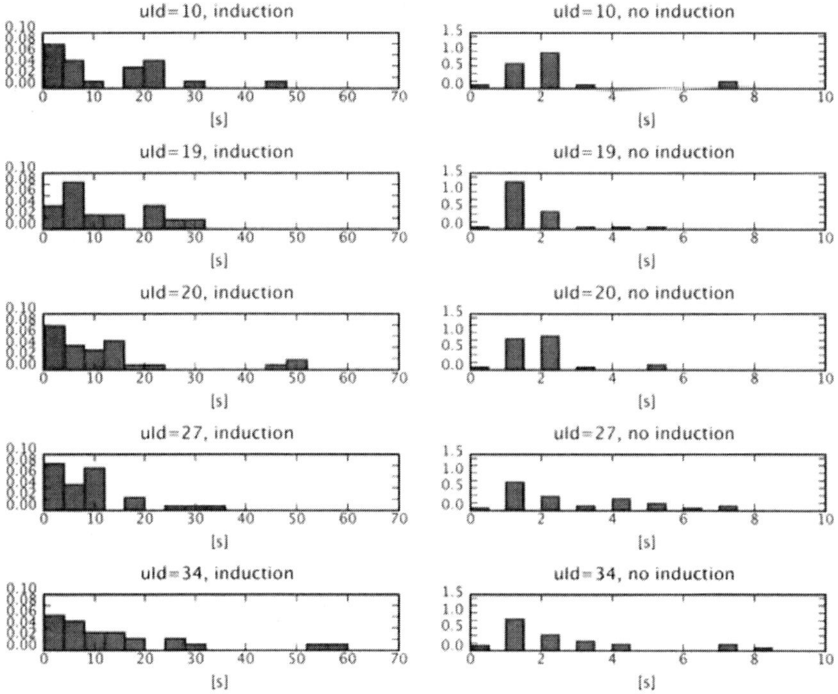


**Figure 5.** Histogram of the time interval lengths for the active vs. inactive reinforcement: valence.

Additional insight is given by the analysis of the learners' error rates throughout the test segment, presented in Figure 7. Again, these results represent the underlying design of the machine emotion model, which only rewards learner's performance. As shown in Figure 7, the average number of errors (through time) is higher for the intervals with no reinforcement (defined by the neutral emoticon (red dot)), compared to the instances when reinforcement is active (positive emoticon (blue dot)). However, note that the occasional short time intervals of good performance are also represented by the neutral emoticon (red dot), due to the delay in the positive reinforcement (see Section 3.3.1). Missing values are due to the self-report (at 30 s) or the default interruption in the tutoring session (see Section 4), or when the typing was paused by the learner.

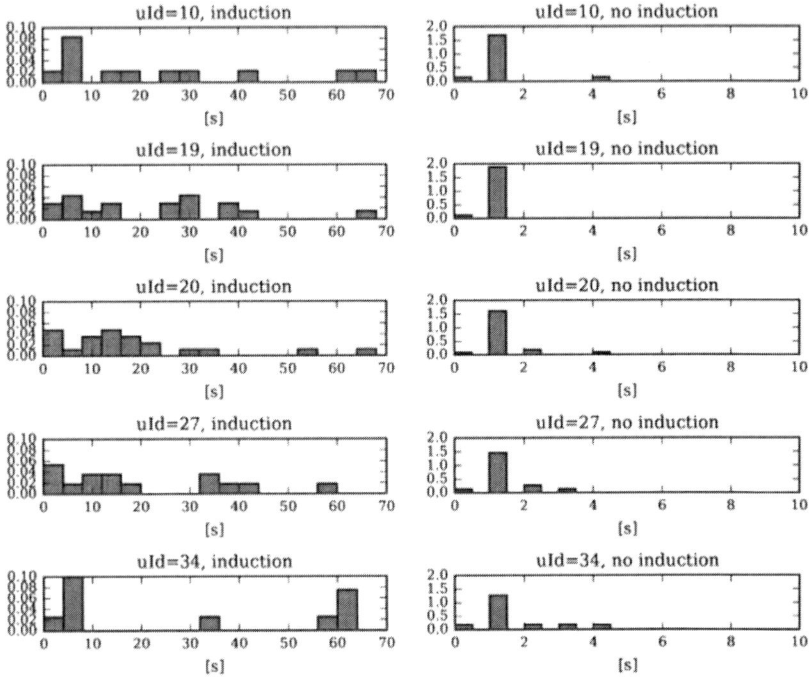


**Figure 6.** Histogram of the time interval lengths for the active vs. inactive reinforcement: arousal.

Presented results give some insight into the dynamics between the learner's affective state and the performance-based positive reinforcement of the machine emotion model. However, these results do not offer a reasonable proof for the influence of the machine emotion elicitation on the learner's affective state. It is impossible to infer what exactly influences learner's affective state—the emoticon or the performance—as they conflate the emoticon with the typing performance. We try to ameliorate this issue in the following section.

## 5.2. The Influence of the Machine Emotion Elicitation on the Learner's Affective State

The machine emotion elicitation model uses error-based performance evaluation as the underlying mechanism to generate the corresponding neutral and positive emoticon responses. This presents inherent limitation: the influence of machine emotion elicitation on learner's affective state is obfuscated by the typing performance. As the machine emotion elicitation is defined exclusively by the learner's typing performance, it is difficult to directly measure the effect that the machine emotion elicitation has on the learner's affective state. That is, it is difficult to argue that the learner's affective state is influenced by the machine generated emoticons and not by the learner's good or bad performance. To test our hypothesis, additional measures are needed.

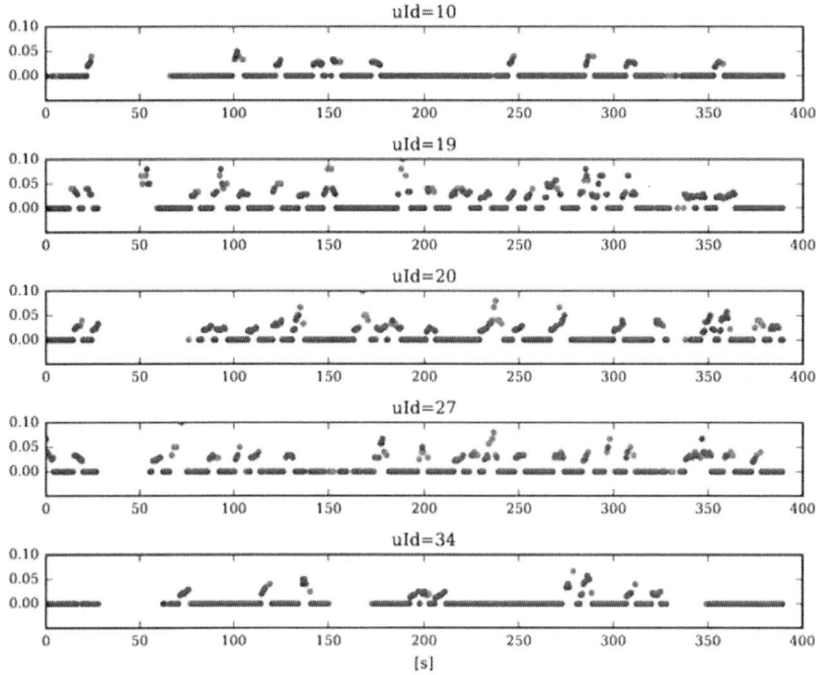


**Figure 7.** The average number of errors per second for the 5 s time interval: neutral (red) vs. positive (blue) emoticon state representing inactive vs. active positive reinforcement.

In this section, additional criteria are given that enable the measurement of the machine emotion elicitation effect on the learner's affective state. We do this by (to an extent) isolating the effect of the typing performance from the effect of the emoticons on the learner's affective state. The argument goes as follows. Emotion elicitation in the touch-typing tutor is defined by the learner's (good vs. bad) performance. Good performance is associated with the positive elicitation and represented by the positive emoticon, whereas the neutral elicitation is represented by the neutral emoticon and by both, bad and good performance. As noted in Section

3.3.1, the threshold for the positive reinforcement to come into effect and reward learner's good performance (with the positive emoticon) is not immediate. Consequently, there are time intervals of neutral elicitation, where the learner's performance is good, but not yet rewarded (the emoticon remains neutral), before the positive reinforcement comes in effect. Thus, we define the neutral elicitation by the instances of good performance where the emoticon is still in its neutral state. This way, we eliminate the effect of bad performance and simultaneously reduce the influence of good performance on the learner's affective state—the learner was already performing well even before the positive reinforcement came in effect.

The procedure goes as follows. First, we define the error-based threshold for the good performance, based on the expert advice and as designed in the machine emotion model. The regression model described in Section 5.1 is used for the fitting. The performance threshold is defined by the number of errors, given the time window and the number of samples. This step is crucial to avoid sampling of the isolated error-free instances, which would skew the results. Based on the predefined error threshold (<20% error-ratio), the instances of bad performance are filtered out. Next, we define the emoticon threshold eT for the neutral and positive emoticons (see also Section 3.3.1). In the machine emotion model, the threshold for the neutral emoticon eT is set to proportionally represent the lower 15% of the total emoticon intensity Φm range [0,1]. This range represents the intensity of the neutral emoticon where the changes in its mouth curvature are visually still perceived as neutral. These criteria isolate the effect of the typing performance from the effect of the emoticons by eliminating the instances of bad performance and only measuring the instances of positive and neutral emotion elicitation where the learner's performance was good.

Table 2 shows the *p*-values for the null hypothesis H0=[R2=0], confirming the correlation between the independent variable (positive emoticon) and the learner's affective state for valence (P_p-val.) and arousal (A_p-val.). The results show the correlation between the positive emoticon and the learner's affective state is significant for all 13 (100%) test participants on the arousal dimension and for 9 (69%) test participants on both dimensions. The hypothesis arguing the influence of the machine emotion elicitation on the learner's affective state is confirmed below.

**Table 2.** Correlation between the positive emoticon and the valence-arousal space: *p*-values for the null hypothesis H0=[R2=0].

| uID | Val. p-val | Arou. p-val. |
|---|---|---|
| 3 | 0.03 | <0.01 |
| 8 | <0.01 | <0.01 |
| 10 | <0.01 | <0.01 |
| 15 | 0.069 | <0.01 |
| 16 | <0.01 | <0.01 |
| 18 | 0.073 | <0.01 |
| 19 | <0.01 | <0.01 |
| 20 | <0.01 | <0.01 |
| 22 | 0.054 | <0.01 |
| 26 | 0.077 | <0.01 |
| 27 | 0.033 | <0.01 |
| 30 | <0.01 | <0.01 |
| 34 | 0.015 | <0.01 |

Table 3 presents the mean valence and arousal values given the neutral (m(V)_neut., m(A)_neut) and the positive emoticon (m(V)_pos., m(A)_pos.), and the significance of the positive emoticon for valence and arousal (V_p-val, A_p-val).

The results presented in Table 3 show that the machine emotion elicitation is significant for 11 (85%) of 13 test participants: among these, for 9 (82%) test participants along the valence dimension and for 7 (64%) test participants along the arousal dimension. Moreover, 5 (45%) of the participants that exhibited significant elicitation effect (uID3, uID10, uID16, uID19, and uID26) were significantly influenced on both affective dimensions. Assuming the worst case scenario that none of the 19 remaining participants exhibit significant elicitation effect, the machine emotion elicitation is still significant with $p<0.05$ for 34% of the participants that had taken part in the study.

**Table 3.** Machine elicitation for valence and arousal.

| uID | m(V) neu | m(V) poz | p val | m(A) neu | m(A) poz | p val |
|---|---|---|---|---|---|---|
| 3 | 0.094 | 0.012 | <0.01 | 0.306 | 0.33 | 0.032 |
| 8 | −0.097 | −0.145 | 0.499 | 0.26 | 0.27 | 0.291 |
| 10 | −0.031 | −0.119 | <0.01 | 0.308 | 0.289 | <0.01 |
| 15 | −0.01 | 0.01 | 0.085 | 0.37 | 0.31 | <0.01 |
| 16 | 0.079 | 0.027 | 0.026 | 0.271 | 0.253 | 0.049 |
| 18 | 0.067 | 0.025 | <0.01 | 0.274 | 0.269 | 0.199 |
| 19 | −0.188 | −0.241 | 0.045 | 0.319 | 0.342 | <0.01 |
| 20 | 0.07 | 0.074 | 0.252 | 0.282 | 0.295 | 0.459 |
| 22 | 0.056 | 0.036 | <0.01 | 0.277 | 0.285 | 0.353 |
| 26 | 0.114 | 0.015 | <0.01 | 0.277 | 0.25 | <0.01 |
| 27 | −0.004 | −0.026 | <0.01 | 0.299 | 0.305 | 0.367 |
| 30 | 0.004 | −0.012 | 0.01 | 0.262 | 0.259 | 0.199 |
| 34 | −0.108 | −0.1 | 0.28 | 0.297 | 0.365 | 0.04 |

## 6. CONCLUSIONS AND FUTURE WORK

The paper evaluated the role of machine emotion elicitation in the intelligent typing tutor. The machine elicitation is based on the notion of positive reinforcement and rewards learner's good performance with emotional feedback via graphical emoticons. The main hypothesis of the paper argued that the machine emotion elicitation can influence learner's affective state during the tutoring session.

We conducted an experimental study with 32 participants and randomly selected 13 participants for the analysis of the experimental results. Given the machine emotion elicitation is performance-based, additional criteria had to be defined to enable the measurement of the emotion elicitation effect on the affective state of the learner. These criteria eliminate the effect of bad performance and simultaneously reduce the influence of good performance on the learner's affective state. Under these criteria, the linear regression model used for the evaluation only samples good performance instances for both modes of (neutral and positive) emotion elicitation.

The experimental results confirm the correlation between the positive emoticon and the learner's affective state with significant correlation for all 13 (100%) test participants on the arousal dimension and for 9 (69%) test participants on both dimensions. The results also confirm our hypothesis that the machine emotion elicitation can influence the affective state of a learner during a tutoring session. The machine emotion elicitation was significant for 11 (85%) test participants: for 9 (82%) on the valence dimension, for 7 (64%) on the arousal dimension, and for 5 (45%) test participants on both affective dimensions.

Capturing any type of behavioral data is difficult. The performance-based emotion elicitation varied strongly and frequently throughout the test segment for all test participants and on both affective dimensions. This is at least in part associated with the difficulty of capturing unstructured and noisy behavioral data. Future work will focus on the reasons for high variation in the machine emotion elicitation. It is also necessary to consider alternative modes of machine emotion elicitation beyond simple graphic emoticons, as well as design more realistic applications to align the notion of positive reinforcement with other aspects, such as attention, motivation, frustration level, and task-load, among others.

## ACKNOWLEDGMENTS

This research was partially supported as part of the programme Creative path to knowledge 2015, funded by Ministry of Education, Science and Sport, Republic of Slovenia.

## AUTHOR CONTRIBUTIONS

The authors contributed equally to the reported research and writing of the paper. Both authors have read and approved the final manuscript.

## CONFLICTS OF INTEREST

The authors declare no conflict of interest.

## REFERENCES

1. Ekman, P. Facial expression and emotion. Am. Psychol. 1993, 48, 384–392.
2. Horstmann, G. What do facial expressions convey: Feeling States, Behavioral Intentions, or Action Requests? Emotion2003, 3, 150–166.
3. Tomasello, M. Origins of Human Communication; MIT Press: Cambridge, MA, USA, 2010.
4. Yiend, J. The effects of emotion on attention: A review of attentional processing of emotional information. Cognit. Emot. 2010, 24, 3–47.

5. Gunes, H.; Schuller, B.; Pantic, M.; Cowie, R. Emotion representation, analysis and synthesis in continuous space: A survey. In Proceedings of the 2011 IEEE International Conference on Automatic Face and Gesture Recognition and Workshops, FG 2011, Barbara, CA, USA, 21–25 March 2011; pp. 827–834.
6. Cowie, R.; Douglas-Cowie, E.; Tsapatsoulis, N.; Votsis, G.; Kollias, S.; Fellenz, W.; Taylor, J.G. Emotion recognition in human-computer interaction. IEEE Signal Process. Mag. 2001, 18, 32–80.
7. Picard, R.W. Affective computing: Challenges. Int. J. Hum. Comput. Stud. 2003, 59, 55–64.
8. Wehrle, T.; Scherer, G.R.; York, N. Towards Computational Modeling of Appraisal Theories; Oxford University Press: New York, NY, USA, 2001; pp. 350–365.
9. Broekens, J.; Bosse, T.; Marsella, S.C. Challenges in computational modeling of affective processes. IEEE Trans. Affect. Comput. 2013, 4, 242–245.
10. Marsella, S.; Gratch, J. Computationally modeling human emotion. Commun. ACM 2014, 57, 56–67.
11. Roda, C.; Thomas, J. Attention aware systems: Theories, applications, and research agenda. Comput. Hum. Behav.2006, 22, 557–587.
12. Chua, R.; Weeks, D.J.; Goodman, D. Perceptual-Motor Interaction: Some Implications for Human-Computer Interaction. In The Human-Computer Interaction Handbook; Jacko, J.A., Sears, A., Eds.; CRC Press: Boca Raton, FL, USA, 2008; pp. 23–34.
13. Peters, C.; Castellano, G.; de Freitas, S. An exploration of user engagement in HCI. In Proceedings of the International Workshop on Affective-Aware Virtual Agents and Social Robots, Boston, MA, USA, 6 November 2009; pp. 9:1–9:3.
14. Marko, T.; Berardina, C.D.; Marco, G.; Ante, O.; Andrej, K. (Eds.) Emotions and Personality in Personalized Services: Models, Evaluation and Applications; Human-Computer Interaction Series; Springer: New York, NY, USA, 2016.
15. Biswas, P.; Robinson, P. A brief survey on user modelling in HCI. In Intelligent Techniques for Speech Image and Language Processing; Springer: New York, NY, USA, 2010.
16. Ahmed, E.B.; Nabli, A.; Gargouri, F. A Survey of User-Centric Data Warehouses: From Personalization to Recommendation. Int. J. Database Manag. Syst. 2011, 3, 59–71.
17. Bobadilla, J.; Ortega, F.; Hernando, A.; Gutiérrez, A. Recommender systems survey. Knowl.-Based Syst. 2013, 46, 109–132.
18. Vinciarelli, A.; Pantic, M.; Bourlard, H. Social signals, their function, and automatic analysis: A survey. In Proceedings of the 10th International Conference on Multimodal Interfaces (ICMI '08), Crete, Greece, 20–22 October 2008; pp. 61–68.
19. Harris, R.B.; Paradice, D. An Investigation of the Computer-mediated Communication of Emotions. J. Appl. Sci. Res.2007, 3, 2081–2090.
20. Thorndike, E.L. Intelligence and its use. Harper's Mag. 1920, 140, 227–235.
21. Gardner, H. Frames of Mind: The Theory of Multiple Intelligences; Basic books Press: New York, NY, USA, 1984.
22. Cantor, N.; Kihlstrom, J. Personality and Social Intelligence; Century Psychology Series; Prentice Hall: Upper Saddle River, NJ, USA, 1987.
23. Kihlstrom, J.F.; Cantor, N. Social intelligence. In The Cambridge Handbook of Intelligence; Cambridge University Press: Cambridge, UK, 2011; pp. 564–581.
24. Vernon, P.E. Some Characteristics of the Good Judge of Personality. J. Soc. Psychol. 1933, 4, 42–57.
25. Albrecht, K. Social Intelligence: The New Science of Success, 1st ed.; John Wiley & Sons: Hoboken, NJ, USA, 2009.
26. Ambady, N.; Rosenthal, R. Thin slices of expressive behavior as predictors of interpersonal consequences: A meta-analysis. Psychol. Bull. 1992, 111, 256–274.
27. Vinciarelli, A.; Valente, F. Social Signal Processing: Understanding Nonverbal Communication in Social Interactions. In Proceedings of the Measuring Behavior, Eindhoven, The Netherlands, 24–27 August 2010.
28. Pantic, M.; Sebe, N.; Cohn, J.F.; Huang, T. Affective multimodal human-computer interaction. In Proceedings of the 13th Annual ACM International Conference on Multimedia—MULTIMEDIA '05, Singapore, 6–11 November 2005; pp. 669–676.

29. Vinciarelli, A.; Pantic, M.; Heylen, D.; Pelachaud, C.; Poggi, I.; D'Errico, F.; Schroeder, M. Bridging the gap between social animal and unsocial machine: A survey of social signal processing. IEEE Trans. Affect. Comput. 2012, 3, 69–87.
30. Richmond, V.P.; McCroskey, J.C.; Hickson, M.L., III. Nonverbal Behavior in Interpersonal Relations, 7th ed.; Allyn & Bacon: Boston, MA, USA, 2011.
31. Pentland, A. Honest Signals: How They Shape Our World; MIT Press: Cambridge, MA, USA, 2008.
32. Fairclough, S.H. Fundamentals of physiological computing. Interact. Comput. 2009, 21, 133–145.
33. Derrick, D.C.; Jenkins, J.L.; Jay, F.; Nunamaker, J. Design Principles for Special Purpose, Embodied, Conversational Intelligence with Environmental Sensors (SPECIES) Agents. AIS Trans. Hum.-Comput. Interact. 2011, 3, 62–81.
34. Allanson, J.; Wilson, G. Physiological Computing. In Proceedings of the CHI '02 Extended Abstracts on Human Factors in Computing Systems, Minneapolis, MN, USA, 20–25 April 2002; pp. 21–42.
35. Allanson, J.; Fairclough, S.H. A research agenda for physiological computing. Interact. Comput. 2004, 16, 857–878.
36. Sandulescu, V.; Andrews, S.; David, E.; Bellotto, N.; Mozos, O.M. Stress Detection Using Wearable Physiological Sensors. In International Work-Conference on the Interplay Between Natural and Artificial Computation; Springer: Heidelberg/Berlin, Germany, 2015; pp. 526–532.
37. Novak, D.; Beyeler, B.; Omlin, X.; Riener, R. Workload estimation in physical human—Robot interaction using physiological measurements. Interact. Comput. 2014, 27, 616–629.
38. McDuff, D.; Gontarek, S.; Picard, R. Remote Measurement of Cognitive Stress via Heart Rate Variability. In Proceedings of the 36th Annual International Conference of the IEEE Engineering in Medicine and Biology Society (EMBC), Chicago, IL, USA, 26–30 August 2014; pp. 2957–2960.
39. Ayzenberg, Y.; Hernandez, J.; Picard, R. FEEL: frequent EDA and event logging—A mobile social interaction stress monitoring system. In Proceedings of the 2012 ACM Annual Conference Extended Abstracts on Human Factors in Computing Systems Extended Abstracts CHI EA 12, Austin, TX, USA, 5–10 May 2012; p. 2357.
40. Jiang, X.; Zheng, B.; Bednarik, R.; Atkins, M.S. Pupil responses to continuous aiming movements. Int. J. Hum.-Comput. Stud. 2015, 83, 1–11.
41. Xia, V.; Jaques, N.; Taylor, S.; Fedor, S.; Picard, R. Active learning for electrodermal activity classification. In Proceedings of the 2015 IEEE Signal Processing in Medicine and Biology Symposium (SPMB), Philadelphia, PA, USA, 12 December 2015; pp. 1–6.
42. Mello, S.K.D.; Craig, S.D.; Gholson, B.; Franklin, S.; Picard, R.; Graesser, A.C. Integrating Affect Sensors in an Intelligent Tutoring System. Available online: https://goo.gl/3EXu8R (accessed on 29 March 2017).
43. Vanlehn, K. The relative effectiveness of human tutoring, intelligent tutoring systems, and other tutoring systems. Educ. Psychol. 2011, 46, 197–221.
44. Partala, T.; Surakka, V. The effects of affective interventions in human-computer interaction. Interact. Comput. 2004, 16, 295–309.
45. Hascher, T. Learning and emotion: Perspectives for theory and research. Eur. Educ. Res. J. 2010, 9, 13–28.
46. Moridis, C.N.; Economides, A.A. Affective learning: Empathetic agents with emotional facial and tone of voice expressions. IEEE Trans. Affect. Comput. 2012, 3, 260–272.
47. D'mello, S.; Graesser, A. AutoTutor and Affective Autotutor: Learning by Talking with Cognitively and Emotionally Intelligent Computers That Talk Back. ACM Trans. Interact. Intell. Syst. 2013, 2, 23:1–23:39.
48. Anderson, J.R.; Corbett, A.T.; Koedinger, K.R.; Pelletier, R. Cognitive Tutors: Lessons Learned. J. Learn. Sci. 1995, 4, 167–207.
49. Aleven, V.; Mclaren, B.; Roll, I.; Koedinger, K. Toward meta-cognitive tutoring: A model of help seeking with a cognitive tutor. Int. J. Artif. Intell. Educ. 2006, 16, 101–128.

50. Azevedo, R.; Witherspoon, A.; Chauncey, A.; Burkett, C.; Fike, A. MetaTutor: A MetaCognitive Tool for Enhancing Self-Regulated Learning. Available online: https://goo.gl/dUMZo9 (accessed on 29 March 2017).
51. Mitrovic, A.; Martin, B.; Suraweera, P. Intelligent Tutors for All: The Constraint-Based Approach. IEEE Intell. Syst.2007, 22, 38–45.
52. Shen, L.; Wang, M.; Shen, R. Affective e-Learning: Using emotional data to improve learning in pervasive learning environment related work and the pervasive e-learning platform. Educ. Technol. Soc. 2009, 12, 176–189.
53. Koedinger, K.R.; Corbett, A. Cognitive tutors: Technology bringing learning sciences to the classroom. In The Cambridge Handbook of the Learning Sciences; Sawyer, R.K., Ed.; Cambridge University Press: New York, NY, USA, 2006; pp. 61–78.
54. VanLehn, K.; Graesser, A.C.; Jackson, G.T.; Jordan, P.; Olney, A.; Rosé, C.P. When are tutorial dialogues more effective than reading? Cogn. Sci. 2006, 30, 1–60.
55. Hone, K. Empathic agents to reduce user frustration: The effects of varying agent characteristics. Interact. Comput.2006, 18, 227–245.
56. Beale, R.; Creed, C. Affective interaction: How emotional agents affect users. Int. J. Hum. Comput. Stud. 2009, 67, 755–776.
57. Marsella, S.; Gratch, J.; Petta, P. Computational models of Emotion. Blueprint Affect. Comput. 2010, 11, 21–46.
58. Rodriguez, L.F.; Ramos, F. Development of Computational Models of Emotions for Autonomous Agents: A Review. Cogn. Comput. 2014, 6, 351–375.
59. Russell, J.A. A circumplex model of affect. J. Pers. Soc. Psychol. 1980, 39, 1161–1178.
60. Yeh, Y.C.; Lai, S.C.; Lin, C.W. The dynamic influence of emotions on game-based creativity: An integrated analysis of emotional valence, activation strength, and regulation focus. Comput. Hum. Behav. 2016, 55, 817–825.
61. Tijs, T.; Brokken, D.; Ijsselsteijn, W. Creating an emotionally adaptive game. In International Conference on Entertainment Computing; Springer: Heidelberg/Berlin, Germany, 2008; pp. 122–133.
62. Plass, J.L.; Heidig, S.; Hayward, E.O.; Homer, B.D.; Um, E. Emotional design in multimedia learning: Effects of shape and color on affect and learning. Learn. Instr. 2014, 29, 128–140.
63. Dryer, D.C. Dominance and Valence: A Two-Factor Model for Emotion in HCI. Available online: https://goo.gl/uJvLhD (accessed on 29 March 2017).
64. Hudlicka, E. Guidelines for Designing Computational Models of Emotions. Int. J. Synth. Emot. 2011, 2, 26–79.
65. Shuman, V.; Clark-Polner, E.; Meuleman, B.; Sander, D.; Scherer, K.R. Emotion perception from a componential perspective. Cogn. Emot. 2015, 9931, 1–10.
66. Shuman, V.; Sander, D.; Scherer, K.R. Levels of valence. Front. Psychol. 2013, 4, 1–17.
67. Ekman, P.; Friesen, W.V. Unmasking the Face: A Guide to Recognizing Emotions from Facial Cues; Prentice Hall: Englewood Cliffs, NJ, USA, 1975.
68. Ekman, P.; Friesen, W.V. Facial Action Coding System: Investigatoris Guide; Consulting Psychologists Press: Sunnyvale, CA, USA, 1978.
69. Ostermann, J. Face animation in MPEG-4. MPEG-4 Facial Animation. The Standard, Implementation and Applications; John Wiley & Sons: Hoboken, NJ, USA, 2002.
70. Essa, I.A.; Pentland, A.P. Coding, analysis, interpretation, and recognition of facial expressions. IEEE Trans. Pattern Anal. Mach. Intell. 1997, 19, 757–763.
71. Rivera, K.; Cooke, N.J.; Bauhs, J.A. The Effects of Emotional Icons on Remote Communication. In Proceedings of the Conference Companion on Human Factors in Computing Systems, Vancouver, BC, Canada, 13–18 April 1996; pp. 99–100.
72. Coan, J.A.; Allen, J.J. (Eds.) Handbook of Emotion Elicitation and Assessment (Series in Affective Science), 1st ed.; Oxford University Press: Oxford, UK, 2007; p. 504.
73. Derks, D.; Bos, A.E.R.; von Grumbkow, J. Emoticons in computer-mediated communication: Social motives and social context. CyberPsychol. Behav. 2008, 11, 99–101.

74. Ganster, T.; Eimler, S.C.; Krämer, N.C. Same Same But Different!? The Differential Influence of Smilies and Emoticons on Person Perception. Cyberpsychol. Behav. Soc. Netw. 2012, 15, 226–230.
75. Lazzeri, N.; Mazzei, D.; Greco, A.; Rotesi, A.; Lanatà, A.; De Rossi, D. Can a Humanoid Face be Expressive? A Psychophysiological Investigation. Front. Bioeng. Biotechnol. 2015, 3, 64.
76. Dunlap, J.; Bose, D.; Lowenthal, P.R.; York, C.S.; Atkinson, M.; Murtagh, J. What sunshine is to flowers: A literature review on the use of emoticons to support online learning. Emot. Des. Learn. Technol. 2015, 163, 1–17.
77. Gross, J.J.; Levenson, R.W. Emotion elicitation using films. Cogn. Emot. 1995, 9, 87–108.
78. Uhrig, M.K.; Trautmann, N.; Baumgärtner, U.; Treede, R.D.; Henrich, F.; Hiller, W.; Marschall, S. Emotion Elicitation: A Comparison of Pictures and Films. Front. Psychol. 2016, 7, 180.
79. Churches, O.; Nicholls, M.; Thiessen, M.; Kohler, M.; Keage, H. Emoticons in mind: An event-related potential study. Soc. Neurosci. 2014, 9, 196–202.
80. Brave, S.; Nass, C. Emotion in Human-Computer Interaction. In Human-Computer Interaction Fundamentals, 2nd ed.; Jacko, J., Sears, A., Eds.; CRC Press: Boca Raton, FL, USA, 2003; Volume 29, pp. 81–96.
81. Jacko, J.A. (Ed.) Human Computer Interaction Handbook: Fundamentals, Evolving Technologies, and Emerging Applications, Third Edition (Human Factors and Ergonomics), 3rd ed.; CRC Press: Boca Raton, FL, USA, 2012.
82. Košir, A. The intelligent typing tutor. 2017. Available online: http://nacomnet.lucami.org/expApp/TypingTutorEng/(accessed on 10 January 2017).
83. Skinner, B.F. Reinforcement today. Am. Psychol. 1958, 13, 94.
84. Amsel, A. Frustrative nonreward in partial reinforcement and discrimination learning: Some recent history and a theoretical extension. Psychol. Rev. 1962, 69, 306.
85. Bandura, A.; Walters, R.H. Social Learning Theory; Prentice-Hall: Englewood Cliffs, NJ, USA, 1977.
86. Stipek, D.J. Motivation to Learn: From Theory to Practice, 2nd ed.; Allyn & Bacon: Boston, MA, USA, 1993; p. 292.
87. Official Unicode Consortium. Official Unicode Consortium code chart. 2017. Available online: http://www.unicode.org/ (accessed 3 January 2017).
88. Mahmood, T.; Mujtaba, G.; Venturini, A. Dynamic personalization in conversational recommender systems. Inf. Syst. e-Bus. Manag. 2013, 12, 213–238.
89. Noldus Information Technology. Noldus FaceReader. 2017. Available online: http://www.noldus.com/ (accessed on 10 January 2017).
90. Kahneman, D. Attention and Effort; Prentice-Hall: Englewood Cliffs, NJ, USA, 1973; p. 246.
91. Hodgson, T.L.; Müller, H.J.; O'Leary, M.J. Attentional localization prior to simple and directed manual responses. Percept. Psychophys. 1999, 61, 308–321.

# CHAPTER 8

# Enterprise 2.0: A Boon or Bane for Entrepreneurial and Innovative Expenditures?

Punita Duhan[1*†] and Anurag Singh[2†]

[1] *Faculty of Management Studies, Banaras Hindu University, 45, ITI Staff Quarters, Ring Road, Maharani Bagh, New Delhi 110 014, India.*

[2] *Faculty of Management Studies, Banaras Hindu University, Varanasi 221 005, India.*

## ABSTRACT

Social media's unabated and unprecedented adoption and growth among masses across the globe and fast emergence of innovative, open, cost effective, at times free of cost, and flexible Social media platforms has opened hitherto unexpected or previously unknown *vistas* for business organizations. Adoption of social media platforms in organizations coupled with the openness, collaboration, interaction, and involvement inherent in social media has led to a state that these organizations are now being termed as Enterprise 2.0. Though social media platforms are being criticized by many for unwarranted attention and importance, embracing these platforms by people worldwide has a different story to tell. This paper is an attempt in this direction to look into the potential of social media for business organizations by focusing the attention on various prospects and problems associated with the adoption of these platforms in pursuing innovative and entrepreneurial expenditures of business organizations and to suggest some ways for effective and smooth incorporation of the same in the organizations. Researchers conclude that as far as the adoption of Enterprise 2.0 technologies is concerned, the most significant issue to deal with is the approach to be adopted for incorporation of these technologies in the organization in an integrative fashion. Research may prove to be beneficial for the academicians by giving them a comprehensive view of various aspects of the Enterprise 2.0 and for the practitioners by providing them guidelines for effective incorporation of the social technologies in their organizations.

**Keywords:** Social media Enterprise 2.0 Challenges Advantages Suggestions for implementation

# INTRODUCTION

According to Mayfield ([2008]), 'Social media is a genie that will not be disappearing back into its bottle'. Whether you like it or not, the enigmatic power of social media does not let you break away from it (Mukherjee [2014]). Having human interaction as its base, it is not a new concept (Edosomwan, Prakasan, Kouame, Watson and Seymour, [2011]), though the intermediation of advanced information technology platforms has led to metamorphosis of interpersonal interactions and communications globally (Edosomwan et al. [2011]; Duhan and Singh [2013]).

Incessant, continual, and unparalleled global expansion and intrusion of social media platforms in our day-to-day activities (Nielsen [2012]; Vehr [2012]; Stanley [2009]; Duhan et al. [2013]) are evidenced by the fact that as per an estimate of Wikipedia (http://en.wikipedia.org/ List_of_ social_networking_websites), more than 200 thriving social communities are available to netizens (Duhan et al. [2013]), out of which Facebook is a front-runner with membership exceeding 517 million across 212 countries (Internet World Stats [2013]). Though interestingly, despite being such a rage, there appears to be no agreement among researchers and scholars as to what encompasses social media, and terms like Web 2.0, social media, and user-generated content (UGC) are often interchangeably used (Constantinides and Fountain [2008]; Kaplan and Haenlein [2010]). Nevertheless, some researchers have attempted to distinguish the three terms (Kaplan et al. [2010]). As per Kaplan and Haenlein [2010]:

Web 2.0 is the ideological and technical foundation based on participatory and collaborative efforts facilitated by tools such as Adobe Flash, Really Simple Syndication (RSS), and Asynchronous Java Script (AJAX).

UGC is the sum total of publicly available media content which is the resultant of creative effort of end-users outside professional realms. And social media, acting as an intermediary between the two, facilitates the creation and exchange of user-generated content by utilizing the ideological and technological foundations of Web 2.0.

On the other hand, Constantinides and Fountain ([2008]), even while acknowledging the emphasis on technical and social dimensions of Web 2.0 and social media, respectively, have used terms the Web 2.0 and social media interchangeably. The term Web 2.0, taken as an umbrella term, has been defined by Constantinides and Fountain ([2008]) as 'a collection of open-source, interactive and user controlled online applications expanding the experiences, knowledge and market power of the users as participants in business and social processes. Web 2.0 applications support the creation of informal users' networks facilitating the flow of ideas and knowledge by allowing the efficient generation, dissemination, sharing and editing / refining of informational content.' In accordance with Constantinides and Fountain ([2008]), for the present paper, researchers have used terms social media and Web 2.0 interchangeably.

However, the multiplicity of social media platforms coupled with their interactive nature, collective wisdom, content creation feature, and easy access (Chaffey et al. [2006]; Duhan et al. [2013]) has led marketers to embrace social media or Web 2.0. Marketers use social media platforms as advertising medium, direct-response medium, sales transaction platform, a lead generation medium, distribution channel, customer service platform, and relationship-building platform (Chaffey et al. [2006]). These platforms are being utilized for a variety of purposes such as to increment brand awareness, brand building, brand exposure, and brand reinforcement. In addition, these platforms are helping organizations in increasing traffic, in gaining marketplace intelligence, in developing loyal fans and in attracting more customers and employees to the organization. Customer service, customer support and productivity improvement are some other areas where these platforms are being taken help of (Mangold and Faulds [2009]; Edosomwan et al. [2011]; Stelzner [2013]; Jagongo and Kinyua [2013]). All of these activities of the organizations are leading to positive results like improved sales, increased exposure, more business partnerships, increased lead generation, reduced marketing and communication expenses, improved search rankings, increased traffic, better market insights and business intelligence, increased effectiveness of marketing, increased speed of access to knowledge, enhanced customer satisfaction, and increased brand reputation and loyal fan base (Buytendijk et al. [2008]; Almeida [2012]; Stelzner [2013]).

The very characteristics of the socio-digital platforms, *viz* connectivity, convergence, collaboration, and transparency, (Duhan et al. [2013]) have transformed the business environment and have helped businesses to increase their worthiness, cultivate strategic partnerships, and increase their contact with customers and suppliers (Jagongo et al. [2013]). The statement of the former director of the National Intelligence, USA, Mike McConnell (as cited in Booz, Allen and Hamilton [2010]) states that survival and effectiveness of the organization are dependent on the comprehension of the functioning of blogs and wikis. This statement once again emphasizes the importance of social media or Web 2.0 for the businesses. Collective information sharing and collaboration at both inter- and intra-organizational levels can lead to making an organization more powerful (Booz et al. [2010]). Accordingly, the induction of Web 2.0 technologies at the work place has given rise to a new business lexicon Enterprise 2.0 or E 2.0 as shown in Figure 1.

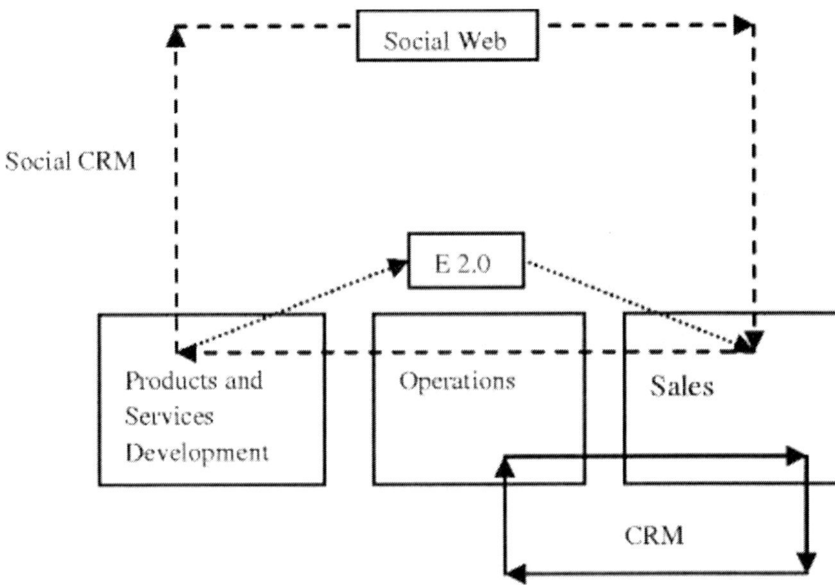


**Figure 1.** RELATIONSHIP BETWEEN ENTERPRISE 2.0 AND SOCIAL WEB. Image adapted from Evans and McKee ([2010]).

## LITERATURE REVIEW

McAfee ([2006]), hailed as the architect of the term Enterprise 2.0, defined and explained the concept with the help of search, links, authoring, tags, extensions, and signals (SLATES), an acronym used for the building blocks or components of E 2.0. The article talked about the ground rules and the role of managers for effectively contesting the accompanied challenges and taking advantage of the opportunities in implementation of E 2.0.

Matuszak ([2007]) cited the real-life usage of E 2.0 in knowledge sharing and management, problem solving, innovation, and collaboration along with the challenges encountered by the organizations while adopting these technologies.

The Economist Intelligence Unit ([2007]) surveyed 406 executives working in diverse industries including financial and professional services, life sciences, IT/telecoms, and media across the world and found that the main reasons for the adoption of Web 2.0 technologies include the desire to cut costs and increase revenue, growth, and profitability. Ten tips were propounded in the report to combat the challenges encountered by organizations and to ensure success.

Mazumder ([2008]) stressed the necessity of adopting the next paradigm of web computing in organizations and defined it as Enterprise 2.0 as it caters to the communicating, collaborating, contributing, and participating needs of various internal and external stakeholders. Mazumder ([2008]) sensing the paucity of ideas to combat with and guide the organizations to deal with attendant challenges resulting due to formative nature of Web 2.0 and immeasurable benefits of its adoption in organizations, put forward an iterative adoption model comprising of four stages (identify, analyze, plan, and implement) for successful adoption of the same.

Terming Enterprise 2.0 as a dynamic journey, an integrative business strategy that is imperative reality to be faced and adjusted to, Buytendijk et al. ([2008]) define E 2.0 as the creation of competitive advantage through interactive, collaborative business models, which lead to organizational effectiveness and drive profitability. Citing the demographic changes and business changes as the main drivers metamorphosing organizations, the paper discusses an Enterprise 2.0 platform offered by the Oracle.

Fuchs-kittowski et al. ([2009]) did a comparative analysis of ten quantitative studies conducted during 2007 to 2008 in Germany. The study reported the diffusion, benefits, barriers, and potential of Web 2.0 technologies in an organization.

Chui et al. ([2009]), after surveying a range of executives, who have adopted Web 2.0 tools for their internal operations, suggested that incorporation of Web 2.0 technologies may result in content generation (mass internal content generation, broadcast solution sourcing, external collaborative contribution), community building such as participatory marketing and decision-support by harnessing information markets. However, in order to realize the same, management must undertake cultural transformation, incorporate technologies in workflow, let users decide the uses, ensure right participation such as by targeting tech savvy and respected opinion leaders, and strike the right balance of freedom and control.

Lennon ([2009]), building upon the concept of Enterprise 2.0 as proposed by Andrew McAfee, discussed various features and tools of social software, which are being utilized or can be utilized by organizations to facilitate collaboration and contribution of external and internal stakeholders of the organizations. Researcher brought to the fore potential advantages (*viz* information access, instant notification, simplicity, and cost effectiveness) and pitfalls (*viz* security, lack of adoption by staff, and loss of productivity) associated with the implementation of E 2.0. Lennon ([2009]) attributes the slow espousal of Enterprise 2.0 to the dynamic and formative nature of Web 2.0 technologies and to the reluctance of managers to adopt tools and services propounded by relatively new and inexperienced software companies to run their organizations.

Hughes ([2010]) distinguished between 'enterprise portals', 'consumer social media', and 'enterprise social networking' (termed as application of social networking techniques and technologies to businesses and 'consumerization of the enterprise'). Researcher asserted that despite some evils associated with the use of social networking, it has potential for delivering productivity benefits, in coexistence with the organizational portals, to the organizations due to its people-centric approach around the content.

Stobbe ([2010]) recognized the superiority of Web 2.0 over Web 1.0 in communication and knowledge management arena in conventional industries and termed the incorporation of Web 2.0 tools in these as the corporate reality. The attendant benefits of Web 2.0 tools in the area of communication, marketing, innovation, and collaboration establish their need and supremacy, but for successful implementation, cultural changes, clear targets, choice of appropriate Web 2.0 tools, and evaluation parameters need to be taken cared of.

Turban et al. ([2011]) developed a framework to deal with the issues related to the amalgamation of social networking in the work places. Based on the analysis of potential risks and opportunities of enterprise social networking, researchers proposed a six-step fit-viability model to guide organizations with the institutionalization of the enterprise social networking.

Schueler ([2011]) investigated the social and organizational uses and effects of E2.0 technologies.

Bughin and Chui ([2011]) evidenced the benefits bestowed upon the organizations by integrating social technologies with their workflows - external as well as internal. Terming such organizations as internally networked, externally networked, or fully networked enterprises, depending upon the extent of usage of social technologies in an organization, the research demonstrated measurable business benefits such as market share gains, operating profits, and market leadership accruing to the networked organizations across a range of regions, industries, and functional areas. Researchers stressed the need for creating fully networked enterprises by integrating the Web 2.0 technologies into employees' day-to-day work activities as well as using these to collaborate with customers, business partners, and suppliers, via continuing adoption and by removing the organizational barriers resisting the change.

Almeida ([2012]) while stressing the need and importance of fast inclusion of web 2.0 systems in the organizations also highlighted the accompanied security threats such as losses in productivity, loss of company reputation, client confidence, vulnerabilities to data leaks, and inherent increased security risks. As blocking access to these new platforms is neither feasible nor sustainable, organizations must adopt a balanced and novel approach to deal with these attack vectors. Some of the solutions to deal with the problem could be the formulation, implementation, and compliance to Web 2.0 policy/IT policy along with the other IT initiatives such as highly customized browse settings, installation of anti-malware software, adoption of strong authentication mechanisms, and establishment of a data loss protection solution.

Leonardi et al. ([2013]) termed the use of social media in organizations as enterprise social media (ESM) and discussed the advantages and disadvantages associated with the incorporation of social media in organizations in specific context of communicative activities. As ESM operates as platform for social interaction and lends the visibility and persistence to communicative actions, more opportunities are accorded to the employees for social learning through instrumental knowledge and metaknowledge. Researchers critically analyzed the implications of ESM for four organizational processes, *viz* social capital formation, boundary work, attention allocation, and social analytics by assigning three metaphors, *viz* leaky pipe, echo chamber, and social lubricant to ESM. The paper attempted to bring to the fore the implications of introduction of social technologies for communicative activities inside the organization.

Booz et al. ([2010]) elaborating on the concept of E 2.0 and its importance propose a structured E 2.0 approach, comprising of two complimentary and integrated service offerings, for quick and successful implementation of E 2.0.

Kopaee and Uppal ([2011]) talked about the paradigm shifts effected by social media technologies in organizations. Authors, while stressing the importance of inclusion of these technologies, do not see the phenomenon as an opportunity in the foreseeable future rather mandate it to keep pace with the competitors. Paper enumerated the potential benefits of social media for various functional areas, antecedent on the very characteristics features of social media fostering collaboration, creativity, innovation, communication, and relationships, alongside attendant risks. A well thought strategic plan, comprising of four iterative steps, has been recommended for intelligent risk management in E 2.0.

Literature review evidences that it is extremely difficult to conjure up an accurate picture of the usage of Enterprise 2.0 due to the dynamic nature of the Web 2.0 coupled with the reluctance of the researchers to differentiate between internal and external usage of Web 2.0 tools. At best, what can be done is to have a cross-sectional view of the situation (Stobbe [2010]). In addition, most of the researches have been conducted in the field of computer-supported cooperative work (CSCW) and human computer-interaction (HCI) communities. The focus of these researches is on specific technologies and their usage by people in organizational settings. The implications for enterprise social media use for organizational actions for internal communication have largely been ignored, and scholars in management and organization studies have not yet begin to explore enterprise social media use (Leonardi et al. [2013]). In addition, the existing research is quite fragmented as most of the researchers have either catered to specific social media tools, particularly wikis and blogs, (Turban et al. [2011]) or have reported only a few of the opportunities/risks/solutions as applicable to the situation being analyzed. The solutions propounded also are quite varied and contextual in nature as substantiated by literature review. Hence, the present study has been proposed in order to have a comprehensive coverage of the advantages, challenges, and suggestions with reference to incorporation of Web 2.0 technologies in the organizations and thereby to fill the research gap.

The present paper is an attempt by the authors to explore the term 'Enterprise 2.0' and the associated advantages and challenges posed to the businesses with the adoption of Web 2.0 technologies in the organizations. An attempt has also been made to suggest some ways to reduce or remove some of the attendant challenges of Web 2.0 technologies, so that organizations can become more effective in their pursuit of innovative and entrepreneurial expenditures. Accordingly, researchers propose the following objectives:

1. To review the concept of Enterprise 2.0.
2. To identify the opportunities and challenges posed by induction of Web 2.0 technologies in organizations.
3. To suggest the ways for effective incorporation of Web 2.0 technologies in organizations in pursuit of innovative and organizational expenditures.

## Originality/value

The paper offers an accessible review of the concept of Enterprise 2.0 along with its attendant value and challenges to the business organizations. The paper will definitely bring to the fore various core issues pertaining to the adoption of techno-social platforms available in the form of Web 2.0 or social media in business organizations. It will create the interest in academicians working in business management and information technology departments in universities and colleges and students studying in these disciplines as well as in the professionals working in diverse functional groups of the organizations.

### Methodology

The paper is based on the secondary literature collected from diverse in-house and proprietary sources available at their websites. Alongside it, various relevant books, journal research papers, and other articles published by news agencies etc. have been taken help of. Information so gathered was suitably analyzed, validated, and adapted as per the requirements of the study.

### Rationale

The characteristics of social media, *viz* connectivity, convergence, collaboration, and transparency are responsible for the fast and global adoption by people and for the transformation of business environment. These developments have prompted the authors to analyze the attendant opportunities and challenges of these social-digital platforms in the metamorphosis of organizations into Enterprise 2.0 and to suggest the ways for effective implementation of Web 2.0 for innovative and entrepreneurial pursuits.

The paper has been organized around five sections. The first section provides a peep into development of the concept of Enterprise 2.0 to the readers. In the second and third sections, the opportunities and challenges posed by induction of Web 2.0 technologies in organizations has been elaborated. The fourth section encompasses the ways for effective incorporation of Web 2.0 technologies in organizations in their pursuit of innovative and organizational expenditures. The concluding remarks emphasizing the major findings regarding the incorporation of Web 2.0 technologies have been given in the final section of the paper.

## WHAT IS ENTERPRISE 2.0?

The term 'Enterprise 2.0' or 'E 2.0', introduced in the business lexicon by Andrew McAfee, Associate Professor, Harvard Business School, in March 2006 (McAfee [2006]; Frappaolo and Keldsen [2008]; [Janssen, n.d.]), is still shrouded in considerable mystery as far as the meaning of the term is concerned (Frappaolo and Keldsen [2008]). In a study carried out by Frappaolo et al. ([2008]), respondents attributed twelve different meanings to E 2.0 concept. These concepts ranged from application of Web 2.0 technologies/new set of technologies/evolving social software platforms in organizations for collaboration, for formation of online communities, for business agility, for democratization of information, and for content-centric systems to the next generation of collaboration/enterprise content management or knowledge management.

McAfee ([2006]) realizing the importance of collaboration of the external efforts with internal efforts for the realization of core organizational goals, put forward the term Enterprise 2.0 to 'focus only on those platforms that companies can buy or build in order to make visible the practices and outputs of their knowledge workers.'

Frappaolo and Keldsen ([2008]) define Enterprise 2.0 as 'a system of Web-based technologies that provide rapid and agile collaboration, information sharing, emergence, and integration capabilities in the extended enterprise.'

The definition highlights that Enterprise 2.0:

➢ is a collection, not a single entity or tool.

➢ leverages Web-based technologies.

➢ needs an (eco)system to thrive.

➢ has low barriers and dynamic nature.

➢ adds value in the shape of collaboration, information sharing, emergence, and integration of capabilities.

➢ positions the functionality within an enterprise setting but encompasses the 'companies, or between companies and their partners or customers' (Frappaolo et al. [2008]).

Enterprise 2.0 is the intersection of technology, social interaction, and content development/management to improve an organization's business processes. The five capability areas for Enterprise 2.0 are communication, collaboration, community, construction, and search as per Booz et al. ([2010]).

Enterprise 2.0 makes use of social software features such as social bookmarking and linking, tagging, rating, user commenting and discussion, open creation and editing policies, and syndication via RSS feeds (Lennon [2009]). The supremacy and the importance of these new technologies in dissemination of knowledge work widely and permanently in organizations can be highlighted by citing an example of Dresdner Kleinwort Wasserstein

(DrKW) European investment bank. DrKW bank incorporated and implemented 'presence display' feature, in the intraorganizational wiki environment of the bank within just 64 minutes (from concept to implementation) without any project definition or planning (McAfee [2006]).

The above discussion evidences that technical aspect of Web 2.0 provides the technological base for Enterprise 2.0 processes and social aspect supports the outreach/culture change required to implement Enterprise 2.0 (Booz et al. [2010]). E 2.0 is the incorporation and ingraining of modern collaborative capabilities into various facets of an organization (Janssen [2014]; Booz et al. [2010]). It is not just a new set of tools but it embodies the commencement and embracing of a new culture, new approach, and new philosophy of conducting business (Booz et al. [2010]; Frappaolo et al. [2008]). Capacities of newer technologies, known as Web 2.0 (also termed as Enterprise 2.0 technologies) technologies, in knowledge capturing and dissemination, in increasing the visibility of knowledge practices and output to others and to knit together the organization, have endeared these to the organizations (McAfee, [2006]).

## BUILDING BLOCKS OF E 2.0

This endearment is the result of six building blocks of the Enterprises 2.0 technologies *viz* SLATES (Search, Links, Authoring, Tags, Extensions, and Signals).

1. Search: refers to the discoverability aspect of the E 2.0 content implying that users should be able to find out what they are looking for. Inherent in this aspect is ability of the collaboration of the content and incorporation of it into other work processes and intellectual endeavors taking place in the organization (McAfee [2006]; Frappaolo et al. 2008)

2. Links: in the form of mash-ups and pointers, guide to what is important and provide structure to online content by providing interconnections between content. Dense link structures (continuously updated and reflecting the opinions of many participants) lead to better search output and help in getting more value from the content (McAfee [2006]; Frappaolo et al. [2008]).

3. Authoring: is the opportunity provided to the people in the form of blogs (cumulative content creation) and wikis (iterative content creation) in order to elicit their contributions in the shape of insight, experience, comment, fact, edit, link, etc. It refers to the

usability and low barrier interactional aspect of the E 2.0 (McAfee, [2006]; Frappaolo et al. [2008]).

4. Tags: refers to the use of metatags (Frappaolo et al. [2008]). Metatags are simple, one word descriptions, accorded to online content which help in its categorization and building of 'folksonomies' (categorization system developed over time by folks) (term popularized by Thomas Vander Wal as cited in McAfee [2006]). Tagging paves the way to make the patterns and processes taking place in the knowledge world more visible (McAfee [2006]) by capturing the individual and collective opinions on the value of the content (Frappaolo et al. [2008]).

5. Extensions: refers to the use of technology to get an insight into user activity patterns and then based on the user search behavior automatically extending the search into other related areas. Use of algorithms automates the some of the work of categorization and pattern making. It is like saying to the user 'if you liked that, then by extension you'll like this' (McAfee [2006]; Frappaolo et al. [2008]).

6. Signals: make the E 2.0 proactively collaborative by pushing newly updated content to interested parties thus saving users from onerous task of checking updates all the time for the new content of interest on sites. RSS is an excellent example of the signals (McAfee [2006]; Frappaolo et al. [2008]).

Dion Hinchcliffe in [2007] coined a new mnemonic FLATNESSES (freeform, links, authorship, tagging, network-oriented, extensions, search, social, emergence and signals) by extending McAfee's SLATES and incorporating four additional key characteristics *viz* freeform, network-oriented, social and emergence to Enterprise 2.0 (Frappaolo et al. [2008]).

7. Freeform: talks about the freedom from all restrictions and barriers in authoring, signals and integration, and interfaces to functionality. Dion ([2007]) emphasizes the need for 'no barrier' over 'low-barrier' as envisaged in SLATES (Frappaolo et al. [2008]).

8. Network-oriented: talks about the Web-addressability of the entire E 2.0 content along with the technology platform and proposes the potential development of a blogosphere within the enterprise (Frappaolo et al. [2008]).

9. Social: dimension emphasizes the importance of incorporation of the transparency (to access), diversity (in content and community members), and openness (to structure) as the core cultural values in the Enterprise 2.0 environment (Frappaolo et al. [2008]).

10. Emergence: stresses the detection and leveraging of the collective wisdom of the community (Frappaolo et al. [2008]).

Although, the collaboration, open access, or collective wisdom predates Enterprise 2.0 and was in use in the past as well, the Enterprise 2.0 enables all this to happen in a far more rapid and agile fashion (Frappaolo et al. [2008]) due to the availability of the technical platforms of Web 2.0. The characteristics of Enterprise 2.0 enumerated above in the SLATES and FLATNESSES frameworks bring to the fore the key value proposition of Enterprise 2.0 evidenced in the example of DrKW bank (McAfee [2006]). The collaborative environments and projects requiring high level of technical know-how and effort are now being effected in hours or minutes. But, simultaneously, a conducive cultural environment is a prerequisite for open and agile sharing, cooperative thinking and development, lest Enterprise 2.0 should result in faster development of ineffective platforms (Frappaolo et al. [2008]).

## Advantages of Enterprise 2.0

Web 2.0 technologies are no longer another 'new media' platforms rather these have turned into vital business tools having wide-ranging capabilities (Chui et al. [2012]). These technologies are being used for diverse array of activities in the organizations ranging from IT to marketing to sales to customer service to public relations to human resources. It is believed that these technologies are poised to become the preferred mode of interpersonal communications in the organizations (Almeida [2012]) as more and more digital consumers enter the work force (Buytendijk et al. [2008]). Given below are some of the advantages of Enterprise 2.0, which have accrued because of the inclusion of these social technologies in the organizations.

1. Improved and flexible organization structure: E 2.0 results in a transparent and flatter organization with lesser bureaucratic processes as it does away with the size and complexity of the earlier system (Miller [2007]; Booz et al. [2010]; Janssen [2014]; Chui et al. [2012]). Reduced size and lessened complexity enables an organization to be more agile and responsive to various environmental changes (Gupta et al. [2013]).

2. Inclusion of distributed workforce: Enterprise 2.0 facilitates the better and enhanced inclusion of distributed workforce especially the remote and 'telework' staff (Booz et al. [2010]).

3. Collaborative decision-making: Enterprise 2.0 results in perpetual, diverse, updated, relevant, efficient, and timely intellectual capital for effective and fast decision-making (Booz et al. [2010]). It helps in 'crowdsourcing' the product ideas and thereby makes the concept of co-creation viable in the organizations, e.g., customers being motivated to upload homemade commercials to YouTube. Collaborations to co-develop a new product or service across different industries (like Nike+ from Nike and Apple and sports shoes with special soles from Adidas and Goodyear) and across competing companies (like Oneworld, SkyTeam, and Star Alliance, the airline industry alliances) are becoming the norm of the day (Buytendijk et al. [2008]).

4. Enhanced searchability and information access: Enterprise 2.0 makes the information more searchable by enabling the various stakeholders to access relevant, timely, and updated information anytime and anywhere with internet enabled devices leading to time saving and enhanced productivity (Lennon [2009]; Fuchs-kittowski et al. [2009]; Bughin et al. [2011]; Chui et al. [2012]).

5. Instant updates notification: RSS subscriptions enable the subscribers to get the instantaneous notification about any website updates saving them lot of time and effort (Lennon [2009]).

6. Simplicity and cost effectiveness: Collaboration, information sharing and communication become simpler and cost effective in Enterprise 2.0 environment due to the Web 2.0 technologies that are simple to set up and use and have open access or are available at nominal prices (Lennon [2009]; Bughin et al. [2011]).

7. Enhanced productivity: E 2.0's result is streamlined communications and collaborations in the organization. It helps in lowering or removing of the functional silos by making the functional borders porous. E 2.0 can even lead to the organizational restructuring for the inclusion of hitherto untapped additional knowledge and expertise in the organization. All this leads to the knowledge workers' productivity enhancement by 20% to 25% (Chui et al. [2012]; Fuchs-kittowski et al. [2009])

8. Market intelligence: E 2.0 serves as an excellent platform for gathering market intelligence either by engaging with customers and other stakeholders through E 2.0 technologies or just by monitoring the conversations taking place on these mediums. Market intelligence so gathered abreast organizations with the latest trends in the market place (Fuchs-kittowski et al. [2009]; Chui et al. [2012]).

9. Open innovation expenditures: Web 2.0 can play a crucial role in innovative expenditures in the organizations especially the open innovation, which is about bridging internal and external resources and acting on those opportunities, to bring better innovation to market faster. Interaction and involvement are the key elements for both - open innovation and Web 2.0. Hence, E 2.0 has the potential to offer tremendous opportunities to entrepreneurs, especially smaller ones, for collaboration with the vast network of different stakeholders in an unimagined way and thereby bring new products and services to the market at faster pace. In addition, the unprecedented growth of the social media paves the way for the emergence of newer and better platforms for interaction, involvement, and collaboration. Though the use of social media in innovative expenditures is in nascent stages, yet the very idea of intersection of social media and open innovation shows tremendous promise for organization to reap future benefits. However, this requires a multi-target approach with many touch points to your innovation community, your innovation ecosystem, customers, and users (Fuchs-kittowski et al. [2009]; Lindegaard [2012]). Kalypso Media, a global innovation-consulting firm, in its survey of over 90 manufacturing firms, found that firms using social media in product innovation have more and better new product ideas, faster time to market, faster product adoption, lower product costs, and lower product development costs (Kenly and Poston [2011]). Bughin et al. ([2011]) and Chui et al. ([2012]) found similar results.

## Challenges of Enterprise 2.0

Though the discussion in the preceding section appears to create an illusion that everything is right with Web 2.0 technologies and E 2.0 is an infallible concept to adopt and implement. Nevertheless, Janus-faced E 2.0 has another facet to it revealing that not all is well. Given below are some of the pitfalls associated with E 2.0:

1. Security: The essence of Web 2.0 lies in its openness, sharing, and transparency, but Enterprise 2.0 does not warrant the same level of openness and transparency. Thus, security and confidentiality of important information is a major area of concern for Enterprise 2.0 as the World Wide Web is fraught of numerous cases of information theft by hackers using viruses and malware. Authoring feature of Enterprise 2.0 technologies can lead to accidental or cognizant leakage of vital information (e.g., new product concept) leading to competitive disadvantages in the market place. Although

major software firms are working on these issues, yet until then, there is a need to strike a right balance between security and openness (Lennon [2009]; Fuchs-kittowski et al. [2009]; Chui et al. [2012]).

2. Loss of productivity: Another impediment in the adoption of Enterprise 2.0 tools in the organizations is the wishful thinking of the management that employing such tools in the organizations would reduce the productivity of the employees, as they will waste a lot of time 'playing' with the features of Web 2.0 technologies. In this regard, organizations may focus on retaining and enhancing those features of the Web 2.0 which lead to increase in productivity (like relationship building) and on removal of time wasters (like 'Poke' applications, customizable layouts, etc.) (Lennon [2009]; Chui et al. [2012]).

3. Lack of ROI metrics: One of the major obstacles in the E 2.0 technologies is related to the lack of appropriate metrics. Science behind the measurement of the results of E 2.0 efforts is in nascent stage and is not fully evolved yet. It is thereby very challenging for organizations to ascertain with accuracy the relationship between E 2.0 investments and returns, using the currently available intermediate measures like engagement (Fuchs-kittowski et al. [2009]; Chui et al. [2012]).

4. Intellectual property rights: Another bone of contention in the E 2.0 is the intellectual ownership of co-created and crowdsourced ideas as the assertion of ownership by an organization may lead to inhibition on the part of contributors (Chui et al. [2012]), and authorizing ownership to the contributors may lead to enhanced costs in the shape of completing legal and consular formalities to acquire intellectual rights or paying royalties etc..

Mazumder [2008] has classified the challenges in the adoption of Enterprise 2.0 into two categories as shown in Figure 2.

1. Challenges related to the formative state of Web 2.0:

5.1 Lack of clarity in Web 2.0 concepts: There is enough ambiguity among the researchers regarding what encompasses Web 2.0 concept (Mazumder [2008]; Constantinides et al. [2008]; Kaplan et al. [2010]).

5.2 Continuously changing Web 2.0 landscape: Fast pace of development of Web 2.0 technologies due to continuous innovations, consolidations, and diversifications in the Web 2.0 landscape makes it difficult for organizations to keep pace with it (Mazumder [2008]).

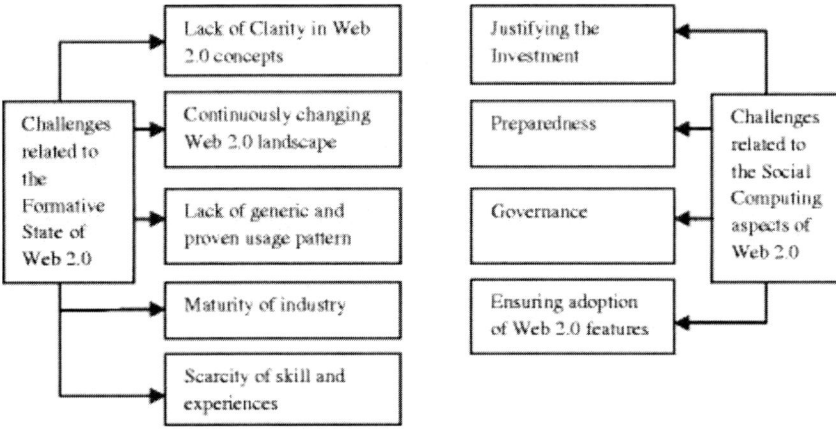


**Figure 2.** CHALLENGES IN ADOPTION OF ENTERPRISE 2.0. Image adapted from Mazumder ([2008]).

5.3 Lack of generic and proven usage pattern: The pattern of usage of these technologies varies from industry to industry and organization to organization resulting into no precedents for the organizations to follow (Mazumder [2008]).

5.4 Maturity of industry: Due to the dynamism of the Web 2.0 technologies, it is difficult to locate a single platform or feature which can support all Web 2.0 related needs (Mazumder [2008]).

5.5 Scarcity of skill and experiences: Scarcity of people with right skills and experience to integrate the Web 2.0 technologies with the enterprise architecture is another challenge for E 2.0 as the people proficient in Web 2.0 technologies are inexperienced in the application of the same in organizations and vice versa (Mazumder [2008]).

*6* Challenges related to the social computing Aspect of the Web 2.0:

6.1. Justifying the investment: Intangible and incremental benefits accruing from Web 2.0 technologies make it an unfit case for justification for fund allocation in the organizations.

6.2. Preparedness: Successful implementation of E 2.0 demands organizational readiness in terms of transformational changes in structure, procedures and practices, as well as cultural readiness in terms of culture characterized by mutual trust, less control, openness, and collaboration (Mazumder [2008]; Chui et al. [2012]; Stobbe [2010]).

6.3 Governance: On one hand, E 2.0 tools empower the employees in unimagined ways whereas on the other hand the absolute authority and control of the managers is reduced. These altered roles at times may lead to unintended outcomes in the form of dissents and negative remarks for management and hence warrant the managers not to react in an exaggerated manner to such criticisms, as they are the ones who primarily motivated the employees to use these platforms. Though in such situations of classical conflict between people's theory-in-use and espoused theory (Argyris [1998]; McAfee [2006]; Chui et al. [2012]), the theory-in-use emerges a clear winner. Accordingly, the lack of judicious application of control and governance on the part of managers turns out to be a big obstacle in proper implementation of this empowerment initiative (McAfee [2006]; Mazumder [2008]).

6.4 Ensuring adoption of Web 2.0 features: Mere implementation of Web 2.0 technologies will not serve the purpose until and unless wholehearted adoption by the staff is not ensured (Mazumder [2008]; Chui et al. [2012]). Demographic (age), psychological (fear of unknown and public ridicule), technological (lack of requisite skills and training), and personal factors of the staff may lead to less or no embracing of the emerging concepts such as Enterprise 2.0 (Lennon [2009]; Fuchs-kittowski et al. [2009]). Problem of nonusage of technologies by knowledge workers even after training and prodding is also quite a prevalent problem (McAfee [2006]) as majority of the people (90%) using internet are only passive audience to the content, 9% are the editors and only 1% are the creators of the content (Owyang [2010]). It remains true even in E 2.0 environment leading to less than desirable contribution from the employees.

So, what should be done by organizations to implement E 2.0 effectively in pursuit of innovative and entrepreneurial efforts?

## SUGGESTIONS FOR EFFECTIVE IMPLEMENTATION OF E 2.0

Mazumder ([2008]) advocates a comprehensive and incremental approach for effective implementation of E 2.0 after a thorough analysis of the needs, preparedness, and benefits already realized by the organization by incorporating some features of Web 2.0. Thorough analysis of the present state of affairs in the organization is advised alongside envisaging of future requirements of the organization. This internal analysis needs to be continuously matched with innovations and changes happening in web 2.0 in order to keep track of the trends and direction, maturity of technology, and the availability of best practices and experiences. Mazumder ([2008]) supports the short implementation phases to be carried out in an iterative fashion. Each iteration should have clearly delineated boundaries as to what results are to be achieved and continuous monitoring and assessment of the result of the previous iteration will be an effective feedback for the future iterations.

Booz et al. ([2010]) have envisaged a formal approach in the form of two complimentary and integrated service offerings, *viz* Enterprise 2.0 adoption framework and Enterprise 2.0 solutions architecture. Enterprise 2.0 adoption framework is comprised of four phases, *viz* baseline analysis, pilot planning, training and piloting, and institutionalizing. Baseline analysis brings to the fore the current collaborative efforts underway in the organization and accentuates the need for improvement. Pilot planning phase, after prioritizing the E 2.0 technologies for adoption, caters to the planning aspects in relation to training, pilot implementation, and institutionalization. The focus of training and piloting phase is on imparting new skills via training modules and pilot testing the induction of Web 2.0 technologies. The fourth and final phase, after analyzing the feedback from the previous stage, modifies the process as per the need and then integrates it in to standard work practices of the organization. Enterprise 2.0 solutions architecture, on the other hand, facilitates the culture of communication and collaboration by the means of social networking, blogs, wikis, and tagging.

Formal approach to E 2.0 is advocated due to the holistic impact of E 2.0, across diverse organizational areas, *viz*policy, governance, resources, and culture which warrants that impacts across change management, systems engineering, technical development, cyber security, risk management, and mission assurance are taken into account (Booz et al. [2010]).

McAfee ([2006]) talks of the ease of use and no preconceived notions about the output structure and work process as the two ground rules for the incorporation of these technologies. In addition, a ten-prong strategy propounded by The Economist Intelligence Unit ([2007]) for effective E 2.0 incorporates the following:

1. Remember, Web 2.0 is omnipresent.

2. Hire young people and learn from them, as internet is their life and blood.

3. Look around and learn from the mistakes of others.

4. Hire the help of professionals in your endeavors.

5. Web 2.0 does not tantamount to online advertising.

6. Do not avoid discussions rather lead these.

7. Make a straightforward business case through cost-benefit analysis.

8. Harness the in-house talent.

9. Avoid being 'me too'.

10. Test the waters before taking a plunge.

As evidenced, different researchers have proposed diverse ways for effective implementation of E 2.0 technologies and thereby for a smooth transition to E 2.0 stage for organizations. However, most of the suggestions put forward by researchers in this regard are generic in nature with no specific industry or sector in consideration. This may be because the concept of E 2.0 is still in nascent stages and the organizations though have embraced the concept realizing its importance but are still to frame any industry specific benchmarks (Fuchs-kittowski et al. [2009]). In addition, the discussion above reveals that even when researchers are proposing different models and approaches, common meeting grounds can be gleaned for effective implementation of E 2.0. Some of these suggestions have been enumerated below:

*1* Precise targets and appropriate tools are crucial: Precisely defined targets, synchronized with corporate strategy, are necessary for successful E 2.0 (e.g., a corporate blog of software development by employees and external developers). Precise targets will in turn help in deciding about the target groups, i.e., are we going to use the tools for employees or customers or suppliers or experts? Choice of Web 2.0 tools is also dependent on the target definition as different tools are appropriate for different functions, like wikis are most suitable for collecting and consolidating knowledge whereas a blog or a forum is more suitable for exchange of ideas (Frappaolo and Keldsen [2008]; Stobbe [2010]).

*2* Receptive culture: Organizational culture's profile, strengths, and challenges impact the execution of a strategy within organizations' domains, same being true for implementation of E 2.0 strategy (McAfee [2006]; Frappaolo et al. [2008]; Stobbe [2010]) as DrKW CIO J.P. Rangaswami says 'I'm not sure wikis would work in a company that did not already have 360 degrees performance review' (McAfee [2006]). Hence, there is an urgent need to assess the cultural dimensions of an organization with respect to attitude toward knowledge capture, collaboration, trust, risk taking, experimentation, innovation, and generational attitudes. Attention needs to be given to the various sub-cultures prevalent in the organizations as their unique characteristics may impede or accelerate the adoption of E 2.0 technologies (McAfee [2006]; Frappaolo et al. [2008]; Stobbe [2010]).

*3* A common platform: A common collaborative platform or infrastructure is necessary. However, the degree of fragmentation permitted in an organization can be decided after evaluating a trade-off between commonality and customization (McAfee [2006]; Chui et al. [2012]). E 2.0 technologies, though completely amorphous and egalitarian, spread more quickly when there is some structure and hierarchy in place (McAfee [2006]).

*4*Organization restructuring and process reengineering: Traditional, centralized, hierarchical, and bureaucratic structures characterized by control and inflexibility are not conducive to the effective implementation of E 2.0 strategy. Instead, what are required are decentralized, flat, flexible, contingent, porous, and continuously learning organizations. There is also a need to make social technologies the part of workers' daily work flow even if the current work flow and processes have to be altered to do the same. The idea is not to let it become a part of their 'To Do' list, e.g., Google has modified the work in order to make web tools most relevant to employees' daily workflow (Chui et al. [2009]; Chui et al. [2012]).

Pander to the employees' ego needs: In order to generate a critical mass of participation for achieving self-sustaining levels of E 2.0, traditional monetary incentives in the shape of bonuses, and individual feedback may not be giving the desired results in unlocking participation. A more effective approach would be to bolster the reputation of participants in relevant communities as done by ArcelorMittal (Chui et al. [2009]; Chui et al. [2012]).

*6*No preaching but help to scale: Organizations should refrain from dictating and publicizing the preferred use of these technologies (McAfee [2006]; Chui et al. [2009]). A better approach would be to let the actual users experiment and then find out the best use on their own. This is because the applications contributing most value in the organization may not be the ones as expected by the management, e.g., at AT&T, support given by the management to spread the awareness about the effective usage of a participatory technology by frontline staffers led to widespread adoption of the technology in the organization (Chui et al. [2009]). So, instead of a formal rollout, it is advisable to observe what works and then scale it up (McAfee [2006]; Chui et al. [2009]; Chui, et al. [2012]). Though some online culture and norms will evolve in the organization with the passage of time so that digital online content can be produced productively and collegially (e.g., Wikipedia). Same may be true for the organizations as well (McAfee [2006]).

*7*Managerial support from the top: Successful implementation and functioning of E 2.0 technologies demands a different leadership approach from the managers. Managers are required to play the role of mentor, enabler, catalyst, and motivator. As actions speak louder than words, they should act as a role model and involve people through deeds and actions but should refrain from interfering too much (McAfee [2006]; Chui et al.

[2009]). At Lockheed Martin, the CIO assured widespread acceptance and collaboration across the company's divisions by establishing his own blog, acting as a role model and setting goals for adoption of E 2.0 (Chui et al. [2009]).

*8*The need to have cyber resilient systems in place: Omni-digitization necessitates weighing the trade-offs between opportunities intrinsic to hyperconnected (Chinn, Kaplan and Weinberg [2014]), networked (Bughin et al. [2011]) enterprises and accompanied threats due to cyber attacks (Chinn et al. [2014]). Security controls, essential for protection against cyber attacks, inhibit the information sharing among employees in inter- as well as intra-organizational Web 2.0 environments. Such restraints are not conducive for the implementation of E 2.0 as the essence of E 2.0 technologies lies in their openness, sharing, and transparency. Hence, there is a need to have cyber resilient systems in place. Successful implementation of E 2.0 demands high-level cyber security entrusted to senior level cross-functional teams and a proper balance between the security and sharing (Lennon [2009]; Fuchs-kittowski et al. [2009]; Chui et al. [2012]; Chinn et al. [2014]).

Various other suggestions for ensuring use and success of E 2.0 technologies include leadership buy-in, bringing right people together, shared understanding of the problem, understanding operating environment, developing a customized solution, incessant updating, continuous drive for adoption and usage, community building, and evaluation and improvement (Chui et al. [2009]; Bughin et al. [2011]; Booz et al. [2010]).

# CONCLUSIONS

In the present paper, researchers reviewed the concept of Enterprise 2.0 based on the definitions propounded by various researchers and concluded that there is no consensus as to what exactly constitutes the concept of E 2.0. This may be attributed to the fact that the concept is still in nascent stage and is yet to be embraced by organizations in entirety. Another important factor contributing to this perplexity may be the dynamic nature of the technological platforms on which the concept has been founded. Researchers hope that the wider acceptance of the concept as well as element of stabilization on the technological front may result in crystallization of the concept in the times to come.

Meanwhile, crystallization or no crystallization of the concept, its antecedent advantages such as more efficient organization structure enabling inclusion of distributed work force, collective decision-making, enhanced information updating and accession, and gathering of market intelligence and innovations has endeared the concept to the organizations. However, inclusion of web 2.0 technologies is not a cakewalk due to the concomitant challenges that organizations have to deal with, *viz* confidentiality of important information, productivity loss due to non-productive features, lack of ROI metrics, ownership of intellectual property rights, and the challenges consequent to formative state of web 2.0. Thus, effective incorporation of organizations necessitates introduction of common collaborative infrastructure for the delivery of precisely defined targets, which are synchronous with corporate strategy. Besides this, organization restructuring, process reengineering, cyber resilient systems, and managerial support are also mandated alongside the effective handling of motivational issues of employees.

Research is beneficial for the academicians as it is a value addition to the existing body of knowledge and provides a comprehensive view of the concept of Enterprise 2.0, its building blocks, attendant advantages, challenges, and suggestions thereof. As the research enumerates advantages and challenges associated with the incorporation of social media tools and practices in the organizations, it may assist practitioners in anticipating the opportunities and hurdles on their way to E 2.0 more realistically. Wide-ranging list of suggestions may also be beneficial by providing them guidelines for effective incorporation of the social technologies in their organizations and helping them to avoid costly errors thereby.

To conclude, it can be said that Enterprise 2.0 may not yet be the 'the future of business' but the super-portal concept, linking social enterprise applications with business enterprise applications such as ERP and CRM, is definitely entering the early majority stage (Miles [2009]). It appears to be no longer whether 'to be or not to be' as far as the adoption of Enterprise 2.0 technologies are concerned rather the issue to be tackled now is 'how' to best incorporate these technologies in the organization as E 2.0 is an integrative business strategy and therefore requires the holistic implementation approach. As change is the only constant in the world of E 2.0, creating an E 2.0 means embarking on a never-ending journey in the pursuit of excellence (Miles [2009]; Buytendijk et al. [2008]). Major software vendors such as IBM, Microsoft, and Oracle are all readying new technology offerings, loaded with Enterprise 2.0 features, to bear a hand to the organizations in their quest for innovation. Though not a panacea for all the dysfunctions of corporate, yet Enterprise 2.0 is ready to take a plunge into mainstream business market, to usher in a new era (McAfee [2006]; Lennon [2009]). An era characterized by a new class of networked organizations working on the socio-technical ideologies of Web 2.0. Networked organizations which are 'learning organizations' with multiplicative benefits, which are more agile, more flexible, more responsive to customer needs, and have improved information flows. These organizations would be permitting decision-making at the lowest levels in hierarchy and right at the point of action (Bughin et al. [2011]). Such organizations will be in tandem with the digital consumer (Chatterjee et al. [2010]). This is because the E 2.0 technologies used by these organizations will help them to understand customers, to connect with them, to forge closer marketing relationships, and to involve customers in product-development efforts in the socially networked world, as has been done by Unilever to co-create Axe Twist brand (Chatterjee et al. [2010]; Bughin et al. [2011]). All this will take the market competition to new levels thereby leading to new benchmarks for competition in coming time across industries (Bughin et al. [2011]).

## COMPETING INTERESTS

The authors declare that they have no competing interests.

## AUTHORS' CONTRIBUTIONS

Both the authors, PD and AS, have contributed almost equally in conception and design of the paper, collection, analysis and interpretation of secondary data and are responsible for the final draft. Both the authors have read and approved the final manuscript.

## REFERENCES


1. Almeida F: Web 2.0 technologies and social networking security fears in enterprises. *International Journal of Advanced Computer Science and Applications* 2012, 3(2):152–156.
2. Argyris, C. (1998). Empowerment: the Emperor's new clothes. Harvard business Review.. Accessed 20 January 2014. https://hbr.org/1998/05/empowerment-the-emperors-new-clothes
3. Booz, Allen, & Hamilton (2010). Ready for what is next. Enterprise 2.0.. Accessed 11 January 2014. http://www.boozallen.com/media/file/enterprise2-west2010.pdf
4. Bughin, J, Chui, M (2011). The rise of the networked enterprise: Web 2.0 finds its payday. McKinsey on Business Technology, 22 (Spring). Accessed 02 February 2014. http://www.mckinsey.com/insights/high_tech_telecoms_internet/the_rise_of_the_networked_enterprise_web_20_finds_its_payday
5. Buytendijk, F, Cripe, B, Henson, R, Pulverman, K. (2008). Business Management in the Age of Enterprise 2.0: Why Business Model 1.0 Will Obsolete You. Oracle. .

Accessed 12 January 2014. http://www.oracle.com/us/solutions/business-intelligence/ 064029.pdf

6. Chaffey D, Chadwick FE, Johnston K, Mayer R: *Internet Marketing: Strategy, Implementation and Practice.* 3rd edition. FT (Financial Times) Prentice Hall, Essex, England; 2006.
7. Chatterjee, I, Küpper, J, Mariager, C, Moore, P, Reis, S. (2010). The decade ahead: Trends that will shape the consumer goods industry. Report on consumer packaged goods practice. McKinsey & Company. Accessed 27 August 2014. http://www.mckinsey.com/.../consumer%20packaged%20goods/.../trends%20t
8. Chinn, D, Kaplan, J, Weinberg, A. (2014). Risk and responsibility in a hyperconnected world : implications for enterprises (pp. 1–5). Report. McKinsey & Company London. . Accessed 28 August 2014. http://www.mckinsey.com/insights/business_technology/risk_and_responsibility_in_a_hyperconnected_world_implications_for_enterprises
9. Chui, M, Manyika, J, Bughin, J, Dobbs, R, Sarrazin, H, Sands, G, Westergen, M (2012). The social economy: unlocking value and productivity through social technologies. McKinsey Global Institute Report. . Accessed 01 January 2014. http://www.mckinsey.com/insights/high_tech_telecoms_internet/the_social_economy
10. Chui, M, Miller, A, Roberts, RP (2009). Six ways to make Web 2.0 work: Web 2.0 tools present a vast array of opportunities - for companies that know how to use them. The McKinsey Quarterly, pp 0–7. . Accessed 02 February 2014. http://www.mckinsey.com/insights/business_technology/six_ways_to_make_web_20_work
11. Constantinides E, Fountain SJ: Special issue papers Web 2.0: conceptual foundations and marketing issues. *Journal of Direct, Data and Digital Marketing Practice* 2008, 9(3):231–244. DOI:
12. Duhan P, Singh A: Social media: a paradigm shift in integrated marketing communication. *Integral Review: A Journal of Management* 2013, 6(2):1–12.
13. Edosomwan S, Prakasan SK, Kouame D, Watson J, Seymour T: The history of social media and its impact on business. *The Journal of Applied Management and Entrepreneurship* 2011, 16(3):1–13.
14. Evans D, McKee J: *Social Media Marketing: The Next Generation of Business Engagement.* Wiley Publishing, Inc, Indiana; 2010.
15. Frappaolo, C, Keldsen, D (2008). Enterprise 2.0: agile, emergent and integrated (underwritten in part by ECM²). A white paper by AIIM. The ECM Association. http://www.aiim.org/PDFDocuments/34464.pdf. Accessed 03 January 2014.
16. Fuchs-kittowski, F, Klassen, N, Faust, D, Einhaus, J (2009). A comparative study on the use of Web 2.0 in enterprises. *Proceedings of I-KNOW' 09 and I-SEMANTICS' 09.* Graz, Austria (pp. 372–378).
17. Gupta, PD, Guha, S, Krishnaswami, SS (2013). Firm growth and its determinants. *Journal of Innovation and Entrepreneurship, 2*:15,
18. Hinchcliffe, D (2007). The state of Enterprise 2.0. Retrieved on December 15, 2013 from http://www.zdnet.com/blog/hinchcliffe/the-state-of-enterprise-2–0/143
19. Hughes, R. (2010). Enterprise social networking : Don't be afraid (pp. 1–8). BroadVision Inc. . Accessed 31 December 2013. http:// www.clearvale. com/clearvale/mkt-nav/en/whitepapers/Enterprise_Social_Networking-Dont_Be_Afraid_2010_02_24.pdf
20. Internet World Stats (2013). Usage and population statistics. . Accessed 05 May 2013. http://www.internetworldstats.com/stats.htm
21. Jagongo A, Kinyua C: The social media and entrepreneurship growth (a new business communication paradigm among SMEs in Nairobi). *International Journal of Humanities and Social Science* 2013, 3(10):213–227.
22. Janssen, C. Techopedia explains Enterprise 2.0. Technopedia. . Accessed 23 January 2014. http://www.techopedia.com/definition/16916/enterprise-20
23. Kaplan AM, Haenlein M: Users of the world, unite! The challenges and opportunities of social media. *Business Horizons* 2010, 53: 59–68.

24. Kenly, A, Poston, B (2011). Social media and product innovation: early adopters reaping benefits amidst challenge and uncertainty. A Kalypso White Paper. Kalypso. . Accessed 05 January 2014. http://kalypso.com/downloads/insights /Kalypso _Social_Media_and_Product_Innovation_1.pdf
25. Kopaee, R, Uppal, S (2011). Enterprise 2.0: harnessing social media. Deloitte Enterprise Risk Service, Emerging Technology Risk Group, Québec, Canada. (pp. 1–12) http://www.slideshare.net/ljubab/enterprise-20-harnessing-social-media Accessed 13 January 2014.
26. Lennon, J (2009). Implementing Enterprise 2.0: balancing social networking and community with collaborative tools and services. A developer works by IBM Corporation. . Accessed 03 January 2014. http://www.ibm.com/developerworks /library/wa-enterprise20/wa-enterprise20-pdf.pdf
27. Leonardi PM, Huysman M, Steinfield C: Enterprise social media: definition, history, and prospects for the study of social technologies in organizations. *Journal of Computer-Mediated Communication* 2013, 19(2013):1–19. d
28. Lindegaard, S (2012). Social media for corporate innovators & entrepreneurs: add power to your innovation efforts. . Accessed 04 January 2014. http:// 15inno.contentrobotllc.netdna-cdn.com/wp-content/uploads/2012/08/Social-Media-for-Corporate-Innovators-and-Entrepreneurs.pdf
29. Mangold WG, Faulds DJ: Social media: the new hybrid element of the promotion mix. *Business Horizons* 2009, 52: 357–365.
30. Matuszak, G. (2007). Enterprise 2.0: Fad or Future? The Business Role for Social Software Platforms (pp. 1–20). A Report by KPMG International. . Accessed 31 December 2013. http://us.kpmg.com/microsite/attachments/ 2007/Enterprise20_WhitePaper.pdf
31. Mayfield, A (2008). What is social media. E-book. . Accessed 06 May 2013. http://www.icrossing.com/ebooks
32. Mazumder, S. (2008). A Web 2.0 adoption model for enterprises. A white paper. Infosys. . Accessed 02 January 2014. http://www.infosys.com/IT-services/ application- services/white-papers/Documents/web-2-adoption-model.pdf
33. McAfee AP: Enterprise 2.0: the dawn of emergent collaboration. *MIT Sloan Management Review* 2006, 47(3):20–29.
34. Miles, D (2009). Collaboration and Enterprise 2.0: work-meets-play or the future of business? A report by AIIM - Find, Control, and Optimize Your Information, MD, Underwritten in part by Allyis, Ektron, EMC[2] and ORACLE. . Accessed 01 January 2014. http://www.aiim.org/PDFDocuments/36789.pdf
35. Miller, R (2007). Enterprise 2.0 definition and solutions. CXO Media. http:// www.cio.com/article/2438467/enterprise-software/enterprise-2–0-definition-and-solutions.html. Accessed 03 January 2014.
36. Mukherjee H: *Share Without a Care. Mind Matters - a Supplement of Sunday Times of India, Bennett.* Coleman & Co. Ltd., Mumbai; 2014.
37. Nielsen nmIncite (2012). State of the media: the social media report 2012. . Accessed 05 May 2013. http://postmediavancouversun.files.wordpress.com /2012/12/nielsen-social-media-report-20122.pdf
38. Owyang, J (2010). Socialgraphics help you to understand your customers: slides and webinar recording. Online document. and http://www.slideshare.net/ charleneli/understand-your-customers-social-behaviors/ and [http://www.web-strategist.com/blog/category/socialgraphics/] Accessed 04 September 2013.
39. Schueler, M (2011). Social effects of Enterprise 2.0 in organizational practice. *WebSci'11*, June, 14–17. . Accessed 28 January 2014. www. websci11.org/fileadmin/websci/Posters/29_paper.pdf?
40. Stanley, M (2009). Mobile internet report. www.ms.com/techresearch. Morgan Stanley. Accessed 24 December 2012.
41. Stelzner, MA (2013). 2013 social media marketing industry report: how marketers are using social media to grow their businesses (pp. 1–42). Social Media Examiner. .

Accessed 02 August 2013. www.socialmediaexaminer.com/ SocialMedia MarketingIndustryReport20

42. Stobbe, A. (2010). Enterprise 2.0: how companies are tapping the benefits of Web 2.0. Deutsche Bank Research. Frankfurt, Germany. . Accessed 02 January 2014. http://www.dbresearch.com/PROD/DBR_INTERNET_EN-PROD/PROD0000000000262287.pdf
43. The Economist Intelligence Unit (2007). Serious business Web 2.0 goes corporate. A Report from Economist Intelligence Unit Sponsored by FAST. . Accessed 01 January 2014. http://www.socialmediagroup.com/wp-content/uploads/ 2007/06/ smg_eiu _web20.pdf
44. Turban E, Bolloju N, Liang T: Enterprise social networking : opportunities, adoption, and risk mitigation. *Journal of Organizational Computing and Electronic Commerce* 2011, 21(3):202–220.
45. Vehr, Nicolas J. (2012). 2012 social media usage survey. Vehr Communications. . Accessed 05 May

# CHAPTER 9

# Video Games Can Develop Graduate Skills in Higher Education Students: A Randomised Trial

**Matthew Barr**

*School of Humanities, University of Glasgow, Glasgow G12 8QQ, Scotland, U*

## ABSTRACT

This study measured the effects of playing commercial video games on the development of the desirable skills and competences sometimes referred to as 'graduate attributes'. Undergraduate students in the Arts and Humanities were randomly assigned to either an intervention or a control group. Previously validated, self-report instruments to measure adaptability, resourcefulness and communication skill were administered to both groups. The intervention group played specified video games under controlled conditions over an eight week period. A large effect size was observed with mean score change 1.1, 1.15, and 0.9 standard deviations more positive in the intervention group than the control on the communication, adaptability, and resourcefulness scales respectively ($p = 0.004$, $p = 0.002$, and $p = 0.013$ for differences in groups by unpaired *t*-test). The large effect size and statistical significance of these results support the hypothesis that playing video games can improve self-reported graduate skills. The findings suggest that such game-based learning interventions have a role to play in higher education.

**Keywords:** Adult learning,Cooperative/collaborative learning,Interactive learning environments,Media in education,Post-secondary education

# 1. INTRODUCTION

Graduate attributes are those generic skills such as problem solving, communication, resourcefulness or adaptability which are considered desirable in graduates, particularly where employability is concerned (Barrie, 2006, 2007; Hughes & Barrie, 2010). However, it may be argued that most higher education courses are not explicitly designed to teach or develop graduate attributes. Many commercial video games, on the other hand, require players to exercise a range of such skills and competences in order to progress (Barr, 2013). Advocates of the learning experience afforded by modern video games include Thomas and Brown (2011), who describe a new "disposition" towards learning that games exemplify, requiring players to be both adaptable ("thrive on change") and resourceful ("marshal all their available resources and experiment with them to find multiple ways of accomplishing a task"). Gee (2007)identifies a range of learning principles present in video game design that encourage, for example, critical thinking and reflective learning, which are also commonly cited as desirable attributes in graduates. However, while there are indications that playing video games may be associated with positive cognitive and social effects (Granic, Lobel, & Engels, 2014), there is little empirical evidence for the efficacy of using commercial video games to develop graduate skills. This work, therefore, was intended to measure the effects of playing commercial video games on the attainment of certain graduate attributes, testing the hypothesis that playing selected games can improve student scores on measures of graduate skills. This general hypothesis may be subdivided into hypotheses relating to each of the areas under investigation: communication, resourcefulness and adaptability. These hypotheses are evaluated by comparing control and intervention group pre- and post-test scores on self-report measures. If these hypotheses are supported, then new opportunities for institutional skills development provision may be revealed, and there are important implications for how video games are perceived by the wider public.

The GAGA Project ("Using games technology to develop graduate attributes") saw the development of a game to help prepare international students for study at the University of Abertay, by introducing that institution's graduate attributes (Lloyd, 2011). However, no empirical evidence of the game's efficacy has been published. Furthermore, this work involved the development of a game for the specific purpose of introducing certain graduate attributes: the study reported here is concerned with the use of existing commercial video games. Adachi and Willoughby (2013), however, demonstrated by means of a four-year longitudinal study that playing strategy and role-playing games predicted self-reported problem solving skills among a sample of 1492 high school-aged participants. Adachi & Willoughby also noted that the empirical evidence for the relationship between playing video games and the development of problem solving skills was limited. Subsequently, Shute, Ventura, and Ke (2015) have shown statistically significant gains in problem solving, spatial skills and persistence in a group of participants asked to play *Portal 2* – one of the titles used in this study – for 8 h, compared with a group asked to play a suite of 2D puzzle games purported to improve such skills.

The Scottish institution at which the study was carried out identifies ten graduate attributes: Investigative, Effective Communicators, Independent and Critical Thinkers, Adaptable, Resourceful and Responsible, Confident, Experienced Collaborators, Subject Specialists, Reflective Learners, Ethically and Socially Aware. As noted by Nicol (2010), the development of graduate attributes in Scotland has drawn heavily on work carried out by Barrie (2006; 2007) in Sydney and Melbourne and, as a result, the attributes extolled by this institution are broadly comparable to those identified by other universities, internationally. Furthermore, it is evident that skills relating to communication, adaptability, and resourcefulness are sought by employers the world over, regardless of the umbrella terms used to describe them.

Since the host institution already purports to develop this list of skills and competencies in its students, this study was designed to determine whether video games offer any advantages for attribute development over-and-above existing university provision. A pilot project indicated that of the attributes listed, effective communication, adaptability and resourcefulness were the most promising candidates for further study, and identified suitable instruments for their measurement.

## 2. GAMES

The games used in the pilot project were selected with assistance from colleagues in industry and academia, who were asked to suggest titles that might relate to the list of graduate attributes provided. These suggestions were necessarily mediated by the financial and technical limitations of the study, which dictated that games must run on very modestly-specified Windows PCs and be relatively inexpensive. An additional consideration was the quality of the games. A poor quality game is of little utility here: well-received titles are more likely to be representative of those which players would choose to play on their own time, and a particularly poor game is likely to impact negatively on the participants' willingness to engage in the study. While game quality is somewhat subjective, review scores aggregated by sites such as Metacritic (Metacritic - Movie Reviews, TV Reviews, Game Reviews, and Music Reviews, 2016) are used by industry and consumers alike to determine a game's excellence (Graft, 2011). Metacritic scores are recognized as imperfect (Dring, 2010) but they undoubtedly provide an easily quantifiable means of determining the relative merits of a game. For the purposes of this study, no game with a Metacritic score of less than 80 out of 100 was considered, with scores ranging from 82 (*Lara Croft and the Guardian of Light*) to 95 (*Portal 2*). All of the games, with the exception of *Gone Home*and *Papers, Please*, include a substantial multiplayer component.

The games used in the study were all commercial titles, designed for entertainment purposes rather than with the intention of developing particular skills in players. The brief descriptions below describe the games in general terms while highlighting some of the features most relevant to this study.

*Borderlands 2* (Borderlands 2-Gearbox Software, 2016) is a co-operative role-playing first-person shooter game developed by Gearbox Software. Players work together to obtain loot and weaponry while defeating a range of foes against a colourful, if violent, cartoonish backdrop and attendant story. A variety of play styles are supported through the choice of character classes presented to the player, ranging from a tank-like "Gunzerker" to a stealthier assassin. The game allows for local area network (LAN) multiplayer, meaning the co-operative elements functioned within the university infrastructure and did not require an internet connection. *Borderlands 2* also permits players to drop in and drop out as required – a participant who arrived after others had already embarked on a mission could straightforwardly join the team without being forced to wait for the beginning of the next mission, or requiring the others to start again from the beginning.

*Minecraft* (Minecraft, 2016) is a procedurally-generated sandbox game with construction, exploration and survival elements. In single player mode, players are free to explore the world and collect ('mine') resources such as stone, wood and metal to create ('craft') a range of buildings, tools and weapons. Multiplayer mode is similarly non-prescriptive in terms of what it permits (or requires) players to do: the main difference is that the world is shared, so players may choose to work together.

Valve's *Portal 2* (Official Portal 2 Website, 2016) is described by the developer as "a hilariously mind-bending adventure that challenges you to use wits over weaponry in a funhouse of diabolical science". The game features a robust co-operative mode, and the co-operative portion of the game allows for split-screen play, meaning two people can play together on the same machine. Participants were asked to play *Portal 2* in pairs and provided with printed instructions on how to host or connect to a co-operative game. The configuration of the game allowed players who had already completed a number of the co-operative levels to advance to subsequent stages and thus minimise repetitious play.

*Lara Croft and the Guardian of Light* (Lara Croft and the Guardian of Light, 2016) was included in the study as a result of the game's emphasis on co-operation to solve puzzles and progress. A fixed isometric view of the action is presented and the game is intended to be played with a collaborator. One player assumes the role of the gun-toting Lara while the other plays as Totec, a Mayan warrior who comes equipped with a spear that may be used to create impromptu ladders and bridges. Co-operative players share the same screen (although online co-op is an option in most versions of the game) and for this study both players were provided with a games controller similar in design to that used with the Xbox 360 games console.

The rationale for the inclusion of *Warcraft III: Reign of Chaos* (Blizzard Entertainment, 2016) was based on its strategic multiplayer mode, which may be played over a local network without an internet connection. The game is played on a three dimensional map with up to four races (Orcs, Humans, Night Elves and Undead) vying for domination. Each player controls one of these races and must collect resources (gold and lumber) to develop and construct buildings, units and weaponry with the ultimate aim of obliterating their opponents from the map. The multiplayer mode of the game supports team play, meaning that participants in the study could work together (even as different races) to defeat a computer-controlled adversary. Unlike *Lara Croft*, many different multiplayer configurations are supported, from the previously described two-versus-one scenario through to any combination of human and computer teams. The computer-controlled adversary may also be handicapped somewhat to accommodate inexperienced human players.

Valve's *Team Fortress 2* (Team Fortress 2, 2016) is a multiplayer-only game that may be hosted on a local server, again avoiding the need for an internet connection to facilitate matchmaking. The game sees the competing teams thrown into conflict on a time-limited or objective-based map. When a team meets the victory conditions – or time runs out – the next map is loaded and a new objective pursued. Each map operates in a pre-determined game mode, such as Capture the Flag or King of the Hill, with the objective of each mode explained by means of a short video shown at the beginning of play. In Capture the Flag mode, for example, both teams are tasked with stealing a briefcase of intelligence from the opposing team's base and transporting it back to their own, with the briefcase standing in for the more traditional flag. The winning team is that which captures the enemy intelligence three times. Players must therefore decide how much emphasis to place on defence of their own intelligence versus making an offensive move to capture the enemy's briefcase, with different team members assuming different roles as agreed.

The Fullbright Company's *Gone Home* ('About Gone Home', 2012) might be described as a first-person interactive story or adventure (the designers term it a "story exploration video game") wherein the player, assuming the role of a young woman returning to her family home after a year-long absence, explores the apparently abandoned house. In doing so, the player may uncover a number of storylines, the most significant of which relates to the protagonist's younger sister. There are no explicit goals and interaction is relatively limited, with plot developments uncovered by reading discarded letters and examining ephemera such as concert ticket stubs and television viewing guides.

*Papers, Please* (Papers, Please, 2016) is a puzzle/simulation game in which the player is cast as an immigration officer, deciding whom to admit and whom to turn away from the border of the fictional former communist state of Arstotzka. The player performs this role by critically assessing the documentation presented by each potential immigrant in light of the ever-changing rules and regulations imposed by the state. As well as exercising critical judgement and adapting to change, the player is presented with an opportunity to reflect on the ethical and social consequences of their in-game actions, not only in terms of the lives of the fictional immigrants and existing citizens of Arstotzka (terrorist attacks are a distinct possibility, should the 'wrong' person be permitted access to the country) but also in terms of the personal price to be paid by the family of the player's character if quotas are missed.

# 3. METHODS

Duran's Communicative Adaptability Scale (CAS) (1983; 1992) is a self-report measure of communication ability, framed in terms of communicative adaptability, which Duran defines as "the ability to perceive socio-interpersonal relationships and adapt one's interaction goals and behaviours accordingly." The scale has been used in a number of studies and produced Cronbach's alpha coefficients between 0.74 and 0.84, indicating good reliability (Duran, 1992). While CAS is here used as a measure of communication skill, a salient feature of this scale is its focus on adaptability. 'Adaptable' is another of the university's identified graduate attributes, and Duran (1992) states that "the most basic form of communication competence is fundamental competence", which may be defined as "an individual's ability to adapt effectively to the surrounding environment over time" (Spitzberg & Cupach, 1984).

The adaptability implicit in Duran's Communicative Adaptability Scale depends upon both "cognitive (ability to perceive) and behavioural (ability to adapt) skills". The scale comprises 30 statements (e.g. "I feel nervous in social situations") that relate to the six dimensions (Social Composure, Social Confirmation, Social Experience, Appropriate Disclosure, Articulation and Wit) of the "social communication repertoire". Respondents are asked to indicate the degree to which each statement applies to them, on a scale from 1 ("never true of me") to 5 ("always true of me") and the responses summed for each dimension. Certain responses (e.g. "I sometimes use words incorrectly") are reversed before summing, e.g. a 2 becomes a 4. The scale was developed and validated by means of two studies: one involving adult teachers, and the other involving university students. It is therefore thought to be highly applicable for use in this study, which involves adult university students.

Building on the work of Pulakos, Arad, Donovan, and Plamondon (2000; 2002), Ployhart & Bliese (2006) suggest a self-report measure of adaptability based on their own Individual ADAPTability (I-ADAPT) theory, in which they define adaptability as an "individual difference construct that influences how a person interprets and responds to different situations". The I-ADAPT-M measure was developed with the practicalities of its use in mind, while addressing all eight of the dimensions of adaptability identified by Pulakos et al. It is, therefore, relatively short (taking around 10 min to complete) and its self-report nature is intended to "simplify administration and scoring, and to enhance applicability to multiple contexts". The measure has been tested and refined in collaboration with subject matter experts and validated by means of a confirmatory factor analysis and a construct validity study of the original 40-item measure "found strong support for convergent and discriminant validity" (Ployhart & Bliese, 2006). Intended for use with adults across multiple contexts, the I-ADAPT-M measure is thought to be highly applicable here.

Ployhart & Bliese present their I-ADAPT theory as a nomological network of knowledge, skill, ability and other characteristics (KSAOs), performances and situations. The I-ADAPT-M measure is a 55-item survey that asks respondents to indicate how well each of the items describes their preferences, styles and habits at work, with each item aligned with a particular dimension of adaptability. For example, the item "I work well with diverse others" relates to cultural aspects of adaptability. The instrument is freely available for research purposes.

While no obvious measures exist for the responsibility aspect of the 'Resourceful and Responsible' attribute, Zauszniewski, Lai, and

Tithiphontumrong (2006) offer a 28-item Resourcefulness Scale, developed and validated in a two-phase study with chronically ill elderly patients. The authors found that the scale had acceptable internal consistency (Cronbach's alpha = 0.85) and state that it may be used with younger and middle-aged adults as well as the elderly, making it applicable for use with the young adults sampled here.

The 28-item Resourcefulness Scale measures resourcefulness along two dimensions: personal ("the ability to independently perform daily tasks") and social ("to seek help from others when unable to function independently"). 16 of the 28 items relate to personal resourcefulness (e.g. "When faced with a difficult problem, I try to approach its solution in a systematic way"), with the remaining 12 designed to measure social resourcefulness (e.g. "When I am feeling sad, it helps to talk to other people"). Items are presented on a 6-point scale ranging from 0 ("not at all like me") to 5 ("very much like me") and respondents asked to indicate how descriptive each of the items is of them.

Student participants were recruited to the study by means of an email invitation with a link to an online form. The email was targeted at year one and year two students in the College of Arts and explained that the study may involve playing video games and completing surveys. The email indicated that participants who completed all assigned tasks would be entered into a prize draw for an Amazon voucher at the end of the semester. Potential participants were not given any advance indication of what the tests might be intended to measure. Participants were randomly assigned to one of two groups: a control group, asked to complete the attribute-measuring tests at the beginning and the end of the study; and, an intervention group that would be asked to play selected video games under controlled conditions and to complete the tests.

Basic demographic information was collected for all participants, including age, gender and subjects studied. In addition, participants were asked to estimate the frequency with which they played video games. A total of 100 students were recruited (mean age 20.45, 52.2% female). Of the 50 students randomly assigned to each group, 36 completed the initial round of testing per group. 20 (40%) of those assigned to the control group completed both pre- and post-tests, while 16 (32%) of the intervention group saw the study through to completion. Groups were broadly comparable in terms of gender, age, year of study and time spent playing video games per week (Table 1).

**Table 1.** Summary of week 1 test scores and demographic information by control/intervention group.

| | | Control | Intervention | *p* |
|---|---|---|---|---|
| N | | 36 | 36 | |
| **Measures** | | | | |
| Communicative Adaptability Scale (mean (SD)) | | 100.14 (8.92) | 99.06 (17.88) | 0.746 |
| I-ADAPT-M (mean (SD)) | | 202.69 (19.70) | 200.36 (37.65) | 0.743 |
| Resourcefulness Scale (mean (SD)) | | 82.75 (19.75) | 81.44 (23.33) | 0.798 |
| **Demographic information** | | | | |
| Note that one participant in both groups did not complete the demographic survey, so N = 35 for these data. | | | | |
| Year of study (%) | Year 1 | 22 (62.9) | 24 (68.6) | 0.801 |
| | Year 2 | 13 (37.1) | 11 (31.4) | |
| Age (mean (SD)) | | 19.80 (3.41) | 21.09 (5.95) | 0.271 |
| Gender (%) | Female | 18 (51.4) | 20 (57.1) | 0.346 |
| | Male | 14 (40.0) | 15 (42.9) | |
| | Other | 3 (8.6) | 0 (0.0) | |
| Hours spent playing video games per week (%) | 0 | 10 (28.6) | 9 (25.7) | 0.973 |
| | 1-4 | 12 (34.3) | 14 (40.0) | |
| | 4-8 | 6 (17.1) | 6 (17.1) | |
| | >8 | 7 (20.0) | 6 (17.1) | |
| Retention (%) | Completed | 20 (55.6) | 16 (44.4) | 0.48 |
| | Lost to follow up | 16 (44.4) | 20 (55.6) | |

The game labs operated on a drop-in basis, open for students to come and play the specified games between the hours of 9am-5pm every Tuesday, Wednesday and Friday. The flexible drop-in structure partially addresses a common criticism of laboratory-based video game studies, where an arbitrarily defined time limit on play does not mirror the circumstances under which players normally play games (Egenfeldt-Nielsen, Smith, & Tosca, 2008). While participants were asked to log 120 min of play on most games (60 min each on *Gone Home* and *Papers, Please*; 14 h total game play across eight games), time management was the students' responsibility, meaning they could choose to play for "just 5 min more" or leave when they had a class to attend. Participants did occasionally opt to play for longer than the prescribed period, either because they were simply immersed in an enjoyable experience, or because it is more natural to stop playing at a suitable juncture in the game, for example, at the completion of a level or mission. In this sense, the lab was arranged to provide better ecological validity than would have been afforded by imposing a rigid temporal structure on proceedings. Under normal conditions, no player would choose to stop when they are in the middle of a game they are enjoying, and many players – particularly those less accustomed to lengthy sessions of video game play – might find being asked to endure 2 h of an unfamiliar game in a single sitting prohibitively tiring.

The control and intervention groups were assessed for similarity at baseline (taken to mean the point at which the first battery of tests was completed, following randomisation) by comparing demographic factors and baseline test scores by attribute (Table 1). Due to concern about retention bias, these baseline features were also compared between those with and without week 8 (end of study) scores (Table 2). All comparisons were by Fisher's exact test for categorical variables, and by unequal variances $t$-test assuming unequal variance between groups for continuous variables (Welch's $t$-test). Total scores for each attribute were calculated, in accordance with the published scoring mechanisms, for each participant at each time point they completed testing.

**Table 2.** Summary of week 1 test scores and demographic information by completed/lost to follow-up.

| | | Completed | Lost to follow-up | *p* |
|---|---|---|---|---|
| N | | 36 | 36 | |
| Group (%) | Control | 20 (55.6) | 16 (44.4) | 0.48 |
| | Intervention | 16 (44.4) | 20 (55.6) | |
| **Measures** | | | | |
| Communicative Adaptability Scale (mean (SD)) | | 97.72 (8.41) | 101.47 (17.94) | 0.26 |
| I-ADAPT-M (mean (SD)) | | 200.22 (19.06) | 202.83 (37.97) | 0.713 |
| Resourcefulness Scale (mean (SD)) | | 80.94 (18.09) | 83.25 (24.60) | 0.652 |
| **Demographic information** | | | | |
| Note that one participant in both groups did not complete the demographic survey, so N = 35 for these data. | | | | |
| Year of study (%) | Year 1 | 19 (54.3) | 27 (77.1) | 0.078 |
| | Year 2 | 16 (45.7) | 8 (22.9) | |
| Age (mean (SD)) | | 21.06 (4.28) | 19.83 (5.36) | 0.293 |
| Gender (%) | Female | 20 (57.1) | 18 (51.4) | 0.714 |
| | Male | 13 (37.1) | 16 (45.7) | |
| | Other | 2 (5.7) | 1 (2.9) | |
| Hours spent playing video games per week (%) | 0 | 7 (20.0) | 12 (34.3) | 0.32 |
| | 1–4 | 14 (40.0) | 12 (34.3) | |
| | 4–8 | 5 (14.3) | 7 (20.0) | |
| | >8 | 9 (25.7) | 4 (11.4) | |

To assess the primary research question, a summary measure of "score change" was calculated for each attribute by subtracting week 1 score from week 8 score for each participant with available data. Thus, each participant is assigned a score change for each attribute, which is negative if their score worsened, and positive if their score improved. The distribution of score changes was assessed in both groups (control and intervention) for each attribute:

- Score changes were assessed for normality graphically by histogram (Fig. 1);
- Each participant's week 1 score was plotted against week 8 score in a scatter plot, such that participants with positive score changes lay above the diagonal, and negative score changes below the diagonal (Fig. 2B);
- Differences in score change between the groups were formally assessed by calculating a Cohen's $d$ for difference in the means for the groups and tested using $t$-test assuming unequal variance (Table 3).

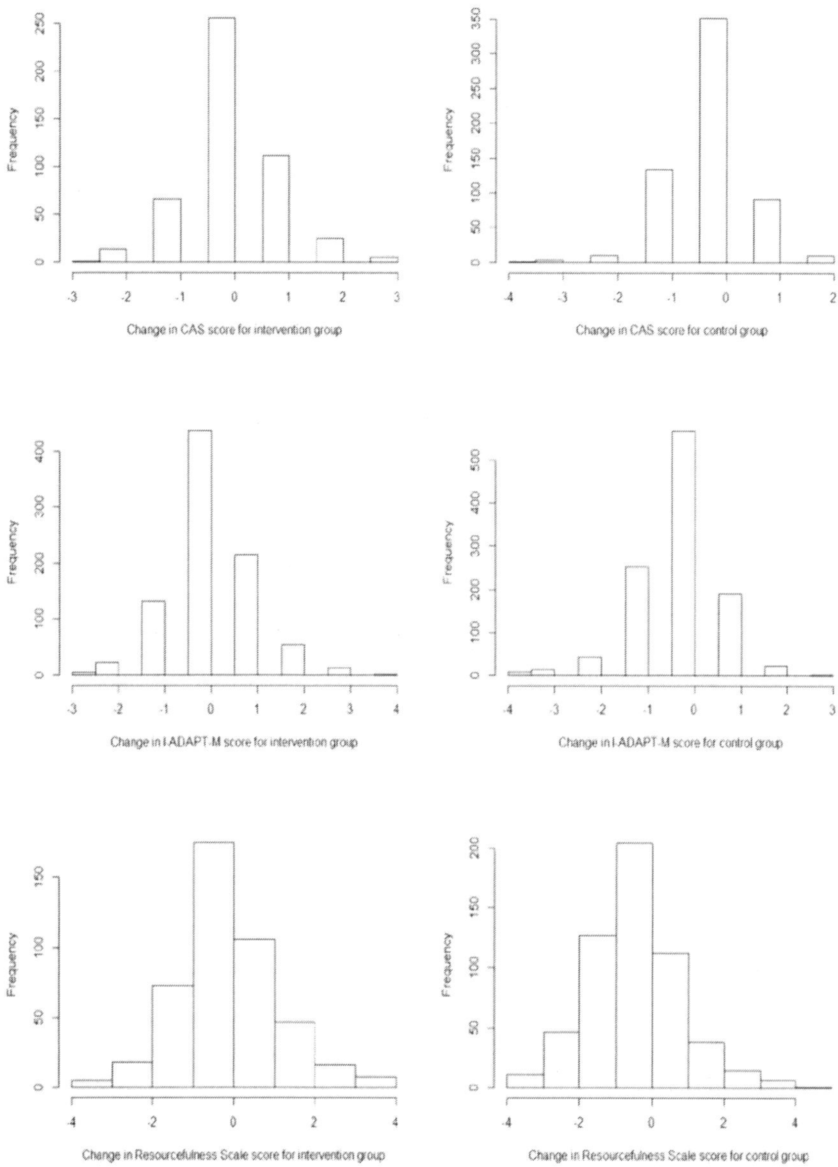


**Fig. 1**. Histograms showing distributions of score change between week 1 and week 8 for each measure (CAS, I-ADAPT-M and Resourcefulness Scale), for both control and intervention groups.

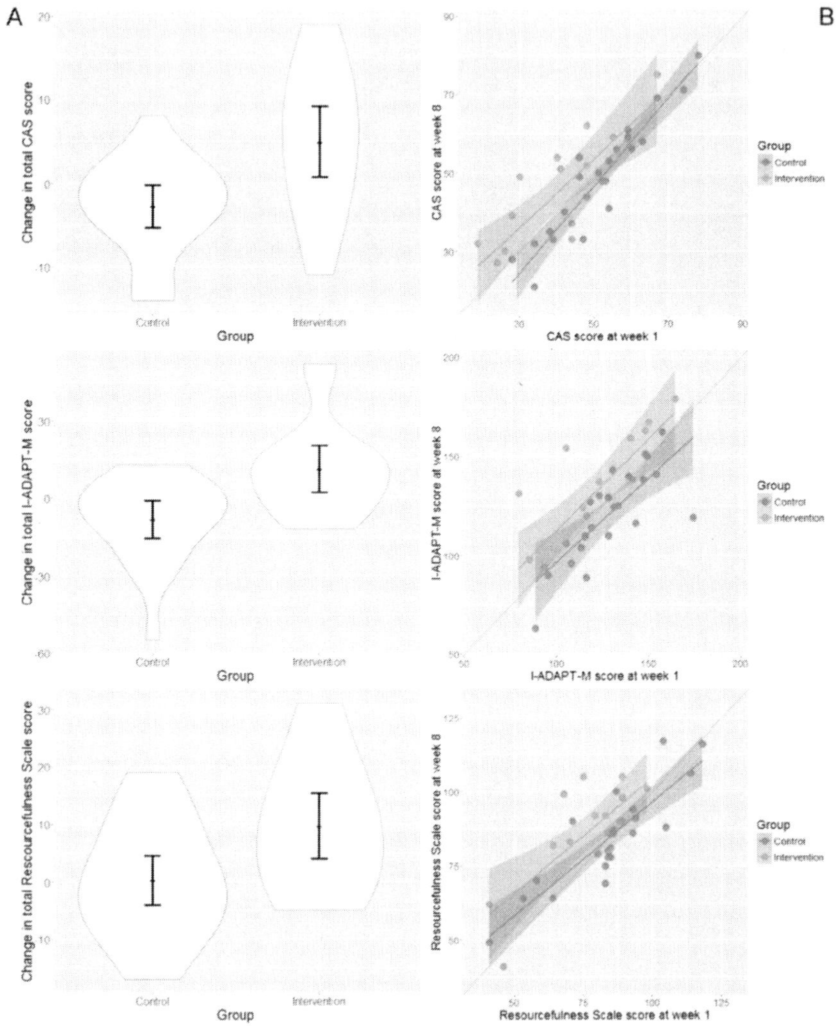


**Figure 2.** Left panel (A) shows distributions of total Communicative Adaptability Scale (CAS), I-ADAPT-M and Resourcefulness Scale score change from week 1 to week 8 by control and intervention groups. Plots are kernel density ('violin') plots. Error bars are 2 standard errors of the mean. Right panel (B) shows scatterplots of scores for the same measures for week 1 and week 8 for both groups. Line of equality for week 1 and week 8 scores is shown (diagonal), and a line of best fit (least squares method) is plotted for each group.

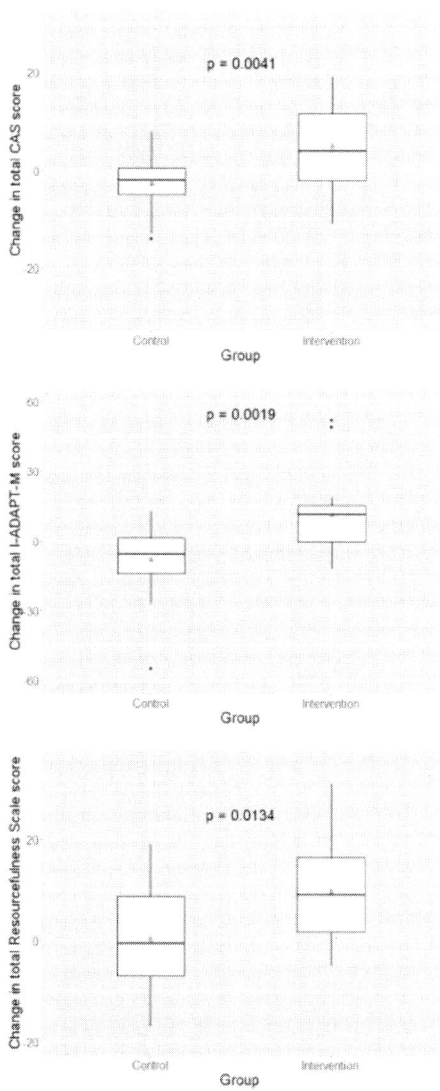


**Figure 3.** Box plots comparing distributions of total Communicative Adaptability Scale (CAS), I-ADAPT-M and Resourcefulness Scale score change from week 1 to week 8 between control and intervention groups. The horizontal line is the median score change for the group, the small red triangle represents mean change, the box represents interquartile range, whiskers show the two standard deviation range used to define outlier, and outliers are plotted as dots. Included as an alternative means of visualizing those data shown in Fig. 2. (For interpretation of the references to colour in this figure legend, the reader is referred to the web version of this article.)

**Table 3**. Summary of score changes from week 1 to week 8.

| | Control | | Intervention | | Difference in means | | | *p* |
|---|---|---|---|---|---|---|---|---|
| | Mean | SD | Mean | SD | Absolute | 95% CI | Cohen's *d* | |
| CAS | −2.8 | 5.65 | 4.94 | 8.41 | 7.74 | 12.79 to 2.69 | 1.1 | 0.004 |
| I-ADAPT-M | −8.25 | 15.99 | 11.31 | 18.07 | 19.56 | 31.32 to 7.8 | 1.15 | 0.002 |
| Resourcefulness | 0.25 | 9.71 | 9.69 | 11.42 | 9.44 | 16.77 to 2.11 | 0.9 | 0.013 |

**Table 4.** Summary of changes in Communicative Adaptability Scale scores for control and intervention groups.

| Change | Group | | Row total |
|---|---|---|---|
| | Control | Intervention | |
| negative (N) | 15 | 5 | 20 (56%) |
| negative (N/row total) | 0.75 | 0.25 | |
| negative (N/column total) | 0.75 | 0.31 | |
| positive (N) | 5 | 11 | 16 (44%) |
| positive (N/row total) | 0.31 | 0.69 | |
| positive (N/column total) | 0.25 | 0.69 | |
| Column Total | 20 (56%) | 16 (44%) | 36 (100%) |

**Table 5.** Summary of changes in I-ADAPT-M scores for control and intervention groups.

| Change | Group | | Row total |
|---|---|---|---|
| | Control | Intervention | |
| negative (N) | 12 | 4 | 16 (44%) |
| negative (N/row total) | 0.75 | 0.25 | |
| negative (N/column total) | 0.60 | 0.25 | |
| positive (N) | 8 | 12 | 20 (56%) |
| positive (N/row total) | 0.40 | 0.60 | |
| positive (N/column total) | 0.40 | 0.75 | |
| Column Total | 20 (56%) | 16 (44%) | 36 (100%) |

**Table 6.** Summary of changes in Resourcefulness Scale scores for control and intervention groups.

| Change | Group | | Row total |
|---|---|---|---|
| | Control | Intervention | |
| negative (N) | 12 | 3 | 15 (42%) |
| negative (N/row total) | 0.8 | 0.2 | |
| negative (N/column total) | 0.6 | 0.19 | |
| positive (N) | 8 | 13 | 21 (58%) |
| positive (N/row total) | 0.38 | 0.62 | |
| positive (N/column total) | 0.4 | 0.81 | |
| Column Total | 20 (56%) | 16 (44%) | 36 (100%) |

# 4. RESULTS

Test scores for communication, adaptability and resourcefulness all showed significant increases for the game-playing invention group over the control group, and 95% confidence intervals calculated for the difference between mean scores for the control and intervention groups did not cross zero (see Fig. 3, Tables 4,5 and 6). All three measures produced approximately normal distributions of scores. Cronbach's alpha coefficients calculated for baseline data indicated very good internal consistency for each measure

($\alpha = 0.88$, $\alpha = 0.91$ and $\alpha = 0.84$ for Communicative Adaptability Scale, I-ADAPT-M and Resourcefulness Scale, respectively).

When normalized by standard deviation, the differences in mean score between week 1 and week 8 indicate a large effect size (Cohen's *d* of between 0.9 and 1.15) for all three measures. Changes in score are summarized in Table 3.

The violin plots below (Fig. 2A) describe the distribution of score change for each measure.

On all three scales, students in the game-playing invention group were more likely to show a positive score change than the control group students. 5 of 20 (25%) students in the control group had improved communication scores versus 11 of 16 (69%) in the intervention group ($p = 0.24$, Fisher's exact test). Similar differences were found for adaptability (8 (40%) versus 12 (75%); $p = 0.03$, Fisher's exact test) and resourcefulness (8 (40%) versus 13 (81%); $p = 0.014$, Fisher's exact test). Thus, the effect was not seen in every intervention group participant, but the group effects were highly significant.

Mean score change on the communication scale was −2.8 (SD = 5.65) in the control group and 4.94 (SD = 8.41) in the intervention group (absolute difference in means = 7.74, 95% CI 2.69 to 12.79, Cohen's *d* 1.1). Mean score change on the adaptability scale was −8.25 (SD = 15.99) in the control group and 11.31 (SD = 18.07) in the intervention group (absolute difference in means = 19.56, 95% CI 7.8 to 31.32, Cohen's *d* 1.15). Mean score change on the resourcefulness scale was 0.25 (SD = 9.71) in the control group and 9.69 (SD = 11.42) in the intervention group (absolute difference in means = 9.44, 95% CI 2.11 to 16.77, Cohen's *d* 0.9). Outliers were observed in both groups, but the measured effect of the intervention was broadly similar across the range of baseline scores (Fig. 2B). As a sensitivity analysis, data was re-analysed with outliers (as defined by > 2 SD from mean) excluded. This made no substantive difference to the results of *t*-tests.

## 5. ISSUES AND LIMITATIONS

Certain challenges were encountered during the study, some of which may be relevant if the ideas described in this paper were to be applied in another formal educational setting. These issues, and limitations of the study in terms of its design and implementation, are discussed here.

As noted above, twelve Windows-based PC workstations were obtained and all games were played on this platform. The predominant – and most cost-effective – means of procuring games on PC is Valve's Steam service, which provides digital downloads (replete with a form of Digital Rights Management, or DRM) at competitive prices, especially during their regular sale events. Thus, this was the mechanism by which most games were obtained. It was known from the pilot project that the network ports required for Steam were not open on the university firewall and a support call to have these ports opened was logged with the relevant IT service. Quite understandably, opening ports is a non-trivial undertaking for a large institution's networking team, which also happened to be engaged in rolling out the IT infrastructure for a recently expanded campus at the time. As a result, these ports were not open at the commencement of the study. For the most part, this issue caused little more than inconvenience – the researcher used a mobile internet hotspot and a USB Wi-Fi dongle to install Steam and the required games on each machine, which simply required time and patience. Potentially more problematic was the use of Valve's Steam service to facilitate matchmaking, mediating the connections between players that are required for multiplayer gaming. By default, Steam is used to facilitate the multiplayer component of *Portal 2* and *Team Fortress 2* – both titles produced by Valve. An unforeseen additional complication with Steam matchmaking related to the limitations placed on newly-created Steam accounts. In order to purchase and install multiple copies of each game, a Steam account with a unique associated email address was created for each machine in the lab and games bought – as gift purchases, via the researcher's own Steam account – for each. However, in order to "protect our users from spamming, phishing, and other abuse, Steam prevents some accounts from accessing certain community and social features" (Limited User Accounts - Managing Your Account Features - Knowledge Base - Steam Suppor, 2016). To this end, Steam limits the ability of accounts which have spent less than five US dollars to engage in multiplayer activity, such as sending friend invites. As all of the purchasing was done through a single account, this restriction remained in place for all of the accounts used in the lab.

However, solutions were found for both games. As noted above, a local dedicated server was created for *Team Fortress 2*, to which participants' games connected instead of looking to Steam for potential matches. This was straightforward to accomplish as LAN play of this nature is supported by default in the game. The solution for *Portal 2* was slightly less straightforward, as LAN co-op is not an option available to players when they launch the game and, while the functionality does exist in the game's code, it may only be accessed by entering command line instructions via a normally-concealed console. A more user-friendly workaround was found on the Steam Users' Forum which, through the modification of one of the game's configuration files, allowed the option to connect to games on specified lab computers to be added to the game's menu. Participants were then instructed to choose the relevant menu option, depending on whether they were to host or connect to a game. In the latter case, they were instructed to choose the option that would connect them to the machine hosting the game, as identified by its IP address, which was clearly displayed on each machine.

MMORPGs *World of Warcraft* (*WoW*) and *Star Wars: The Old Republic* were also considered for inclusion but these games both require still more network ports to be opened, so this was not a realistic aim. While technical issues precluded any experimentation with these titles, the learning curve and overall complexity of such MMORPGs was also taken into consideration. Certainly, in the 2 h allocated to most of the other games, it seems unlikely that newcomers to the MMORPG genre would have progressed much beyond the most rudimentary stages of the game and thus would not experience the most relevant aspects of the genre, particularly the group-based questing. Further, if existing *WoW* players in the experimental cohort wished to use their own characters – an understandable desire if they have invested many hours into their creation and development – this might also have been problematic, as high level characters are generally prevented from grouping with new players in the first place.

More mundane were the issues relating to the available hardware. As noted above, the machines used in the lab were not remarkably well-specified, and certainly not intended for gaming. They did, however, prove perfectly usable for most games, especially when graphical options were adjusted to reflect the limited capabilities of the machines' graphics cards. The exception to this was *Lara Croft and the Guardian of Light* which, even on the lowest performance settings, was somewhat sluggish and occasionally unresponsive. *Lara Croft* was also one of the few games to rely on the supplied games controllers rather than the keyboard and mouse, and the build quality of the controllers – styled after the very popular Xbox 360 controller – was such that the effects of sluggish controls were amplified by the peripherals' shortcomings. These shortcomings, which mostly related to the left analogue stick typically used for movement, were not immediately obvious. On delivery, the controllers appeared to be of excellent quality and offered a more than acceptable recreation of the experience afforded by the rather more expensive Xbox-branded version of the peripheral. However, after a period of use, the analogue stick became unreliable, particularly in the diagonal directions – the very directions in which a player of an isometrically-presented game is likely to wish to move.

Such issues were not critical, however. They might have been considered so if they had resulted in a significant number of participants abandoning the study in response to hardware or software problems but, while several participants passed comment on the unsatisfactory nature of their experience with *Lara Croft*, none stated that it was unplayable or that they wished to abandon play. Of the 20 participants who completed the surveys associated with the preceding game (*Portal 2*), 17 completed those associated with *Lara Croft*.

In general, then, technical issues were of relatively little concern, although the nature of the potential problems outlined here should be borne in mind by educators considering similar projects. Other limitations relate to the experimental design of the study.

While the demographic information collected at the beginning of the study was thought sufficient, and is complete enough to account for important variables such as gender and year of study, it might have been useful to collect data on participants' previous study and work experience. For example, a student who has previously attended university or college, or was employed for any substantial period, would presumably possess more finely-honed graduate or work-related skills. The randomised nature of the study addresses concerns about the potential effects that variations in such experience might have, but questions remain about the impact of the game-playing intervention on these participants. Could gains in attribute attainment resulting from the intervention be tempered by previous exposure to opportunities for attribute development, for example?

The experiment was designed with ecological validity in mind, but even the more relaxed, drop-in structure of the lab-based game play is not an accurate reflection of how games are played at home. This is of little concern if this work is viewed as a potential model for introducing selected commercial video games to the higher education experience, as the arrangements in such cases would necessarily be similar to those described here. However, the nature of the intervention means it is difficult to make claims about the effects of playing video games more generally. The lab experience was often quite social in nature, with participants typically surrounded by those with whom they were playing, or who were playing the same game, and thus had a common interest. It is possible that the effects would be different if the games were played online, which might be more typical of the multiplayer games used here.

Participants were also aware that they were being measured by means of the online tests, and observed – however informally – by the researcher in the room. As such, the Hawthorne Effect (French, 1953) must be considered. The Hawthorne Effect, particularly where educational interventions are concerned, has been dismissed by some (see Deslauriers, Schelew, & Wieman, 2011 for a refutation of the phenomenon) but there is little doubt that the atypical circumstances under which the games were played, and their effects measured, could have had some subtle impact. However, given the nature of the study – which was not concerned with how the participants played the games or otherwise behaved under lab conditions – any such effect is considered by be negligible.

The limitations of self-report measures, in general, should also be borne in mind: such measures are susceptible to complications including social desirability bias, response bias, and issues related to participants' understanding of the language used to construct the surveys.

Any future work should also attempt to identify the specific types of game – or game features – that are most effective in raising communication, adaptability and resourcefulness scores. This might be achieved by modifying the experimental design to include multiple intervention groups, each playing a particular game for an extended period of time. However, the titles used here were carefully selected to ensure that there was a focus on multiplayer co-operation and it is likely that this is the most salient feature of the games played, certainly where communication is involved. In this respect, that a game features a co-operative multiplayer mode is probably a more important consideration than the nature of the game play involved.

## 6. CONCLUSION

This work demonstrates that playing commercial video games can have a positive effect on communication ability, adaptability and resourcefulness in adult learners, suggesting that video games may have a role to play in higher education. The study also suggests that graduate skills may be improved in a relatively short amount of time, with the gains reported here achieved over a period of eight weeks and representing just 14 h of game play. Certainly, the results of the randomised controlled trial described here suggest that the popular discourse around games' alleged ill-effects should be tempered by considerations of the potential positive outcomes of playing video games. There is a need for further, similarly robust study of these effects, and such work may only be hampered by ill-informed attitudes to the ubiquitous and immensely popular medium of video games.

## FUNDING

The pilot project on which this work is based received seed funding from the RCUK Digital Economy Communities & Culture Network+(EP/K003585/1).

## ACKNOWLEDGMENTS

I wish to thank Dr. Steve Draper for advice on experiment design, Dr. David Barr for his contribution to statistical analysis and Dr. David Wilson for feedback on this manuscript.

## REFERENCES

1. About Gone Home. 2012, June 19. Retrieved from https://fullbright. Company /gonehome/.
2. Adachi, P. J. C., & Willoughby, T. (2013). More than just fun and games: The longitudinal relationships between strategic video games, self-reported problem solving skills, and academic grades. Journal of Youth and Adolescence, 42(7), 1041e1052.
3. Barr, M. (2013). Can playing video games help develop graduate attributes?. In Proceedings of the 6th annual university of Glasgow learning and teaching conference. Glasgow, UK. Retrieved from http://eprints.gla.ac.uk/78489/.
4. Barrie, S. C. (2006). Understanding what we mean by the generic attributes of graduates. Higher Education, 51(2), 215e241.
5. Barrie, S. C. (2007). A conceptual framework for the teaching and learning of generic graduate attributes. Studies in Higher Education, 32(4), 439e458.
6. . Blizzard Entertainment. (2016). Warcraft III. Retrieved 25 April 2016, from http://us.blizzard.com/en-us/games/war3/. Borderlands 2-Gearbox Software. (2016). Retrieved 25 April 2016, from http://www.gearbox software .com/games/borderlands-2.
7. Deslauriers, L., Schelew, E., & Wieman, C. (2011). Improved learning in a large-enrollment physics class. Science, 332(6031), 862e864.
8. Dring, C. (2010, July 20). EA's Moore: Metacritic mania a 'slippery slope'?. Retrieved 24 March 2016, from http://www.develop-online.net/news/ea-s-mooremetacritic-mania-a-slippery-slope/0107404.
9. Duran, R. L. (1983). Communicative adaptability: A measure of social communicative competence. Communication Quarterly, 31(4), 320e326.
10. Duran, R. L. (1992). Communicative adaptability: A review of conceptualization and measurement. Communication Quarterly, 40(3), 253e268.
11. Egenfeldt-Nielsen, S., Smith, J. H., & Tosca, S. P. (2008). Understanding Video Games: The Essential Introduction (New Ed). Routledge.
12. French, J. R. P. (1953). Experiments in field settings. In F. J. Gravetter, & L.-A. B. Forzano (Eds.), Research methods for the behavioral sciences (pp. 98e135). New York: Holt, Rinehart & Winston.
13. Gee, J. P. (2007). What video games have to teach us about learning and literacy. New York: Palgrave Macmillan.
14. Graft, K. (2011). Take-Two's zelnick stresses importance of metacritic scores. Retrieved 24 March 2016, from http://www.gamasutra.com/view/news/33092/TakeTwos_Zelnick_Stresses_Importance_Of_Metacritic_Scores.php.
15. Granic, I., Lobel, A., & Engels, R. C. M. E. (2014). The benefits of playing video games. American Psychologist, 69(1), 66e78.
16. Hughes, C., & Barrie, S. (2010). Influences on the assessment of graduate attributes in higher education. Assessment & Evaluation in Higher Education, 35(3), 325e334.
17. Lara Croft and the Guardian of Light. (2016). Retrieved 25 April 2016, from http://www.laracroftandtheguardianoflight.com/.

18. Limited User Accounts - Managing Your Account Features - Knowledge Base - Steam Support. (2016). Retrieved 8 June 2016, from https://support. Steampowered .com/kb_article.php?ref¼3330-IAGK-7663.
19. Lloyd, R. (2011). The GAGA project: Using games technology to develop graduate attributes. University of Abertay Dundee. Retrieved from http://www. enhancementthemes.ac.uk/pages/docdetail/docs/case-studies/the-gaga-project-using-games-technology-to-develop-graduate-attributes. Metacritic - Movie Reviews, TV Reviews, Game Reviews, and Music Reviews. (2016). Retrieved 25 April 2016, from http://www.metacritic.com/.
20. Minecraft. (2016). Retrieved 25 April 2016, from https://minecraft.net/.
21. Nicol, D. J. (2010). The foundation for graduate attributes: Developing self-regulation through self and peer-assessment. The Quality Assurance Agency for Higher Education. Retrieved from http://qmwww. enhancementthemes.ac. uk/docs/publications/the-foundation-for-graduate-attributes-developing-selfregulation-through-self-and-peer-assessment.pdf. Official Portal 2 Website. (2016). Retrieved 25 April 2016, from http://www.thinkwithportals.com/.
22. Papers, Please. (2016). Retrieved 25 April 2016, from http://papersplea.se/.
23. Pulakos, E. D., Arad, S., Donovan, M. A., & Plamondon, K. E. (2000). Adaptability in the workplace: Development of a taxonomy of adaptive performance. Journal of Applied Psychology, 85(4), 612e624.
24. Pulakos, E. D., Schmitt, N., Dorsey, D. W., Arad, S., Borman, W. C., & Hedge, J. W. (2002). Predicting adaptive Performance: Further tests of a model of adaptability. Human Performance, 15(4), 299e323.
25. Ployhart, Robert E., & Bliese, P. D. (2006). Individual adaptability (I-ADAPT) Theory: Conceptualizing the antecedents, consequences, and measurement of individual differences in adaptability. In Understanding adaptability: A prerequisite for effective performance within complex environments (Vol. 6, pp. 3e39). Emerald Group Publishing Limited. Retrieved from http://www.emeraldinsight. com/doi/full/10.1016/S1479-3601%2805%2906001-7.
26. Shute, V. J., Ventura, M., & Ke, F. (2015). The power of play: The effects of Portal 2 and Lumosity on cognitive and noncognitive skills. Computers & Education, 80, 58e67.
27. Spitzberg, B. H., & Cupach, W. R. (1984). Interpersonal communication competence. SAGE Publications.
28. Team Fortress 2. (2016). Retrieved 25 April 2016, from http://www. teamfortress.com/.
29. Thomas, D., & Brown, J. S. (2011). A new culture of learning: Cultivating the imagination for a world of constant change. Lexington, Ky: CreateSpace.
30. Zauszniewski, J. A., Lai, C.-Y., & Tithiphontumrong, S. (2006). Development and testing of the resourcefulness scale for older adults. Journal of Nursing Measurement, 14(1), 57e68. http://doi.org/10.1891/jnum.14.1.57

# CHAPTER 10

# A Cloud Based Mobile Dispatching System with Built-in Social CRM Component: Design and Implementation

**Cosmina Ivan * and Razvan Popa**

*Department of Computer Science, Faculty of Automation and Computer Science, Technical University of Cluj Napoca, Baritiu 26, 400027 Cluj, Romania*

## ABSTRACT

*Mobile dispatching applications* have become popular for at least two major reasons. The first reason is a more mobile-centric usage pattern, where users relate to apps for fulfilling different needs that they have. In this respect, a vehicle dispatching application for mobile phones is perceived as a modern way of booking a vehicle. The second reason has to do with the advantages that this method has over traditional dispatching systems, such as being able to see the vehicle approaching on a map, being able to rate a driver and the most importantly spurring customer retention. The taxi dispatching business, one of the classes of dispatching businesses, tends to be a medium to lower class fidelity service, where users mostly consider the closest taxi as opposed to quality, which is regarded as being at a relatively consistent level. We propose a new approach for the taxi ordering application , a mobile dispatching system, which allows for a more engaged user base and offers fidelity rewards that are used to enhance the customer retention level based on a built in social customer relationship management (CRM) component. With this approach, we argue that in a business world which is shifting from a consumer-centric marketing to a human-centric model, this apps will allows taxi businesses to better interact with their clients in a more direct and responsible manner. Also this distributed system helps taxi drivers, which can receive orders directly from their clients and will be able to benefit from offering quality services as they can get higher ratings.

**Keywords:** mobile computing; cloud; dispatching system; social CRM

# 1. INTRODUCTION

The growth of *mobile computing* has outpaced any previous consumer electronic in terms of growth speed. This has enabled traditional expensive equipment to be displaced by easy to use Software as a Service product. We have seen the smartphone becoming the interface for anything that can be remotely controlled and the center of the entire online presence including email, social networks and professional activities [1]. This growth of software designed for mobile devices is set to continue over the course of the following decades. The mobile revolution brought changes in consumer behavior and the way people interact. New mobile devices come equipped with sensors such as GPS, accelerometer, gyroscope, altimeter, camera and thermometer. It also generates huge amount of metadata that can be captured and analyzed for discovering useful hidden patterns. Not to mention that they make use of a large bandwidth Internet connection that over 4G LTE (Long Term Evolution) can reach speeds of tens of megabits per second.

The rise of the *cloud* has changed from being a novelty in five years ago, to being the default deployment choice for most software products. While scalability was one of the top concerns five years ago, it has been now elegantly addressed by virtualization. Also, the price of cloud hosting has decreased with increased competition in the field, from both large enterprises such as Amazon, Microsoft or Google but also new organizations that found a niche with specific programming languages or types of software such as Digital Ocean or SoftLayer [2]. Competition between the cloud providers has become extremely sharp across all layers of the cloud, especially PAAS (Platform as a Service) and SAAS (Software as a Service), but we also observed that all IAAS (Infrastructure as a Service) vendors have included tools that compete with platform offerings, this is due to commoditization of the IAAS layer, which makes all providers want to raise on the ladder of technology offerings and extend their services into higher margin areas.

Given the ubiquity of smartphone devices, we are seeing an increased integration between different systems in the sense of reducing the time between activities required to be performed by people who are part of the same process. In this respect, CRM applications have integrated real time filtering of social networking data, in order to identify possible risks and opportunities as early as possible. These features have become a common component of any customer-facing B2C system. In this respect is not enough anymore to just have a working system, but to have a complete ecosystem that can track users from acquisition towards using the product and being able to reactivate them. The smartphone install base will continue to expand and this creates opportunities for mobile based systems to displace traditional more expensive systems. One of these systems is *mobile dispatching.* Traditional dispatching systems have been expensive as they required both hardware and software purchases. The hardware system is composed of a mobile data terminal with either an Internet connection or a radio connection, now these hardware terminals can be completely replaced with a smartphone or a tablet, which offers the same functionality. Dispatching applications were the first candidates for displacing a higher cost existing technology. By using cheap consumer level mobile devices it is possible to offer complex dispatching systems on a SAAS basis. With the rising adoption of smartphones by the consumer base, a large variety of applications meant at simplifying users daily life and enhancing productivity are appearing. Vehicle booking applications have first become popular in western countries, as this region offered a higher income level that determined a larger smartphone penetration.

Modern dispatching systems can now be built purely using software, and using mobile devices as the in-vehicle hardware. Furthermore the dispatching system can be hosted in a *public cloud*, which offers built in scalability and reliability. In this case, when hardware cannot be seen as a differentiator between systems and considering the rapid review cycle that an application such as a *taxi booking engine* usually receives, having an *integrated customer analysis solution* is extremely important. The dispatching system can be offered as white label product and sold on a monthly subscription. While the margins on selling software are generally high (80%–90%), the competition can also be very tough. Also when addressing current customers that have implemented traditional dispatching systems that use proprietary hardware equipment, the sale proposition will be weak unless the current offering includes *strong marketing or CRM (Customer relationship management) capabilities* that can be correlated to revenue growth. One important feedback mechanism which can be used in such a system is social networks. Considering for example a taxi ordering application, drawing new clients to using the service is strongly connected to the influence their network of friends have on promoting this service.

This paper is organized as follows: Section 2 encompasses the research we have done on existing dispatching systems with the aim of understanding the current enterprise and technological landscape and be able to contribute with new improvements. Section 3 describes the architectural design decisions and implementation considerations for the system, based on the integration of two subsystems: the *Dispatching application* and the *Social CRM component.* Section 4 describes the testing scenarios that we have envisaged and considered for an initial evaluation and Section 5 make conclusions and presents future developments.

# 2. BIBLIOGRAPHIC RESEARCH

## 2.1. Similar Systems and Applications

Traditional dispatching applications have incurred high costs attributed to purchases of physical equipment and revolving licensing fees. The first attempts to use mobile devices for logistic activities took place in the last decade, with GPRS based positioning. However the potential complexity of the applications built on this infrastructure was extremely low and they did not succeed on taking enough market share. Also these systems required a human operator that would manually insert or confirm the orders into the system. As more automation was necessarily, some logistic companies started using voice recognition and SMS as a more efficient way of placing an order into the system. In the last years, the number of proprietary dispatching apps has skyrocketed, with Uber being the most visible international player in the space. However the market remains segmented, with very few companies offering complete dispatching solutions.

We present here a set of similar services that we have analyzed from the literature based on their functionalities, and then in Table 1 creating a comparison matrix. We have inspired form these systems in determining the specifications of the system we are building.

**Table 1.** Similar services comparison matrix.

| Criteria/Service | *T Dispatch* | *SAP-SCM* | *DDS* | *Hailo* | *Taxi Magic* | *Uber* | *MTData* | *OUR SYSTEM* |
|---|---|---|---|---|---|---|---|---|
| Web presence | https://tdispatch.com | http://Go.sap.com | http://digital-dispatch.co.uk | https://www.hailoapp.com | http://gocurb.com | https://www.uber.com | http://www.mtdata.com.au | www.taxiarmy.com |
| iOS support | X | - | X | X | X | X | X | X |
| Android support | X | - | X | X | X | X | X | X |
| Cross platform support | X | - | - | - | - | - | - | X |
| Client Usage Analytics | X | X | - | - | X | X | X | X |
| Show nearby vehicles | - | - | - | X | X | X | - | X |
| Calculate shortest route | - | X | - | - | X | X | - | X |
| API available | - | X | X | X | - | - | - | X |
| Customizable design | X | X | X | - | - | X | - | X |
| Management panel | X | X | X | - | - | - | - | X |
| Geofencing | - | X | - | X | - | - | X | X |
| Shared vehicle ownership | - | - | - | - | - | - | - | X |
| Payment processing | X | X | X | X | X | X | X | X |
| Social Media integration | - | - | - | X | X | - | - | X |
| User satisfaction dashboard | - | - | - | - | - | - | - | X |
| Customer lifecycle management | - | - | - | - | - | - | - | X |

- *T-Dispatch* is the most similar system to our project, offering emerging taxi companies the ability to offer their users a modern app based dispatching solution. They have both driver and user apps.
- *SAP SCM* is a product line offered by the largest software enterprise in Europe. SAP enhanced their logistic module with the ability to book, track and dispatch vehicles using mobile devices and

management boards. Their entrance into this space was generated by demands from their costumers that required lower cost alternatives for managing their logistics. SAP does not offer the dispatching system as a separate product, but as an extension to their mature logistics system.

- *DDS* is a UK based company that has been focused on dispatch technology for over two decades. They have clients around the world and until mobile devices became available, they were one of the leading global suppliers of Mobile Dispatch Terminals (MDT). They entered into the mobile dispatching market in 2013 with a lower cost dispatching system. The key differentiator for our product versus DDS is the powerful management dashboard. DDS is not focused on customers, preferring to push forward their dispatching technology and not focusing on user retention and other metrics that are important for smaller companies.
- *Hailo* is an app that has attracted attention in UK, Ireland and North America, offering a simpler way for users to book a taxi using their mobile phone. They use the existing taxis and operated at a level equal to taxi dispatch companies. Their model is similar to other common apps as GetTaxi and MyTaxi.
- *Taxi Magic* was one of the first services that offered the ability to order a vehicle without calling, a system in which ordering a taxi is fairly simple: after launching Taxi Magic, your iPhone will use GPS or triangulation to determine your general location, and will present a list of nearby cab services (some listings are only phone numbers, while others fully support Taxi Magic's ordering system). After choosing a supported cab company, the application will ask for your exact street address and will then take you to a status screen that will alert you once your ride is dispatched (wait times can vary depending on the time of day and location). The status screen also allows you to view how far away the cab is and the driver's name. From this system we make use of ideas on localization.
- *Uber* . Luxury transportation in sleek black car is based on the business model of offering private drivers as taxi. It is available in largest cities around the world. The app offers functionalities of ordering a taxi by getting the users GPS positions, it allows tracking the driver as he approaches and when the ride is over, it allows for payment using credit card. While TaxiMagic operates by simply displacing the telephone as the ordering channel with an order sent from the smartphone, other services have appeared which work differently. This service also operate by having both a driver app and a client app. When the client orders a taxi, the order is submitted to

the closest driver, instead of going through an operator. By having a mobile app, the driver can be tracked by the client so the client can see when his taxi arrives.

- *MTData* is another traditional dispatch system provider that has entered the mobile dispatch market. They are still pushing their traditional dispatch technology including physical MDT (Mobile Data Terminal), but they also adopted SAAS products that can be offered independently on in conjuncture with their traditional systems.

From the Table 1 we can conclude that our system plan to include functionalities from analyzed solutions on the market, emphasizing on the specific CRM component which offer a unique characteristic to the proposed approach.

## 2.2. Social CRM Component

As the dispatching marketplace is becoming overcrowded with both providers that have tailored their existing systems to offer mobile dispatching and new providers, we needed a way to differentiate our product. We identified that most enterprise clients interested in accessing the technology that we offer have two primarily goals:

- Better understanding of their clients, retention levels, marketing analytics, customer activation levels.
- New marketing channel and consumer feedback mechanism that can be used to improve the product and the customer experience.

We are differentiating ourselves from the other alternatives by being a more lightweight system, that is easy to set up and which provides the business with actionable insights on their customers. The strong integration between the *dispatching component* and the *marketing-purposed customer analytics dashboard* provides a unique selling point. Most companies already have a mechanism of handling each of these two use cases, but the problem is that the systems are decoupled. This makes automation of some processes impossible. Our system is able to aggregate data on the users, create actionable metrics and automate specific tasks that offer maximum benefit to the business.

One such scenario is gathering data across all major social networks for a specific filter. For example we can filter for any mentions of the company name. After all the data is gathered, it is normalized and aggregated into our data stores in real time. At this point we also analyze the data, for example we analyze what kind of sentiment is associated to the data, and scale the sentiment on a −20 to +20 scale. If the sentiment is highly negative, we can automate the system to reply to the users post, offering him a coupon or apologizing for any inconvenience he faced using the system. If the sentiment is highly positive, we might encourage the user to invite his friends by offering discount rates or free coupons.

Statistics show that is four times harder to regain a lost customer than to get a new one. However, if the company is able to respond quickly to a negative experience suffered by the client, it can avoid losing the customer. With customer satisfaction increasing in importance every day across all enterprises, this is to become a major incentive for adoption of our system. For example if a client booked a vehicle but experienced any kind of frustration, there is a large chance this user will tweet about it or post it on Facebook. Our system will capture this negative comment within less than 10 s and offer any customer support people the means to identify what the issue was in the specific case and convince the client to retry the service. Our analytics dashboard can also be used for monitoring the impact of specific marketing campaigns. In order for this data to provide actionable insights, it is important to have a minimum delay between the moment any comment is published on the Internet and the moment an action is taken, being it an automatic action (such as a *thank you note*) or a customer support call meant at retaining a user that has gone through a negative experience.

Most of this data is gathered across social networks, but we are not limited to them. Twitter is one place where customers express their frustration or excitement within seconds, thus we needed access to the Twitter dataset. Facebook is another social network that can offer important information on the user, but as we mentioned we are not limited to using social networks. The service also allowed the enterprise to access any information matching the specific filters anywhere the Internet, such as Blog posts or comments written on news websites. In order to have access to all this data sources, we are using DataSift [3], which together with Gnip [4] are the only two companies in the world that have access to all the Twitter data in real time, and also their systems span across Twitter, offering access to over 20 data sources including Facebook, Blogs, Q&A websites and many other.

# 3. SYSTEM DESIGN

After analyzing the currently available systems and the functionalities they offer, we started analyzing the infrastructure that should back our system. According to [1] we opted for a Cloud-based service to offer the infrastructure for data synchronization between the apps and the operator panel. We also make use of the best practices of developing mobile applications by migrating data and processing power inside the

Cloud. We have studied how to realize the integration between the service and the Cloud and the benefits of this approach and we analyzed the means of implementing web services for fulfilling this goal.

We developed an API for our service which would be consumed inside the mobile application. We decided on using REST web services as they preferred when working with mobile applications. We needed the application to be available on as many mobile phone operating systems as possible, so we continued by analyzing cross platform mobile development solutions. After comparing Titanium development with other development frameworks we decided on using this platform because it offered a series of advantages such as compiling natively and being able to be extended in order to support more advanced functionality available for iOS or Android.

One important requirement was that the cross platform development supports *GPS*. According to [5] we make use of how to implement *GPS* into our application and how to determine *GPS* coordinates with various precisions. We can still determine the approximate user position when *GPS* is not available, such as when the user is located inside a building, which is a very common use case for our system. The way to identify the position of the user in such condition is by *GPS*triangulation. Even without a *GPS* receiver, the cell phone can provide information about your location. A computer can determine the location based on measurements of your signal, such as: its angle of approach to the cell towers, how long it takes the signal to travel to multiple towers and the strength of your signal when it reaches the towers.

The specific system that we are developing allows clients (users) to book vehicles directly from their mobile device without having to call through an operator. Having an app for this use case opens the doors for a wide variety of marketing strategies such as offering promotions, coupons, paying by credit card, offering subscriptions. This allows users to have an alternative to the traditional method of booking a vehicle by phone calling, based on the new and powerful trend of mobile cloud applications.

## 3.1. Functional and Nonfunctional System Characteristics

Software is becoming critical in driving the information-based economy. Time-to-market, robustness, and quality are important factors for measuring the success of systems in competitive economies and environments. There is also a need to evolve and adapt rapidly in an environment of continuous changes of business requirements. Therefore, there are stronger needs for standards and formalizations of the processes by which we specify and capture these requirements. Requirements capture is one of the initial phases to undertake in the system development process.

The functional requirements (FR) have been decomposed into low-level functional specifications that are depicted in Table 2. These specifications have been assigned priorities which are consistent with the iterative approach of development that we are following.

**Table 2.** Functional Requirements.

| | | |
|---|---|---|
| **FR1** | **Booking a vehicle by clients** | High |
| FR1.1 | Ordering based on GPS location | High |
| FR1.2 | Add precise location | High |
| FR1.3 | Remember used locations for suggestions | High |
| FR1.4 | Display map with user location | High |
| FR1.5 | Allow dragging the position marker on the map | Medium |
| FR1.6 | Get GPS location based on wireless | High |
| FR1.7 | Handle cases when GPS location cannot be obtained by allowing only exact address input | High |
| **FR2** | **Vehicle Dispatching** | High |
| FR2.1 | View active orders | High |
| FR2.2 | Respond to active order | High |
| FR2.2.1 | Respond with car id and time until it arrives | High |
| FR2.2.2 | Mark initial car position on a map | Medium |
| FR2.3 | Blink and sound alert on new order | High |
| FR2.4 | Call phone for order not processed within 1 min | Low |
| **FR3** | **Order confirmation** | High |
| FR3.1 | Display vehicle id and time until it arrives | High |
| FR3.2 | Allow order canceling | High |
| FR3.3 | Allow vehicle check-in | Medium |
| FR3.4 | Allow push notification if app is closed | High |
| **FR4** | **Authentication** | High |
| FR4.1 | Allow Facebook authentication | High |
| FR4.2 | Allow authentication with username, password and phone number | High |
| FR4.3 | Verify phone number | Low |
| **FR5** | **App promotion trough social networks** | High |
| FR5.1 | Allow Facebook sharing of app use | High |
| FR5.2 | Prompt for app review after 1 successful ride | High |
| **FR6** | **Feedback** | High |
| FR6.1 | Allow feedback from button in tab bar | High |
| FR6.2 | Allow vehicle check-out | Low |
| **FR7** | **User post-ride functionalities** | High |
| FR7.1 | Allow distance displayed on check out | Low |
| FR7.2 | Prompt user for driver rating on check out | Low |
| **FR8** | **Management Dashboard and Social CRM** | High |
| FR8.1 | Filter data in real time across multiple social networks | High |
| FR8.2 | Get an overall sentiment analysis of the service provided for specific time intervals | High |
| FR8.3 | Data augmentation in real time and Metadata generation | High |
| FR8.4 | Export data to a data store | High |

Non-functional requirements (NFR) are properties and qualities the software system must possess while providing its intended functional requirements or services. These types of requirements have to be considered while developing the functional counterparts. They greatly affect the design and implementation choices a developer may make. They also affect the acceptability of the developed software by its intended users. In the following, we briefly describe the three categories of non-functional requirements that may be imposed on a software system.

**System-related NFRs:** These types of requirements impose some criteria related to the internal qualities of the system under development and the hardware/software context in which this system will operate.

- Operational requirements: The Dispatching Application will be running on iOS and Android phones, and will be using Cloud services for data synchronization and storage.
- Manageability requirements: The manager will be able to administer customer complaints and to scan social networks for potential issues regarding the service. He should also be able to use the information in the system databases regarding clients previous booking in order to direct advertising campaigns and monitor the overall client satisfaction with the service.
- Performance requirements: For our system these requirements are considering the response time of data synchronization.
- The response time to an order is dependent of the other user inserting the response manually (the operator or the driver being a human not a system that can respond automatically). Data synchronization must be assured to take place bellow 2 s.
- Maintainability requirements: The system must be designed in such a way that it allows a modifiable, component based system that allows future modifications and functionality extensions without breaking the present working version. This requirement is especially valid for our mobile application, as different mobile application versions installed on smartphone must communicate effectively with the Cloud-based API. In order to achieve maintainability we relied on API versioning for this specific requirement.
- Portability requirements: The system must work on a variety of mobile OS, of which iOS and Android are mandatory. A cross platform solution must be implemented to allow maximum code reuse with little adaptation.

- Security requirements: The application must use the .NET security framework for assuring authentication and authorization security constraints, and must also allow for SSL communication.

**Process and Project-related NFRs:** These types of NFRs impose criteria to be followed while developing the project.

- Conformance to standards requirements: The standard developing pattern for Titanium applications is MVC, which should be followed in order to assure maximum code reusability and maintainability.
- Development process requirements: The project needs to be developed in an iterative method, allowing for partial system components development and testing.
- Testing requirements: The API for the Cloud infrastructure needs to be tested using a unit testing approach, while the mobile vehicle booking application need to be tested using use-case testing.
- Installation and deployment requirements: The mobile applications need to be deployed to the AppStore and GooglePlay accordingly.

**Human-related NFRs:** These types of requirements deal with constraints related to the stakeholders and the social and societal context in which the system is deployed.

- Usability requirements: The application needs to be easy to understand and use by new users. It must also feature a demo the first time the application is launched.
- Look and Feel requirements: The mobile application needs to adhere to the usual UI components and not define custom components that might reduce the learnability of the system.
- Legal requirements: The application should not allow for malicious uses of personal data required by the application such as mobile phone numbers. This data must be stored on the Cloud and should be accessible only for specific users, if needed.

**Device-related NFRs**

- GPS: The device must feature GPS capable services for approximate user position identification.
- Internet: The device must allow for Internet connection for sending order, receiving responses and for the overall interconnection with the Cloud services.
- Operating system: The device must work with any iOS or Android version.

- Screen resolution: The application must work properly on any screen resolution. The application must be compatible with both the Retina display and the lower resolution display screens.

**Social Network related NFR**

- Completeness: The system must be able to scan for customer feedback across multiple social networks.
- Metadata: The data should be augmented in order to provide location context to the social network posts.
- Usability: The dashboard should be easy to operate and with meaningful.

## 3.2. Technological Perspective

### 3.2.1. Cross Platform Mobile Applications

According to Gartner, at the beginning of 2014, Android had 78.4% market share, while iOS had 15.6% of new worldwide sales. This means that their combined market share is more than 90% of all new smartphone sales. However, even if the two players dominate the market, developing for two frameworks is time consuming as very little work can be reused, the programming language and development environment for *Android* and *iOS* being very different. Also if another *OS* must be targeted in the future, this would require rewriting the application. In order to increase productivity a cross platform approach can be used. There is currently a wide range of cross platform solutions available including *Appcelerator Titanium*, *RhoMobile* and *PhoneGap*. *Appcelerator Titanium* [6] is an open source project and has integrated most common functionalities of *iOS* and *Android*. Developing with Titanium compared to other Cross Platform solutions is that it allows for native development. When using *Titanium* you are programming in *JavaScript* and the framework translates the code into native *Java* or *Objectual-C*. The development environment for Titanium is using its own *IDE* based on *Eclipse*, *Titanium Studio*, and it uses the JavaScript development language. It can also be extended using module in order to offer complete native functionality, which is not supported by the Titanium platform, and the recommended way of development is using a *MVC* pattern.

### 3.2.2. Windows Communication Foundation (WCF)

Windows Communication Foundation [7] is a framework for building service-oriented applications. Using *WCF*, applications can send data or asynchronous messages from one service endpoint to another. An endpoint can be a client of a service that requests data from a service endpoint. The messages can be as simple as a single character or word sent as XML, or as complex as a stream of binary data. In WCF all the communication details are handled by channel, it is a stack of channel components that all messages pass through during runtime processing. When are calling WCF service through a proxy class on the client side, it will send message (request soap message mainly includes some parameter values of method) and first the message will go through protocol Channels which mainly supports for security, transactions and reliable messaging, and second the message will go through encoder which convert messages into an array of bytes for transport, finally, the encoder message will go through the bottom transport channel which are responsible for transporting raw message bytes. WCF provides a number of transport protocols, including HTTP, TCP, MSMQ, peer-to-peer, and named pipes. In summary, *WCF* is designed to offer a manageable approach to creating Web services and Web service clients.

### 3.2.3. Microsoft Entity Framework

The Microsoft ADO.NET Entity Framework [8] is an Object/Relational Mapping (ORM) framework that enables developers to work with relational data as domain-specific objects, eliminating the need for most of the data access plumbing code that developers usually need to write. Using the Entity Framework, developers issue queries using LINQ, then retrieve and manipulate data as strongly typed objects. The Entity Framework's ORM implementation provides services like change tracking, identity resolution, lazy loading, and query translation so that developers can focus on their application-specific business logic rather than the data access fundamentals.

### 3.2.4. SignalR

Traditionally web applications used a polling technique for getting updates. For the client application this is not feasible as the polling interval is unknown. For example the driver could wait for hours without receiving an order, so he would poll thousands of times to receive one favorable result. Also the polling interval would have to be below 2 s (to offer a response time as low as possible), which would mean a high demand on the server and low scalability.

SignalR [9] is an Asynchronous library for .NET to help build real-time, multi-user interactive applications and is based on long polling techniques. Long polling is a variation of the traditional polling technique and allows emulation of an information push from a server to a client. With long polling, the client requests information from the server in a similar way to a normal poll. However, if the server does not have any information available for the client, instead of sending an empty response, the server holds the request and waits for some information to be available. Once the information becomes available (or after a suitable timeout), a complete response is sent to the client. The client will immediately re-request information from the server, so that the server will always have an available waiting request that it can use to deliver data in response to an event. Long polling is not a push code, but can be used under circumstances where a real push is not possible. Using long polling in the client mobile application gets notified to update its data, and thus to synchronize with the server, exactly as the new data is available. Using a long polling approach there is a very low demand on the server which translates into a high scalability, as new users and drivers are added to the distributed dispatching system.

In the .NET framework SignalR represents an implementation of long polling. However SignalR does not rely only on the long polling technique. SignalR has a concept of transports, each transport decides how data is sent/received and how it connects and disconnects. Transports build into SignalR are: WebSockets, Server Sent Events, Forever Frame, Long polling. SignalR tries to choose the "best" connection supported by server and client.

### 3.2.5. Push Notifications

Mobile apps are allowed to perform only very specific activities in the background, so battery life is conserved. However, it is required that there is a way to alert the user of interesting things that are happening even if the user is not currently inside the app. Mobile OS have provided a solution to this. Instead of the app continuously checking for events or doing work in the background, a server-side component for doing this can be written. When an event of interest occurs, the server-side component can send the app a push notification, which is intended for signaling the app that there are event pending on the server. Push Notifications are not intended for transmitting data to the client app, but are used as a signaling mechanism when the app is not running. Push Notifications makes no guarantee about delivery or the order of messages. Apps need to register with the Notification Service that is APNS (Apple Push Notifications Service) [10] for Apple and C2DN for Android [11]. This assigns a specific ID called device token that the app can send to the server. If the server needs to perform a push notification, it uses this device token to specify the app it want to send the notification to. Device tokens change so it is advisable to perform device token updates on the mobile preferably every time the app is opened. The Notification service offers an API that the server can poll periodically to determine what device tokens are still active. Because communication between the server and the notification Service is not trivial, 3rd party services are available such as Urban Airship [12].

### 3.2.6. Social Network Data Filtering

DataSift [3] is a platform that enables cost efficient and simple retrieval of data cross platform with built in augmentation for data. The main usage of this data at the moment is for marketing purposes, for example a marketer might be interested in how a specific new product is received by the market, the sentiment towards various functional aspects or some specific idea. DataSift bridges all this different data sources and delivers insights, and as this data is created and analyzed in real time, it is possible to respond with very low latency to the current public sentiment. Because some specific search queries might be too complex for search engines, this is the point where search technology can be improved by using crowd-sourced data across a multitude of systems. This data can be combined in order to respond to more complex queries. DataSift can be configured to act as the query engine for answers to question that come from various data sources.

### 3.2.7. Data Sources

Twitter was the first Data Source supported by DataSift and still is the most important. However once the infrastructure was created, DataSift has added more data sources that can be analyzed in real time.

- Facebook—license cost FREE—With more than 1.1 Billion active users, Facebook public data provides a unique view into what the world is watching, sharing and interested in.This data source provides access to the stream of public Facebook status updates, which include text-updates, links, photos and videos. Location names (e.g. restaurants) are added if the status update includes a location or check-in. This provides valuable insights to help market researchers. Author information including full name, profile photo and Facebook user-id is removed in accordance with Facebook's Platform Policies on Data Collection and Usage.

- Twitter—license cost $0.10 per 1000 interaction—The Twitter source delivers the text of Tweets plus more than 40 other pieces of data associated with Tweets. With more than a quarter of a billion Tweets every day, Twitter is an immensely significant source of data, delivering both breadth and depth of coverage. With this source you can receive data such as the author's name and screen name, their location, their preferred language, the number of people they follow on Twitter and how many people follow them. Other examples include filtering for Retweets, or for Tweets sent in reply to a particular author, or for particular keywords in users' bios.

- Wordpress—license cost $0.50 per 1000 interactions—WordPress powers 20 percent of blogs and sites on the web and has more than 1 million posts per day from blogs on wordpress.com, as well as content from sites hosted elsewhere that utilize WordPress as a content management platform if they enable the Jetpack plug-in. Comments and likes are also available from this data source.
- Blogs—license cost $4.00 per 1000 interactions—The Blog data source combines material from a wide variety of sites, ranging from well-known hosts such as Blogger with very large numbers of active users to small, single-user sites that run as blogs or incorporate a blog. You want to count mentions of a competitor's brand across as many social media sites as possible. Activate the Blog data source and use the interaction content target in your filter to capture posts from every available source. By spreading your "net" in this way you can add extra volume to your input data, to make your statistical analysis more significant.

## 3.3. System Use Cases

There are four types of actors that the system supports, each having specific capabilities. We will analyze each actor together with the associated use cases.

The client actor is the user that has the booking application installed on his mobile phone. He uses the application to order taxis by sending his location to the server that consists of the *Cloud*. This is the main functionality of the system, which we will be presenting later on in a more detailed fashion. We note that this use case is composed of two elements: getting the *GPS* position of the user, which is used by the system to identify the address of the user, and it also offers the possibility of fix tuning this location to specify it more precisely, as this location will be sent to the operator or the driver. The User use cases are presented in Table 3.

The vehicle tracking functionality allows the user to see the taxi approaching on a map. In addition to this time estimation will be displayed together with a distance approximation. In case the response to an order comes from the operator, this functionality will not be available, as the taxi will not have GPS capabilities that allow tracking. The Share on Social networks use case allows the user to share the current ride with his friends on social media. This is an element that enhances the marketing potential for the app and a key component in attracting new users. There are two types of services which users can use with the app: Facebook and Twitter. One of the main benefits of using this app is the possibility of accumulating points, as a rewards program envisioned to spur app usage and attract new users. Each time the user will be making orders using the app, he will accumulate points which can be converted into free apps.

**Table 3.** Client Use Case specifications.

| Category | Use case |
| --- | --- |
| Book vehicle | Access map view of nearby vehicles |
| Book vehicle | Specify exact location |
| Book vehicle | Get time and cost estimates |
| Book vehicle | Specify advance booking time |
| Book vehicle | See vehicle details |
| Track Vehicle | Track vehicle on map |
| Track Vehicle | Get notifications |
| Pay for the ride | In app payment |
| Rate vehicle | Rate vehicle |
| Share on Social Network | Share on social networks |

The Driver is responsible for responding to incoming orders. It does this by accepting or declining an order using a simple two buttons interface. The orders are assigned to drivers based on the proximity of the client to the driver. In addition to these functionalities, the Driver can also call the client in case he cannot see him at the specified pick up location or if he needs additional information. The driver cannot see the clients phone number, but only a call button. The rate client functionality allows the driver to rate the client based on his behavior. The rating is based on considerations such as: was the client present at the meeting point, did he leave a tip, was he loudly *etc.* The rating is based on a 5 star system subjective to the driver. Future orders placed by the client will show the overall rating that this client has.

The operator is responsible for responding to orders that were not answered by drivers directly. This allows companies to use the traditional mechanism for finding a taxi and send a response to the client. Using this mechanism, the client always gets a response to his order, even if no driver is available in his proximity that is active.

Responding to a client involves two things. First, an identifier for the taxi must be specified. This consists of the car number or some other way for the client to identify the taxi. Also the operator must specify the approximate location where the taxi is at the moment, by selecting it from a map. This creates a more visual context for the client and creates a sense of consistency between orders answered by the driver and the operator. Similar to the driver, the operator can call the client to ask him more details. Distinctly from the driver, the operator can see the users number. As we earlier specified, when a response to an order is set, the operator selects an address from the map which will display the initial taxi position to the client. It is possible for the operator to cancel an order from the client, in which case can write a cancelation message explaining the decision. The operator use cases are illustrated in Figure 1.

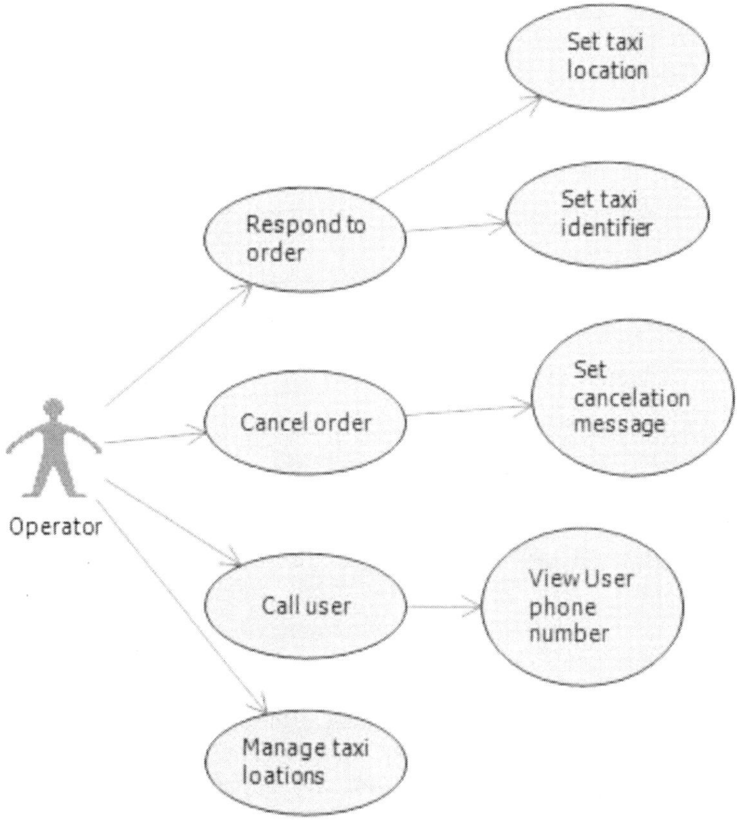


**Figure 1.** Operator use case.

The Manager actor is responsible with registering taxi companies into the system, setting the areas in which they operate, adding drivers and creating operator accounts. The manager is a role comparable with the administrator of the system. It has the power to change accounts, activate or deactivate them.

The Social CRM can provide valuable information regarding the user satisfaction level with the service and the potential direct improvement points. The person responsible for the Social CRM management will have access to a dashboard offering metrics such as overall customer satisfaction levels for specific time intervals, highly negative or positive comments in real time and automation and filtering tools. Also the Social CRM component will augment user data with statistics obtained using DataSift. The list of Social CRM use case is presented in Table 4.

**Table 4.** Social Customer Relationship Management (CRM) Use Case specifications.

| Category | Use Case |
|---|---|
| User data augmentation | See user satisfaction metric |
| User data augmentation | Segment users by activity levels |
| User data augmentation | Identify promotion targets |
| Data filtering | Identify comments in real time |
| Data filtering | React to comments in real time |
| Customer satisfaction | Create promotion |
| Customer satisfaction | Assign to-do items |

## Social CRM—React to Comment Use Case Detailed

When a highly positive or negative comment regarding the service is published on the web either on a social media website such as Twitter or Facebook, or through a blog comment or even an article, DataSift will extract that interaction and will deliver it to our application in real time as presented in Figure 2. The complete process through which DataSift is capable of extracting this interactions and augmenting them in real time will be explained in the following section.

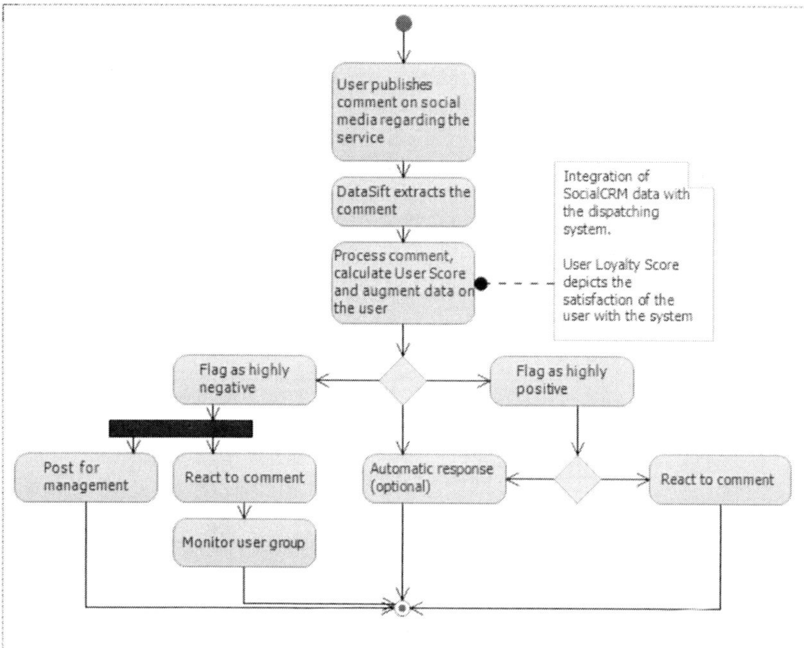


**Figure 2.** Social CRM react to comment use case.

Once the interaction enters our system, it is already augmented with sentiment analysis, which means it can easily be catalogued by our application. The comments that have a sentiment rating between 15 and 20 (20 being the maximum) are tagged as highly positive. Comments having a rating between −20 and −15 (−20 being the minimum) are tagged as highly negative. Both of this categories are extremely important from a marketing perspective.

If a comment is highly positive, the marketer is interested in building on the positive experience of the user and will offer him bonus point or extra credit for inviting new people to the platform.

## 3.4. Conceptual Design

The proposed system is a complex solution which can be decomposed into multiple components. From a high level architectural point of view, the core of the product is represented by the *Cloud Engine*, which is stored on Windows Azure. The Cloud Engine uses a *relational SQL database* for persistence and interacts with third party services. The mobile applications for clients and drivers access the service through the *custom built API*. The *management panel* is also a separate component that is built on the Cloud service. The *social media analysis tool* cuts across both the cloud service and the operator management panel, providing insights and automating social media data augmentation. A high level representation of the system can be observed in Figure 3.

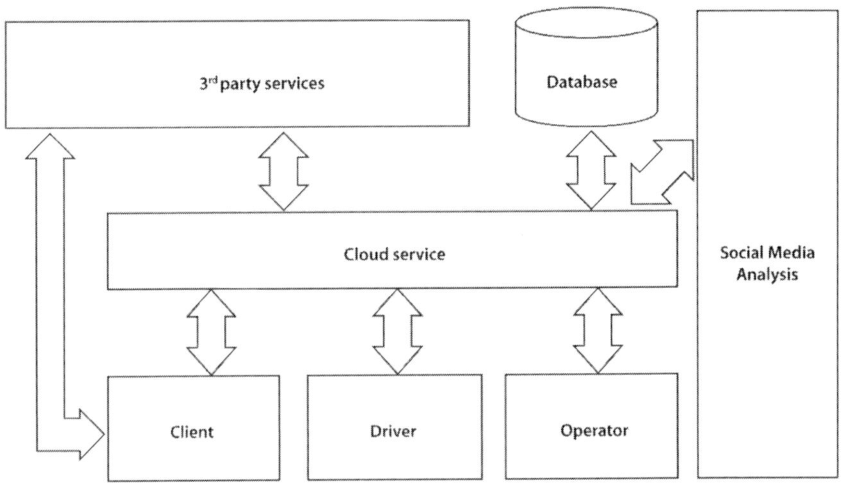


**Figure 3.** The block diagram of the system.

Client and Driver apps and the Operator web interface are the consumers of the *API* exposed by the Cloud service. The Cloud Service acts as the intermediary between all communication that takes place between these components and handles the data synchronization. The Cloud service relies on its functionality on using a database for persisting information such as orders, responses, users *etc*. The Cloud service also interacts with external services for performing specific tasks. Examples of this include sending *push notifications* or *reverse geocoding*. The client mobile applications can also access external services. For example the Client app accesses Facebook and analytics services.

The Cloud service acts as *a hub* and intermediating all communication between the clients. While for a client booking a vehicle seems as a P2P operation, it actually constitutes a client-server operation. As illustrated, numerous operators, divers and Clients can connect to the Cloud, new ones can be added, or some can be removed at any time. For example a taxi driver that terminates his work schedule for the day, can disconnect from the Cloud service and will not receive any new orders until he checks in again with the service.

All data is stored into a proprietary SQL database, and specific tasks that have been delegated to external services are managed by the Cloud service. When a client books a vehicle, the Cloud service checks through the fleet of vehicles that are available on that area at that moment and selects one for being dispatched to the client. In case no vehicle is received, the Cloud service sends the order to a specific vehicle company in order to be processed. Not all mobile applications are required to have a server component. However applications that require a higher degree of complexity need to create their own model and an API for exposing the services. *Cloud* computing is known to be a promising solution for mobile computing due to reasons including mobility, communication, and portability, reliability, security. In the following, we describe how the Cloud can be used to overcome obstacles in mobile computing, thereby pointing out advantages of *Mobile Cloud Computing (MCC)* [15] MCC refers to an infrastructure where both the data storage and the data processing happen outside of the mobile device. Mobile Cloud applications move the computing power and data storage away from mobile phones and into the Cloud, bringing applications and mobile computing to not just smartphone users but also a much broader range of mobile subscribers.

Figure 4 depicts a high level overview of the Social media analysis tool as implemented by DataSift. Facebook, Twitter, Blogs and other online data sources are monitored in real time and processed by the DataSift Engine.

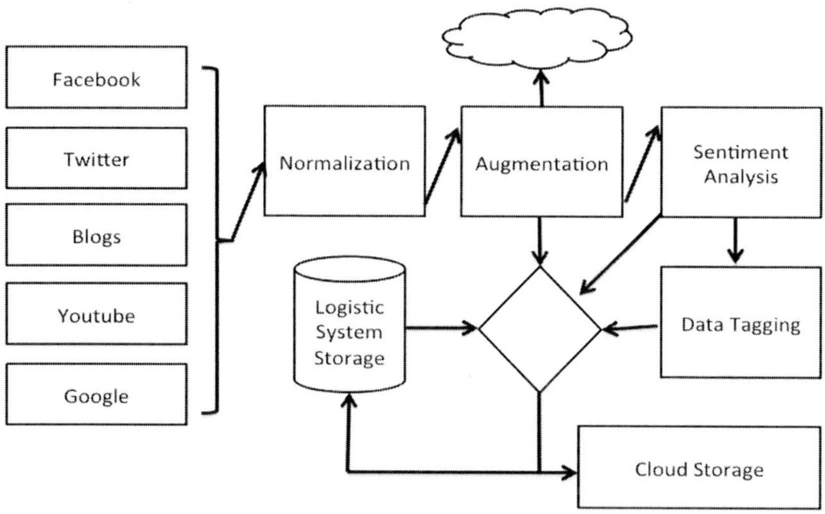


**Figure 4.** Social CRM components built on DataSift.

The process of augmentation of the user data in our system and the insights provided to the customer relationship responsible goes through a pipeline of steps. The normalization step converts all interactions into a similar format independent of their source, whether it is Facebook, Twitter or a blog post. Augmentation provides additional data on the interaction such as location context and fetching of the content of a link. The sentiment analysis tool provides a mean of grading the sentiment associated with a given post on a scale from −20 to +20. The sentiment analysis is provided by a Lexalytics algorithm that is offered as a black box solution. Data integration with the dispatching system is handled in the Logistic System Storage, where the data is stored into one common database.

We have analyzed the theoretical approaches and the frameworks required for implementing the proposed application. In the following chapter we are detailing how we implemented the vehicle booking application.

## 3.5. System Implementation

In this section we will present the system architecture and some implementation deign concerns for all major components. As we have stated in the previous sections, our system consists in a dispatching system which is vertically integrated with a Social CRM system. The Social CRM system is responsible for aggregating information about our users from online data sources and are used for improving the customer relationships or better targeting the users using advertising.

In Figure 5 we have represented the two systems in more detail. The Social CRM system is built on top of the DataSift platform. The dispatching system is responsible for controlling the DataSift platform using the API it exposes. Through the API we can use filters for sifting only the interactions we need, and then integrating the two systems using a common SQL Azure database.

Next we will analyze both of the two systems and the integration between them. First we will address the dispatching system, and in the second half of this chapter we will analyze the DataSift platform in detail.

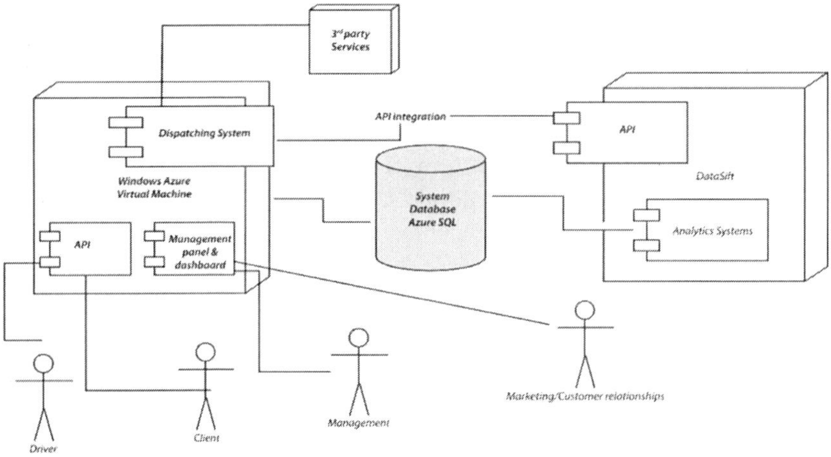


**Figure 5.** System integration.

### 3.5.1. General Mobile Dispatching System Architecture and Implementation

The Dispatching System can operate as a standalone application. There can be identified two types of components. The first type includes the proprietary components. This need to be developed by the developers, are based on specific frameworks and include: the components constituting the Cloud service (designating the service built by the developers), the mobile application, the browser client and the management interface. The second type of components are represented by the 3rd party services (distinctly from proprietary services, 3rd party services or external services are built by other organizations and are made available to the public for use) are exposed trough certain API.

In this example we are using five types of external services: The Notification Service—used for sending Push Notifications (a way of alerting a mobile device), social services that offer integration with Facebook and Twitter, Analytics services for tracking usage patterns, SMS gateway service for sending the user an SMS with the activation code (required by the business rules), and a geocoding and reverse geocoding service for converting GPS position into street address. All of these components will be explained together with their implementation technologies and internal working

A request is serialized as *JSON*, signed using the user key and sent to the server through the server *API*. The server determines the nearest driver to the user, by interrogating the database based on the business logic. Once the nearest driver is determined, the *Signaling Framework* (used to alert the mobile application) is used to determine the selected driver's app to download or update the order sent by the client. After the driver confirms the order, the server uses the same approach to inform the user that his order was responded. All requests sent to the proprietary server components need to use SSL for proving security to the system. The dispatching application exposes *JSON REST* services using *WCF* Framework. Working with *JSON* in the context of *WCF* is easy as the framework automatically serializes *JSON* request and responses and performs data binding between *JavaScript* and *CLR* objects. Once the data is received on the server, the server performs some security check on the request. This usually implies authentication and authorization of the request. As there is no password required for the Taxi Ordering application, signing the data using a key, which is known only by the client and the server, and is unique for each client mobile application, does this.

Figure 6 depicts the integration between the client mobile application and the server. On The client we have the *MVC*pattern. The view sends an event to the controller, which calls the send order operation on the *Model*. The model component responsible for sending the request (implemented in Titanium using an *HTTP Socket*), serializes the data and sends them to the specified service endpoint exposed by the API. Once the request arrives on the server, the reverse process occurs as the JS data objects are translated into *CLR* objects by the *WCF* framework. The security component is responsible for checking the signature of the user in the case of Order Taxi applications. In other applications a username and password approach can be used for obtaining the same result. It is essential to observe that once the request passes the security verification, it is recorded and the registration key for the order is returned to the client. Further on the client uses this registration key for referring to his order. At this point there is no response available for the client yet.

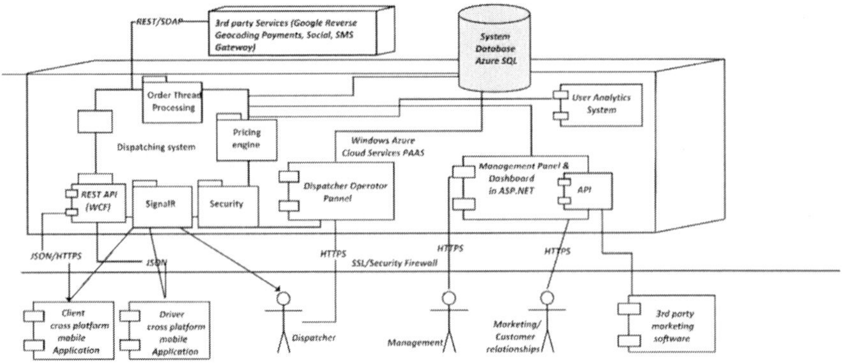


**Figure 6.** General Dispatching System Architecture.

The order placed by the user in the system is assigned to the nearest driver. When the driver confirms the order, a response is sent to the client mobile application. This response can come after a variable amount of time which can be anywhere between a few seconds and 3 min. In consequence *SignalR* is used to inform the client when the response is ready. SignalR is not used to pass the response directly to the user, but rather the user applications download the response once it receives the update signal.

An important characteristic of the service is that it should offer scalability. All the components depicted can be hosted in the *Cloud*. This allows an elastic hosting environment, which can be used easily. For Order Taxi application, we are using *Windows Azure*. Using *Windows Azure* we can easily deploy the server component as it was built completely on the *.NET*framework.

**Location determination.** Titanium offers the possibility of interacting with device capabilities such as using the GPS and allows for specific parameter to be set on the GPS such as the precision of positioning, as a balance between time and required accuracy. When the app starts the coordinates are the ones cached on the device, in other words the ones detected at the last time you used the geolocation on your device. Detecting the current position takes time so if you have an app based on geolocation you might want to take this in account to improve the user experience and avoid to get false results. Titanium.Geolocation [6] provides the necessary methods to manage geolocation.

**Implementation of the Model.** The business logic of the system is implemented in the model. The service model is composed of a set of classes representing the implementation of the domain model. Figure 7 represents the most important objects that constitute the domain model. Because Entity Framework was used for mapping CLR objects to database records, these entities have a corresponding implementation in the SQL server database. We are outlining the most important entities presented in our system:

*Order*: represents an order placed by the client into the system. The Order has a set of attributes representing:

- State of the order: *IsResolved, IsCanceled, IsPendingResponse*. This attributes are used for identifying the current status of the order.
- Modification time: Each modification of the state of the order also sets a time stamp on the object, which is used by the system. For example when an order is created, it is displayed to the operator together with a label showing how much time has passed since the order was submitted.

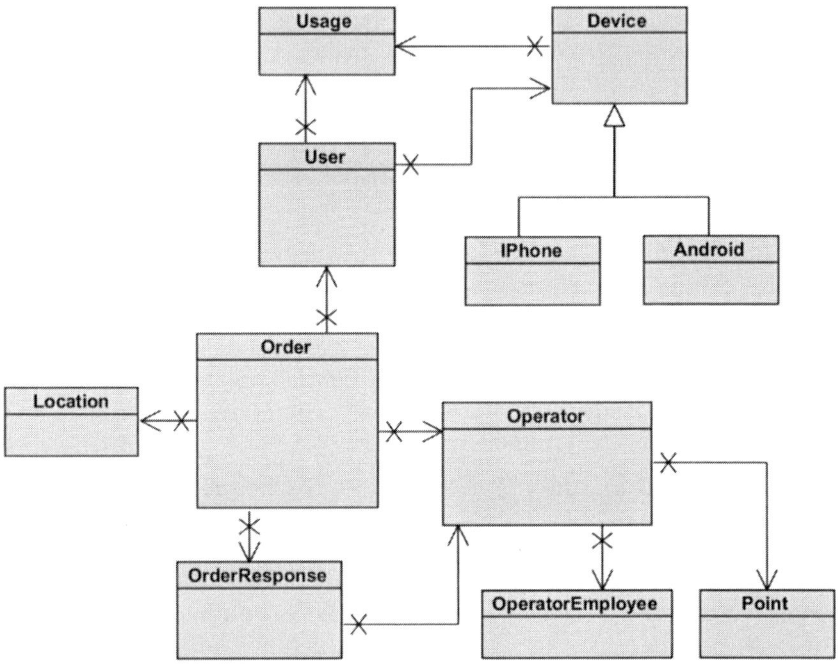


**Figure 7.** The entities of the system model.

- Data associated with an order: Represent information such as the rating of the taxi driver or the feedback of the client following the ride.
- Associated data such as the pick-up location or the owner is represented as references to the specific entities.

*User*: represents the client who is placing orders into the system. The user has the following attributes associated with him:

- Name represents the name chosen by the person submitting orders.
- Registration date the date when this user registered by submitting his phone number and name
- Phone number is used for contacting the person in case he does not show up at the pick-up location
- Phone is validated is used to determine whether the specific user was validated by the validation code sent through the *SMS*.

- The user must be marked as active in order to be able to place orders into the system. A user state can be changed to inactive in case abuse has been observed for this particular user.
- The confirmation code is the activation code sent to the user through *SMS* that is used to determine if the phone number is valid.

*Location*: Represents the position where an order is set. It contains the *GPS* coordinates for the location together with an optional name for it. There is also a property used for counting how often that location is used. The more frequent locations will be displayed first in the location suggestion list.

*Operator:* This entity represents an operator, which might me understood as a taxi company or a collection of taxi companies unified as a group. This entity presents the following properties:

- Activation date and time, when this operator has been registered
- A perimeter that represents where the operator is active, represented by a collection of points.
- Stations represent predefined locations on the map where taxis are expected to be present.

*OperatorEmployee:* This class represents the operator that responds to orders.

The name is the real name of the operator.

*IsActive* property is set to true for those *Operators* which are active, meaning having permission to access the system, permission set the manager.

*OrderResponse:* created by the *OperatorEmployee* and represents the response the user receives for his order. It contains the necessary information required by the client such as the car number, the name of the driver, and the expected waiting time for the user. It also has an *IsRead* property which is used for determining whether the response has been read by the user application. If the Response is not read in a certain amount of time, this means that that the client application is closed and as a consequence the response needs to be delivered using push notifications.

*Point:* This class is used for defining perimeters in which an operator activates. Ay order placed within this perimeter might come to the operator. The number represents the count for the point, so that given a collection of points and their orders, the system can check whether a specific point is inside that perimeter or outside of it.

The entities are mapped by Entity Framework into the CLR classes which are further extended in functionality by means of partial classes, by adding extra functionality.

**Service Database.** The service relies on a SQL rational database. The service database is generated using *Entity Framework*, and we designed the *Entity Framework* entities directly mapped to the tables, and providing the same properties as columns in the rational database.

*UserSet* table represents the client who is placing orders into the system. The most important columns of this table include the name which represents the name chosen by the person submitting orders, the registration date – the date when this user registered by submitting his phone number and name. The phone number is used for contacting the person in case he does not show up at the pick-up location, and is represented as an nVarChar.

We used this representation especially because phone number formats are very different for distinct regions. *IsPhoneValidated* column is used to determine whether the specific user was validated by the validation code sent through SMS. The user must be marked as active in order to be able to place orders into the system, this column being represented as a non-nullable Boolean type. A user state can be changed to inactive in case abuse has been observed for this particular user. The confirmation code is the activation code sent to the user through SMS that is used to determine if the phone number is valid. This column is also represented as an nVarChar.

The table *OrderSet* has the foreign key represented by *User_id* that specifies the User which placed the order inside the system. *OrderSet* and *OrderResponseSet* have a one to one relationship between them. We decided to separate these two tables, even though there is a synonymy relationship between them as there can be order, which do not have a response, such as for example an order that was canceled.

We can observe that there was no case for splitting entities in our model. In this mapping scenario, properties from a single entity in the conceptual model are mapped to columns in two or more underlying tables. In this scenario, the tables must share a common primary key. In our mapping scenario each entity in the conceptual model is mapped to a single table in the storage model. This is the default mapping generated by Entity Data Model tools. Each operator can define multiple stations which represent positions on the map which an associated name (records in the *LocationsSet* Table) that are by the operator to specify the initial taxi position easily, by clicking the marker on the map associated to that specific location. The mapping of a list of stations (defined as actually being of type location) to the *OperatorSet* is done by *EntityFramework* by introducing a new table called *OperatorLocation*, as can be observed in Figure 8.

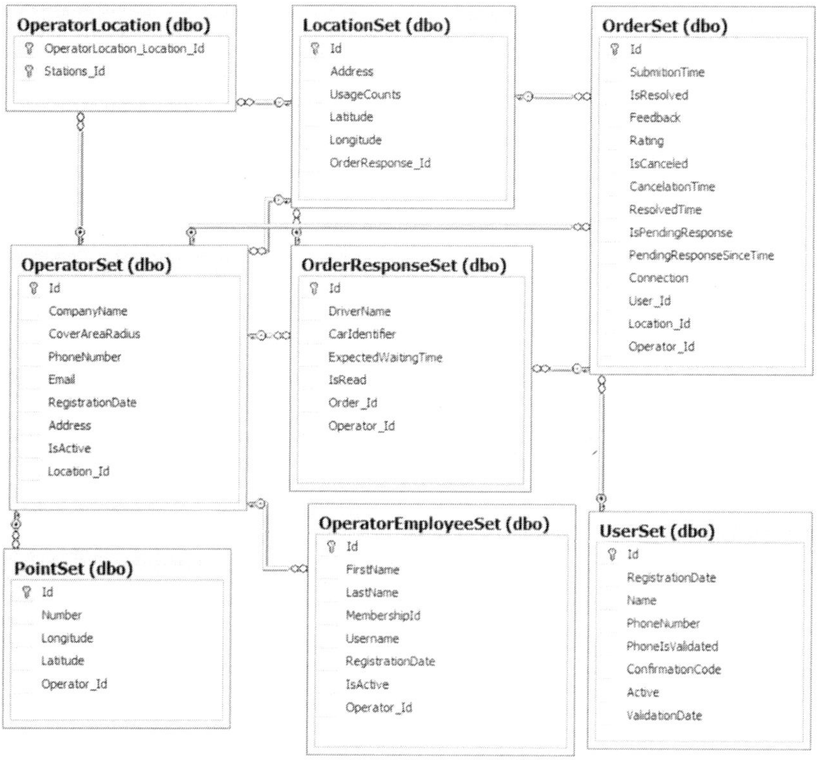


**Figure 8.** The MS-SQL database.

We are using this database model representing the conceptual model of the system inside *SQL Server 2010*. We have decided on implementing our database using Entity Framework generate Database from Model approach, as it offered a productive environment where changes in the model could be easily translated into updates of the database. We also notice that there is a balance between the numbers of read and write operations as every record inserted into the database needs to be read usually just one time, processed and then archived. For example an Order is created, added to the system, it is answered by the operator, and the response is sent back to the client and after this there response is no longer used actively and constitutes solely a history used for creating suggestions such as, for example, suggesting pick up locations.

**System API specification.** The interaction between the client mobile and the server is performed through the means of a *REST* API and we implemented the *REST* API trough WCF. For example, IApi is the interface which is implemented by the API class. IApi exposes multiple methods including: UserOrderNew, UserOrderCancel, UserOrderResponse and UserNew.

*UserOrderNew*—this method is exposed as a resource using the verb POST and is available by invoking the service at the location /Api/user/order/new. The data passed to the method are encoded as JSON and consist of the User name and phone number. Once this data are received on the server the system sends the user an SMS message at the specified phone number. At this moment the user status is set as invalidated. In order to validate the phone number the user needs to send the confirmation code sent to him through SMS by using the next method described, ValidatePhone.

*UserOrderCancel*—this method is used to validate the users phone number by sending using the POST verb the code sent to him by SMS. This rest resource is available at /Api/user/order/cancel. The data needs to be submitted in the JSON format, as with all API calls to our service. When the code reaches the server, it is checked whether the code matches the one in the system. If the code is correct, the user is allowed to submit the order.

*UserOrderResponse*—this method allows for creating a new order inside the system. This is performed by sending the information required the order to the address /Api/user/order/response using the POST verb. Once an order is received on the server, it is recorded inside the database; it gets displayed on a specific operator panel. Once the operator responds to the order, an OrderResponse entry is created and an update signal is sent to the client. Among the attributes in a create order request the most important are:

- The location where the order was sent for. This consists of the GPS position
- The user who submitted the request
- The date and time the order was created
- The device information

*GetOrderResponse*—allows the client to read the response to his order. It is accessible using the GET verb at the address /Api/order/response. The request contains the identity of the order. The response is encoded as JSON and contains the information for the client such as:

- The car number which was assigned for the order
- The information regarding the driver

- The estimated arrival time of the driver

*UserOrderCancel*—allows an order to be canceled by the user. The cancelation is performed by the client, and is accessible at /Api/user/order/cancel. The request verb is POST, as the submitted information contains the identity of the order that should be canceled. We note that we decided on not implementing the DELETE verb combined with the call at /Api/order as some Api best practices recommend as in our case there is no associated delete operation on the server. When an order is canceled what happens is that the IsCanceled property is set for the order, and an update notice is sent to the subscribers, such as the operator.

**Security and Membership Framework.** The API is secured using ASP.NET Membership Framework that handles the authentication and authorization logic of the application. The benefit of the Membership Framework is that a robust and throughout tested framework offers much better security than self-implemented framework. As a consequence, the Security framework was not extended and was allowed to operate as it is. By not extending or close integrating any services of the Membership framework with our system, we decoupled the two subsystems and allowed for further changes.

Also, all API calls are authenticated. The authentication is done using the user id, password and the session id. Each session is started when a user logs in. This prevents users to run the application on multiple devices in parallel and improves the overall security of the system. For the driver application authentication is done using tokens that are valid for a specific time interval. When a token expires, it needs to be renewed. Using tokens we are able to reduce the resource utilization on the server. If a call fails to authenticate, an error code is retuned. All communication is forced to use SSL, which eliminates or reduces the chance of Man in the middle attacks.

**SignalR.** It is not feasible to implement data synchronization using a polling interval, as the polling interval is both unknown and will generate large amount of data and CPU usage. In the .NET framework SignalR represents an implementation of long polling. However SignalR does not rely only on the long polling technique. SignalR has a concept of transports, each transport decides how data is sent/received and how it connects and disconnects. SignalR uses two concepts on the server implementation: *Hubs* and *persistent connections*. The Client app uses *Hubs*. Extending the *Hub* class represents the implementation of a hub on the server. Each method defined inside this class is mapped to a JavaScript implementation at compile time. The JavaScript document is saved on the project root folder and the client must reference it. It is possible to have broadcast events, which alert all the clients or only one in particular. It is also possible to group client and inform a whole group at a time. When the mobile application registers using SignalR, on the server a session ID called client ID is given to it. We are storing this client ID for each order. When a response is available and needs to be sent from the server to the client, we are sending an update request to the mobile app, using the client ID stored earlier.

There are three components of the system that need to be updated from the server. This are the client app, the driver app and the operator panel. The update scenario for the driver app is similar to the one for the client app. We note that the client app and the driver app are components that need to be independently updated, so having groups in this scenario is unnecessarily. However for the operator panel we need multiple operators to be able to respond to an incoming order. In this scenario it is more feasible to group the operators in groups, a group representing one operating company. When a new order is registered into the system the first operator who sees the new order will be able to respond to it.

### 3.5.2. Management Panel For Human Aided Dispatch

Some orders need to be inserted by the dispatcher, or might come from an external API that integrates with other SCM or ERP systems. Management Panel represents a web interface intended for responding to orders through a human actor acting as a dispatcher. The webpage is developed using *ASP.NET* and is secured using *.NET Membership Framework Forms Authentication*. A logged in user will be displayed a panel consisting of the current orders. Color codes are used for different order statuses. Brown is used for canceled orders, Green for orders that were responded successfully. No color is used for orders which have not been responded yet. The webpage uses AJAX techniques for receiving new orders and sending them without requiring complete page reloads. When a new order is inserted into the system, *SignalR* is used to notify the browser webpage to reload its orders panel. Partial page reloads are designed using the *ASP.NET UpdatePanel* and the *AJAX* functionality is built on JQuery. Using the Operator panel website the operator is able to respond to client orders. Whenever a new order that is destined for that operator is inserted into the system, SignalR that the orders grid needs to be updated notifies the webpage. Using an update panel control, as we specified earlier, does the update.

We implemented the operator panel in such a way to allow multiple operators to work on the same set of orders without worrying of responding to the same order. Whenever an operator views the content of an order, the order is marked as pending. When this happens a message is sent to the user notifying him that the operator viewed his order. Also another operator is announced that his colleague is already processing the specific order. If he tries to process the same order he will get an alert.

*Feature usage metrics using Analytics*. Analytics provide the means of measuring user experience inside the app and becomes a key component of the mobile ecosystem. Analytics provide the means of observing how users are interacting with the app and this provides the information required for further updates. Traditionally two analytics were used: *daily active users* and *user session time*. However it has been observed that user engagement falls sharply few days after the app first installation. As a consequence another key metric has become the *user retention level* after one day, one week and one month. Unless the app uses analytics it cannot understand its users base accordingly.

Analytics provide information regarding usage statistics such as new users, active users (which combines new and returning users into one stat), and sessions (how many times your app is used over a time period). You can grow this stat several ways such as acquiring new users, getting existing users to use more often or retaining users longer), session length (Session Length is a key engagement metric. Although different kinds of apps have different average session lengths, you would like this stat to improve over time with each additional update), frequency of use (this stat reveals the intensity with which your app is used), retention level, and app versions. It is also possible to track custom events such as the user clicking a menu button or completing a game level. We are tracking the address textbox editing feature, the map marker move, the amount the map marker is moved, the amount of time spent editing the address textbox, the amount of time until the order is placed.

*Social media integration*. Using Social Networks such as Facebook and Twitter we provide a mean of authentication using *OAuth v2*. For example if the app requires the users email address it can prompt the user to authenticate in the app using his *Facebook* account. If the user agrees to allow *Facebook* to share the email address with the app, the app is authorized to retrieve the users email from the Facebook service using the *Facebook* API. *OAuth* is an open standard for authorization, it allows users to share their private resources stored on one site with another site without having to hand out their credentials, typically supplying username and password tokens instead.

The other common use of *social services* integration is for marketing purposes. Many apps allow users to post messages to *Facebook* or to post on the users behalf. The posted messages should be based on users intention to share them, but they also often serve as a marketing strategy inside the users social network. *Order Taxi* application uses *social services* for marketing purposes by sharing the users ride information with the users consent. In order to use social services, as with most third party *APIs* an *API* key must be obtained by registering on the providers website. For *Facebook* this is available in the developers section of their website. Titanium offers modules for integrating *Facebook* and *Twitter* services and encapsulating the communication with the REST *API*. In our Taxi Ordering Application, we are integrating Facebook in order to allow people to post messages on their wall to inform their friend they are using Order Taxi application. They can also invite friends to join the application and earn points.

*Management and configuration* .There are three types of components that need to be managed: The proprietary server, the mobile client and the third party services. Managing the third party services is usually done by a management panel on the providers' website. A management panel for changes that have a high occurrence rate manages the proprietary server. For example new drivers are added manually to the system from this management panel. The hardest component to be managed is the mobile client application as there is no direct control over it. If major changes to the system are required for implementing new functionalities and this requires a change in the API it is important that API versioning is used to secure reliability for old clients that do not install the last updates. Backward compatibility of the system must always be respected. If the changes made to the system do not require any change in the API, but rather a change in the address, this can be resolved if the client was designed to adapt to such changes. Otherwise an update of the client app is required.

### 3.5.3. Social Crm System Using Datasift

DataSift [3] supports a variety of datasources. However the idea and first implementation addressed just one datasource, which is the most active of them, all that being the Twiter Firehose. Twitter does allow anyone to access its streaming API. However only a subset of all tweets are available through the streaming API, which are less than 1%. Twitter does however have two affiliated companies which get all the tweets through the Twitter Firehose, those being DataSift and Gnip (which is now a subsidiary of Twitter).

In this section we will describe how the DataSift architecture is implemented and build for a massively scalable requirements. DataSift implemented both their software and hardware solution because the large amount of data required to process offered both technical and economic challenges. DataSift runs on Hadoop and has one of the largest Hadoop clusters in the world. By creating their own hardware cluster they were able to take advantage of more low level performance optimizations than if they had used a public cloud provider such as Amazon, Google or Microsoft. Also considering the massive explosion in Big Data over the past few years, their infrastructure is expanding massively which would have been much more costly if they decided to use a public clod solution.

The DataSift architecture can be broken up in three large areas as follows that being *data extraction, filtering and delivering*.

(1) Data Extraction and Preprocessing

We call data preprocessing the act of extracting or receiving data from the defined datasources. Given the multitude of data sources one important aspect of this step is normalizing the data. The Redis Queue is used as a buffer during high peak usage. This allows the DataSift architecture to remain reliable at all times. Data is extracted out and normalized. Twitter data is highly dimensional, it has 30 plus attributes and you get access to them all. These attributes include geolocation, name, profile data, the tweet itself, timestamp, number of followers, number of retweets, verified user status, client type, *etc*.

The Interaction Generation thus acts similar to a JOIN operation over multiple streams of proprietary data structures and formats. As one can see the data sources are received using both Push and Pull HTTP requests and the formats are ranging from JSON and XML to Binary Streams. The result of the Interaction Generation block is a normalized object. This object is further augmented with data extracted from third party sources or by analyzing the data using proprietary or licensed algorithms such as Sentiment analysis or Language Detection. Entity extraction and natural language processing is applied to the tweet. Language is determined, for example, and that result is made available in the meta-data. Each link is resolved and the contents fetched so filters can be applied to content and the links themselves. Data is fully elaborated before the filtering process occurs.

Bringing the datasets into their system they needed to form close partnerships. Their sentiment analysis engine was licensed, made fast, made clusterable, and made suitable to handle 500 million hits a day with low latency. Each service must have < 100 ms response time. After 500 ms it is thrown away. In order to respect this they needed to cache the augmentation data sources locally. Also one in 10 tweets is a link, so the system creates a request for fetching the content of the referenced page in order to allow filters against it. So if a brand is mentioned it can be resolved against the actual content to figure out what it all means. This can provide quick insights into new blog posts or product reviews mentioned on social media.

Metadata Generation.

- Tagging allow adding custom metadata to interactions. For example, a specific car model can be tagged as luxury or economy. This information can be very useful later on into post processing. Adding tags based on conditional rules gives you the power to code business rules directly into your CSDL code. Normalized data is augmented in order to provide more context into the application. By enrichment the interactions will gather more metadata that can be queried using CSDL. The supported Enrichment engines are Demographics, Sentiment, Gender, Entities, Topics and Trends.
- Sentiment scoring allows a computer to consistently rate the positive or negative assertions that are associated with a document or entity. The scoring of sentiment (sometimes referred to as tone) from a document is a problem that was originally raised in the context of marketing and business intelligence, where being able to measure the public's reaction to a new marketing campaign (or, indeed, a corporate scandal) can have a measurable financial impact on your business.
- The Salience Sentiment data source delivers a measure of the positive or negative sentiment in a post. Within DataSift, sentiment is typically scored from –20 to 20 although values outside this range do sometimes occur. A score of zero is neutral, scores below zero indicate negative sentiment, and scores above zero indicate positive sentiment. For example, a score of –1 is mildly negative while a score of 15 is strongly positive.
- The Salience Topics data source lists the topics it finds in a post. Salience Topics are derived from an analysis of all the content in Wikipedia. As such, they allow for robust detection of content that is "about" a particular topic. A major advantage of this approach is that the topics analysis engine can easily be extended. The engine independently analyzes the content and the title.
- The Salience Entities data source lists the entities it finds in a post. Entities are typically proper nouns (people, companies, products, places) but can also include special patterns like URLs, phone numbers, addresses, currency amounts, and quotes. It can also recognize entities that we have never seen before. Each entity has sentiment associated with it so, if there is a Tweet that says "I really like Brand X, but don't like Brand Y", the entity discovery feature will correctly associate the sentiment with the individual entities. Sentiment analysis is also able to understand emoticons and nuances in the language. Only English is available however.

- Classifiers take a large sample of interactions from the platform, manually classify the interactions and use machine learning to learn key signals, which dictate which category interactions should belong to. The result is a set of scoring rules that form the classifier. The resulting classifier can be run against live or historic data ongoing. For example a classifier can be used to asses a user's probability of preaching a specific product or to route specific interactions to specific customer support or marketing teams inside a company.

(2) Filtering the Interactions

The cost of licensing the Twitter Firehose is extremely high and would become an inefficient investment for the majority of companies. Datasift created a declarative language called CSDL is order to filter out the Interaction (such as Tweets, Facebook posts, blog entries *etc.*) you do not want and keep the Interactions you do want. As we have explained in the previous sections the cost of running a queue includes both a licensing fee and a processing fee. The licensing fee is based on the number of interactions that match the defined query.

CDSL language CDSL allows for defining filtering conditions that specify what information the stream will include and augmenting the objects in the stream with data from third-party sites. A filtering condition has three elements: target, operator and argument. The target specifies the operand such as the content of a Twitter post. The operator defines the comparison Datasift should make. For example, it might search for Tweets from authors who have at least 100 followers. More complex filters can be built by combining simple filters using the logical operators: AND, OR, and NOT. Once a result stream has been defined through a filter, it can be reused as part of the definition of another stream by using the stream keyword to combine it with further filtering conditions. The argument can be any value, as long as the type of the argument matches the type of the target.

All interactions matching a filter form a stream. Each stream is assigned an identifier such as "4e8e6772337d0b993391ee6417171b79. Stream identifiers are included in rules to further qualify which tweets should be in a stream. Rules build on filters and other rules: rule "4e8e677 2337d0b993391ee6417171b79" and language.tag = "en" This allows filters to grow on one another. DataSift also pushes for public streams which are more cost effective to process because of resource sharing the computation of a specific rule.

In order to create scalable filters DataSift uses a compiler to schedule filters efficiently across a cluster. Rules are made from a combination of filters and can have 1000 s or millions of terms. Millions of rules can be evaluated simultaneously, scheduled across hundreds of machines. Rules can be reused and hierarchically order. Filters include regular expressions, you can filter out tweets based on text in the profile, for example. There are many different targets and operators. The core filter engine is in C++ and is called the Pickle Matrix and is depicted in the Figure 9 below. The filtering engine is implemented using a custom built compiler and virtual machine based on Distributed Complex Event Processing with Query Rewriting.

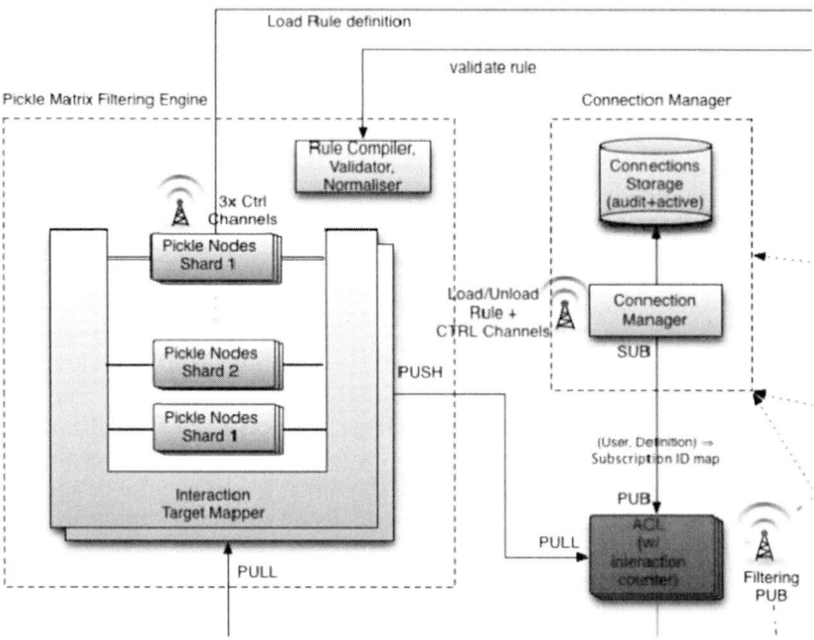


**Figure 9.** Real time filtering of normalized posts based on precompiled rules [3].

A compiler takes filters and targets a Hadoop cluster with a Manager and Node servers. The Manager's job is to determine that if a rule is loaded anywhere else and if can be put somewhere that is highly optimized, like close to someone else that is running a similar stream. Node's job is filter tweets by rules, get a list of matches, and push the matches down the pipeline.

Custom algorithms are built so rules are shared as much as possible. No filter is run in isolation. The filters form a shared space. If there is a filter that filters only for "computer" references then that filter is run on each tweet once and the result is shared between all rules using the same filter. Instead of continually running duplicate filters they are only run once. Rules can be a hierarchical and the compiler is merges them together so that they share rule evaluations. If a node already has a rule then it will attract filters that use that rule. That rule is run just once for all the filters on the node.

By combining workloads of multiple customers together they can exploit any commonality in the filters. DataSift is paid for every operation even though they only run it once. If a regular expression is shared, for example, it is only run once. It cannot always work this way, perhaps a node is loaded so cannot take another client, so it must run on another machine.

The entire configuration dynamically changeable at runtime. The scheduling algorithm is constantly looking at monitoring data. If latency crosses a threshold then the system will be reconfigured. Filters are processed immediately in memory. Each server, for example, can run 10,000 streams. Nodes have a rule cache so they can be shared.

Compiler supports short circuiting to optimize filters. If a regular expression is bigger than an entire machine, for example, then they will automatically load balance across nodes.

The filtering engine is sharded. Each shard receives the full firehose and every "interaction" (*i.e.* a "tweet" or "FB status" or "blog post") is processed by all shards, the results of which are collated before being sent downstream. Each of the N nodes in a single shard (which are replicas of each other) receives 1/N of the hose on a round robin basis. So, supposing there are two shards, with three nodes each, 50% of the filters would be found on each shard. Each node in a shard would receive 1/3 of the hose (and would have 50% of the filters on it). And it would be a replica of the other nodes in that shard. Thus, if a very heavy filter is loaded, that will be balanced by adding more nodes to the shard the heavy rule is loaded into, thus reducing the amount of data that a single node has to process.

A big push is for customers to create reusable public rules to encourage the reusability of data streams. People can use any of the public streams in their own rules. For example, someone could make a word filter that creates a stream. You can build off that stream by using it. Everyone shares that same stream so if a 1000 users are using the dirty word filter the filter is not getting evaluated 1000 times. The filter is getting evaluated once for everyone, which is highly efficient. The platform will thus offer even better performance for a higher number of workloads and become highly scalable with resource usage relative to processing requirement being reduced.

(3) Loading and Delivering the Results

Once the filtering process identifies an interaction that matches the specified query, the interaction is delivered to the specific stream. It is important to mention that DataSift buffers the data it receives for up to one hour. During this time it is possible to request specific interactions from DataSift. The data is stored in Hadoop HBase. However most implementations will require specific custom processing on the results created by DataSift. For example a client might be interested in extracting information such as addresses or mentions of specific users or places and store them later in their own database.

When creating a DataSift Stream running task it is possible to specify a specific output location. Tweets that match the filter are accessible to external applications via a REST API, HTTP Streaming, or Web sockets with a client library exists for: PHP, Ruby, C#, Java, Node.js. The results are JSON objects containing all the data in a normalized, fully augmented format. Augmentations include gender, geolocation, point-of-interest, country, author, the tweet, follower count, Klout score, *etc.* in the stream. There up to 80 fields for each message. Tweets are not guaranteed to arrive in any order and you are not guaranteed to see all the tweets ever sent. This is because Hadoop MapReduce jobs are used to extract the data out of HBase, which involves sharding and thus change the order. However Hadoop does offer solutions for persisting the order of the analyzed data.

## Recording interactions on DataSift

DataSift records the result of the Filtering Task in HBase tables. When data is streamed out of DataSift, Hadoop MapReduce jobs will extract the data in the specific desired format. Most of the time this format will be JSON. DataSift took the decision of storing the normalized data in HBase table instead of pure JSON because it allows further querying if necessarily or exporting it in other formats such as CSV or Excel documents as depicted in the Figure 10. This storage component is fundamental to DataSift for two reasons. First it is used as an Achiever, where all the Interactions that came through the system are stored in a normalized form and can be later processed using the Historic Task Services. The recorder is used for buffering the data until it is transferred to the client in the specified way (live stream, push to a specific data source, download using HTTP *etc.*) The recording table uses entries similar to <interaction ID><recording ID> in order to map the interactions that should be exported to a specific stream.

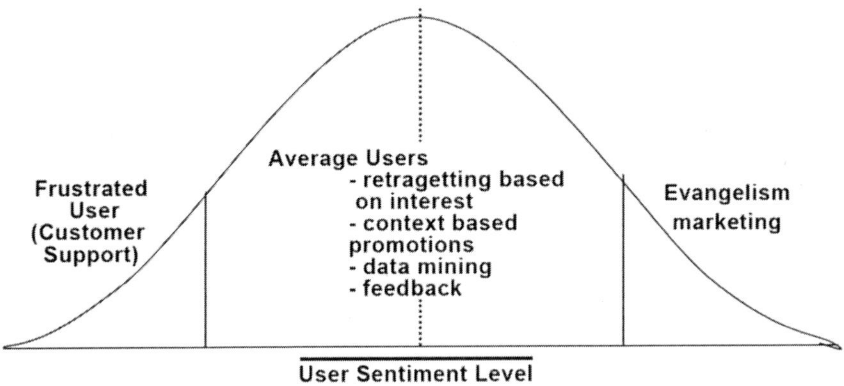


**Figure 10.** Bell Curve of our User Base. Social CRM has the purpose of moving the curve to the right and increasing the number of users.

The content of each interaction is only stored once, and will be archive by DataSift. When DataSift introduced Historic Queues, it bought the data from Twitter for the previous two years. This data amounted to 300 TB, which was delivered over the Internet and normalized according to the way all interaction objects are processed, including augmentations.

## Social CRM integration with the Dispatching System

The dispatching system is offered as a SAAS product to enterprise clients. The Social CRM system builds upon it and has the purpose of aggregating as much information about the users as possible. The most important data that we extract using DataSift and utilize in our system is presented below.

**User sentiment score**—describes the sentiment the user has towards the application. This metric is closely monitored as it groups the users into three major categories.

The first category is composed of users that are neither highly enthusiastic about using the system nor highly negative. They are the regular users and compose 80%–90% of the user base. In general no human interaction with these users is performed. They are advertised and retargeted using their profile and interests, as we will describe bellow. The second category is composed of users that are negative on the system. They have probably experienced either a problem with the system or in the interaction with the driver for example. Whatever the cause, the problem should be addressed so that it will not affect other users or have a spillover effect. The most effective way of dealing with highly negative users is an apologetic customer support phone call during which the user is offered free credit for retrying the system and with the promise that his problem will be addressed as soon as possible.

This method has been used effectively by Uber for monitoring their drivers. The last category is composed of users who are extremely positive on using the system, which we will be calling evangelizers. This category should be enticed to promote the system by offering them a more privileged role that allows better service and social recognition. This method of gamification at the high levels of the customer spectrum has been proven by numerous companies including Foursquare, Path, Quora and StackExchange.

**Interaction History**—this provides anyone interested in a specific user the ability to see the exact posts that constitute the sentiment index, or to identify what the pain points of a highly negative user are. All the interactions provided by DataSift are stored in our database and augment the user profile.

**Promotions History**—all the promotions and advertising campaigns that have ever been targeted to a specific user are recorded. This is for two reasons. One of them is to see the conversion and activation factors of specific campaigns. The other is to aid us in future campaigns by selecting only those users that have or have not been targeted previously within a specific program.

**More information on the users**—by aggregating more information about each user such as age, locations, interests, network of friends *etc.*, we are able to understand the user base better and it helps with categorizing them better. The purpose of the entire Social CRM component is to improve the service and increase the success rate of our marketing campaigns by better targeting which will reduce the total cost. We can thus create online marketing campaigns that can be extremely targeted and still benefit from low CPC rates.

In this section we have detailed the implementation of the proposed system and explained the functionality of the complete architecture by breaking it up into the composing parts. We also analyzed how we managed to integrate the two systems in an efficient and scalable manner by using Windows Azure Cloud Computing as the underlying architecture for our system. We decomposed the system into two large subsystems: the dispatching system and the Social CRM system.

We explained how a cross platform approach can be used to developing mobile application and we have proved the native capacities of the system by using the GPS API. We also presented how the mobile application can be integrated with the Cloud and how the Cloud can act as a data synchronization mechanism between the client mobile application, the driver application and the operator panel. Regarding the Social CRM system, we explained how it can be built to extract and augment the data in our database and bring more value and customer engagement.

# 4. TESTING AND VALIDATION

## 4.1. Mobile based Client Application Testing

Testing of the mobile applications has been performed, covering usability testing and integration testing. Usability testing of software applications developed for mobile devices faces a variety of challenges due to their unique features, such as limited bandwidth, unreliability of wireless networks, as well as the changing context. For assuring the system correctness Use Case Driven Testing of the functionalities of the system must be addressed in various environmental contexts such as no Internet access, no GPS signal *etc.* The client application was designed with these considerations in mind and the testing approach was by using Use Case Driven testing in various conditions. The following issues have been tested:

- **Mobile application context.** It can be defined as "any information that characterizes a situation related to the interaction between users, applications, and the surrounding environment [2]." For our client application we have tested how the app was performing in different times and places, especially how GPS was acting inside buildings and how well wireless networks aided the positioning based on the accuracy of position determination. It is very difficult to select a methodology that can include all possibilities of mobile context in a single usability test. If the user position cannot be obtained and the GPS was turned off, we asked the user to turn it on or input the address manually.

- **Connectivity and Mobile Internet Coverage.** Logistic Systems are characterized by very high availability constraints. Lack of connectivity or slow Internet speed is common with mobile applications. We tested whether the application can identify this situation and alert it to the user, notifying him that the app cannot work properly and he has to either turn on internet (if this is not turn on already), or just report that the app cannot work in the absence of an internet connection. According to Ericsson, 85% of the world population will have access to 3G coverage by 2017. In the

European Union, over 95% of the metropolitan areas are covered by 3G. According to the same report from Ericsson, by 2017 50% of the world population will have access to 4G which will enable even richer interactions in terms of data synchronization and reach media content, especially voice and video streaming.

- **UI/UX testing for different screen sizes.** The mobile screen resolution is extremely fragmented. We also realized that many mobile devices that will be used as dispatching terminals will range from small 3 inch diagonal low resolution devices, up to tablets reaching over 10 inch in diagonal. These concerns affect mobile applications. We tested the applications on multiple devices and also used UI elements that can adapt proportionally to screen sizes. We have observed that for some small screens the application was not displayed properly because we have implemented some minimum size attributes in order to display the text completely. In order to resolve the issue we added test cases for small screen displays, and if the screen width was bellow a specific value, we used a smaller font and minimum width, which solved the problem. In order to test the aspect of the application rendered on different devices, virtualization tools such as Samsung Remote Test Lab. The Remote Test Lab is a free service from Samsung Developers. With it, you can access a remote physical device through a network, install an application and test it remotely.
- **CPU and Memory performance considerations.** Mobile devices have a high diversity of performance specifications. As we intend to support old and new devices as well, we need to test how the application performs on different hardware environments. These requirements must be tested especially if the work is not mitigated to the Cloud. For our system this was less of a concern as we perform the processing and storage on the Cloud. The order history and user data are all stored in the Cloud, and is consumed using the service API. Because we do not have access to all hardware devices, we used pCloud platform [18], which allows virtualization of different devices using screen streaming. Using their service we were able to deploy the application to a large variety of Android handsets and test the behavior of the system on both old and new devices.

## 4.2. API Testing and Validation

The API was implemented using the REST protocol and the JSON data passing format. All communication between the Cloud System and other systems is done using the API (excluding the integration with the Social CRM System which is also done using the database). In the first instance the validation of the service was performed by adding a new project to the solution and creating *Unit Test* classes. Inside this class specific methods for testing functionalities have been defined. Sending JSON requests required a series of step including creating the JSON request data from the CLR object, sending the request using a selected verb, and handling the HTTP specific errors, we defined a method called SendRequest.

Using this method we specified the resource we wanted to test, the verb and the data.

The data object was defined as dynamic to allow for easier operation with encoding and decoding JSON data. We designed the system to return specific error codes for specific errors such as duplicate telephone number. When designing the Unit Test we have tested if this error codes are returned appropriately. For example when creating a new user we tested different combinations of telephone and user name.

As we added new functionality to the system we expended the test scenarios and we rerun the test periodically to ensure that the system remains valid after performing modifications.

## 4.3. Load Testing for Scalability and Synchronization

For Load Testing, we were interested in how the system would reach to a high increase in usage. As we built the System on Windows Azure, we were certain that the scalability aspect will be mitigated effectively as long as we did not have any bottlenecks. Load testing also allowed for an efficient way of discovering errors in the system that occurred in scenarios such as concurrent access to shared resources and overriding of data that was not protected using locks. For Load Testing we first used a number of 10000 concurrent threads that were fired from a virtual machine in the cloud. We used as virtual machine in the Windows Azure Cloud as the communication latency would be minimized and it would help us discovering synchronization issues.

Once we handled all synchronization issues that have arisen through our testing, we needed a better way of testing the scalability beyond what we could have obtained using simple threads. For this we relied on LoadStorm, which is a cloud based tool that can create multiple client virtual machines firing requests at the test server requests can be customized with specific automate trigger based on the received responses. Up to 250 requests/second Windows Azure used just one medium size virtual machine. As the stress on the server reached over 90% CPU usage, automatic scaling was performed, which increased the number of virtual machines and decreased the response time to around

0.5 s. The time required for a virtual machine to launch was around 3–4 min.

## 4.4. Social Media Analysis

For the Social CRM component, the data is received in real time. However delays are to be expected. According to DataSift SLA (Service level agreement), the maximum delay between a Tweet being posted by a user and the time it is processed by DataSift should be less than 4 s. In this respect we analyze what is the average delay we will encounter from a tweet being posted on Twitter and the time it is analyzed by our Social CRM component.

In order to calculate the time delay we fired a number of 300 threads that each posted a message on Twitter. Then we used a stopwatch to obtain the time interval between when the message was posted and the moment the interaction was delivered from DataSift into our system. It is important to understand that the delays between the time the user publishes an interaction on other dataset such as blogs or discussion groups and the time DataSift processes this interaction can be much larger and span up to one hour.

## 4.5. Coverage Ratio of Matching Interactions

While analyzing the processing lag described in the previous paragraph we observed that for the 300 interactions we submitted on twitter using Twitters public API, DataSift received only 248. This means that 52 interactions were not identified by DataSift. Further investigation revealed that the reason why this was happening was because we had a sudden burst in activity that lasted only a few seconds. In this test case we tried to identify if the DataSift platform provides a high enough coverage ratio. For this we fired a number of 1000 Twitter posts over a range of 10 different accounts. Each interaction was submitted at a time interval ranging randomly between 1 and 10 s from the last one. A number of 10 threads were used for posting the threads. In this scenario the number of interactions captured by DataSift have been of 972, which translates into a 97.2% coverage ratio.

In conclusion we have tested the various components of the system and we concluding that the system is valid and works according to the initial functional and non-functional requirements.

# 5. CONCLUSIONS AND FURTHER DEVELOPMENTS

We have detailed the implemented the system according to the specifications. We started by analyzing the requirements for our system by comparing similar applications in order to identify the most important features. We than stated the functionalities which the system was designed to offer and we created the use cases for our actors. We explained the two large subsystems that constitute our project: the dispatching system and the Social CRM system. Before implementation we created the conceptual model and listed the suitable technologies necessarily for meeting our requirements. In this respect we used DataSift as the underlying platform for building the Social CRM engine and Titanium as the best solution for developing cross platform mobile applications We also analyzed what the main threats to REST security are and we have enumerated some actions that we have taken in order to lower the chances of an attacker breaking the system or to help identify and mitigate an attack. We identified what are the main differences in terms of security between running the applications on premise *vs.* Cloud, as this has been a particular controversial topic. We than analyzed what methods can be used to secure REST services.

The Social CRM component of our application was designed in order to augment the information on our users and enhance the performance of our marketing campaigns. For this we used DataSift as the underling platform for extraction of interactions from Social Networks and other online public data sources. We than detailed the implementation of DataSift and how it extracts, normalizes and delivers the data into our system. We also examined some technical challenges that DataSift has encountered and explained the solutions that were applied such as defining time intervals for processing historic content. The Datashift remains a good option which is able to sustain a growing level of scalability for our system.

In conclusion we have tested the various components of the system and we are affirming that the system is valid and works according to the initial specified functional and non-functional requirements. The system is for now up and running [19], but as for any real system there are a lot of further developments and improvements which are determined by production usage.

As further developments, we would like to explore some other aspects for improving the system as elaborating on the dispatch strategy [20], integrating a solution for cruising mile reduction as presented in [21], or even a component for finding potential passengers as proposed in [22]. We also plan in the next release to complement our services with other services such as for example Google traffic API [23] or Skyhook [24] in order to create some new functionalities. Concerning the data, we started the project with relational database, but also we take into account the alternative of transferring the data persistence layer to a noSQL solution (such as for example Redis or Couchdatabase) as a more scalable solution. As a potential problem from a real world environment perspective exploitation of the system, capturing massive data from social networks could represent a possible problem, but designing appropriate filters for data, must be able to solve such a prospective bottleneck.

## AUTHOR CONTRIBUTIONS

This paper was a result of a collaboration between the two authors. Razvan Popa came with the idea and implemented the system software. Cosmina Ivan refined the initial idea, supervised the project and contributed to the writing and editing of the manuscript. Both authors have read and approved the final manuscript.

## CONFLICTS OF INTEREST

The authors declare no conflict of interest.

## REFERENCES

1. Ericsson Mobility Report. 2014. Available online: http://www.ericsson.com/res/docs/2014/ericsson-mobility-report-june-2014.pdf (accessed on 25 September 2014).
2. Sharma, A.; Soni, P. Mobile Cloud Computing (MCC) Open Research Issues. *IJIET*, 2013. Available online: http://ijiet.com/wp-content/uploads/2013/02/ 5.pdf (accessed on 29 September 2014). []
3. DataSift Guide. Available online: http://dev.datasift.com/docs (accessed on 29 June 2015).
4. Gnip, Social Media in Financial Markets. 2013. Available online: http://gnip.com/docs/social-media-and-markets-the-coming-of-age.pdf (accessed on 15 November 2014).
5. Wilson, T. "How GPS Phones Work". 2011. Available online: http://www.howstuffworks.com/gps-phone.htm(accessed on 15 January 2015). []
6. Titanium. Available online: http://www.appcelerator.com/product/ (accessed on 29 June 2015).
7. Microsoft WCF Feature Details. Available online: http://msdn.microsoft.com/en-us/library/ms733103.aspx (accessed on 29 June 2015).

8. Microsoft ADO.NET Entity Framework At-a-Glance. Available online: http://msdn.microsoft.com /en-us/data/aa937709 (accessed on 5 December 2014).
9. ASP.NET SignalR. Available online: http://signalr.net/ (accessed on 29 June 2015).
10. Apple Push Notification Service. Available online: https:// developer .apple.com /notifications/ (accessed on 15 December 2014).
11. Android Cloud to Device Messaging. Available online: https://developers .google.com/android/c2dm/ (accessed on 15 January 2015).
12. Urban Airship. Available online: http://urbanairship.com/ (accessed on 29 June 2015).
13. Alonso, G.F.; Casati, F.H.; Kuno, H. *Web Services: Concepts, Architectures, Applications*; Springer: Berlin, Germany, 2004. []
14. Dinh, H.T.; Lee, C.; Niyato, D.; Wang, P. A survey of mobile cloud computing: Architecture, applications, and approaches. *Wirel. Commun. Mobile Comput.* **2013**, *13*, 1587–1611. [] []
15. Tyree, J.; Akerman, A. Architecture decisions: Demystifying architecture. *IEEE Softw.* **2005**, *22*, 19–27. [] []
16. Schultz-Møller, N.P.; Migliavacca, M. Distributed Complex Event Processing with Query Rewriting, Imperial College London. In Proceedings of the Third ACM International Conference on Distributed Event-Based Systems, Nashville, TN, USA, 6–9 July 2009. []
17. Bass, L.; Clements, P.; Kazman, R. *Software Architecture in Practice*; Wesley: Boston, MA, USA, 2003. []
18. Pcloud. Available online: www.pcloud.com (accessed on 29 June 2015).
19. Taxy Army. Available online: www.taxiarmy.com (accessed on 29 June 2015).
20. Hou, Y.; Li, X.; Zhao, Y.; Jia, X.; Sadek, A.W.; Hulme, K.; Qiao, C. Towards efficient vacant taxis cruising guidance. In Proceedings of the 2013 IEEE Global Communications Conference (GLOBECOM), Atlanta, GA, USA, 9–13 December 2013; pp. 54–59.
21. Zhang, D.; He, T. pCruise: An On-demand Cruising Miles Reduction for Taxicab Networks. In Proceedings of the 2012 IEEE 33rd Real-Time Systems Symposium, San Jan, PR, USA, 4–7 December 2012; pp. 85–94.
22. Yuan, N.J.; Zheng, Y.; Zhang, L.; Xie, X. T-finder: A recommender system for finding passengers and vacant taxis. *IEEE Trans. Knowl. Data Eng.* **2013**, *25*, 2390–2403. [] []
23. Google Traffic API. Available online: https://developers.google.com/maps/documentation/javascript/exampl es/layer-traffic (accessed on 26 June 2015).
24. Skyhook Technology. Available online: http://www.skyhoo kwireless.com / (accessed on 26 June 2015).

# CHAPTER 11

# Towards Guidelines for Building a Business Case and Gathering Evidence of Software Reference Architectures in Industry

**Silverio Martínez-Fernández[1]*, Claudia P Ayala[1], Xavier Franch[1], Helena Martins Marques[2] and David Ameller[1]**

*[1]GESSI Research Group, Universitat Politècnica de Catalunya, Jordi Girona, 1-3, 08034 Barcelona, Spain.*

*[2]Everis, Diagonal, 605, 08028 Barcelona, Spain.*

## ABSTRACT

### Background

Software reference architectures are becoming widely adopted by organizations that need to support the design and maintenance of software applications of a shared domain. For organizations that plan to adopt this architecture-centric approach, it becomes fundamental to know the return on investment and to understand how software reference architectures are designed, maintained, and used. Unfortunately, there is little evidence-based support to help organizations with these challenges.

### Methods

We have conducted action research in an industry-academia collaboration between the GESSI research group and *everis*, a multinational IT consulting firm based in Spain.

### Results

The results from such collaboration are being packaged in order to create guidelines that could be used in similar contexts as the one of *everis*. The main result of this paper is the construction of empirically-grounded guidelines that support organizations to decide on the adoption of software reference architectures and to gather evidence to improve RA-related practices.

### Conclusions

The created guidelines could be used by other organizations outside of our industry-academia collaboration. With this goal in mind, we describe the guidelines in detail for their use.

**Keywords:** Software architecture Reference architecture Empirical software engineering Business case Cost-benefit analysis Reference architecture context Industry-academia collaboration

## 1 BACKGROUND

Nowadays, the size and complexity of information systems, together with critical time-to-market needs, demand new software engineering approaches to design Software Architectures (SA) (Nakagawa et al. [2011]). One of these approaches is the use of software Reference Architectures (RA) that allows to systematically reuse knowledge and components when developing a concrete SA (Cloutier et al. [2010]; Galster and Avgeriou [2011]). Hence, RAs provide guidance for the development and evolution of a class of software systems in a cost-effective manner (Martínez-Fernández et al. [2013b]).

As defined by Bass et al. ([2003]), a Reference Model (RM) is "a division of functionality together with data flow between the pieces" and an RA is "a reference model mapped onto software elements and the data flows between them". It is important to denote that this RA definition already emphasizes two fundamental assets of an RA: the RM that defines its fundamental properties, and the software elements that makes the RM operational by its implementation (Bass et al. [2003]; Galster and Avgeriou [2011]).

A more detailed definition of RAs is given by Nakagawa et al. ([2011]). They define an RA as an architecture that encompasses the knowledge about how to design SAs of systems of a given application or technological domain. Therefore, an RA must address: business rules; architectural styles that address quality attributes; best practices of software development such as architectural decisions, domain constraints, legislation, and standards; and the software elements that support development of systems for that domain. All of this must be supported by a unified, unambiguous, and widely understood domain terminology (Nakagawa et al. [2011]).

In this paper, we consider that an RA may have the elements that these two RA definitions state. We show the relationships among RM, RM-based RA and RA-based concrete SA in Figure 1. Throughout the paper, we use the term RM to refer to industry-specific RM, although RMs can also be defined by other agents such as research centers or non-profit organizations. Also, we use the term RA to refer to RM-based RA and SA to refer to RA-based concrete SA. Angelov et al. have identified the generic nature of RAs as the main feature that distinguishes them from concrete SAs (Angelov et al. [2012]). Every application has its own and unique SA, which is derived from an RA. This is possible because RAs are abstract enough to allow their usage in differing contexts (Angelov et al. [2012]).

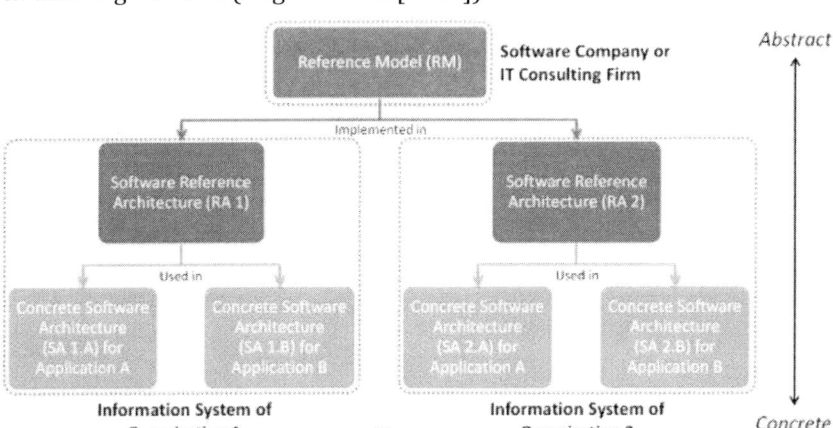


**Figure 1.** RELATIONSHIPS AMONG RM, RA AND SA. A reference model (RM) could be the baseline of many software Reference Architectures (RA). Likewise, RAs serve as a reference for the concrete Software Architecture (SA) of the applications of an information system. These three artifacts go from a high level of abstraction to a low level of abstraction.

The motives behind RAs are: to facilitate reuse, and thereby harvest potential savings through reduced cycle times, cost, risk and increased quality (Cloutier et al. [2010]); to help with the evolution of a set of systems that stem from the same RA (Galster and Avgeriou [2011]); and to ensure standardization and interoperability (Angelov et al. [2012]). Due to this, RAs are becoming a key asset of organizations (Cloutier et al. [2010]).

## 1.1 Research problem

Although the adoption of an RA might have plenty of benefits for an organization, it also implies several challenges, such as the need for an initial investment (Martínez-Fernández et al. [2013b]) and getting real evidence for driving its design and use (Angelov et al. [2013]). Currently, organizations have little support for dealing with these two challenges.

First, there is a shortage of economic models to precisely evaluate the benefit of RAs in order to make informed decisions about their adoption in an organization (Martínez-Fernández et al. [2013b]). Organizations with a wide portfolio of applications, which may consider adopting an existing or new RA to create and maintain such applications, lack an approach to know whether it is worth for them to invest on the adoption of an RA. This situation could be addressed by making a business case with the help of an economic model that perform cost-benefit analysis about the adoption of an RA (Reifer [2002]).

Second, there is also a shortage of experience reports disseminating the context of RAs in industry. For instance, a recent literature review about evidence in software architecture, in which only two papers were about RAs, shows that there is limited knowledge about RAs (Qureshi et al. [2013]). As a result, practitioners usually find the current literature about RA scarce and abstract (Angelov et al. [2012]), limiting the industrial uptake of research results in the field. In this context, we argue that in order to enable practitioners to fully exploit the benefits of RA adoption and usage, the research community must clarify the context of RA in practice. We propose conducting empirical studies to accumulate real evidence for understanding the context of RAs from essential types of stakeholders. Such evidence aims to help practitioners to better understand RA-related practices and, then, to identify the current challenges to improve these practices in their organization. Throughout the paper, we use the term "RA-related practices" to refer to common practices in RA projects, such as defining the goals of an RA, RA design, RA review, RA use and so on.

## 1.2 Research goals and contribution

In this context, the goal of this research is to support organizations (i.e., software companies, information technology consulting firms) to deal with the following Research Questions (RQ):

- RQ 1: Is it worth for an organization to invest on the adoption of an RA?
- RQ 2: How can an organization get corporate evidence that is useful for RA-related practices?
- In addition, we aim for a third research question:
- RQ 3: How the results from RQ1 and RQ2 could be articulated to provide prescriptive support utilities (i.e., guidelines and artifacts) to support organizations in such endeavors?

These support utilities aim to allow organizations to set up and carry out empirical studies aimed to extract evidence to support RQ1 and RQ2.

## 1.3 Paper structure

The paper is structured as follows. In Section 2, we explain the research methodology used. In Section 3, we report the details of how RQ 1 was approached and its results. In Section 4, we report the details of how RQ 2 was approached and its results. In Section 5, we report how the results from RQ 1 and RQ 2 have been packaged to answer the RQ 3, and we present the guidelines for building a business case and gathering evidence of RAs and their context of use. Finally, in Section 6, we end up with conclusions and future work.

The work presented in this paper is a follow-up of the work presented in (Martínez-Fernández et al. [2013a]). It substantially extends such work by:

- Providing further details of the research methodology applied (see Section 2).
- Adding results obtained in RQ 1 (see Section 3): providing new results about the application of an economic model to build a business case of an RA (see new Section 3.2).
- Making more narrow the scope of RQ 2 (see Section 4), updating the set of criteria to understand and evaluate RAs (see Section 4.1), and providing new results about why RAs are used in organizations (see new Section 4.2.1).
- Providing details of the formative and summative stages of the guidelines obtained from the RQ 1 and RQ 2 results (see Section 5). To

analyze if the proposed guidelines could be used by other organizations, we also add the context of RA projects as reported by other researchers and practitioners (see new Section 5.1.1).

# 2 METHODS

This section explains the research methodology used, and the context of this research. The research is being done under an industry-academia collaboration (Martínez-Fernández and Marques [2014]) between the GESSI research group and *everis*, a multinational IT consulting firm based in Spain.

The architecture group of *everis* faced the two problems stated in Section 1.1. The main motivation of *everis* for conducting this research is twofold:

- strategic/organizational: providing quantitative evidence to its clients about the potential economic benefits of applying an RA;
- technical: identifying strengths and weaknesses of RA-related practices in RA projects in order to disseminate them and, if necessary, to improve them.

## 2.1 Action research

This research consists of an ongoing action research initiative among the GESSI research group and *everis*. Action research is "learning by doing" - a group of people identify a problem, do something to resolve it, see how successful their efforts are, and if not satisfied, try again (Brydon-Miller et al. [2003]). The action research cycle consists of: 1) diagnosis of a problem, 2) examination of options to solve the problem, 3) selection of options and execution, 4) analysis of the results, and, 5) repetition for improvement.

However, the idea behind this research is not only to help *everis* to cope with RQ 1 and RQ 2. With the goal of RQ 3 in mind, we also aim to package the solution in such a way that it can be easily used by other organizations dealing with similar problems as *everis*. The guidelines that will be proposed in this paper are shaped throughout our involvement with *everis* to cope with the RQ 1 and the RQ 2.

## 2.2 Context of RAs in everis

We analyze the context of RA projects from our experience with *everis*. We focus on the case in which *everis* has designed an RA with the purpose of deriving concrete SAs for each application of a client organization. This usually happens when *everis* is regularly contracted to create or maintain information systems in client organizations. Each information system of the client organization is built upon the RA and includes many software applications (see Figure 2). RAs enable reuse of architectural knowledge and software components (normally associated to particular technologies) for the design of concrete SAs in client organizations. Therefore, RAs provide a baseline that facilitates standardization and interoperability as well as the attainment of business goals during applications' development and maintenance.

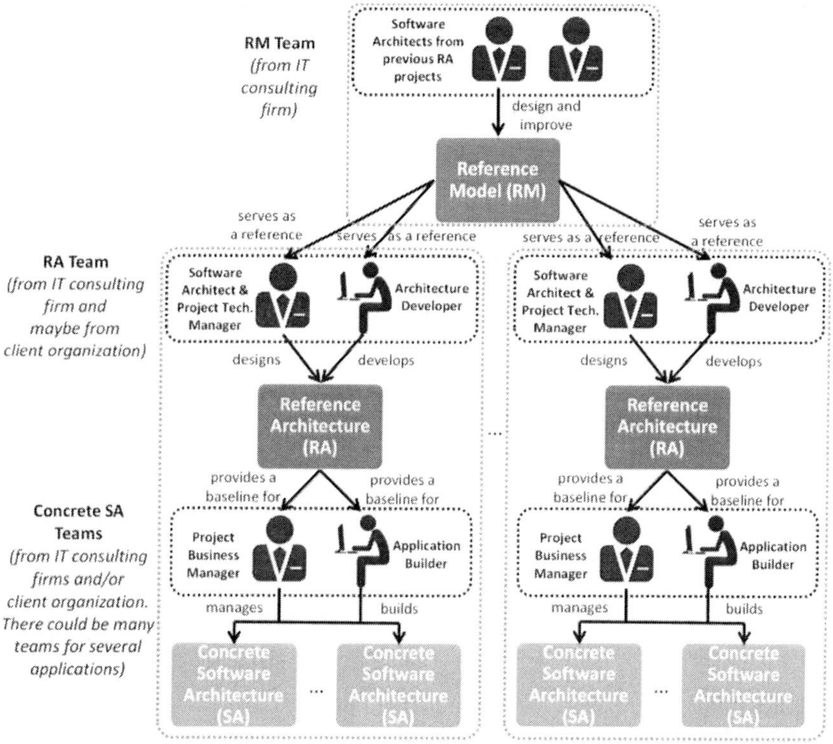


**Figure 2.** RELEVANT STAKEHOLDERS FOR RA ANALYSIS. The figure explains which types of stakeholders and their roles in each type of project (RM, RA and SA projects).

Besides, a special characteristic of *everis* is its previous experience in multiple RA projects. This experience allows *everis* to build a more abstract industry RM. This RM includes best practices from previous successful experiences, which serve as a reference for new RAs that inherit a certain level of quality.

The context of *everis* is very similar to other IT consulting firms. As a recent Gartner report shows, IT consulting firms "leverages industry-specific or industry reference models to accelerate client delivery and ensure quality and consistency across client engagements" (Brand [2014]). However, "clients must ensure that generic industry or reference models [...] are sufficiently customized and tailored to enable their unique business capabilities and environments" (Brand [2014]), so that the RM does not stifle competitive advantage of the RA.

Next subsections respectively show the types of projects that can be found on the *everis* context and the stakeholders that participate in each project.

***Types of projects***

There are three types of projects with different targets (Figure 2).

*1.* RM projects.

*2.* RA projects.

*3.* SA projects.

***Stakeholders for RA analysis***

Stakeholders need to be clearly defined for RA assessment purposes (Angelov et al. [2008]). The people involved in an RA assessment are the evaluation team, which conducts the empirical studies of the guidelines, and stakeholders from architectural projects. In the three types of projects defined above performed by IT consulting firms, we consider the following five stakeholders essential for RA assessment: project business manager, project technological manager, software architect, architecture developer, and application builder. Each of these stakeholders has a vested interest in different architectural aspects, which are important to analyze and reason about the appropriateness and the quality of the three types of projects (Gallagher [2000]). However, there could be more people involved in an architectural evaluation, as Clements et al. indicate in ([Clements et al. 2001]). As a consequence, although this context is generic for IT consulting firms, projects' stakeholders may vary between firms. Below, we describe to which type of project essential stakeholders belong and their interests.

*RM project* It is composed of software architects from the IT consulting firm that worked in previous successful RA projects. They are specialized in architectural knowledge management. Their goal is to gather the best practices from previous RA projects' experiences in order to design and/or improve the corporate RM.

*RA projects* RA projects involve people from the IT consulting firm and likely from the client organization. Their members (project technological managers, software architects and architecture developers) are specialized in architectural design and have a medium knowledge of the organization business domain.

Project technological managers from the IT consulting firm are responsible for meeting schedule and interface with the project business managers from the client organization.

Software architects (also called as RA managers) usually come from the IT consulting firm, although it may happen that the client organization has software architects in which organization's managers rely on. In the latter case, software architects from both sides cooperatively work to figure out a solution to accomplish the desired quality attributes and architecturally-significant requirements.

Architecture developers come from the IT consulting firm and are responsible for coding, maintaining, integrating, testing and documenting RA software components.

*SA projects* Enterprise application projects can involve people from the client organization and/or subcontracted IT consulting firms (which may even be different than the RM owner) whose members are usually very familiar with the specific organization domain. The participation of the client organization in RA and SA projects is one possible strategy for ensuring the continuity of their information systems without having much dependency on subcontracted IT consulting firms.

Project business managers (i.e., customer) come from client organizations. They have the power to speak authoritatively for the project, and to manage resources. Their aim is to provide their organization with useful applications that meet the market expectations on time.

Application builders take the RA reusable components and instantiate them to build an application.

# 3 BUILDING THE BUSINESS CASE OF RAS IN EVERIS

This section details our action research initiative with regard to RQ 1, which is intended to quantify the benefits and costs of RAs through a business case. "A business case is a tool that helps you make business decisions by predicting how they will affect your organization. Initially, the decision will be a go/no-go for pursuing a new business opportunity or approach" (Northrop and Clements [2014]). A useful economic function for business cases is the Return On Investment (ROI). The ROI is a "measure of how much profit an investment earns computed by dividing net income by the assets used to generate it" (Reifer [2002]). Although the ROI is the most popular function in business cases, there are many others (Ali et al. [2009]). For instance, Net Present Value (NPV) estimation with discounted cash flow is mostly used to address the time value of money, and the Internal Rate of Return (IRR) compares the profitability of investments. Sarmad Ali et al. summarize the economic functions used for software product lines (Ali et al. [2009]).

Figure 3 shows the action research cycles conducted in order to answer RQ 1.

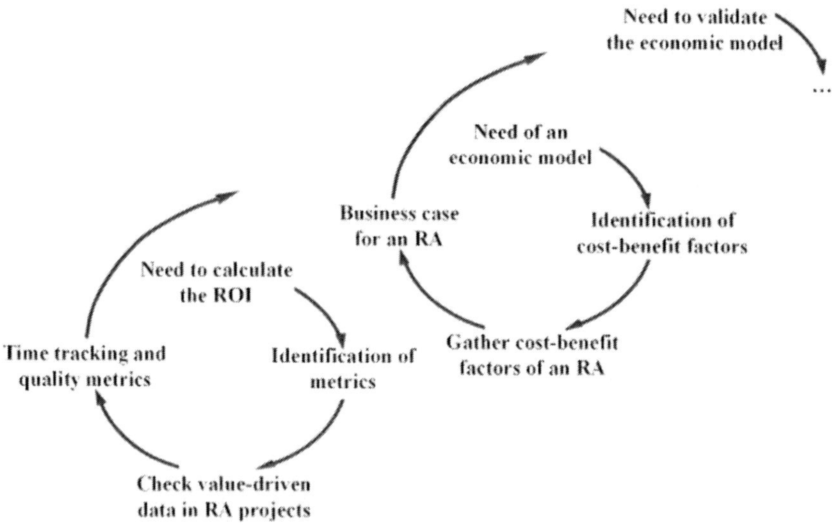


**Figure 3.** ACTION-RESEARCH CYCLES TO SHAPE THE GUIDELINES THAT SUPPORT RQ 1. The figure expl1ains the formative stage to create the checklist of value-driven data in RA projects and the REARM economic model.

In the first cycle of the RQ 1, we diagnosed the problem of the lack of approaches to justify the investment on RAs to *everis*' clients in monetary terms. As a consequence, we designed online questionnaires to ask stakeholders the metrics available in RA projects and conducted them in several RA projects. As a result, we observed that effort metrics could be derived from time tracking practices and that cost-benefit factors could be computed by using reuse-based metrics from the source code of the RA projects. The results from the online questionnaires to study the metrics available in RA projects are reported in Section 3.1.

In the beginning of the second cycle of action research, we diagnosed the need of having an economic model that would use the available data. Then, we identified economic functions meaningful to *everis* to justify RA investments. We also identified cost-benefits factors from the literature that can be calculated from the available metrics. Later, we computed these cost-benefit factors for a real RA project. At the end of this second cycle, we could build the business case for that RA project. In Section 3.2, we report an application of REARM, which is the economic model that we created.

Currently, we are at the beginning of a third cycle in which we diagnosed the problem of validating the economic model in another RA project.

## 3.1 First cycle: survey to check existing value-driven data in RA projects

In this survey, a sample of 5 *everis*' RA projects and 5 SA projects were selected on the basis of their suitability and feasibility to contact at least with one person that participated in the projects.

The main perceived economic benefits on the use of RAs are the cost savings in the development and maintenance of systems due to the reuse of software elements, and the adoption of best practices of software development that increase the productivity of developers (Martínez-Fernández et al. [2013c]). To quantify these cost savings, we used online questionnaires to ask project technical managers and application builders about existing information from past projects. An excerpt of the questions of this survey is shown in Table 1, whereas Additional file 1 includes all the questions. When the client organization has no experience in RAs, these data need to be estimated, which could be potentially error-prone.

### 3.1.1 Results: costs and benefits metrics for RAs

In this section we describe the information that was available in order to calculate the costs and benefits of adopting an RA. We divide existing information in two categories: effort and software metrics. First, the invested effort from the tracked activities allows the calculation of the costs of the project. Second, software metrics help to analyze the benefits that can be found in the source code.

#### *Effort metrics to calculate projects' costs*

In RA projects, 4 out of 5 client organizations tracked development efforts, while maintenance effort was tracked in all 5. In SA projects, 4 out of 5 client organizations tracked development and maintenance effort.

**Table 1.** An excerpt of the template survey for software architects to check existing value-driven data in ra projects

| Type of question | Question |
|---|---|
| Questions about data available for the RA. | Is it possible to access to a code quality management tool (e.g., Sonar) used in the RA project? If not, is it possible to install Sonar to take metrics from the source code of the RA? |
| | Would it be possible to estimate the degree of reuse in each of the modules of the RA with respect to the RM? (optional) |
| | Did the RA stakeholders track the time spent on each task in the development of the RA? If so, with which granularity? |
| | Is there data about personnel and time invested in maintaining the RA? If so, with which granularity? |
| | Would it be possible to give an estimate of the additional training time that an application builder needs to use the RA? |
| | Would it be possible to specify a standard hourly rate of performing tasks on the RA? |
| Questions about data available for the applications based on the RA. | How many applications are (or will be) based on the RA? Make a list of the applications with a contact person. |
| | Do you have an overview of the development of applications based on the RA? If so, go on. If not, we will contact the person who you indicated in the previous answer. |
| | For which of the above applications is it possible to know which RA modules have been reused and the degree of reuse? |
| | Is additional effort needed to reuse RA modules? |
| | Can you estimate how long it would take to develop RA modules instead of reusing them? |
| | Is it possible to access to a code quality management tool (e.g., Sonar) used for the RA-based applications? If not, is it possible to install Sonar to take metrics from the source code of the applications? |
| | Please, indicate the generic characteristics (e.g., reuse percentage of RA modules, size of applications) of three ideal types of RA-based applications with low, medium and high complexity. |
| | Did the RA stakeholders track the time spent on each task in the development of the RA-based applications? If so, with which granularity? |
| | Is there data about personnel and time invested in maintaining the RA-based applications? If so, with which granularity? |
| | Would it be possible to specify a standard hourly rate of performing tasks on the RA-based applications? |
| | Have you done any comparison between the costs and the benefits between RA-based applications and ad-hoc applications? |
| | Currently, are there indicators or metrics to evaluate the improvement of the quality attributes in the applications because of the RA usage? |
| Questions for adding comments and propose metrics to calculate the ROI of the RA. | In addition to the information discussed above, do you think that there is other available information to evaluate how the RA affects the applications development? |
| | Do you think that other metric, not mentioned above, could be useful to calculate the ROI of building applications based on the RA? |
| | Our economic model to calculate the ROI of an RA is based on the reuse and maintenance of code. Do you think there are other quality attributes or important factors for evaluating an RA? |
| | Before sending the survey, would you like to add any comments that may help to understand the context of your answers? |

The development effort is the total amount of hours invested in the development of the RA and the SAs of applications. It could be extracted from the spent time for each development's activity of the projects. The maintenance effort is the total amount of hours invested in the maintenance of the RA and the SAs of applications. Maintenance activities include changes, incidences, support and queries.

#### *Software metrics to calculate benefits in reuse and maintainability*

Source code in RA and SA projects was obviously available in all projects. However, due to confidentiality issues with client organizations, it is not always allowed to access source code.

The analysis of the code from RA and SA projects allow quantifying the size of these projects in terms of LOC or function points (e.g., number of methods). Having calculated the project costs as indicated above, we can calculate the average cost of a LOC or a function point. Since the cost of applications' development and maintenance is lower because of the reuse of RA modules, we can calculate the benefits of RA by estimating the benefits of reusing them. Poulin defines a model for measuring the benefits of software reuse (Poulin [1997]). Maintenance savings due to a modular design could be calculated with design structured matrices (MacCormack et al. [2012]). For a detailed explanation about how such metrics can be used in a cost-benefit analysis, the reader is referred to (Martínez-Fernández et al. [2013b]).

### 3.1.2 Lessons learned

Improvements in the quality attributes of an RA (e.g., reuse, maintainability, security) are extremely difficult to evaluate in an analytic and quantitative fashion contrary to the efficacy of the business (e.g., sales) (Carriere et al. [2010]). This is because software development is a naturally low-validity environment and reliable expert intuition can only be acquired in a high-validity environment (Erdogmus and Favaro [2012]). In order to evaluate RAs based on an economics-driven approach, software development needs to move to a high-validity environment. The good news is that it could be done with the help of good practices like time tracking, continuous feedback, test-driven development and continuous integration. In order to get the metrics defined above, tools such as JIRA (Atlassian [2014]) and Redmine (Redmine [2014]) allow managing the tasks and their invested time, general software metrics (like LOC) and percentages of tests and rules compliance can be calculated by Sonar (SonarSource [2014]) and (Jenkins [2014]). We think that adopting good and repeatable practices to collect data is the basis for moving software development to a high-validity environment and consequently being able of performing an accurate cost-benefit analysis.

## 3.2 Second cycle: a case study to apply an economic model to calculate the ROI of adopting an RA

In this case study, a sample of 1 *everis*' client organization RA project in a public administration and 1 SA project was selected. These projects were selected because the public administration that adopted the RA was interested in the study results. Besides, by the time we conducted the study, *everis*' started the aforementioned SA project, being highly feasible to collect quantitative data. Although we were aware of other SA projects with participants that do not belong to *everis*, it was not possible to contact with them.

Results from the previous survey (see Section 3.1) revealed that the data available in order to calculate costs and benefits were effort and software metrics. We collected these metrics, which are presented in (Martínez-Fernández et al. [2013b]), from two types of tools. In order to collect data, JIRA (Atlassian [2014]) was used to collect the invested effort from training, development and maintenance activities. Keeping track of activities is common in practice for project management and auditing. In addition to that, Sonar (SonarSource [2014]) was used to gather software metrics to analyze the benefits that can be found in the source code. Sonar offers tool support for obtaining general software metrics such as LOC, dependencies between modules, technical debt, and percentages of tests and rules compliance.

### 3.2.1 Results

After retrospectively collecting the data of the past RA and SA projects, we analyzed which cost-benefit factors of adopting an RA could be calculated and envisaged the REARM economic model (Martínez-Fernández et al. [2013b]) in order to calculate the ROI of the RA investment. By the time we conducted the study, the public organization had already: (1) adopted an RA designed by *everis*, (2) created an application using the RA, and (3) fixed errors discovered in the RA software elements that were reused by the application.

We calculated a three-year ROI of 42% with a payback period of 16,5 months and 7 applications in the public organization (see Figure 4).

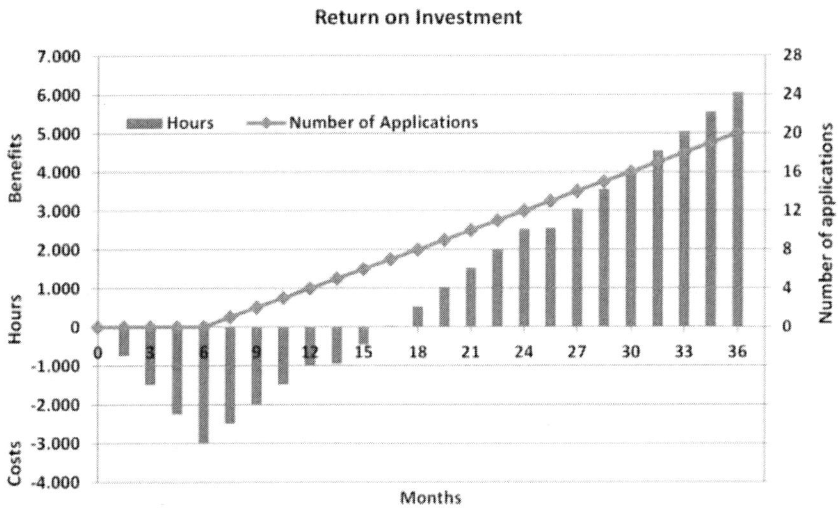


Figure 4 Roi of developing and maintaining ra-based applications versus stand-alone fashion in a public administration.The public administration of this study will realize a three-year ROI of 42% with a payback period of 16,5 months and 7 applications.

Moreover, applications are introduced into the market earlier from the seventh month on. This is due to the effort avoidance of reusing the RA in the development of new applications.

The results of this study are further reported in (Martínez-Fernández et al. [2013b]).

### 3.2.2 Lessons learned

As Clement et al. point out in their book (Clements and Northrop [2002]), experts agree that the number of applications you need to build for a reuse-based architecture-centric approach to pay off is between 2 and 3. We also agree with that statement. In our study it turned out to be 7 because the application from which we collected data was small and only 20% of the RA was reused. However, in applications in which this percentage is higher, the benefit from the RA is greater. If we perform sensitivity analysis to REARM, with a higher reuse of the RA in applications (for instance higher than 70%, which is likely in medium to large applications), the RA pays off with 2 applications.

# 4 GATHERING EVIDENCE OF RAS IN EVERIS

This section details our action research initiative with regard to the RQ 2. Figure 5 shows the action research cycles conducted in order to answer RQ 2.

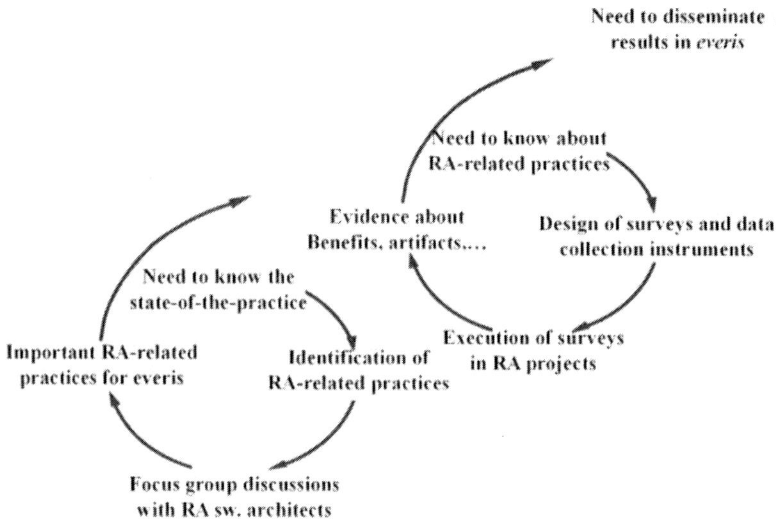


**Figure 5.** ACTION-RESEARCH CYCLES TO SHAPE THE GUIDELINES THAT SUPPORT RQ 2. The figure explains the formative stage to create the template survey that aims to gather relevant evidence from RA projects.

In the first cycle of the RQ 2, we diagnosed the need of knowing about the state of past and present RA projects in *everis* in order to reuse architectural knowledge and improve RA-related practices in prospective RA projects. As a consequence, we planned to identify a set of criteria about RAs that are relevant for practitioners. Finally, we identified five aspects that indicate what evidence to gather in order to support RA-related practices, which are presented in Section 4.1.

In the second cycle of this action research, we planned to gather evidence about these aspects. We designed surveys to gather mostly qualitative evidence about such aspects. Then, we executed these surveys in a case study with several RA projects in *everis*. As a consequence, we obtained results about why *everis*' clients adopted RAs, and the benefits and drawbacks of RAs. These results are reported in Section 4.2.

Currently, we are at the beginning of a third cycle of the RQ 2 in which we diagnosed the problem of disseminating these results in *everis*.

## 4.1 First cycle: identifying practical review criteria for RAs

In order to gather evidence of RAs, it becomes necessary to previously identify the aspects that are relevant for practitioners about RAs. In this section we identify an initial set of criteria, which might be further refined after gathering evidence from RAs. To do so, we analyzed the key criteria mentioned by *everis*' software architects during the meetings and focus group discussions of our action research initiative, and we also studied the literature. We prioritized the *everis*' vision to make a more practitioner-oriented set of criteria.

Although a commonly accepted set of criteria to evaluate RAs does not exist (Angelov et al. [2008]; Gallagher [2000]; Graaf et al. [2005]), it has been claimed that RAs have to be evaluated for the same aspects as SAs (Angelov et al. [2008]). For this reason, we started by analyzing some available works on SA evaluation (Bass et al. [2008]; Clements et al. [2001]; Falessi et al. [2010]). However, existing evaluation methods for SAs are not directly applicable to RAs or other architecture-centric approaches such as product lines architectures because they do not cover their generic nature (Angelov et al. [2008]). The development of a family of software systems has some characteristics that distinguish it from the development of software systems (Montagud et al. [2011]). Therefore, existing evidences for product line architectures can be also used to evaluate RAs, namely: generic characteristics such as "variability, reusability, commonality, and compositionality" (Montagud et al. [2011]); the propagation of architectural decisions while reusing common assets (Montagud et al. [2011]); and lower development costs with respect to developing systems individually (Ali et al. [2009]; Linden et al. [2004]; Montagud et al. [2011]).

Due to these reasons, the authors of the paper and two more software architects from *everis* elaborated further this analysis considering the specific characteristics of RAs as described in (Angelov et al. [2008], [2012]; Galster and Avgeriou [2011]; Graaf et al. [2005]; Nakagawa et al. [2011]), commonalities with other architecture-centric approaches such as product line architectures (Ali et al. [2009]; Deelstra et al. [2005]; Linden et al. [2004]; Montagud et al. [2011]), and experience from *everis*. The resulting aspects for understanding and evaluating RAs are detailed below and summarized in Table 2.

**Table 2.** Summary of relevant aspects for software reference architecture understanding and evaluation as seen by practitioners

| Aspect | Description of the RA Aspect |
|---|---|
| 1 | Overview and classification of an RA |
| 2 | Requirements and quality attributes analysis |
| 3 | Architectural knowledge and decisions |
| 4 | Supportive technologies |
| 5 | Business qualities and architecture competence |

Aspect 1 refers to the need of determining the context and classifying an RA. As Angelov et al. point out (Angelov et al. [2012]), there are five types of RAs depending on their characteristics. Among the most important characteristics are (Angelov et al. [2012]):

- the organization(s) that will use the RA (e.g., a *single organization* or *multiple organizations* that share a domain),
- who defines the RA (e.g., *software companies* as IT consulting firms, *software groups* from the organization that use the RA, and so on),
- the origin and motivation of the RA (e.g., *preliminary* when the RA solves a new problem or *classical* when it is based on previous experiences),
- the goal of the RA and the domain of the RA-based applications (e.g., *standardization* of SAs or *facilitation* of the design of SAs),
- and the RA elements it may include (e.g., *components and connectors, policies and guidelines,* and so on).

The classification of an RA is vital to better understand its limits, to ensure its congruency, and to facilitate its evaluation.

Aspect 2 consists of the quality attributes targeted by an RA. The achievement of quality attributes is in fact an SA most compelling reason for existence (Bass et al. [2003]). However, SAs and RAs do not strictly determine all of an application's qualities. One example is usability: "whether the user sees red or blue backgrounds, a radio button or a dialog box" (Clements et al. [2001]) is not determined by an SA or an RA. A list of quality attributes that lie squarely in the realm of SAs is defined by the architecture tradeoff analysis method (Clements et al. [2001]): performance, reliability, availability, security, modifiability, portability, functionality, variability, subsetability and conceptual integrity. For instance, variability shows how well an RA could be expanded or modified to produce new SAs of applications. Besides, an RA could address more architectural qualities than an SA (e.g., variability, reusability, commonality, compositionality, and applicability) (Angelov et al. [2008]; Montagud et al. [2011]). Quality attributes analysis should be wider for RAs in this sense.

Aspect 3 comprises architectural decisions. Many prominent researchers (Angelov et al. [2008]; Falessi et al. [2010]) highlight the importance of architectural decisions for the SA design process and the architectural evaluation. For RAs, architectural decisions are even more important than in a single software system since, owing to systematic reuse, an inadequate design decision could be propagated to several software systems (Montagud et al. [2011]).

Aspect 4 consists of the supportive technologies such as methods, techniques and tools (Falessi et al. [2010]; Nakagawa et al. [2011]) that aim to improve the RA design process and support the use of the RA during the development of applications. Moreover, this aspect is very important for practitioners, since they are interested in knowing the latest versions of technologies and tools used in the RA projects, and providing application builders with tools that improve their productivity.

Aspect 5 refers to business qualities of an RA. SAs also address business qualities (Angelov et al. [2008]) (e.g., cost, time-to-market) that are business goals, i.e. the objectives of an organization that affect their competence (Bass et al. [2008]). These business qualities are even more important in the context of families of applications, such as RAs: "the main arguments for introducing software product family engineering are to increase productivity, improve predictability, decrease the time to market, and increase quality (dependability)" (Linden et al. [2004]).

We recommend gathering evidence about these five aspects, which are summarized in Table 2, in order to improve RA-related practices. Next, Section 4.2 explains how we are gathering evidence about these aspects. Currently, there are no guidelines to support the gathering of these aspects altogether. This has motivated our work.

## 4.2 Second cycle: surveys to gather evidence to improve RA-related practices

In these surveys, the target populations were RA projects and SA projects executed by *everis*. A sample of 9 representative *everis*' projects in client organizations were selected. All these projects were from Europe (7 from Spain).

In order to collect data, semi-structured interviews were used for project technological managers, software architects, and client's project business managers. The reason of using interviews is that these roles have higher knowledge than the other roles about the architectural aspects of the Table 2, or another perspective in the case of client's project business managers, so we wanted to collect as much information as possible from them. Prior to the interviews, questionnaires were delivered to collect personal information about the interviewee and to inform him/her about the interview. On the other hand, online questionnaires were used for architecture developers and application builders, since most of their questions are about supportive technologies and their responses can be previously listed, simplifying the data collection process.

To perform data analysis, the research team held several discussion meetings during and after data collection, and established specific protocols and templates for data analysis. In the case of the interviews, we used an Excel-based template to organize each participant's answer to each question using tables. For doing this, we used the interview transcripts and individual notes taken by different researchers during the interviews. Then, we analyzed the data from two perspectives that lead us to a better understanding and interpretation of the results. First, we analyzed the answers at the project level, in order to understand the specific context of each project and the perspective of its stakeholders. Second, we analyzed the answers at whole by assessing all participants' answers related to each question, in order to categorize their answers using template tables that described (in each column): the name of the category, a detailed description of the cases covered by the category, the participant, and the explicit sentences that support the category. Such categories were then further discussed and analyzed by the entire team in order to better analyze the evidence and improve our understanding until reaching an agreement. As a result, some categories were split, modified, discarded or added to ensure that all answers were well-represented.

The complete version of the surveys protocol, which contains interview guides and questionnaires, is available at the Additional file 2. An excerpt of the questions for software architects of this survey, which only includes the questions used for the results described in the next two subsections, is shown in Table 3.

### 4.2.1 Results: motivations to use RAs for designing SAs of applications

In this subsection, we present results about the Aspect 1, which was defined in Section 4.1. Such results answer why RAs were adapted for creating SAs of *everis* client organizations' applications. Next, we report the motives that trigger the origin behind each RA project. These results can help organizations to analyze if they need an RA. Table 4 shows the characteristics and objectives of each RA project.

**Table 3.** An excerpt of the template survey for software architects to gather evidence about aspects 1 and aspect 5 of ra projects

| Type of question | Question |
|---|---|
| Questions about the classification of the RA. | What do you understand by RA? |
| | What was the objective of the project? |
| | Which was the client organization's problem that motivated the project? |
| | What was the relationship with the client organization during the design and maintenance of the RA? |
| Questions about the business qualities of the RA for the client organization. | What benefits does the client organization experience from adopting your RA? And developers from using it? |
| | Which problems does the client organization experience from adopting your RA? And developers from using it? |
| | How the training for the client organization was conducted in order to them use your RA? |
| | Did the use of your RA cause any organizational change in the client organization? |
| | How does the use of your RA reduce the time-to-market of RA-based applications in the client organization? |
| | What types of non-functional requirements are reinforced because of using your RA in applications? |
| | To sum up, what conclusions do you draw from the facilities provided by your RA for the client organization? |
| Questions about the business qualities of the RA for the IT consulting firm (optional). | How is your RA based on an RM and any other existing architectural knowledge and software components in your company? |
| | What do you think should be replaced, included or updated in prospective versions of the RM? |
| | To sum up, what conclusions do you draw from the facilities provided by the RM for the IT consulting firm? |

The motivations why *everis*' client organizations adopted an RA are shown below. We report between brackets the identifier of the client organization that indicated such motivation (see Table 4).

- 5 out of 9 projects (B, C, D, F, H) reported the update of technologies to develop applications since they were obsolete or application maintenance was costly.
- 4 out of 9 projects (A, B, G, H) mentioned the need to homogenize the development of similar applications and identify their common elements to foster reuse.
- 4 out of 9 projects (C, D, F, G) aimed to simplify application development (e.g., use of widely-known technologies) and improve productivity of application builders in order to hire profiles less specialized and reduce development time.

**Table 4.** OVERVIEW AND CHARACTERISTICS OF SELECTED *everis*' RA PROJECTS

| Id. | Domain | RA objective | Examples of applications | RA project type |
|---|---|---|---|---|
| A | Industry | Web-based applications to allow vendors updating information about clients in a department store. | Application that allows vendors to manage client information. | Design |
| B | Banking | Multi-platform applications that are fast, satisfy practices of the market and support transaction processing. | Application for online banking. There are approximately 300 applications. | Design, Evolution |
| C | Banking | Multi-platform applications of a bank. To improve the productivity of applications builders and to facilitate the development of applications. | Application to integrate some existing applications with the same look and feel. Application to improve the business process of depositing money. There are approximately 10 applications. | Design, Evolution |
| D | Insurance | Applications that satisfy internal request for proposals. | Applications to hire insurance policy (home insurance, life insurance...). | Design, Evolution |
| E | Public sector | Java web applications, with flexible front-end, integration and batch processes. | Application to support billing and technical services. | Design, Evolution |
| F | Public sector | Web-based applications for the different departments of a public administration. | Application to deliver forms and pdfs. There are around 50 applications of different departments of a public administration. | Design, Evolution |
| G | Public sector | Applications with enhanced reuse and reduced development costs. | Application for enterprise resource planning and customer relationship management. | Design |
| H | Insurance | Applications integrated with services of an insurance company. | Application to manage health care and payments. | Design |
| I | Public sector | Applications that include the business processes of a utility organization. | Application for urban management reports. | Design |

- 2 out of 9 projects (C, I) needed to improve business processes of the organization because of organizational changes or applications misalignment with business needs.
- 2 out of 9 projects (C, E) were started because the client organization had difficulties in developing applications without the help of a software vendor.
- 2 out of 9 projects (A, B) mentioned the need to support and enable application development in any platform (e.g., web, smartphone, POS terminal, ATM).

- 2 out of 9 projects (B, D) stated the need to migrate functionality from legacy systems to new systems (also known as "downsizing") to reduce maintenance costs.
- 1 out of 9 projects (A) reported the lack of products on the market adapted to its needs and business processes.

### 4.2.2 Results: strengths and weaknesses of RAs

In this section we present preliminary results about the Aspect 5 defined in Section 4.1. Such results answer how the adoption of RAs provide observable benefits to the different involved actors in RA projects in *everis*. Below, the resulting benefits and aspects to consider are reported, and it is indicated between brackets the identifier of the client organization that mentioned such benefits (see Table 4).

#### *Benefits in* everis' *RA projects*

We grouped benefits in four categories. Below each category, explicit sentences from software architects are also indicated.

- 7 out of 9 projects (A, B, C, E, F, G, I) stated "reduction of the development time and faster delivery of applications".
    - o An RA allows starting developing applications since the first day by following architectural decisions already taken.
    - o An RA decreases the development time of applications since the RA's modules that implement needed functionality are reused in the application.
- 7 out of 9 projects (A, B, C, D, E, H, I) mentioned "increased productivity of application builders".

  An RA facilitates material and tools for the development, testing and documentation of applications, and for training application builders.

    - o An RA generates or automatizes the creation of code in the applications.
    - o An RA indicates the guidelines to be followed by the application builders.
    - o An RA reduces the complexity of applications' developments because part of the functionality is already resolved in the RA.
    - o An RA facilitates the configuration of its modules and the integration with legacy systems or external systems.

- 6 out of 9 projects (A, B, C, D, E, G) stated "cost savings in the maintenance of the applications".
    - An RA increases the control over applications through their homogeneity.
    - An RA maintains only once reused services by all applications.
    - An RA allows adding or changing functionalities by means of a modular design.
    - An RA establishes long term support standards and "de facto" technologies.
- 4 out of 9 projects (C, F, G, I) mentioned "increased quality of the enterprise applications".
    - An RA helps to accomplish business needs by improving key quality attributes.
    - An RA helps to improve the business processes of an organization.
    - An RA reuses architectural knowledge of previous successful experiences.

***Aspects to consider that eventually could become risks in* everis' *RA projects***

- 5 out of 9 projects (B, C, E, F, H) considered "additional learning curve". An RA implies an additional training for their own tools and modules, even if its technologies are standard or "de facto" already known by the application builder.
- 4 out of 9 projects (B, C, D, E) stated "dependency on the RA". Applications depend on the reused modules of the RA. If it is necessary to make changes in a reused module of the RA or to add a new functionality, application builders have to wait for the architecture developers to include it in the RA for all the applications.
- 2 out of 9 projects (A, D) considered "limited flexibility of the applications". The use of an RA implies following its guidelines during the application development and adopting its architectural design. If business needs require a different type of application, the RA would limit the flexibility of that application.

The results of this study are further reported in (Martínez-Fernández et al. [2013c]).

### 4.2.3 Lessons learned

During the pilot of the survey, we learnt the following lessons about its design:

- The same term could have slightly different meaning in the academia and in the industry (for instance, the term "enterprise architecture" is sometimes used in the industry to mean "RA for a single organization").
- The software development methodology used during the development of applications is seldom prescribed by the RA, so we removed it as relevant aspect for RAs (it was an aspect in previous versions).
- Contacting stakeholders from client organizations was harder than contacting interviewees from *everis*. This is mainly because it was *everis* who requested the study, so they had a clear interest on it.

# 5 RESULTS AND DISCUSSION

In this section, we present how the results from RQ1 and RQ2 have been articulated into guidelines to support organizations building a business case and gathering evidence of RAs. The guidelines have been incrementally constructed based on our action research approach with *everis*. For its shaping and validation, the construction of the guidelines is respectively divided in two stages: the formative and the summative stages.

## 5.1 Formative stage: shaping the guidelines

In the formative stage, the goal is to incrementally shape the guidelines from the feedback of the action research. In order to analyze whether other organizations deal with similar problems as *everis*, we highlight the similarities of RAs designed by *everis* with other RA contexts that have been reported in the literature and by practitioners. After this analysis, we will only package into the guidelines the material that could be used under other organizations context.

### 5.1.1 Similar contexts of RAs in practice

The results from our action research in *everis* are particular to the context described in Section 2.2. IT consulting firms, such as Accenture (Brand [2014]) and Capgemini (Herold and Mair [2013]) also fit into such context (i.e., they use industry-specific RM, and they carry out the three types of projects described there). However, to properly create the guidelines for other RA contexts, it is vital to first characterize RA projects conducted by other companies.

Architecture-centric approaches to develop families of software applications are not new. Deelstra et al. give a classification of these approaches with respect to the level of reuse (Deelstra et al. [2005]): 1) standardized infrastructure; 2) platform: 3) software product line, and 4) configurable product family. In this classification, RAs can be positioned as standardized infrastructures or platforms (Graaf et al. [2005]), whereas software product lines and configurable product families are based on Product Lines Architectures (PLA). Several authors has stated that RAs are more generic than PLAs (Martínez-Fernández et al. [2013b]). Next, we classify RAs in the industry under the two former categories.

On the one hand, standardized infrastructures have been used by public administrations in Germany (Herold and Mair [2013]), in the Netherlands (Galster et al. [2013]), and in Spain (García-Alonso et al. [2010]). These RAs provide software assets as inspiration for the design of applications, but little domain engineering effort is performed (i.e., little domain specific functionality is included in the RA). They are popular in public administration because there is a need to cover multiple organizations from different business domains (i.e., ministries or departments of the government) and little common functionality exist. Also, the high distribution of development teams implies that these RAs play only an informative or instructive role rather than regulative.

On the other hand, platforms additionally "require a certain amount of domain engineering to create and maintain the assets that implement the common functionality" (Deelstra et al. [2005]). There are several business domains that have used this type of RAs.

In the space domain, the NASA has detected that "many Earth science data system components and architectural patterns are reconstructed for each mission" (Mattmann and Downs [2010]). In order to reuse these assets in new systems, they created the NASA's ESDS RA (NASA [2012]).

In the banking domain, RAs are usually used to integrate legacy systems and migrated service-oriented systems that contain the business logic. The common scenario is that these RAs provide common services that then may be reused in the different front-ends or channels (e.g., desktop applications, web client applications, mobile applications, ATMs and so on). An example is Credit Suisse (Murer and Hagen [2013]).

The most mature domain for RAs may be the embedded systems domain. For instance, Océ, one of the world's leading copier manufacturers, uses an RA to derive an SA for engines incorporated in a specific series of Océ printers (Graaf et al. [2005]). Besides, in the automotive industry, car manufacturers such as Volvo (Eklund et al. [2005]) and BMW (Reichart and Haneberg [2004]) started to use RAs to develop the software of electronic/engine control unit based on basic software components that were unique to them. As a further step, AUTOSAR has become popular later because it standardizes basic software components for many car manufacturers, suppliers and other related companies (AUTOSAR [2014]). This enables the reuse of software developed by original equipment manufacturers in multiple car manufacturers. This has led to software ecosystems that are characterized by a network of developers rather than a single organization providing the final product to the customer (Eklund and Bosch [2014]).

To sum up, we can conclude that core idea of using an RA for the development and maintenance of a family of software products is common in all these contexts. However, RM are only commonly used in IT consulting firms. As a consequence, the study of RM during the application of the guidelines will be optional so that it can be used in these other contexts.

It is also important to note that all RAs described in this section are based on practical experience in the industry. The guidelines will target this type of RA, also known as *classical* (Angelov et al. [2012]). Conversely, the guidelines would be hardly applicable in *preliminary* RAs, i.e., those that are "defined when the technology, software solutions, or algorithms demanded for its application do not yet exist in practice by the time of its design" (Angelov et al. [2012]).

### 5.1.2 Packaging the guidelines

*everis*' results are being suitably packaged with the aim of being applied in prospective RA projects and also in similar organizations. Figure 6 summarizes the guidelines for building a business case and gathering evidence of RAs in industry.

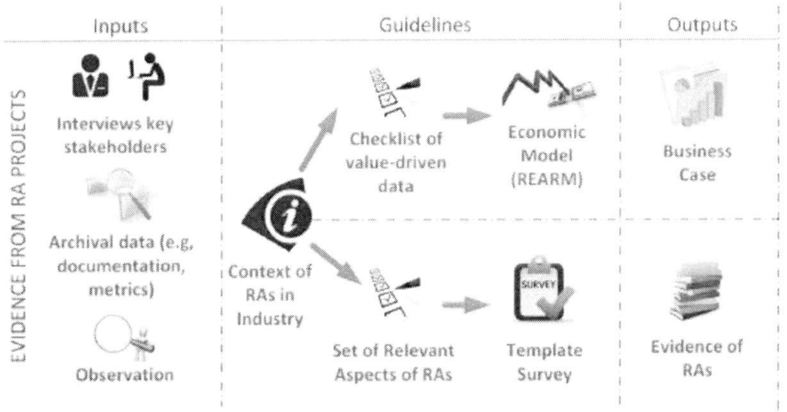


**Figure 6: EMPIRICAL STUDIES OF THE GUIDELINES FOR BUILDING A BUSINESS CASE AND GATHERING EVIDENCE OF RAS IN INDUSTRY.** The guidelines are composed of the context of RAs in industry, and four

empirical studies. The four empirical studies are used as follows. To answer RQ 1, there are two studies: a survey to check existing value-driven data in organizations and a case study to calculate the ROI of adopting an RA. To answer RQ 2, there are two studies: a focus group to determine the set of criteria about RAs important for an organizations and a template survey to gather evidence about the previously identified relevant aspects of RAs.

First of all, organizations that may want to use these guidelines need to fit into the context depicted in Section 5.1.1. This means that they need to design an RA based on practical experience, and to use such RA for the development and maintenance of a family of applications in industry. This is because the input for using the guidelines is evidence from real RA projects.

The guidelines support organizations:

*1.* To decide whether to invest on an RA by providing them with:

- A checklist to analyze existing value-driven data in RA projects.
- An economic model that uses such value-driven data to calculate the ROI of adopting an RA.

*2.* To improve RA-related practices based on corporate evidence by providing them with:

- A practitioner-oriented set of criteria to understand and evaluate an RA.
- Templates of interview guides and online questionnaires to gather relevant evidence.

On the one hand, to analyze whether it is worth to invest on an RA, a checklist of value-driven data that an organization might have is facilitated to check if the provided economic model provided can be executed. On the other hand, to improve RA-related practices with evidence, a set of relevant aspects for RAs is facilitated to check which ones are important for an organization and then use the provided template surveys to gather evidence.

To gather evidence with the help of the aforementioned artifacts, empirical studies can be set up and carried out. Several data collection techniques exist (Lethbridge et al. [2005]). We propose surveys that use interviews and questionnaires, case studies that require documentation analysis and metrics gathering, and focus groups. Below, we explain the dimension, context, objective and method applied in each empirical study of the guidelines. To see the threats to validity in *everis*, the reader is referred to (Martínez-Fernández [2013]).

***I) A survey to check existing value-driven data in RA projects***

***Dimensions***

RQ 1.

***Context***

Typically, organizations do not have resources to compare the real cost of creating applications with and without an RA and historical data may be scarce. Thus, alternatives should be considered.

***Objective***

The objective of this survey is to identify the quantitative information that can commonly be retrieved in RA projects in order to quantitatively calculate the costs and benefits of adopting an RA in an organization. This is an initial step to create repeatable techniques for performing a cost-benefit analysis.

***Method***

Exploratory surveys with personalized questionnaires applied to relevant stakeholders (e.g., manager, architect, developer) to find out the quantitative data that has been collected in RA projects and SA projects. An example of conducting this empirical study and its approach for data collection is described in Section 3.1.

***II) A case study to apply REARM to calculate the ROI of adopting an RA***

***Dimensions***

RQ 1.

***Context***

Before deciding to launch an RA, organizations need to analyze whether to undertake or not the investment. Offering organizations an economic model that is based on former RA projects data can help them to make more informed decisions.

***Objective***

The objective is to analyze whether it is worth investing on an RA with the help of an economic model, in order to improve the communication among architects and management, and to improve their decisions.

***Method***

A case study that applies an economic model to calculate the ROI of adopting an RA. Depending on the maturity of the organization, two approaches can be applied. If the organization does not have experience with an RA, the economic model should be fed with estimated data. Nevertheless, when the organization already has experience with RAs (i.e., the case of IT consulting firms), real data can be gathered by means of an exploratory quantitative post-mortem analysis. Then, the economic model quantifies the potential advantages and limitations of using an RA. Some related works explain how to calculate the ROI of a product (Forrester [2014]), software reuse (Frakes and Terry [1996]; Poulin [1997]), and software product lines (Ali et al. [2009]). We suggest the use of REARM, which is an economic model specific for RAs presented in (Martínez-Fernández et al. ([Martínez-Fernández et al. 2013b])). An example of conducting this empirical study and its approach for data collection is described in Section 3.2.

***III) A focus group to study the relevant criteria of RAs for an organization***

***Dimensions***

RQ 2.

***Context***

Typically, organizations drive the design and use of RAs in an unsystematic manner (Eklund et al. [2005]). To drive RA-related practices based on evidence, it becomes fundamental to identify the relevant aspects of RAs as seen by practitioners.

***Objective***

The objective of this study is to identify the aspects that are important for each organization in order to support RA-related practices.

***Method***

A focus group with relevant stakeholders (e.g., manager, architect, developer) to find out which aspects of RAs are important to them. A focus group is considered a proven and tested technique to obtain the perception of a group of selected people on a defined area of interest (Lethbridge et al. [2005]). An example of conducting this empirical study and its approach for data collection is described in Section 4.1.

***IV) Surveys to gather evidence to improve RA-related practices***

***Dimensions***

RQ 2.

***Context***

To reuse architectural knowledge and improve RA-related practices in prospective RA projects, organizations need to understand RA's characteristics, as well as its potential benefits and limitations. Gathering evidence from previous RA projects is a feasible way to start gaining such an understanding.

***Objective***

The purpose of the survey is to understand the impact of using RAs for designing the SAs of the applications of an information system of a client organization. This is a descriptive survey that measures what occurred while using RAs rather than why. The following questions are important for organizations in order to understand relevant Aspects 1 to 5 of RAs (defined in Table 2):

*1.* Why is an RA adapted for creating SAs of the organizations' applications? What type of RA is being designed and used in the organization?

*2.* What is the state of practice in requirement engineering for RA projects in the organization?

*3.* What is the state of practice in architectural design for RA projects in the organization?

*4.* Which tools and technologies are currently being used in RAs projects by the organization?

*5.* How does the adoption of RAs provide observable benefits to the different actors involved in RA projects in the organization?

***Method***

Exploratory surveys with personalized questionnaires applied to relevant stakeholders (e.g., architects, developers) to gather their perceptions and needs. An example of conducting this empirical study and its approach for data collection is described in Section 4.2.

Finally, the output for using guidelines for RQ 1 is a business case that evaluates whether it is worth or not to invest on an RA. On the other hand, the output of gathering evidence about Aspects 1 to 5 of Table 2 is a corporate knowledge base about these aspects. It is important to note that, although it is not strictly necessary, it is recommended to gather Aspects 1 to 5 for building the business case. In other words, guidelines are complementary and support each other (e.g., results from a preceding study can be used to corroborate or further develop other results). For instance, in our industry-academia collaboration, the qualitative results about the benefits and drawbacks of RAs supported the unquantifiable benefits, and uncertainties and risk of the business case.

## 5.2 Summative stage: validating the guidelines

The summative stage will take place once the guidelines will have been adequately shaped and improved. The primary role of this stage will be to validate the version of the guidelines after applying it in *everis* with more practitioners. This evaluation consists of the use of the guidelines in other organizations to design and conduct empirical studies. Organizations analyzing whether to make the strategic move to RA adoption and organizations that face the design and use of RAs based on evidence will benefit from these guidelines.

# 6 CONCLUSIONS

Conducting empirical studies is becoming one of the main sources of communication between practitioners and the academia. We are conducting an action research initiative in *everis*. This has allowed gathering industrial evidence:

- To build a business case of adopting an RA in a public administration of Spain, which is an *everis*' client (Martínez-Fernández et al. [2013b]). The feedback from this study improved the checklist of value-driven data and the REARM economic model. We learned the importance of good practices like time tracking, continuous feedback, test-driven development and continuous integration in order to quantitatively evaluate RAs. We performed a cost-benefit analysis of an RA adoption in a public administration and it showed that the RA pays off after creating 7 small applications. With medium to large applications, this number could be reduced to 2 applications.
- To create an evidence-based information about RAs in *everis*. It includes evidence about: (a) the motivations of *everis*' client organizations to adopt RAs; (b) benefits and drawbacks of using RAs (Martínez-Fernández et al. [2013c]); and (c) artifacts of RAs (Martínez-Fernández et al. [2014]). The feedback from these studies improved the set of relevant criteria of RAs, and our template survey to gather evidence about RAs. Among the main benefits, stakeholders indicated

that the adoption of an RA bring cost savings in the development and maintenance of applications and improved productivity during the design of concrete SAs.

These results have been evaluated by the *everis*' managers involved in the research. Besides, for their widespread use in *everis*, they have been published in form of proposed solutions, internal reports, executive summaries, and pilots run in real projects (Martínez-Fernández and Marques [2014]).

The main contribution of this work is the formulation of guidelines for conducting empirical studies to support building a business case and gathering evidence of RAs. These guidelines consist of stating the context of RAs in industry and their stakeholders, and an assortment of four complementary empirical studies that allow understanding and evaluating RAs. The created guidelines could be used by other organizations outside of our industry-academia collaboration. With this goal in mind, we describe the guidelines in detail for their use. However, practitioners should be aware that conducting empirical studies is time consuming and they should dedicate proper effort.

Future work spreads into two directions. In terms of shaping the guidelines (the formative stage), we need to validate REARM in another *everis*' RA project and to analyze the rest of qualitative data from the survey to gather evidence about RAs. With respect to validation (the summative stage), we plan to apply the guidelines in other organizations if possible.

## ACKNOWLEDGEMENTS

This work has been supported by "Cátedra *everis*" and the Spanish project TIN2010-19130-C02-01. We would also like to thank all participants of the surveys for their kind cooperation.

## COMPETING INTERESTS

The authors declare that they have no competing interests.

# AUTHORS' CONTRIBUTIONS

Every author was important for the completion of this article, however, their previous activities are also important to reach the research results, then, these activities are listed in this section. SMF, CA and XF envisaged the guidelines and the protocol of the studies. HM was responsible of looking for RA projects at *everis*, contacting the participants of the studies to schedule meetings with SMF and DA and provide more information when necessary. The guidelines have been shaped in periodic meeting at *everis* among SMF, CA, XF and HM. SMF and DA performed the face-to-face interviews to the survey participants. All authors read and approved the final manuscript.

# REFERENCES

1. Ali, MS, Babar MA, Schmid K (2009) A comparative survey of economic models for software product lines. In: Software Engineering and Advanced Applications, 2009. SEAA'09. 35th Euromicro Conference on, 275–278.. IEEE. ., [http://ieeexplore.ieee.org/xpl/login.jsp?tp=&arnumber=5349963&url=http%3A%2F%2Fieeexplore.ieee.org%2Fxpls%2Fabs_all.jsp%3Farnumber%3D5349963]
2. Angelov S, Trienekens JJ, Grefen P: Towards a method for the evaluation of reference architectures: Experiences from a case. In *Software Architecture*. Springer, Berlin Heidelberg; 2008:225–240. http://link.springer.com/chapter/10.1007\%2F978-3-540-88030-1_17
3. Angelov S, Grefen P, Greefhorst D: A framework for analysis and design of software reference architectures. *Inform Software Tech* 2012, 54(4):417–431.
4. Angelov S, Trienekens J, Kusters R: Software reference architectures-exploring their usage and design in practice. In *Software Architecture*. Springer, Berlin Heidelberg; 2013:17–24. http://link.springer.com/chapter/10.1007\%2F978-3-642-39031-9_2.
5. Atlassian (2014) Jira: Issue and project tracking software. Accessed 12 Feb 2014., [https://www.atlassian.com/es/software/jira]
6. AUTOSAR (2014) Automotive open system architecture (autosar). . Accessed 12 Feb 2014., [http://www.autosar.org/]
7. Bass, L, Clements P, Kazman R (2003) Software architecture in practice. Addison-Wesley Professional., [http://resources.sei.cmu.edu/library/asset-view.cfm?assetid= 30659]
8. Bass, L, Clements P, Kazman R, Klein M (2008) Evaluating the software architecture competence of organizations. In: Software Architecture, 2008. WICSA 2008. Seventh Working IEEE/IFIP Conference on, IEEE, 249–252., [http://ieeexplore.ieee.org/xpl/login.jsp?tp=&arnumber=4459163&url=http%3A%2F%2Fieeexplore.ieee.org%2Fiel5%2F4459128%2F4459129%2F04459163]
9. Brand, S (2014) Accenture has business-outcome-driven ea capabilities, but doesn't automatically begin with this approach. . Accessed 25 Feb 2014., [https://www.gartner. com/doc/2651816/accenture-businessoutcomedriven-ea-capabilities-doesnt]
10. Brydon-Miller M, Greenwood D, Maguire P: Why action research? *Action Res* 2003, 1(1):9–28.

11. Carriere, J, Kazman R, Ozkaya I (2010) A cost-benefit framework for making architectural decisions in a business context. In: Software Engineering, 2010, ACM/IEEE 32nd International Conference on, IEEE, vol 2, 149–157. ., [http://ieeexplore.ieee.org/xpl/login.jsp?tp=&arnumber=6062148&url=http%3A\%2F%2Fieeexplore.ieee.org%2Fxpls%2Fabs_all.jsp%3Farnumber%3D6062148]
12. Clements, P, Northrop L (2002) Software product lines: practices and patterns. Addison-Wesley Professional., [http://www.addison-wesley.de/9780201703320.html]
13. Clements, P, Kazman R, Klein M (2001) Evaluating software architectures: methods and case studies. Addison-Wesley Professional. ., [http://resources.sei. cmu.edu/library/asset-view.cfm?assetid=30698]
14. Cloutier R, Muller G, Verma D, Nilchiani R, Hole E, Bone M: The concept of reference architectures. *Syst Eng* 2010, 13(1):14–27.
15. Deelstra S, Sinnema M: Product derivation in software product families: a case study. *J Syst Soft* 2005, 74(2):173–194.
16. Eklund, U, Bosch J (2014) Architecture for embedded open software ecosystems. J Syst Softw.
17. Eklund U, Askerdal Ö, Granholm J, Alminger A, Axelsson J: Experience of introducing reference architectures in the development of automotive electronic systems. In *ACM SIGSOFT Software Engineering Notes, vol 30*. ACM, New York; 2005:1–6.
18. Erdogmus, H, Favaro J (2012) The value proposition for agility–a dual perspective. Accessed 3 Mar 2014., [http://www.infoq.com/presentations/Agility-Value]
19. Falessi D, Babar MA, Cantone G, Kruchten P: Applying empirical software engineering to software architecture: challenges and lessons learned. *Empir Software Eng* 2010, 15(3):250–276.
20. Forrester (2014) Forrester's total economic impact (tei). [http://www.forrester.com/ marketing/product/consulting/tei.html], Accessed 12 Feb 2014.
21. Frakes W, Terry C: Software reuse: metrics and models. *ACM Comput Surv (CSUR)* 1996, 28(2):415–435.
22. Gallagher, BP (2000) Using the architecture tradeoff analysis method to evaluate a reference architecture: A case study. Tech. rep., Software Engineering Institute, CMU/SEI-2000-TN-007.
23. Galster M, Avgeriou P: Empirically-grounded reference architectures: a proposal. In *Proceedings of the joint ACM SIGSOFT conference–QoSA and ACM SIGSOFT symposium–ISARCS on Quality of software architectures–QoSA and architecting critical systems–ISARCS*. ACM, New York; 2011:153–158.
24. Galster M, Avgeriou P, Tofan D: Constraints for the design of variability-intensive service-oriented reference architectures–an industrial case study. *Inf Softw Technol* 2013, 2(55):428–441.
25. García-Alonso, J, Olmeda JB, Murillo JM (2010) Java para aplicaciones corporativas de la administración. In: Teniente E Abrahão S (eds)JISBD. IBERGARCETA Pub. S.L. 2010, 263–266. ., [http://www.informatik.uni-trier.de/~ley/db/ conf/jisbd/jisbd2010.html#Garcia-AlonsoOM10]
26. Graaf, B, Van Dijk H, van Deursen A (2005) Evaluating an embedded software reference architecture. industrial experience report In: Software Maintenance and Reengineering, 2005. CSMR 2005. Ninth European Conference on, IEEE, 354–363. ., [http://ieeexplore.ieee.org/xpl/articleDetails.jsp?arnumber=1402153]
27. Herold, S, Mair M (2013) Checking conformance with reference architectures: a case study In: Enterprise Distributed Object Computing Conference (EDOC)2013 17th IEEE International. ., [http://ieeexplore.ieee.org/xpl/ articleDetails. jsp?arnumber=6658265].
28. Jenkins (2014) An extendable open source continuous integration server. . Accessed 12 Feb 2014., [http://jenkins-ci.org/]
29. Lethbridge, T, Sim S, Singer J (2005) Studying software engineers: data collection techniques for software field studies. Empir Software Eng: 311–341. ., [http://link.springer.com/article/10.1007/s10664-005-1290-x]

30. Northrop, LM, Clements PC (2014) A framework for software product line practice, version 5.0. . Accessed 1 Mar 2014., [http://www.sei. cmu.edu/ productlines /frame_report/index.html]
31. Linden FVD, Bosch J, Kamsties E: Software product family evaluation. In *Software Product Lines*. Springer, Berlin Heidelberg; 2004:110–129. http://link.springer .com/chapter/10.1007\%2F978-3-540-24667-1_27.
32. MacCormack A, Baldwin C, Rusnak J: Exploring the duality between product and organizational architectures: a test of the mirroring hypothesis. *Res Pol* 2012, 41(8):1309–1324.
33. Martínez-Fernández, S (2013) Towards supporting the adoption of software reference architectures: an empirically-grounded framework In: Proceedings 11th International Doctoral Symposium on Empirical Software Engineering (IDoESE) at the Empirical Software Engineering International Week; Baltimore, Maryland, USA. available at . Accessed 12 Feb 2014., [http://umbc.edu/eseiw2013/ idoese/pdf /eseiw2013_IDoESE_180.pdf]
34. Martínez-Fernández S, Marques H: Practical experiences in designing and conducting empirical studies in industry-academia collaboration. In *Conducting Empirical Studies in Industry (CESI), 2014 2nd International Workshop on*. ACM, New York; 2014:15–20.
35. Martínez-Fernández, S, Ayala C, Franch X, Ameller D (2013a) A framework for software reference architecture analysis and review In: Memorias del X Workshop Latinoamericano de Ingeniería en Software Experimental ESELAW2013; Montevideo, Uruguay. available at: . Accessed 12 Feb 2014., [http://cibse2013. ort.edu.uy/pdf/ESELAW-ISBN-978-9974-8379-3-5.pdf]
36. Martínez-Fernández, S, Ayala C, Franch X, Marques H (2013b) Rearm: a reuse-based economic model for software reference architectures. In: Favaro J Morisio M (eds) Safe and Secure Software Reuse, Lecture Notes in Computer Science, vol 7925, 97–112. doi:10.1007/978-3-642-38977-1_7.
37. Martínez-Fernández, S, Ayala C, Franch X, Martins Marques H (2013c) Benefits and drawbacks of reference architectures. In: Drira K (ed) Software Architecture, Lecture Notes in Computer Science, vol 7957, 307-310. doi:10.1007/978-3-642-39031-9_26.
38. Martínez-Fernández, S, Ayala C, Franch X, Marques H (2014) Artifacts of software reference architectures: a case study In: Proceedings of the 18th International Conference on Evaluation and Assessment in Software Engineering. doi:10.1145/2601248.2601282.
39. Mattmann, C, Downs R (2010) Reuse of software assets for the NASA Earth science decadal survey missions. Geoscience and Remote Sensing Symposium (IGARSS)2010 IEEE International, vol 1. [http://ieeexplore. ieee.org/xpls /abs_all.jsp?arnumber=5653018]
40. Montagud S, Abrahão S, Insfran E: A systematic review of quality attributes and measures for software product lines. *Software Qual J* 2011, 20: 425–486.
41. Murer, S, Hagen C (2013) 15 Years of Service Oriented Architecture at Credit Suisse: 1–30. . Accessed 25 Feb 2014., [http://ieeexplore.ieee. org/xpls/abs_ all.jsp? arnumber=6654116] Murer, S, Hagen C (2013) 15 Years of Service Oriented Architecture at Credit Suisse: 1–30. . Accessed 25 Feb 2014.
42. Nakagawa EY, Antonino PO, Becker M: Reference architecture and product line architecture: a subtle but critical difference. In *Software Architecture*. Springer, Berlin Heidelberg; 2011:207–211. http://link.springer.com /chapter /10.1007\ %2F978-3-642-23798-0_22
43. NASA (2012) Esds reference architecture working group: Esds reference architecture for the decadal survey era. . Accessed 12 Feb 2014., [https://e arthdata.nasa.gov/sites/default/files/field/document/ESDS%20Reference%20Arch itecture%20v1.1.pdf]
44. Poulin JS: *Measuring software reuse: principles, practices, and economic models*. Addison-Wesley Longman Publishing Co., Inc., Boston; 1997.

45. Qureshi N, Usman M, Ikram N: Evidence in software architecture, a systematic literature review. In *Proceedings of the 17th International Conference on Evaluation and Assessment in Software Engineering*. ACM, New York; 2013:97–106. 10.1145/2460999.2461014
46. Redmine (2014) A flexible project management web application. . Accessed 12 Feb 2014., [http://www.redmine.org/]
47. Reichart, G, Haneberg M (2004) Key drivers for a future system architecture in vehicles In: Convergence International Congress & Exposition On Transportation Electronics. SAE International. [http://papers.sae.org/2004-21-0025/]
48. Reifer, DJ (2002) Making the software business case: improvement by the numbers. Pearson Education. [http://books.google.es/books?id=W61QAAAAMAAJ]
49. SonarSource (2014) Continuous inspection of code quality. . Accessed 12 Feb 2014., [http://www.sonarsource.com/]

# CHAPTER 12

# Application of Informatics for the Enhanced Management of Robotic Operations

**Jungwan Hong, Yongjin (James) Kwon**

*Department of Industrial Engineering, Ajou University, Suwon, South Korea*

## ABSTRACT

In the past, the proposed concept-the application of informatics for robot operations-was difficult to implement due to technological limitations. With the advancement of ICT technologies, the production robots can be integrated within the information network, and the critical data can be processed to reveal the very important information. From the information, better managerial decisions are expected that will ultimately contribute to the organizations' efficiency and competitiveness. In this context, this study explains the merits of quality informatics in the domain of networked robots that are the essential tools for the global production companies. Even though this study merely presents the outcome of robot joint replacement period estimation, the foreseeable advantages of using the proposed method can be numerous. The future environment of global business will even push the boundaries of multinational, distributed production systems, and accelerate the implementation at a faster rate. Accordingly, the brand value of the product is expected to be greater than the country of the manufacturing. The survival of the company will be dependent on the optimized quality level that is encompassing the entire distributed production systems located throughout the whole. Under such circumstances, it can be foreseeable that the innovative ideas and the smart application of advanced technologies should be the priority.

**Keywords:** Informatics for Robotics, Process Information, Visibility, Data Processing, Robot Management

# 1. INTRODUCTION

In South Korea, smartphone and automobile companies are global operations, where a number of production facilities situated in foreign countries are involved. To increase their competitiveness, advanced automated production equipment, such as robots, became a critical component. The foreign production facilities are also interconnected with their headquarters, and the key production activities, such as defect rates and condition of production equipment, are being monitored 24 hours. One of the critical quality control activities is the robot maintenance. However, it is being resorted to the scheduled plan, and this contains the inherent risk of premature spending on replacement. Such is true even for today. Robot operators can hardly relate the robot conditions with the record of robot operations. This situation can be viewed as a consumer trying to purchase a used car without knowing any previous history. The lack of operational history data prohibits the users from taking the robot conditions into consideration [1]. In this context, the purpose of this study is to develop a novel quality informatics system for the networked production robots. The novelty includes 1) the application of informatics concept to the production robots in an effort to attain the component-level data that has not been previously considered; and 2) the robot usage data are directly linked to the managerial decision process that is defined as the quality informatics for the operational aspect of production robots. For that purpose, the proposed quality informatics system collects the robot status data from each axis motor, and process the data to extract the critical information that has not been possible in the past. The critical information is directly related to the decision of motor replacement period, which has a serious financial consequence to the organizations. The robot operational data are collected in real-time, from which the usage and status are monitored. The data represent the motor pulse signals, motor on/off time, motor malfunction data, and motor rotation data of each axis. The work cycle and idle time, and other ancillary data are also recorded in the database. Such data received from the component level have not been previously considered, when the product quality is of concern [2] [3]. Our initial analysis also shows that the robot programming can be adjusted to evenly assign the motion commands over all axes. Therefore, no premature or concentrated wear occurs on one axis, which can seriously hamper the robot positioning accuracy along specific directions. In the past, the inaccurate count for the movement of robot arm means that the robot status is not considered with the product quality. Now, with the ability to collect and analyze the robot axis motion data, a better managerial decision can be materialized. The underlying justification is that the product quality is affected by the equipment status. From the managerial aspects of robot operations, the engineers can instantly identify the robot status; hence a more pragmatic plan can be developed in terms of setting up a new production plan or initiating a critical maintenance for the robots. The overall idea is presented in Figure 1, depicting the new form of QC scheme that has evolved over the existing statistical techniques. This is centered on the notion of informatics [4] [5].

## 2. THE API DEVELOPMENT

To collect the data, the robot control system structure needs to be defined. It is shown in Figure 2. We developed the API (application programming interface) to extract the critical data, which in turn processed into important information. The information will be ultimately used in making a critical decision. The API connects remotely to the networked robots to perform the operations, such as programmed robot executions and robot servo motor on/off. The API extracts and analyzes the data from the robots, and displays the meaningful information to the operator. Finally, the API provides the real-time status as well as the replacement period of the robot axes. This provides only the critical information that directly contributes to the product quality. The structure of API is illustrated in Figure 3.

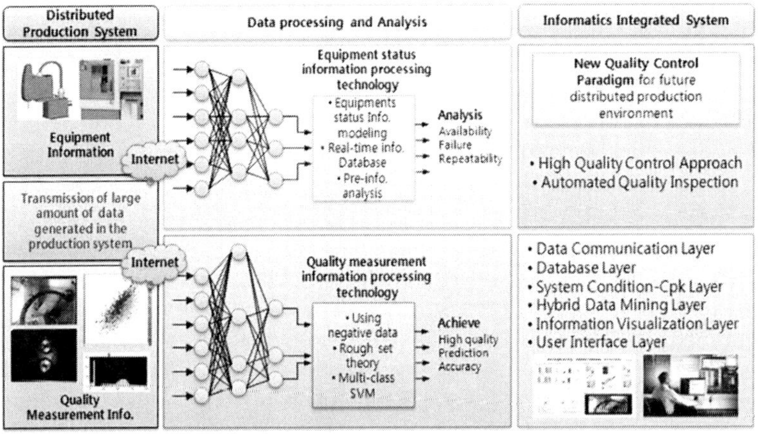


**Figure 1**.A concept of informatics-based quality control approach.

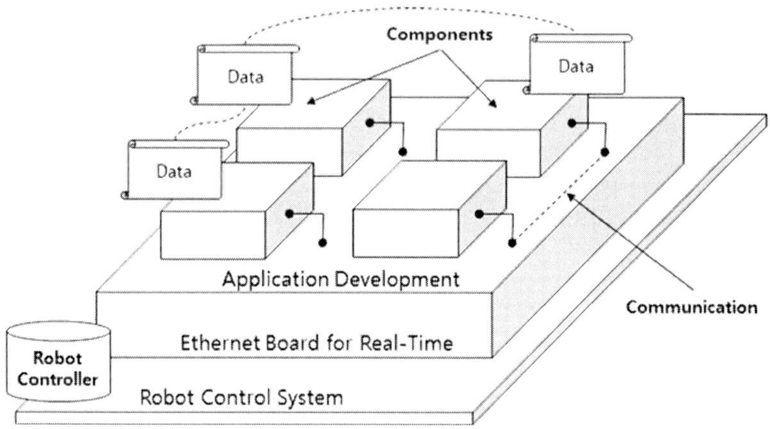


**Figure 2**. Robot control system structure.

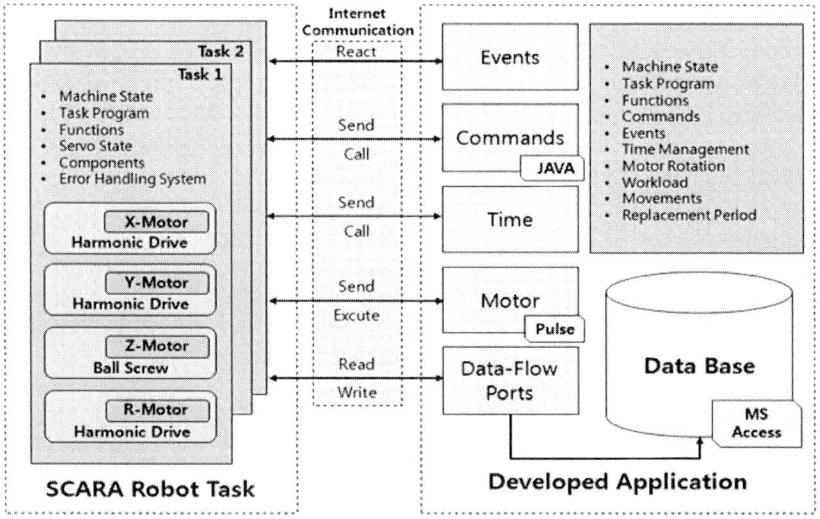


**Figure 3**. The workings of the application.

The API also executes a process of converting from the quality measurement information into knowledge. The quality measurement information to be handled in this layer can be classified in motor speed and various time data. The most notable quality information in this study is the number of revolutions of the motor/harmonic drive. To calculate the number of rotation of the motor/harmonic drive, the pulse movement values stored in the database for each-axis have to be trimmed. For the SCARA robot used in this study, the resolver pulse values are defined per one rotation of each axis. And speed reduction gear (harmonic drive) reduction ratio is also defined. Table 1 shows the reduction ratio and resolver pulse value per degrees of axis for the SCARA robot.

# 3. EXPERIMENTAL RESULTS

To calculate the robot maintenance period, this study focuses on the most critical component, namely the harmonic drive assembly. The harmonic drive converts the torque from the electric servo motor into a higher value with the use of reduction gears, while at the same time, provides a structural rigidity between the motor and the rotating robot arm. Therefore, it should be replaced at a regular interval and the care must be exercised in order to precisely track the usage of it. The replacement period can be set at a regular interval.

For example, the user may replace it once every 6 year, or it can be replaced as a result of actual usage. It's much better to replace it based on actual usage, and in order to do that, the moving distance of each axis must be calculated. This process is shown in Figure 4. In the work envelope of X/Y plane, when the robot moves from P1 to P2, the pulse variation values

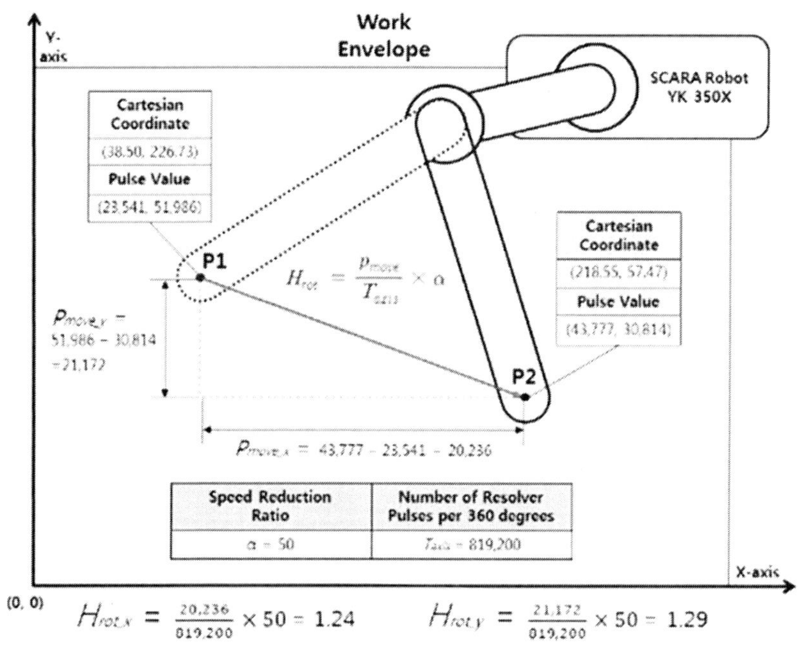


**Figure 4**. The workings of the application.

**Table 1**. Speed reduction ratio and resolver pulses per degrees/movement.

| Axis | Speed Reduction Ratio ($u$) | No. of Resolver Pulses per 360 Degrees | No. of Resolver Pulses per Lead Movement |
|---|---|---|---|
| X | 50 | 819,200 | N/A |
| Y | 50 | 819,200 | N/A |
| Z | 50 | N/A | 16,384 |
| R | 50 | 819,200 | N/A |

of X/Y-axis represent $P_{move\_x}$ = 20,236 and $P_{move\_y}$ = 21,172, respectively. B by applying the reduction ratio of 50 and the number of resolver pulses for 360 degrees (i.e., $T_{axis}$ = 819,200), it is possible to obtain the number of harmonic drive rotations. Then, the analytical results are shown to the operator. Figure 5 illustrates the algorithm and source code for the calculation. As shown, it processes the rotation and time data of motor/harmonic drive stored in the database. Then, the results are visually presented to the operator with analysis. Figure 6 illustrates some of the screen shots of the API. Integrated monitoring system indicates the current status of all components in the robot cell (two SCARA robots, one linear robot, a vision sensor, a web cam, etc.), while the second image shows the detailed usage information of the YK-220X SCARA robot. Just by simply looking at the display, it is possible to grasp the details of each robot at a component level. Figure 7(a) shows the results of motor rotation, using the original program instructions. Upon analysis, the operator can notice the excessive burden on the Y-axis motor, which will eventually wear out the Y-axis motor earlier than other motors. This also creates the positioning accuracy problem, when a specific motor accumulates too much rotational work.

To counter this problem, a minor adjustment to the program has been made to balance the work among the motors. With the new program, the robot has been running for many hours and the outcome is derived from the data. The result is illustrated in Figure 7(b), which shows the more even distribution of work among the axes in order to prevent an excessive wear on a single axis. At the same time, the replacement period has been substantially shortened, which will save a lot of money for the companies. The comparison is also provided in Table 2 and Table 3.

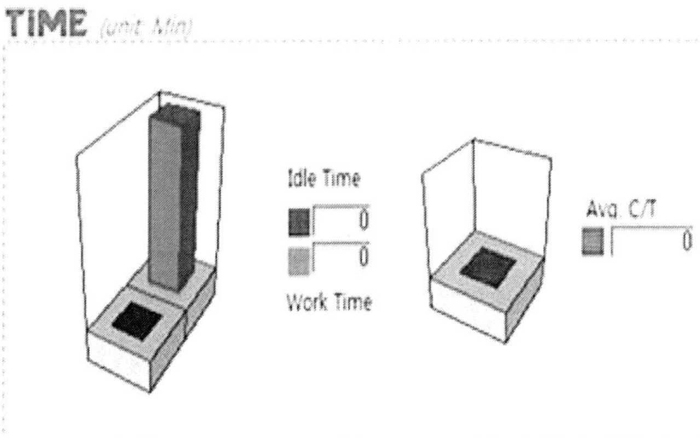


```
Private Sub wxWinsock1_OnDataArrival(ByVal bytesTotal As Long) 'display data

  Dim sBuffer As String
  Dim sBuffer2 As String

  Dim rotation As Variant
  Dim rx As Variant
  Dim ry As Variant
  Dim rz As Variant
  Dim rr As Variant


  wxWinsock1.GetData sBuffer
  sBuffer = Trim(StrConv(sBuffer, VbStrConv.vbUpperCase))
  If (InStr(sBuffer, "LOGIN")) Then
          wxWinsock1.SendData (txtScaraUser.Text & vbCrLf)
  End If
  If (InStr(sBuffer, "PASSWORD:")) Then
          wxWinsock1.SendData (txtScaraPassword.Text & vbCrLf)
          authenticate = True
  End If
  If (InStr(sBuffer, "OK")) And robotbusy = True Then
        If countOK <= 3 Then
        countOK = countOK + 1
        If countOK = 3 Then
        countOK = 0
        robotbusy = False
        End If
        End If
  End If
```

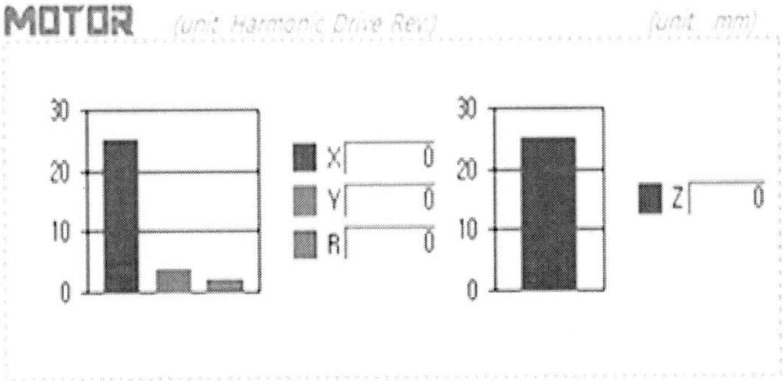


```
Private Sub cmdScaraConnect_Click() 'connection to Ethernet card

Dim nPort As Long

nPort = txtScaraPort.Text

If cmdScaraConnect.Caption = "Connect" Then

 sServer = Trim(txtScaraIP.Text)

 If InStr(sServer, "://") > 0 Then sServer = Mid(sServer, InStr(sServer, "://") + 3)
  If InStr(sServer, "/") > 1 Then
   sPage = Mid(sServer, InStr(sServer, "/"))
   sServer = Left(sServer, InStr(sServer, "/") - 1)
    If InStr(sPage, "#") > 1 Then sPage = Left(sPage, InStr(sPage, "#") - 1)

    Else
     sPage = "/"
    End If

     If InStr(sServer, ":") > 1 Then
      nPort = Mid(sServer, InStr(sServer, ":") + 1)
      sServer = Left(sServer, InStr(sServer, ":") - 1)
     End If

   wxWinsock1.Connect sServer, nPort 'connection to Ethernet card (sServer is IP address.
  Else
   wxWinsock1.SendData "LOGOUT" & vbCrLf
   controlButton cmdScaraConnect, "Connect"
   txtScaraSend.Enabled = False
   cmdScaraSend.Enabled = False
   cmdServoOn.Enabled = False
   txtScaraIP.Enabled = True
   txtScaraPort.Enabled = True
   txtScaraUser.Enabled = True
   txtScaraPassword.Enabled = True
```

**Figure 5**. The source code and algorithm for calculation.

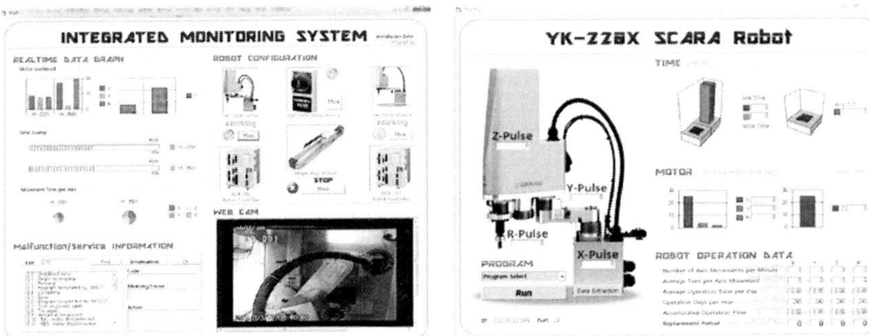


**Figure 6**. Snapshots of the developed API. (a) Integrated monitoring application; (b) Detailed robot status information.

**Table 2**. Comparative analysis for YK-220X robot: before improvement.

| | Before Improvement-YK-220X | | | |
|---|---|---|---|---|
| Axis | X | Y | Z | R |
| No. of axis movements per min (n) | 10 | 21 | 15 | 9 |
| Average turn per axis movement ($\theta$) | 0.06 | 0.18 | 0.07 | 0.10 |
| Speed (%) | 100 | 100 | 100 | 100 |
| Speed reduction ratio (N) | 50 | 50 | 12 mm | 50 |
| Operation time/day (h) | 24 | 24 | 24 | 24 |
| Operation time/year (d) | 365 | 365 | 365 | 365 |
| **Replacement period (years)** | **9** | **2** | **5** | **6** |

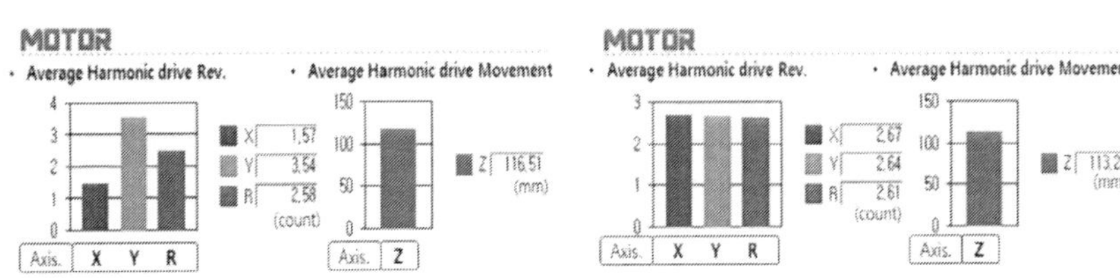


(a) (b)

**Figure 7**. Actual usage of each axis for the YK-220X SCARA robot. (a) YK-220X robot: before improvement; (b) After improvement as a result of applying the quality informatics concept.

**Table 3**. Comparative analysis for YK-220X robot: after improvement.

| Before Improvement-YK-220X | | | | |
|---|---|---|---|---|
| Axis | X | Y | Z | R |
| No. of axis movements per min (n) | 11 | 18 | 15 | 5 |
| Average turn per axis movement ($\theta$) | 0.07 | 0.05 | 0.06 | 0.15 |
| Speed (%) | 100 | 100 | 100 | 100 |
| Speed reduction ratio (N) | 50 | 50 | 12 mm | 50 |
| Operation time/day (h) | 24 | 24 | 24 | 24 |
| Operation time/year (d) | 365 | 365 | 365 | 365 |
| **Replacement period (years)** | 7 | 6 | 6 | 8 |

# 4. CONCLUSION

In the past, the proposed concept was difficult to implement due to technological limitations. With the advancement of ICT technologies, the production robots can be integrated within the information network, and the critical data can be processed to reveal the very important information. From the information, better managerial decisions are expected that will ultimately contribute to the organizations' efficiency and competitiveness. In this context, this study explains the merits of quality informatics in the domain of networked robots that are the essential tools for the global production companies. The future environment of global business will even push the boundaries of multinational, distributed production systems, and accelerate the implementation at a faster rate. Accordingly, the brand value of the product is expected to be greater than the country of the manufacturing. The survival of the company will be dependent on the optimized quality level that is encompassing the entire distributed production systems located throughout the whole. Under such circumstances, it can be foreseeable that the innovative ideas and the smart application of advanced technologies should be the priority.

# ACKNOWLEDGEMENTS

This research was supported by the Basic Science Research Program through the National Research Foundation (NRF), funded by the Ministry of Education, Republic of Korea (Grant No. NRF-2013R1A1A2006108). The authors wish to express sincere gratitude for the financial support.

## CITE THIS PAPER

Jungwan Hong, Yongjin (James) Kwon (2015) Application of Informatics for the Enhanced Management of Robotic Operations. *Journal of Computer and Communications*,**03**,71-77.

## REFERENCES

1. Committee on Visionary Manufacturing (1998) Visionary Manufacturing Challenges for 2020. National Academic Press, Washington DC.
2. Shi, J.J. and Zhou, S.Y. (2009) Quality Control and Improvement for Multistage Systems: A Survey. IIE Transactions, 41, 744-753.
3. Chan, H.K. (2011) Supply Chain Systems: Recent Trend in Research and Applications. IEEE Systems Journal, 5, 2-5.
4. Stepanskiy, L. and Kwon, Y. (2010) Modeling of Robot Availability for the Network-Controllable Production System, Journal of Concurrent Engineering: Research & Applications, 18, 303-310.
5. Sarkisov, L. and Kim, J. (2013) Computational Structure Characterization Tools for the Era of Material Informatics. Special Issue on Molecular Modelling in Chemical Engineering, 121, 322-330.

# CHAPTER 13

# The impact of Information Technology on Job Related Factors lik e Health and Safety, Job Satisfaction, Performance, Productivity and Work Life Balance

**Ratna R[1] and Kaur T[2*]**

*[1]PhD Scholar (IIT Kharagpur) and Assistant Professor (HR and OB), Amity Business School, Amity University, Noida-201301, Uttar Pradesh, India*

*[2]Academic Co-ordinator, Quality Assurance and Enhancement Cell, Amity University, Amity Lucknow Campus, Uttar Pradesh, India*

## ABSTRACT

The impact of Information Technology on workplaces, individuals and society as a whole has increased dramatically during the last two decades of the 21st century. This period has seen maturation in the field of digital computing, combined with the use of telecommunications technology, in order to link many computers into what is 'virtually' a very large single network, the Internet. Data has become widely accessible, and readily inter-related. Implementation of new technology has lead to many changes in the workplace. This paper aims to study the impact of technology on various Job related factors, 5 shortlisted for the study i.e. Health and Safety, Job Satisfaction, Performance, Productivity and Work Life Balance. Which Job factor is getting affected to maximum extent with the introduction of technology? The study was done with the help of questionnaire based on Likert scale. Data was collected from 100 employees of Barco and CMC Ltd. Convenience sampling method was used. Data was analyzed through SPSS Software and excel to find out that Performance is the most impacted factor by introduction of new technology, followed by Job Satisfaction, Health and Safety, Productivity and work life balance. The factor analysis converted them into three components in which component 1 contributed more towards the impact of technology.

**Keywords:** Information technology; Workplace; Digital computing; Internet; Health and safety; Job satisfaction; Performance; Productivity; Work life balance

# INTRODUCTION

## INTRODUCTION TO INFORMATION TECHNOLOGY

IT, short for Information Technology, and pronounced as separate letters, Information Technology is the application of computers and various techniques, to handle masses of data. This broad subject is concerned with all aspects of managing and processing information, especially within a large organization or company. Computers and communications technologies form the backbone of Information Technology (IT). To a large extent it underlies the rise of modern business and economy.

Constantly, such a technology forces an industry to learn, to acquire, to adapt and to change its very mindset, let alone its technical knowledge. The impact of IT on workplaces, employment relations, individuals and society as a whole has increased dramatically during the last two decades of the 21st century. This period has witnessed maturation in the field of **DIGITAL COMPUTING**, with the combined usage of telecommunications technology, in order to link many computers, into what is 'virtually' a very large single network, the Internet. It is invading the very core of the way things are being done including industrial relations.

As stated by Peter Drucker, recognized management guru:

"Management has to recognize that there is no one technology that pertains to any industry, on the contrary, all technologies are capable to have an impact on any industry."

Data has become widely accessible, and readily inter-related. This matrix of widely inter-connected computers is being slowly but steadily augmented by the incorporation of robotics and artificial intelligence. This phenomenon can best be described as "digital business" or "digital economy", embracing e-commerce and the **INTERNET**, but extends much further. This makes IT a sole object that has the most pervasive effect on the modern society today. Organisations at global level are changing the way they do business in adopting the information revolution. Its impact can be seen in terms of:

- Changing relationships between companies and their customers and suppliers.
- The way they organize themselves.
- The very core of the business itself – the labour force.
- Its internal processes as well.

## IMPACT OF TECHNOLOGY ON HEALTH AND SAFETY

Occupational **HEALTH AND SAFETY** is a discipline with a broad scope aiming at "Promotion and maintenance of the highest degree of physical, mental and social well-being of workers that is the "whole person" in all occupations; prevention among workers of adverse effects on health caused by their working conditions; the protection of workers in their employment from risks resulting from factors adverse to health; the placing and maintenance of workers in an occupational environment adapted to physical and mental needs; the adaptation of work to humans.

Successful occupational health and safety practice requires the collaboration and participation of both employers and workers in health and safety programmes, and involves the consideration of issues relating to occupational medicine, industrial hygiene, toxicology, education, engineering safety, ergonomics, psychology, etc. With the introduction of new technology human health and safety can be well protected against:

- Communicable Diseases - Vector borne diseases (e.g. malaria), sanitary hygiene diseases, risk associated with handing of infectious wastes;
- Injury - Risk of accidents from traffic, explosions, falls, heat stress, operation of machinery, handling of physically hazardous wastes and resources (e.g. sharps), minimize loss of hearing; and
- Exposure to hazardous chemicals - Inhalation (e.g. air pollution), avoid dermal contact, ingestion of contaminated food and water (e.g. pesticide residue) of hazardous chemicals and of radioactive material.

## IMPACT OF TECHNOLOGY ON JOB SATISFACTION

**Job Satisfaction** is the favourableness or un-favourableness with which the employee views his work. It expresses the amount of agreement between one's expectation of the job and the rewards that the job provides. The nature of one's job environment is an important part of life because ultimately Job Satisfaction influences one's general life satisfaction. Job Satisfaction, thus, is the result of various attitudes possessed by an employee. In a narrow sense, these attitudes are related to the job under condition with such specific factors such as Wages, Employment Supervision, Working conditions, Social/Human relation on the job, Prompt settlement of grievances and Fair treatment by employer. However, more comprehensive approach requires that Inter and Intra Personal factors to be included before a complete understanding of job satisfaction can be obtained. Such factors as employee's age, health temperature, desire and level of aspiration should be considered. Further his family relationship, social status, recreational outlets, activity in the organizations etc. contribute deeply to job satisfaction.

Information Technology (IT) has played an important role in business since the 1950s and the use of technology to reduce costs, improve operations, enhance customer service, and improve communications has progressed rapidly over the past four decades.

Job satisfaction is an important criterion for the success of an organization where it is closely associated with job turnover and life satisfaction. Using new technologies such as Computer-Aided Manufacturing (CAM), Virtual Reality (VR), Expert Systems (ES), and the Internet can give companies an edge. New technologies can result in employees "working smarter" as well as providing high-quality products and more efficient services to customers. Companies that have realized greatest gains from new technology have human resource management practices that support the use of technology to create what is known as high-**PERFORMANCE** work systems. Work, training, programs and reward systems often need to be reconfigured to support employees' use of new technology.

## IMPACT OF TECHNOLOGY ON PERFORMANCE

Performance is the accomplishment of a given task measured against preset known standards of accuracy, completeness, cost, and speed. Use of technology within the ethical limits definitely benefits the organisation, along with improvisation in individual and group performance. On one hand, employee workload reduces through technological advancement; on the other number of employees to perform a task is also reduced, thus reducing job opportunities. Companies use advanced technologies to check and evaluate employee's performance via Human resource management department. To drive **PRODUCTIVITY** and manage human capital, HR department leverages emerging technology to keep up with the market trend. Current technology trends impacting HR are Outsourcing and focus on value that HR brings to the organisation. The demand for better service performance has driven a technological trend towards more powerful, integrated and scalable system components.

## IMPACT OF TECHNOLOGY ON PRODUCTIVITY GROWTH

Productivity is one of the most closely watched indicators of longterm economic prospects. Rising productivity is the key to making possible permanent increases in the standard of living. Changes in technology are the only source of permanent increase in productivity, but a number of transient factors can affect both true and "measured" productivity. For example, workers may work harder during periods of high demand and firms may use their capital assets more intensively by running factories for extra shifts; both factors can lead measured productivity to be too high relative to actual technological progress. Similarly, during periods of high demand, productivity can rise because firms take advantage of increasing returns to scale; however some people argue that this effect is not permanent and should be discounted when measuring long-run technical change.

## IMPACT OF TECHNOLOGY ON WORK-LIFE BALANCE

Work- Life Balance is a comfortable state of equilibrium achieved between a person's primary priorities of their employment position and their personal lifestyle. To put it in simple words demands of a working individual's career should not overwhelm his ability to enjoy a satisfying personal life beyond the business environment. These days, we have so many potentially labour saving technological devices, which we have deeply inculcated in our daily practices but with a logical question: to what extent do such advances increase rather than decrease workload and stress? New technology can clearly enable us to work faster and more efficiently, and it facilitates flexible and remote working e.g. work from home, preparing quick presentations and reports with use of cell phones besides computers and laptop but it can also mean that we cannot ever really get away and switch off.

# LITERATURE REVIEW

Derks et al. examined the impact of work related smartphone use on daily recovery from work-related efforts to which workhome interference (WHI) is an important inhibitor. Contrary, to their hypothesis it was found out that smartphone user did not experience more overall work-home interference (WHI) than nonusers. For control group WHI was positively related to psychological detachment, relaxation, mastery and control activities, implying that being connected to work in evening hours through smartphone's had consequences only to the extent to which employees succeed in recovering [1].

Mazmanian et al. studied how wireless e-mail devices specifically the Blackberry were incorporated into daily lives of professionals and its consequent social impact. Findings suggested these Blackberry communication entailed 3 important dualities having conflicting consequences for work and lives of plymouth members: continuity and asynchronicity, engagement and withdrawal, autonomy and addiction, making it diffcult for memebers to dis-engage from work and blending among people [2].

Ali analysed employment relation systems of three Asian countries-China, India, and Korea. He made a case for diversion in employment relation systems that technological advances, improved communications, economic liberalization, and increased international competition has brought in an era of economic, institutional and cultural integration. Under globalization the workplace practices are under a constant state of movement. Academicians not only analysed the benefits and the deleterious effects of this phenomenon on the employment relations of developed and under-developed nations, but also stirring up the debate whether the industrial relations systems of countries are converging or diverging [3].

Bakker gives an overview of research on the impact of e-mail provided by personal computers and smart phone devices based on Job-demands resources (JD-R) model as a framework. The results of the studies were interpreted to show which aspects of e-mail communication can be considered as demands and resources, and hence complicate or facilitate our working life. Increasing pressure of excessive amounts of e-mail and prompt reply seems to be disproportionally loading the recipient, moreover a smart phone on one hand increases the flexibility of an employee on the other hand facilitates long working hours with a risk of disturbed work-home balance [4].

Bill identified contributing influences of an individual's attitude towards a technological innovation/ improvisation in the **WORKPLACE**. Multiple factors stemming from individuals knowledge, beliefs, values, cognitive/

mechanical ability, gender, organisational culture and social information processing tend to influence an individual's attitude. Now, since an organisation comprises of many individuals with various combination of above, careful consideration must be given before introducing any innovation. The study observes higher adoption rates where employees have control over the innovation and its implementation therefore the organisation must provide information sharing, risk-free environment and evolve a system of learning [5].

Morris and Dillon focussed on understanding the factors which influence user acceptance of information technology. They reviewed literature that demonstrates the nature of technological acceptance, which is mediated by distinct factor groups related to: the psychology of the users, the design process of information technology, and the quality of the technology in user terms. The research offered insights that could support the derivation of reliable predictions of user acceptance. However, potentially overlapping theories seem to exist, though independent of each other creating possibilities for unifying this framework to extend innovation diffusion concepts and systems design models (particularly user-centered design) into a formal theory of user acceptance of information technology [6].

Gudmundsdottir investigated that great changes have been discovered with the introduction of technology in the last decade, regarding the organization of work. The results show that when dividing fishing factories into three technological stages; low technology, middle technology and high technology, the job strain was highest and the decision authority by the employee was lowest in the high technological factories. This even had an impact on health and atmosphere at the workplace, where the employees in the high technological factories were more likely to complain about several health problems as well as about low degrees of cheerfulness at the workplace and tiresome jobs. However, initially these same people were most positive towards the implementation of the high technology and the new way of organizing their job that the technology introduced. This effect has made the psychosocial and physical working environment tougher, especially for women [7].

Bresnahan investigated that information technology (IT) and associated changes in work organization were important causes of shift in labour demand in favour of high-wage, high-skill work, which contributed to a substantial rise in income inequality in the United States. Specifically, it was found out that IT use is correlated with a new workplace organization that includes broader job responsibilities for line workers, more decentralized decision-making and more self-managing teams. Therefore, both IT and new organization are correlated with worker skill, measured in a variety of ways. Significantly, firms which attempt to implement only one of the hypothesized complements without the others are less productive than firms which invest in all the complements. Taken together, the results highlight the importance of organizational changes stimulated by IT in the changing demand workers of different types [8].

Vintangcol stresses on the importance of Information Technology (IT) and that computers and communication technologies form the backbone of IT. To a large extent it underlies the rise of modern business and economy; however on a continuous basis such a technology forces an industry to learn, to acquire, to adapt, to change its very mindset, let alone its technical knowledge. IT has invaded the very core of the way things are done - including industrial relations, which is grooming the work place as well as the employment relations [9].

## MATERIALS AND METHODS

### OBJECTIVES

a) To study the impact of technology on various job related factors 'Job Satisfaction', 'Productivity', 'Performance', 'Health and Safety' and '**Work Life Balance**' respectively via correlation.

b) To study which factor is most affected by the implementation of new technology via Factor Analysis.

### RATIONALE OF THE STUDY

The significance of the study is to understand the impact of technology on various factors like job satisfaction, productivity etc. and which factor is the most affected by the implementation of new technology.

### QUESTIONNAIRE DESIGN

The questionnaire measures the impact of technology on various factors like Performance, Job Satisfaction, Productivity, Health and Safety, Work Life Balance. Questionnaire is based on Likert Scale and designed according to the objectives of the present study.

### RESEARCH DESIGN

Descriptive Research: Through Survey Method

## STATISTICAL TOOLS

**SAMPLE SIZE:** The overall sample size in this study is one hundred (100).

**SAMPLING TECHNIQUE:** The sampling technique used is convenience sampling.

**SAMPLE DESCRIPTION:** The employees working with IT sector.

## DATA COLLECTION TECHNIQUES

**PRIMARY DATA:** It was collected by personally interviewing the employees with the help of the questionnaire made for the purpose.

**SECONDARY DATA:** It was collected from newspapers, magazines journals, online resources etc.

## PILOT TEST

A pilot study was done on 40 samples to analyze the process and the possible outcomes of the questions to be asked.

## RELIABILITY

The data collected by the employees working in IT sector was analyzed with the help of SPSS (**TABLES 1** and **2**).

**TABLE 1:** Case processing summary.

| | | N | % |
|---|---|---|---|
| Cases | Valid | 40 | 72.7 |
| | Excluded[a] | 15 | 27.3 |
| | Total | 55 | 100.0 |

[a]Listwise deletion based on all variables in the procedure.

**TABLE 2:** Reliability statistics.

| Cronbach's Alpha | N of Items |
|---|---|
| 0.825 | 25 |

# RESULTS

## ANALYSIS PART-1

The new technology implemented in the organisations was found with the help of personal interviews of HR Managers of various companies like CMC and Barco. The various new technologies implemented were:-

- New software like Taleo, SAP etc
- Introduction of HRIS

## ANALYSIS PART-2

The questionnaire was broken into 5 major sections each having 25 questions. The first five questions determined the impact of technology on 'Job Satisfaction', then 'Productivity', 'Performance', 'Health and Safety' and 'Work Life Balance' respectively.

The answers to the questions of 100 employees were analysed based on Likert Scale, where answers were graded as per the following **TABLE 3**.

**TABLE 3:** Likert scale.

| | Score |
|---|---|
| Strongly Disagree | 1 |
| Disagree | 2 |
| Neither Agree nor Disagree | 3 |
| Agree | 4 |
| Strongly Agree | 5 |

Thereafter, average of the sections was taken into consideration and a correlation between the sectional average and the overall average was calculated.

Here we are assuming that if the sectional average is higher, the impact of technology is going to be much higher. For e.g. if the sectional average of 'Job Satisfaction' is 4 and the overall average is 3.6, then we infer that Job Satisfaction is much higher that Productivity of the employee (**TABLE 4**).

**TABLE 4:** Correlation among various parameters as per feedback of 100 respondents.

| Job Satisfaction | Productivity | Performance | Health and Safety | Work Life Balance | Average All |
|---|---|---|---|---|---|
| 1.4 | 1.6 | 2.4 | 1 | 1.8 | 1.64 |
| 1.4 | 1.6 | 2 | 2 | 1.2 | 1.64 |
| 1.4 | 1.6 | 2.8 | 2 | 1.2 | 1.8 |
| 1 | 1 | 2.8 | 2 | 2.8 | 1.92 |
| 1 | 1 | 3.8 | 3 | 3.8 | 2.52 |
| 1.6 | 1.4 | 3 | 3 | 3 | 2.4 |
| 1.6 | 1.4 | 3.2 | 4 | 4 | 2.84 |
| 1.6 | 1.4 | 2.4 | 1 | 1 | 1.48 |
| 2.6 | 2.4 | 2.8 | 2 | 1.2 | 2.2 |
| 1.4 | 1.6 | 3.2 | 1 | 1.8 | 1.8 |
| 1.6 | 1.4 | 2.4 | 1 | 1.8 | 1.64 |
| 1.6 | 1.4 | 2 | 2 | 2 | 1.8 |
| 1.6 | 1.4 | 3 | 3 | 1.4 | 2.08 |
| 1.4 | 1.6 | 2.8 | 2 | 1.2 | 1.8 |
| 1.4 | 1.6 | 2 | 2 | 1.2 | 1.64 |
| 1.6 | 1.4 | 2 | 2 | 1.2 | 1.64 |
| 1 | 1 | 3 | 3 | 2.2 | 2.04 |
| 1 | 1 | 3 | 3 | 2.2 | 2.04 |
| 2.2 | 1.8 | 2.8 | 2 | 2 | 2.16 |
| 2.8 | 2.2 | 2 | 2 | 1.2 | 2.04 |
| 2.2 | 1.8 | 2.4 | 1 | 2.6 | 2 |
| 2.8 | 2.2 | 4 | 1 | 2.6 | 2.52 |
| 1 | 1 | 2.4 | 1 | 1 | 1.28 |
| 1 | 1 | 2.8 | 2 | 1.2 | 1.6 |
| 1.6 | 1.4 | 3.6 | 2 | 1.2 | 1.96 |
| 2.4 | 2.6 | 2.8 | 2 | 1.2 | 2.2 |
| 1.6 | 1.4 | 2.8 | 2 | 1.2 | 1.8 |
| 1 | 1 | 2.4 | 1 | 1 | 1.28 |
| 1.4 | 1.6 | 2.4 | 1 | 1 | 1.48 |
| 1.4 | 1.6 | 3.2 | 1 | 1 | 1.64 |
| 1.8 | 2.2 | 3.2 | 1 | 1 | 1.84 |
| 2.4 | 2.6 | 2.4 | 1 | 1.8 | 2.04 |
| 2.8 | 3.2 | 2.4 | 1 | 1.8 | 2.24 |
| 2.8 | 3.2 | 3.2 | 1 | 1.8 | 2.4 |
| 1.8 | 2.2 | 2.8 | 2 | 2 | 2.16 |
| 3 | 3 | 2.8 | 2 | 2 | 2.56 |
| 2.2 | 1.8 | 2 | 2 | 2 | 2 |
| 1 | 1 | 2.2 | 3 | 2.2 | 1.88 |
| 1.4 | 1.6 | 3.8 | 3 | 2.2 | 2.4 |
| 1.4 | 1.6 | 2.2 | 3 | 2.2 | 2.08 |
| 4 | 4 | 4 | 4 | 4 | 4 |
| 4 | 4 | 4 | 4 | 4 | 4 |
| 3 | 3 | 3 | 3 | 3 | 3 |
| 3 | 3 | 3 | 3 | 3 | 3 |
| 5 | 5 | 5 | 5 | 5 | 5 |
| 3 | 3 | 3 | 3 | 3 | 3 |
| 3 | 3 | 3 | 3 | 3 | 3 |

| | | | | | |
|---|---|---|---|---|---|
| 2 | 2 | 2 | 2 | 2 | 2 |
| 4 | 4 | 4 | 4 | 4 | 4 |
| 3 | 3 | 3 | 3 | 3 | 3 |
| 4 | 4 | 4 | 4 | 4 | 4 |
| 3 | 3 | 3 | 3 | 3 | 3 |
| 3 | 3 | 3 | 3 | 3 | 3 |
| 2 | 2 | 2 | 2 | 2 | 2 |
| 1 | 1 | 4 | 1 | 1 | 1.6 |
| 2 | 2 | 2 | 2 | 2 | 2 |
| 1 | 1 | 4 | 1 | 1 | 1.6 |
| 1 | 1 | 4 | 1 | 1 | 1.6 |
| 1 | 1 | 4 | 1 | 1 | 1.6 |
| 2 | 2 | 2 | 2 | 2 | 2 |
| 3 | 3 | 3 | 3 | 3 | 3 |
| 1 | 1 | 4 | 1 | 1 | 1.6 |
| 1 | 1 | 4 | 1 | 1 | 1.6 |
| 2 | 2 | 2 | 2 | 2 | 2 |
| 2 | 2 | 2 | 2 | 2 | 2 |
| 2 | 2 | 2 | 2 | 2 | 2 |
| 1 | 1 | 4 | 1 | 1 | 1.6 |
| 1 | 1 | 4 | 1 | 1 | 1.6 |
| 1 | 1 | 4 | 1 | 1 | 1.6 |
| 4 | 4 | 4 | 4 | 4 | 4 |
| 4 | 4 | 4 | 4 | 4 | 4 |
| 5 | 5 | 5 | 5 | 5 | 5 |
| 4 | 4 | 4 | 4 | 4 | 4 |
| 4 | 4 | 4 | 4 | 4 | 4 |
| 5 | 5 | 5 | 5 | 5 | 5 |
| 4 | 4 | 4 | 4 | 4 | 4 |
| 3 | 3 | 3 | 3 | 3 | 3 |
| 3 | 3 | 3 | 3 | 3 | 3 |
| 4 | 4 | 4 | 4 | 4 | 4 |
| 4 | 4 | 4 | 4 | 4 | 4 |
| 5 | 5 | 5 | 5 | 5 | 5 |
| 5 | 5 | 5 | 5 | 5 | 5 |
| 3 | 3 | 3 | 3 | 3 | 3 |
| 4 | 4 | 4 | 4 | 4 | 4 |
| 4 | 4 | 4 | 4 | 4 | 4 |
| 5 | 5 | 5 | 5 | 5 | 5 |
| 4 | 4 | 4 | 4 | 4 | 4 |
| 4 | 4 | 4 | 4 | 4 | 4 |
| 5 | 5 | 5 | 5 | 5 | 5 |
| 5 | 5 | 5 | 5 | 5 | 5 |
| 4 | 4 | 4 | 4 | 4 | 4 |
| 3 | 3 | 3 | 3 | 3 | 3 |
| 2 | 2 | 2 | 2 | 2 | 2 |
| 3 | 3 | 3 | 3 | 3 | 3 |
| 1 | 1 | 4 | 1 | 1 | 1.6 |
| 3 | 3 | 3 | 3 | 3 | 3 |
| 4 | 4 | 4 | 4 | 4 | 4 |
| 4 | 4 | 4 | 4 | 4 | 4 |
| 5 | 5 | 5 | 5 | 5 | 5 |
| 3 | 3 | 3 | 3 | 3 | 3 |
| 1281 | 1279 | 1636 | 1320 | 1296 | 5531 |
| 23.16% | 23.12% | 29.58% | 23.87% | 23.43% | 1 |

Interpretation: it is observed that the correlation numbers for each of the sections were very much similar, showing strong correlation between 'Job Satisfaction', 'Productivity', 'Health and Safety' and 'Work Life Balance' as compared with the total sum of all the answers, except 'Performance' which is showing a stronger correlation against total sum, concluding that 'Technology' has the highest impact on 'Performance' of the employees (**TABLES 5A** and **5B**).

**TABLE 5A:** Average overall correlation among various parameters.

| Correlation Factor Against | Job Satisfaction | Productivity | Performance | Health and Safety | Work Life Balance |
|---|---|---|---|---|---|
| Total Sum | 0.92 | 0.90 | 0.93 | 0.91 | 0.89 |

**TABLE 5B:** Detailed workout of average correlation among various parameters.

| | Job Satisfaction | Productivity | Performance | Health and Safety | Work Life Balance | Average All |
|---|---|---|---|---|---|---|
| Job Satisfaction | 1 | | | | | |
| Productivity | 0.985121223 | 1 | | | | |
| Performance | 0.805863384 | 0.788482095 | 1 | | | |
| Health & Safety | 0.734803452 | 0.70025149 | 0.881448331 | 1 | | |
| WorkLife Balance | 0.744412714 | 0.71774545 | 0.77128782 | 0.870706485 | 1 | |
| Average All | 0.926722 | 0.908803 | 0.930373 | 0.919592 | 0.896507 | 1 |

Interpretation: The correlation was calculated in excel and the result is shown above. It is observed that after the implementation of new technology, performance was the most impacted (**TABLE 6**).

**TABLE 6:** Percentage contribution of various parameters [Impact of technology on various factors (correlation)].

| | Job Satisfaction | Productivity | Performance | Health and Safety | Work Life Balance |
|---|---|---|---|---|---|
| Total % | 23.16% | 23.12% | 29.58% | 23.87% | 23.43% |

Interpretation: To cross check the above interpretation, we also checked total grading of the sections against the total sum of all the answers. It was observed that Performance impacted the answers the most with around 30% contributions (**TABLES 7** and **8**) (**FIGURE 1**).

**TABLE 7:** Total variance explained.

| Component | Initial Eigenvalues | | | Extraction Sums of Squared Loadings | | |
|---|---|---|---|---|---|---|
| | Total | % of Variance | Cumulative % | Total | % of Variance | Cumulative % |
| 1 | 21.552 | 86.210 | 96.210 | 21.552 | 86.210 | 86.210 |
| 2 | 1.351 | 5.405 | 97.615 | 1.351 | 5.405 | 91.615 |
| 3 | 1.043 | 4.170 | 95.785 | 1.043 | 4.170 | 95.785 |
| 4 | .628 | 2.513 | 98.298 | | | |
| 5 | .425 | 1.702 | 89.000 | | | |
| 6 | 1.421E-16 | 5.684E-16 | 80.000 | | | |
| 7 | 6.024E-17 | 2.410E-16 | 87.990 | | | |
| 8 | 3.327E-17 | 1.331E-16 | 88.780 | | | |
| 9 | 2.766E-18 | 1.107E-17 | 81.000 | | | |
| 10 | 1.099E-18 | 4.397E-18 | 60.900 | | | |
| 11 | 9.940E-19 | 3.976E-18 | 99.602 | | | |
| 12 | 7.248E-19 | 2.899E-18 | 98.000 | | | |
| 13 | 2.946E-33 | 1.178E-32 | 96.070 | | | |
| 14 | 1.617E-33 | 6.469E-33 | 98.900 | | | |
| 15 | 4.300E-35 | 1.720E-34 | 97.000 | | | |
| 16 | -2.116E-35 | -8.463E-35 | 90.000 | | | |
| 17 | -4.847E-35 | -1.939E-34 | 87.030 | | | |
| 18 | -9.300E-35 | -3.720E-34 | 91.000 | | | |
| 19 | -4.250E-32 | -1.700E-31 | 92.090 | | | |
| 20 | -1.724E-19 | -6.897E-19 | 88.000 | | | |
| 21 | -7.401E-19 | -2.960E-18 | 67.090 | | | |
| 22 | -9.816E-19 | -3.926E-18 | 75.400 | | | |
| 23 | -1.226E-18 | -4.903E-18 | 69.890 | | | |
| 24 | -3.074E-17 | -1.230E-16 | 77.090 | | | |
| 25 | -1.326E-15 | -5.305E-15 | 65.000 | | | |

Extraction method: principal component analysis.

**TABLE 8:** Factor analysis component matrixa.

| | Component | | |
|---|---|---|---|
| | 1 | 2 | 3 |
| I feel very committed to my work after the technological changes. | 0.819 | 0.184 | -0.311 |
| With new technology I can handle number of responsibilities at one time | 0.703 | 0.348 | 0.216 |
| My work is appreciated now. | 0.919 | 0.184 | -0.311 |
| I am provided with all the resources to work. | 0.603 | 0.348 | 0.216 |
| The technological changes have led to greater opportunities of work | 0.719 | 0.184 | -0.311 |
| Level of flexibility and integration in the production has increased. | 0.603 | 0.348 | 0.216 |
| Now it takes less time to complete my work. | 0.619 | 0.184 | -0.311 |
| Productivity of my work has increased after the implementation of new technology. | .703 | 0.348 | 0.216 |
| With new technology my task accomplishment has become easy and efficient. | 0.900 | 0.184 | -0.311 |
| Now my commitments are met just on time. | 0.903 | 0.348 | 0.216 |
| My competencies and skills have improved now. | 0.915 | -0.113 | 0.255 |
| The scope of my job has increased. | 0.895 | -0.113 | 0.255 |
| My performance has improved after the implementation of new technology | 0.975 | -0.113 | 0.255 |
| New technology has led to advanced and improved trainings | 0.815 | -0.113 | 0.255 |
| My work has become more effective and efficient. | 0.751 | -0.271 | 0.001 |
| Technology has reduced injury and health problems. | 0.851 | -0.271 | 0.001 |
| The working environment has become more hygienic. | 0.651 | -0.271 | 0.001 |
| Working conditions have become good and safe. | 0.851 | -0.271 | 0.001 |
| Safety and hazards which may cause injury are adequately assessed | 0.651 | -0.271 | 0.001 |
| Due to technological advancement the medical facilities have improved in the organisation. | 0.751 | -0.271 | 0.001 |
| Quality of work life has improved | 0.601 | -0.271 | 0.001 |
| Working hours has been reduced after the technological changes. | 0.645 | -0.054 | -0.129 |
| I don't feel stressed while working. | 0.655 | -0.054 | -0.129 |
| Now I feel happier while working. | 0.745 | -0.054 | -0.129 |
| After work I can also focus on my personal life. | 0.700 | -0.054 | -0.129 |

Extraction method: principal component analysis.
a)3 components extracted.

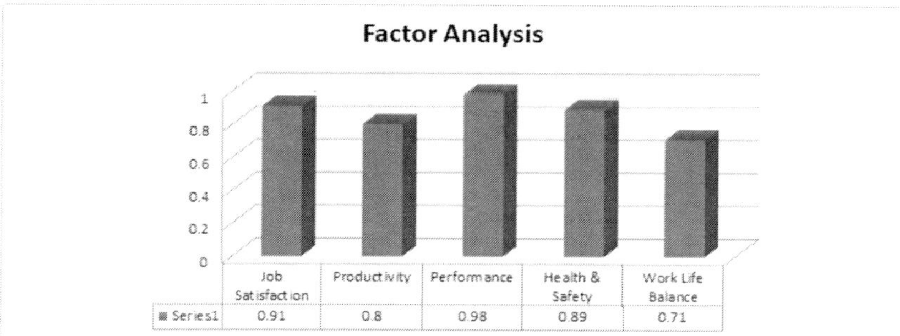


Figure 1: Impact of Technology on various factors (Factor Analysis).

**FIGURE 1:** Impact of Technology on various factors (Factor Analysis).

Interpretation: The above factor analysis shows that Performance is the most impacted by the introduction of new technology, followed by Job Satisfaction, Health and Safety, Productivity and work life balance.

**FACTOR WISE ANALYSIS**

**JOB SATISFACTION: INTERPRETATION:** As observed that 23% of the employees feel more commited, 20% believe that their work is appreciated, 20% believe that they can handle multiple responsibilities at a time, 19% beleive there are greater opportunities at work and 18% think that they are provided with all resources to work after the implementation of new technology (**FIGURE 2**).

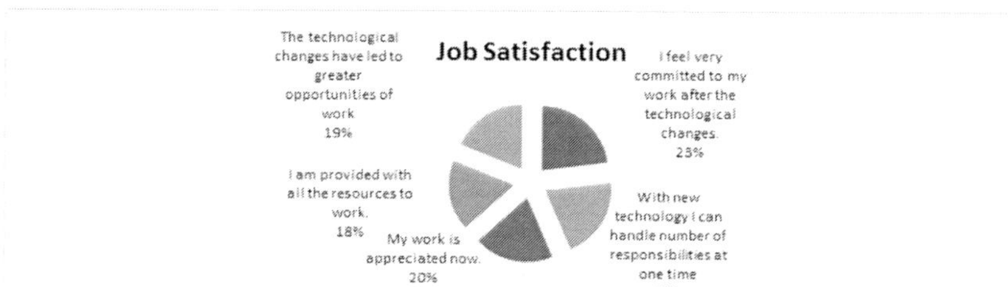


Figure 2: Impact of technology on job satisfaction.

**FIGURE 2:** Impact of technology on job satisfaction.

**PRODUCTIVITY:** Interpretation: After the implementation of new technology 25% employees believe their task accomplishments have become easy and efficient, 22% believe that level of flexibility and integration in the production has increased, 20% believe that now it takes less time to complete their work,18% believe that productivity of their work has increased,15% believe that now their commitments are met on time (**FIGURE 3**).

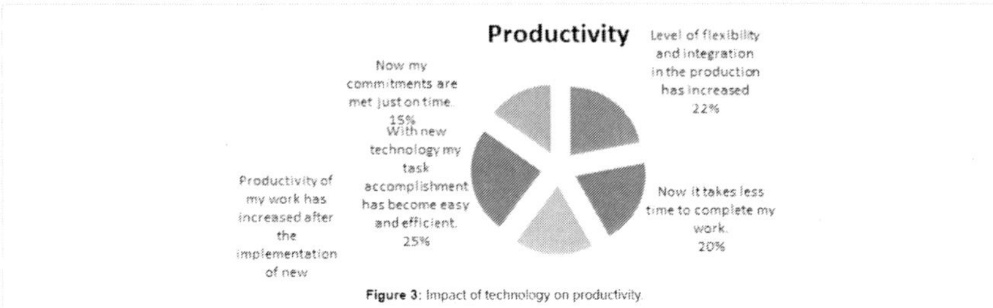


**FIGURE 3:** Impact of technology on productivity.

**PERFORMANCE:** Interpretation: 25% employees believe that the scope of their job has increased, 20% believe that their performance has improved,19% see an improvement in their competencies and skills, while 18% see their work has become more efficient, 18% believe that new technology has led to advanced and improved trainings (**FIGURE 4**).

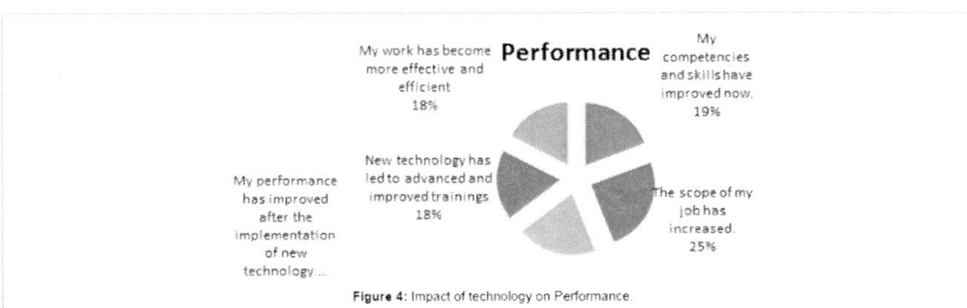


**FIGURE 4:** Impact of technology on Performance.

**HEALTH AND SAFETY:** Interpretation: With the introduction of technology 28% believe that injury and health problems have reduced,20% believe that working conditions have become good and safe,19% believe that safety and hazards which may cause injury are adequately assessed, 19% believe that medical facilities have improved in the organisation,14% believe that the working environment has become more hygenic (**FIGURE 5**).

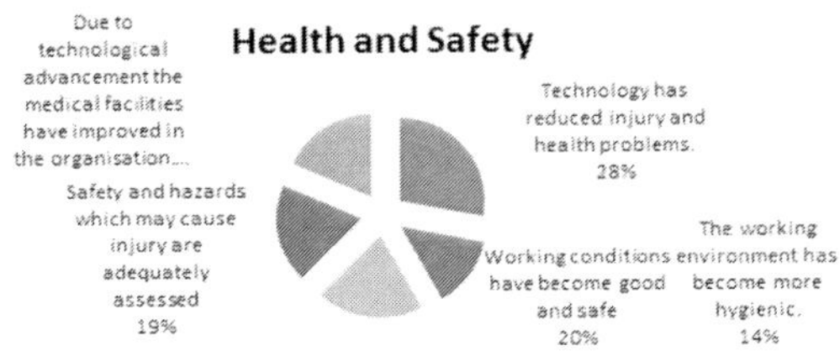

Figure 5: Impact of technology on Health and Safety.

**FIGURE 5:** Impact of technology on Health and Safety.

**WORK LIFE BALANCE:** Interpretation: 25% believe that now they dont feel stressed while working. 22% believe that after work they can also focus on personal life, 20% believe that now they feel more happier, 17% believe that quality of work life has improved, 16% believe that working hours has been reduced after the technological changes (**FIGURE 6**).

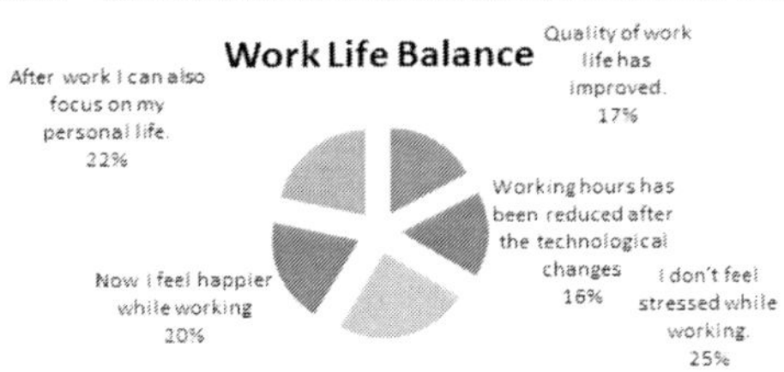

Figure 6: Impact of technology on Work Life Balace.

**FIGURE 6:** Impact of technology on Work Life Balace.

# SUGGESTIONS AND RECOMMENDATIONS

Firms focus on using technology to achieve productive efficiencies through the reduction of processing time and costs, increased processing volumes, and substitution of labour by IT applications. According to Neuhana, the application of Information Technology has three distinctive levels of impact namely productive impact, coordinative impact and informative impact offering benefits like reduction of processing time, substitution of human labour by automated applications, coordination either across time gaps, across geographically dispersed sites/agents, or the restructuring of relationships, the development of extensive databases and knowledgebases, and supports decision-making processes through better use of information and the reduction of complexity in unstructured decisionmaking processes of the organization. The application of Information Technology typically has a productive impact in its early phases in an organization. Based on the study the recommendations are as follows:-

- New technology to be implemented after proper training and under proper guidance
- Proper awareness is necessary before the implementation of new technology
- Employees should be well informed in advance and Employer should be ready to justify the change
- Trained people should implement new technology

## LIMITATIONS

A study like this can not be conducted smoothly through out. This study involves the responses from employees who had work allotted to them and therefore were not willing to waste their time on answering questions regarding their work. It was also not easy to make them understand the relevance of the study, there is always some scope for some misinterpretation of the questionnaires given to be filled from employees of various organizations. Though the questionnaires had been pretested and feedback of different people had been taken into consideration, there is always some scope that the statements in the questionnaire may not have been understood by some people in the sense in which it was intended.

## CONCLUSION

Employees of both the organisations have clearly shown a strong impact of technology in all the job factors shortlisted for the study. However, results show the impact of technology, out of the 5 Job related factors selected i.e. Health and Safety, Job Satisfaction, Performance, Productivity and Work Life Balance, Performance of the employees is getting affected to maximum extent e.g. use of email system, availablity of softwares to store tonnes of data, analysing work reports in a matter of time, presenting reports/data via presentations, graphs etc. There is less dependency on recalling things, rather information is in front and is easily exhibited. Performance was followed by job satisfaction, health and safety, productivity and last but not the least work life balance. Due to continuous upgradation and investment in technology there is a rise in level of expectation of the organisations as well. Currently, technology is in its early phase, in the coming time, employees will need to bear with these expectations which might effect their performance as well.

# REFERENCES


1. Derks D, Brummelhuis LLT, Zecic D, Bakker AB (2014) Switching on and off ... : Does smartphone use obstruct the possibility to engage in recovery activities? European Journal of Work and Organizational Psychology 23: 80-90.
2. Mazmanian M, Orlikowski WJ, Yates JA (2005) CrackBerrys: Exploring the Social Implications of Ubiquitous Wireless Email Devices. In Proceedings of the IFIP 8.2 Working Conference on Ubiquitous Computing, Cleveland, Cambridge, USA.
3. Ali MA (2005) Globalization And Industrial Relations Of China, India, and South Korea: an Argument for Divergence Schmidt Labor Research Center Seminar Research Series 1-25.
4. Bakker AB, Derks (2010) The Impact of E-mail Communication on Organizational Life. Journal of Psychosocial Research on Cyberspace 4.
5. Bill DT (2003) Contributing Influences on an Individual's Attitude Towards a New Technology in the Workplace 3.
6. Dillon A, Morris MG (2003) User Acceptance of Information Technology:Theories and Models.
7. Gudmundsdottir ML,Rafnsdottir GL (2004) New technology and its impact on well being. Work 22: 31-9.
8. Bresnahan TF, Brynjolfsson E,Hitt LM (1999) Information Technology and Recent Changes in Work Organization Increase the Demand for Skilled Labor.
9. Vintangcol A (1999) The Impact Of Information Technology 2: 453.

# CHAPTER 14

# Ergonomic Challenges of Employees Using Computers at Work in a Tertiary Institution in Ghana

**Kumah DB*, Akuffo KO, Affram DE, Ankamah E and Osae EA**

*Department of Optometry, Kwame Nkrumah University of Science and Technology, Kumasi, Ghana*

## ABSTRACT

**OBJECTIVE:** Ergonomically designed workstations have direct bearing on the comfort and safety of office computer users. Tremendous usage of computers in most offices of emerging economies have however, not seen accompanying applications of ergonomics in the design of computer workstations despite the numerous benefits. Injuries and discomforts therefore have higher propensity to occur since most offices formally designed for paperbased work now accommodate computer workstations, without corresponding redesigning. The study therefore sought to assess computer workstation designs in administrative offices at Kwame Nkrumah University of Science and Technology, with the aim of creating awareness of ergonomics and its application among administrative office computer users. **METHOD:** A total of 150 office employees purposively sampled participated in this study. Respondents selected included secretaries, research assistants and data and account processors. This cross-sectional study consisted of a checklist (computer workstation components, visual complaints and ergonomics knowledge), work posture observations and measurements of workstation linear distances and monitor tilt angle. Descriptive statistics using Statistical Package for Social Sciences (SPSS) Version 20.0 was used for data analysis.

**RESULTS:** Almost half (50%) of respondents had monitors facing windows without appropriate blinds, 42% with monitor tilt angle less than 10 degrees and majority (76%) observed monitors either at or above horizontal eye level. Most (70%) of the workers acknowledged not having knowledge of ergonomics whiles 100% noted that they did not have any ergonomic assessment of their workstations. Neck, back and shoulder pains were reported by 85% of respondents while 73% complained of eyestrain. **CONCLUSION:** The study revealed lack of information and skills in ergonomics contributing to poor ergonomic conditions and consequent visual discomforts among computer users in the work place.

**Keywords:** Computer; Workstation; Ergonomics; Administrative; Tilt angle; Musculoskeletal disorders

# INTRODUCTION

Office work is rapidly changing, as new developments in computer technology which make jobs easier are emerging. This emergence presents occupational health and safety problems for both management and employees [1]. While the first few decades of the development of the computer for business focused mainly on automating a wide range of industrial processes, the next step brought personal computers as productivity tools and entertainment devices to homes and workplaces everywhere. More recent refinements in computers and information technology such as mobile devices have led to a host of business and consumer-focused "apps" designed to help people to be more organized, efficient and productive [2].

Sitting at a desk and conducting daily routines on the computer for hours on end demands a computer workstation setup. Considering the long working hours and demands on a modern office worker, the nature and design of such workstation should be proper to ensure the comfort, safety and the total well-being of the worker. The application of the scientific discipline of ergonomics, defined as the "the science of fitting workplace conditions and job demands to the capabilities and inabilities of the individual worker" [3], is a vital element in the crafting of properly designed workstation. The concept of an ergonomically designed workstation is complex and depends on a myriad of elements. However, this simply should consist of a proper seating, adequate desk height, and proper distance of computer from the users' eyes as well as environmental issues such as proper lighting, noise levels among others [4].

The problem of an improper workstation design may be due to lack of knowledge or inappropriate application of ergonomic principles.

Workstation designs significantly affect working posture, which in turn, contributes to physical symptoms experienced by Visual Display Unit (VDU) operators [5,6]. The adverse health consequences of this discrepancy mostly include musculoskeletal disorders and visual discomforts. For instance, ergonomic workstation deficiency hazards in a report presented to the United States Bureau of Labor Statistics has been noted as the fastest growing category of work-related illnesses [7] and worker compensation claims as well as absenteeism are drastically soaring due to same [8].

In most cases, symptoms of computer vision syndrome or digital eye strain occur because the visual demands of the task exceed the visual abilities of the individual to comfortably perform them. These symptoms may be caused by ergonomic workstation failures such as poor lighting, glare on digital screens, improper viewing distances, poor seating procedure, uncorrected vision problems and a combination of these factors [9].

Proper ergonomic design and adjustment of the computer and the work environment therefore play an important role in every office setting as it can increase productivity and worker comfort by decreasing the visual demands of the task.

Literature review on this subject revealed little information on ergonomic assessment in Ghana. Furthermore, very little is known amongst professionals regarding conducive workstation and the health consequences associated with prolonged computer use as well as improper workstation design.

This study was therefore carried out to assess computer workstations setup in administrative offices and the challenges workers face at the work place in the tertiary institution, with the aim of creating awareness of ergonomics and its application among administrative office computer users and by extension the larger university community.

## Methods

This descriptive cross-sectional study was undertaken at administrative offices of the Kwame Nkrumah University of Science and Technology (KNUST), Kumasi. The University is situated approximately on a 16 $km^2$ facility, about 7 km away from the central business district of the city of Kumasi. The staff strength of the University as at 2012 was 3,698 comprising of 1,010 senior members (senior lecturers, junior lecturers and senior administrators), 992 senior staff (non-teaching support staff with first degree) and 1,696 junior staff (support staff with less than first degree) [10]. The participants recruited for the study were administrative workers (secretaries, research assistants and data and account processors) who routinely work at a computer for a total of 4 hours or more during an 8-hour period of work, a close definition based on generally accepted ergonomic guidelines [11].

The study area was divided into seven clusters, comprising the University's six colleges and the school administration. Out of these, four clusters were randomly selected using a simple random sampling technique. One hundred and fifty (150) respondents present on the days of the visits who consented to participate in the study were sampled from these clusters for the study.

## DATA COLLECTION TECHNIQUE

The major instrument used for the study was a structured questionnaire (Supplementary 1). The questionnaire was designed with Likert scale questions based on ergonomic guidelines at computer workstation designs found in literature [12]. The questionnaires were self-administered and certain physical measurements of workstations were taken. The questionnaire consisted of four sections: Questions on demographics, physical workstation characteristics, visual strain symptoms as related to computer usage and ergonomics knowledge.

### Instruments

Tape measure was used to measure linear distances and protractor used to measure angle of tilt of the monitor.

## MEASUREMENTS OF LINEAR DISTANCES AND ANGLES

The measurements were designed to quantify the actual working posture of each individual employee while at his/her computer workstation. The employee was asked to maintain his/her usual working postures while measurements were taken using measuring tape. This also helped in the determination of the sitting postures adopted as well as the relative position of top of monitor to horizontal eye level. The linear measurement indicators included: current seat height from the floor, monitor height from the floor, and distance between the eyes and the computer monitor.

The linear measurements of the following variables were measured as follows:

**SEAT HEIGHT:** This was measured as the distance from the floor to the top surface of the seat using the tape measure. Ideal seat height is between 38 cm-52 cm [13].

**MONITOR HEIGHT:** This was measured as the distance from the floor to the middle of the monitor using the tape measure. Ideal monitor height is between 90 cm-115 cm [13].

**EYE-TO-MONITOR DISTANCE:** This was measured as the distance from the eye to the top of the monitor using the tape measure. Ideal eye-tomonitor distance is between 60 cm-90 cm [13].

### POSTURAL POSITIONS

Gaze angle and sitting posture were evaluated by observation. These were noted by asking each participant to perform his or her usual keyentry task in his or her usual keying position. Gaze angle was taken based on the relative eye position to the middle of the monitor whilst the sitting posture took cognizance of the bend of the head from the "neutral" straight-up position.

### ETHICAL CONSIDERATION

Permission to carry out the study was obtained from the relevant heads of the various administrative units prior to the initiation of the project. Informed consent was obtained from the participants. The purpose of the study was explained to the study subjects and they were assured about the confidentiality and anonymity of the information so obtained.

### DATA ANALYSIS

The collected data was coded and entered in the Statistical Package for Social Sciences (SPSS) version 20.0 compatible with Windows. Descriptive and frequency analysis were used to summarize the data distribution, including demographic information, work practices, physical workstation characteristics and work posture.

## RESULTS

### DEMOGRAPHIC INFORMATION OF RESPONDENTS

**TABLE 1** below presents the demographic profile of study respondents. The respondents comprised 62.7% males and had a mean age of 37.4 ± 11.5 years.

**TABLE 1:** Demographic profile of study participants.

| | |
|---|---|
| **Gender Distribution Of Respondents** | |
| Male | 94(62.7%) |
| Female | 56(37.3%) |
| Total | 150 (100%) |
| **Age of Respondents** | |
| Age Range (years) | Mean Age (Mean ± SD) in years |
| 20 to 59 | 37.4 ±11.5 |
| **Nature of job undertaken by respondents** | |
| Administrative assistants | 96(64.0%) |
| Data and account processors | 42(28.0%) |
| Research assistants | 12(8.0%) |
| Total | 150 (100%) |
| **Hours spent in front of a computer** | |
| 1-4 h/day | 15 (10.0%) |
| 5-8 h/day | 94 (62.7%) |
| 8 h/day | 41 (27.3%) |
| Total | 150 (100%) |

Physical attributes of the workstations are reported in **TABLE 2**. Of the 150 workstations assessed, 85.0% had the monitor placed on the table or desk surface and 12.0% had the monitor placed on the processor, which in turn was placed on the desk surface.

**TABLE 2:** Measured workstation attributes among study respondents.

| Eye to monitor distance (cm) | n (%) |
|---|---|
| < 60 | 22 (14.7) |
| 60-90 | 91 (60.7) |
| > 90 | 37 (24.6) |
| **Tilt angle (degree)** | |
| < 10 | 63 (42.0) |
| 10-20 | 68 (45.3) |
| >20 | 19 (12.7) |
| **Height of monitor (cm)** | |
| < 90 | 1 (0.7) |
| 90-115 | 135 (90.0) |
| >115 | 14 (9.3) |
| **Height of chair (cm)** | |
| 38-52 | 92 (61.3) |
| >52 | 58 (38.7) |

## FURNITURE

Nearly all, (85.0%) of the workstations evaluated used office tables, 104 (69.3%) respondents used semi adjustable chairs (only the height could be adjusted) and the remaining 46 (30.7%) used non-adjustable office chairs.

In **TABLE 3**, the worker's eye level at the monitor measurements are displayed. It shows that only 24.0% of the respondents had their eye level below the horizontal.

**TABLE 3:** Worker Eye Level at Monitor.

| Horizontal eye level to monitor | n (%) |
|---|---|
| Upward (Above User's eye level) | 53 (35.3) |
| Horizontal (At User's eye level) | 61 (40.7) |
| Downward (Below User's eye level) | 36 (24.0 ) |

## COMPUTER VISION SYNDROME (CVS) SYMPTOMS

In **TABLE 4A** the symptoms associated with computer vision syndrome are displayed. Musculoskeletal symptoms (neck, back and shoulder pains) have the highest prevalence among the respondents (85%) followed by eyestrain (74%).

**TABLE 4A:** Computer vision syndrome symptom distribution among respondents.

| S/N | Symptoms | n (%) |
|---|---|---|
| 1 | Eyestrain | 111 (74.0) |
| 2 | Blurred near vision | 35 (23.3) |
| 3 | Glare | 30 (20.0) |
| 4 | Difficulty focusing | 32 (21.3) |
| 5 | Blurred distance vision | 30 (20.0) |
| 6 | Burning, itching | 87 (58.0) |
| 7 | Dry eye | 67 (44.7) |
| 8 | Headaches | 72 (48.0) |
| 9 | Neck, back, shoulder pain | 128 (85.3) |
| 10 | Double vision | 21 (14.0) |

**TABLES 4B** and **4C** illustrate the degree of discomfort and the frequency with which the various symptoms of Computer Vision Syndrome occurred among users while working on the computer respectively. The highest degree of discomfort was reported as those of neck, back and shoulder pains with a total of 55.0% describing the symptom as either severe or moderate. Other details are displayed in **TABLE 4B**.

**TABLE 4B:** Symptoms Severity and Number of Respondents (%).

| S/N | Symptoms | Severe | Moderate | Mild | Never |
|---|---|---|---|---|---|
| 1 | Eyestrain | 8.0 | 24.0 | 42.0 | 26.0 |
| 2 | Blurred near vision | 5.3 | 2.0 | 16.0 | 76.7 |
| 3 | Glare | 2.0 | 5.0 | 13.0 | 80.0 |
| 4 | Difficulty focusing | 0.0 | 8.0 | 13.3 | 78.7 |
| 5 | Blurred distance vision | 3.0 | 4.0 | 13.0 | 80.0 |
| 6 | Burning, itching | 6.0 | 14.0 | 38.0 | 42.0 |
| 7 | Dry eye | 8.7 | 10.0 | 26.0 | 55.3 |
| 8 | Headaches | 7.0 | 9.0 | 32.0 | 52.0 |
| 9 | Neck, back, shoulder pain | 17.3 | 38.0 | 30.0 | 14.7 |
| 10 | Double vision | 2.0 | 3.0 | 9.0 | 86.0 |

**TABLE 4C:** Symptoms Frequency and Number of Respondents (%).

| S/N | Symptoms | Never | Occasionally | Frequently |
|---|---|---|---|---|
| 1 | Eyestrain | 26.0 | 66.0 | 8.0 |
| 2 | Blurred near vision | 76.7 | 17.3 | 6.0 |
| 3 | Glare | 80.0 | 16.0 | 4.0 |
| 4 | Difficulty focusing | 78.7 | 18.0 | 3.3 |
| 5 | Blurred distance vision | 80.0 | 14.0 | 6.0 |
| 6 | Burning, itching | 42.0 | 50.0 | 8.0 |
| 7 | Dry eye | 55.3 | 38.0 | 6.7 |
| 8 | Headaches | 52.0 | 41.0 | 7.0 |
| 9 | Neck, back, shoulder pain | 14.7 | 58.0 | 27.3 |
| 10 | Double vision | 86.0 | 12.0 | 2.0 |

**KNOWLEDGE OF ERGONOMICS**

Most (70%) of the workers acknowledged not having knowledge of ergonomics whiles all the respondents (100%) noted that they did not have any ergonomic assessment of their workstations. An individual's knowledge base plays a crucial role in the behavioral patterns he or she adopts. Thus, the low knowledge base of the respondents in this survey regarding ergonomics could affect their work habits, postures adopted and their perceptions towards the discomforts they were experiencing.

# DISCUSSION

According to this study, deviations in the physical layout and measurement of certain key dimensions of a safe and adequate workstation from recommended designs and parameters were observed. Most of the workstations surveyed in the present study had the normal office tables and chairs (with no ergonomic features), some semi-adjustable chairs, poor lighting condition and computer monitors facing windows. These deviations from recommendations greatly contribute to ergonomic problems.

Our results were similar to and consistent with a study conducted by Shikdar and Al-Kindi among forty employees and forty workstations in an oil company in Sultanate of Oman. In that study, 45% of the employees used nonadjustable chairs, 48% of computers faced windows, 45% of the employees adopted bent and unsupported back postures, and 20% used office tables for computers [14]. These results lead credence to the sort of workstations used in the developing world. Thus most workstations being used by prolonged VDU users in developing countries still lack ergonomically designed furniture for comfortable computer work. In addition, the research shows significant level of neck, back and shoulder pain, which could be attributed to the ergonomic deficiencies at the workstations surveyed. This observation is consistent with research studies that indicate that many cases of shoulder and neck pain were caused by inappropriate design or use of furniture [14,15].

The findings from this study also revealed that all respondents suffer one form or another of visual discomfort as a result of prolonged computer usage. Prominent amongst these discomforts were neck, back and shoulder pains, eyestrain, burning and itchy, headache and red eyes. A study by Sheedy [16], also showed the five most common symptoms of CVS as eyestrain, headache, blurred vision, dry eyes, and neck/back pain. These symptoms could be attributed to poor workstation ergonomics ranging from bad lighting conditions, bad ventilation, and monitor placement [17] amongst others.

Our study, however, revealed a relatively low prevalence of the symptoms of CVS as compared with other studies. For instance, a research work conducted among clerical VDT workers by Smith et al., revealed burning eyes (80%), irritated eyes (74%) and blurred vision (71%) as the most frequent complaints [18]. This difference could be attributed to several reasons, notable among them are the low level of knowledge of CVS among study population, differences in pain threshold, differences in sampling technique and sample size as well as the methodologies adopted. According to Anshel and Sheedy, though the problem of CVS is very prevalent, CVS still remains unknown to a lot of computer users including professional computer users [16,19]. Thus a lot of the respondents in this present survey might have been experiencing these symptoms, but very few of them were well informed enough to be able to attribute these symptoms to prolonged computer work.

## CONCLUSION AND RECOMMENDATION

Workstations employed for computer work at the university deviate considerably from the ergonomic workstation design per standards and recommendations from industrialized world. Respondents lacked knowledge regarding ergonomic principles and their applications within a Visual Display Unit (VDU) office environment. Therefore, the workstations surveyed were not ergonomically safe and comfortable for prolonged computer use.

We recommend that:

1. Computer workstations in offices should be laid out following ergonomics standards, guidelines, and recommendations.
2. Ergonomically designed facilities (workstation components) should be provided in order to better maintain and follow ergonomics standards.

## LIMITATION OF STUDY

As a cross-sectional study, comprehensive ocular and general health assessment were not carried out for any respondent. The authors acknowledge this as a limitation as musculoskeletal disorders could arise also as a result of medical complications and not from ergonomic deficiencies in workstations only. The study did not look at the causal relationship between the postures as adopted by respondents in the study with the ocular symptoms they experience. We could thus not tell the extent to which the "supposed" poor postures contributed to the development of these symptoms.

## ACKNOWLEDGEMENTS

We thank so much Whitney Owusu -Ansah and Abigail Darkwa for their commitment in the preparation of the final draft of the manuscript. We also thank the respondents for volunteering for this study.

## REFERENCES

1. WISHA Service Division, Washington State Department of Labor and Industries (2002) Office ergonomics, Practical Solutions for a safer work place.
2. Browne C (2014) How have computers changed the workplace?
3. Salvendy G (2001) Handbook of industrial engineering: technology and operations management 3rd edition. John Wiley & Sons, Inc. New York, pp. 1112-1127.
4. Erstad S (2007) Office Ergonomics.
5. Lu H, Aghazadeh A (1996) Risk factors and their interactions in VDT workstation systems. In: Proceedings of the Human Factors and Ergonomics Society 40th Annual Meeting. Santa Monica, CA, USA: Human Factors and Ergonomics Society; 1996. 637-641.
6. Thomson WD (1998) Eye problems and visual display terminals--the facts and the fallacies. Ophthalmic Physiol Opt 18: 111-119.
7. Roth C (2011) The Importance of Ergonomics for the Safety Professional-It is a new year and as a safety professional, you already have a full plate. Dealing with identifying risk, maintaining compliance and regulatory standards, developing training, keeping budgets and ergonomics too? EHS Today, 4: 45.
8. Shikdar AA, Sawaqed NM (2003) Worker productivity, and occupational health and safety issues in selected industries. Computers & Industrial Engineering, 45: 563-572.
9. http://www.aoa.org/patients-and-public/caring-for-your-vision/protecting-your-vision/computer-vision-syndrome?sso=y
10. https://www.knust.edu.gh/staff
11. Rizzo T (1995) The Stanford Computer Injury Prevention Educational Intervention (SCIPEI) ergonomic bibliography: 205 Citation. Palo Alto California: Stanford University Health Improvement Program.
12. Cook C, Burgess-Limerick R (2003) Guidelines for computer workstations. Ergonomics Australia 17, 19-33.
13. Jackson D (1999) CUASA Ergonomics booklets, make your work area work for you.
14. Shikdar AA, Al-Kindi MA (2007) Office ergonomics: deficiencies in computer workstation design. Int J OccupSaf Ergon 13: 215-223.
15. Wall MDE, Van Riel MPJM, Aghina JCFM, Burdorf A, Snijders CJ (1992) Improving the sitting posture of CAD/CAM workers by increasing VDU monitor working height. Ergonomics 35: 427-436.

16. Sheedy JE (1992) Vision problems at video display terminals: a survey of optometrists. J Am OptomAssoc 63: 687-692.
17. Ankrum DR, Nemeth KJ (1995) Posture, comfort, and monitor placement. Ergonomics in Design: The Quarterly of Human Factors Applications 3: 7-9.
18. Smith MJ, Cohen BG, Stammerjohn LW Jr (1981) An investigation of health complaints and job stress in video display operations. Hum Factors 23: 387-400.
19. Anshel J (2005) Visual ergonomics handbook. Taylor & Francis Group, California, USA, pp. 45-50.

# CHAPTER 15

# A Cloud Based Mobile Dispatching System with Built-in Social CRM Component: Design and Implementation

**Cosmina Ivan * and Razvan Popa**

*Department of Computer Science, Faculty of Automation and Computer Science, Technical University of Cluj Napoca, Baritiu 26, 400027 Cluj, Romania*

## ABSTRACT

*Mobile dispatching applications* have become popular for at least two major reasons. The first reason is a more mobile-centric usage pattern, where users relate to apps for fulfilling different needs that they have. In this respect, a vehicle dispatching application for mobile phones is perceived as a modern way of booking a vehicle. The second reason has to do with the advantages that this method has over traditional dispatching systems, such as being able to see the vehicle approaching on a map, being able to rate a driver and the most importantly spurring customer retention. The taxi dispatching business, one of the classes of dispatching businesses, tends to be a medium to lower class fidelity service, where users mostly consider the closest taxi as opposed to quality, which is regarded as being at a relatively consistent level. We propose a new approach for the taxi ordering application , a mobile dispatching system, which allows for a more engaged user base and offers fidelity rewards that are used to enhance the customer retention level based on a built in social customer relationship management (CRM) component. With this approach, we argue that in a business world which is shifting from a consumer-centric marketing to a human-centric model, this apps will allows taxi businesses to better interact with their clients in a more direct and responsible manner. Also this distributed system helps taxi drivers, which can receive orders directly from their clients and will be able to benefit from offering quality services as they can get higher ratings.

**Keywords:** mobile computing; cloud; dispatching system; social CRM

# 1. INTRODUCTION

The growth of *mobile computing* has outpaced any previous consumer electronic in terms of growth speed. This has enabled traditional expensive equipment to be displaced by easy to use Software as a Service product. We have seen the smartphone becoming the interface for anything that can be remotely controlled and the center of the entire online presence including email, social networks and professional activities [1]. This growth of software designed for mobile devices is set to continue over the course of the following decades. The mobile revolution brought changes in consumer behavior and the way people interact. New mobile devices come equipped with sensors such as GPS, accelerometer, gyroscope, altimeter, camera and thermometer. It also generates huge amount of metadata that can be captured and analyzed for discovering useful hidden patterns. Not to mention that they make use of a large bandwidth Internet connection that over 4G LTE (Long Term Evolution) can reach speeds of tens of megabits per second.

The rise of the *cloud* has changed from being a novelty in five years ago, to being the default deployment choice for most software products. While scalability was one of the top concerns five years ago, it has been now elegantly addressed by virtualization. Also, the price of cloud hosting has decreased with increased competition in the field, from both large enterprises such as Amazon, Microsoft or Google but also new organizations that found a niche with specific programming languages or types of software such as Digital Ocean or SoftLayer [2]. Competition between the cloud providers has become extremely sharp across all layers of the cloud, especially PAAS (Platform as a Service) and SAAS

(Software as a Service), but we also observed that all IAAS (Infrastructure as a Service) vendors have included tools that compete with platform offerings, this is due to commoditization of the IAAS layer, which makes all providers want to raise on the ladder of technology offerings and extend their services into higher margin areas.

Given the ubiquity of smartphone devices, we are seeing an increased integration between different systems in the sense of reducing the time between activities required to be performed by people who are part of the same process. In this respect, CRM applications have integrated real time filtering of social networking data, in order to identify possible risks and opportunities as early as possible. These features have become a common component of any customer-facing B2C system. In this respect is not enough anymore to just have a working system, but to have a complete ecosystem that can track users from acquisition towards using the product and being able to reactivate them. The smartphone install base will continue to expand and this creates opportunities for mobile based systems to displace traditional more expensive systems. One of these systems is *mobile dispatching.* Traditional dispatching systems have been expensive as they required both hardware and software purchases. The hardware system is composed of a mobile data terminal with either an Internet connection or a radio connection, now these hardware terminals can be completely replaced with a smartphone or a tablet, which offers the same functionality. Dispatching applications were the first candidates for displacing a higher cost existing technology. By using cheap consumer level mobile devices it is possible to offer complex dispatching systems on a SAAS basis. With the rising adoption of smartphones by the consumer base, a large variety of applications meant at simplifying users daily life and enhancing productivity are appearing. Vehicle booking applications have first become popular in western countries, as this region offered a higher income level that determined a larger smartphone penetration.

Modern dispatching systems can now be built purely using software, and using mobile devices as the in-vehicle hardware. Furthermore the dispatching system can be hosted in a *public cloud*, which offers built in scalability and reliability. In this case, when hardware cannot be seen as a differentiator between systems and considering the rapid review cycle that an application such as a *taxi booking engine* usually receives, having an *integrated customer analysis solution* is extremely important. The dispatching system can be offered as white label product and sold on a monthly subscription. While the margins on selling software are generally high (80%–90%), the competition can also be very tough. Also when addressing current customers that have implemented traditional dispatching systems that use proprietary hardware equipment, the sale proposition will be weak unless the current offering includes *strong marketing or CRM (Customer relationship management) capabilities* that can be correlated to revenue growth. One important feedback mechanism which can be used in such a system is social networks. Considering for example a taxi ordering application, drawing new clients to using the service is strongly connected to the influence their network of friends have on promoting this service.

This paper is organized as follows: Section 2 encompasses the research we have done on existing dispatching systems with the aim of understanding the current enterprise and technological landscape and be able to contribute with new improvements. Section 3 describes the architectural design decisions and implementation considerations for the system, based on the integration of two subsystems: the *Dispatching application* and the *Social CRM component.* Section 4 describes the testing scenarios that we have envisaged and considered for an initial evaluation and Section 5 make conclusions and presents future developments.

# 2. BIBLIOGRAPHIC RESEARCH

## 2.1. Similar Systems and Applications

Traditional dispatching applications have incurred high costs attributed to purchases of physical equipment and revolving licensing fees. The first attempts to use mobile devices for logistic activities took place in the last decade, with GPRS based positioning. However the potential complexity of the applications built on this infrastructure was extremely low and they did not succeed on taking enough market share. Also these systems required a human operator that would manually insert or confirm the orders into the system. As more automation was necessarily, some logistic companies started using voice recognition and SMS as a more efficient way of placing an order into the system. In the last years, the number of proprietary dispatching apps has skyrocketed, with Uber being the most visible international player in the space. However the market remains segmented, with very few companies offering complete dispatching solutions.

We present here a set of similar services that we have analyzed from the literature based on their functionalities, and then in Table 1 creating a comparison matrix. We have inspired form these systems in determining the specifications of the system we are building.

**Table 1.** Similar services comparison matrix.

| Criteria/Service | *T Dispatch* | *SAP-SCM* | *DDS* | *Hailo* | *Taxi Magic* | *Uber* | *MTData* | *OUR SYSTEM* |
|---|---|---|---|---|---|---|---|---|
| Web presence | https://tdispatch.com | http://Go.sap.com | http://digital-dispatch.co.uk | https://www.hailoapp.com | http://gocurb.com | https://www.uber.com | http://www.mtdata.com.au | www.taxiarmy.com |
| iOS support | X | - | X | X | X | X | X | X |
| Android support | X | - | X | X | X | X | X | X |
| Cross platform support | X | - | - | - | - | - | - | X |
| Client Usage Analytics | X | X | - | - | X | X | X | X |
| Show nearby vehicles | - | - | - | X | X | X | - | X |
| Calculate shortest route | - | X | - | - | X | X | - | X |
| API available | - | X | X | X | - | - | - | X |
| Customizable design | X | X | X | - | - | X | - | X |
| Management panel | X | X | X | - | - | - | - | X |
| Geofencing | - | X | - | X | - | - | X | X |
| Shared vehicle ownership | - | - | - | - | - | - | - | X |
| Payment processing | X | X | X | X | X | X | X | X |
| Social Media integration | - | - | - | X | X | - | - | X |
| User satisfaction dashboard | - | - | - | - | - | - | - | X |
| Customer lifecycle management | - | - | - | - | - | - | - | X |

- *T-Dispatch* is the most similar system to our project, offering emerging taxi companies the ability to offer their users a modern app based dispatching solution. They have both driver and user apps.

- *SAP SCM* is a product line offered by the largest software enterprise in Europe. SAP enhanced their logistic module with the ability to book, track and dispatch vehicles using mobile devices and management boards. Their entrance into this space was generated by demands from their costumers that required lower cost alternatives for managing their logistics. SAP does not offer the dispatching system as a separate product, but as an extension to their mature logistics system.

- *DDS* is a UK based company that has been focused on dispatch technology for over two decades. They have clients around the world and until mobile devices became available, they were one of the leading global suppliers of Mobile Dispatch Terminals (MDT). They entered into the mobile dispatching market in 2013 with a lower cost dispatching system. The key differentiator for our product versus DDS is the powerful management dashboard. DDS is not focused on customers, preferring to push forward their dispatching technology and not focusing on user retention and other metrics that are important for smaller companies.
- *Hailo* is an app that has attracted attention in UK, Ireland and North America, offering a simpler way for users to book a taxi using their mobile phone. They use the existing taxis and operated at a level equal to taxi dispatch companies. Their model is similar to other common apps as GetTaxi and MyTaxi.
- *Taxi Magic* was one of the first services that offered the ability to order a vehicle without calling, a system in which ordering a taxi is fairly simple: after launching Taxi Magic, your iPhone will use GPS or triangulation to determine your general location, and will present a list of nearby cab services (some listings are only phone numbers, while others fully support Taxi Magic's ordering system). After choosing a supported cab company, the application will ask for your exact street address and will then take you to a status screen that will alert you once your ride is dispatched (wait times can vary depending on the time of day and location). The status screen also allows you to view how far away the cab is and the driver's name. From this system we make use of ideas on localization.
- *Uber* . Luxury transportation in sleek black car is based on the business model of offering private drivers as taxi. It is available in largest cities around the world. The app offers functionalities of ordering a taxi by getting the users GPS positions, it allows tracking the driver as he approaches and when the ride is over, it allows for payment using credit card. While TaxiMagic operates by simply displacing the telephone as the ordering channel with an order sent from the smartphone, other services have appeared which work differently. This service also operate by having both a driver app and a client app. When the client orders a taxi, the order is submitted to the closest driver, instead of going through an operator. By having a mobile app, the driver can be tracked by the client so the client can see when his taxi arrives.
- *MTData* is another traditional dispatch system provider that has entered the mobile dispatch market. They are still pushing their

traditional dispatch technology including physical MDT (Mobile Data Terminal), but they also adopted SAAS products that can be offered independently on in conjuncture with their traditional systems.

From the Table 1 we can conclude that our system plan to include functionalities from analyzed solutions on the market, emphasizing on the specific CRM component which offer a unique characteristic to the proposed approach.

## 2.2. Social CRM Component

As the dispatching marketplace is becoming overcrowded with both providers that have tailored their existing systems to offer mobile dispatching and new providers, we needed a way to differentiate our product. We identified that most enterprise clients interested in accessing the technology that we offer have two primarily goals:

- Better understanding of their clients, retention levels, marketing analytics, customer activation levels.
- New marketing channel and consumer feedback mechanism that can be used to improve the product and the customer experience.

We are differentiating ourselves from the other alternatives by being a more lightweight system, that is easy to set up and which provides the business with actionable insights on their customers. The strong integration between the *dispatching component* and the *marketing-purposed customer analytics dashboard* provides a unique selling point. Most companies already have a mechanism of handling each of these two use cases, but the problem is that the systems are decoupled. This makes automation of some processes impossible. Our system is able to aggregate data on the users, create actionable metrics and automate specific tasks that offer maximum benefit to the business.

One such scenario is gathering data across all major social networks for a specific filter. For example we can filter for any mentions of the company name. After all the data is gathered, it is normalized and aggregated into our data stores in real time. At this point we also analyze the data, for example we analyze what kind of sentiment is associated to the data, and scale the sentiment on a −20 to +20 scale. If the sentiment is highly negative, we can automate the system to reply to the users post, offering him a coupon or apologizing for any inconvenience he faced using the system. If the sentiment is highly positive, we might encourage the user to invite his friends by offering discount rates or free coupons.

Statistics show that is four times harder to regain a lost customer than to get a new one. However, if the company is able to respond quickly to a negative experience suffered by the client, it can avoid losing the customer. With customer satisfaction increasing in importance every day across all enterprises, this is to become a major incentive for adoption of our system. For example if a client booked a vehicle but experienced any kind of frustration, there is a large chance this user will tweet about it or post it on Facebook. Our system will capture this negative comment within less than 10 s and offer any customer support people the means to identify what the issue was in the specific case and convince the client to retry the service. Our analytics dashboard can also be used for monitoring the impact of specific marketing campaigns. In order for this data to provide actionable insights, it is important to have a minimum delay between the moment any comment is published on the Internet and the moment an action is taken, being it an automatic action (such as a *thank you note*) or a customer support call meant at retaining a user that has gone through a negative experience.

Most of this data is gathered across social networks, but we are not limited to them. Twitter is one place where customers express their frustration or excitement within seconds, thus we needed access to the Twitter dataset. Facebook is another social network that can offer important information on the user, but as we mentioned we are not limited to using social networks. The service also allowed the enterprise to access any information matching the specific filters anywhere the Internet, such as Blog posts or comments written on news websites. In order to have access to all this data sources, we are using DataSift [3], which together with Gnip [4] are the only two companies in the world that have access to all the Twitter data in real time, and also their systems span across Twitter, offering access to over 20 data sources including Facebook, Blogs, Q&A websites and many other.

# 3. SYSTEM DESIGN

After analyzing the currently available systems and the functionalities they offer, we started analyzing the infrastructure that should back our system. According to [1] we opted for a Cloud-based service to offer the infrastructure for data synchronization between the apps and the operator panel. We also make use of the best practices of developing mobile applications by migrating data and processing power inside the Cloud. We have studied how to realize the integration between the service and the Cloud and the benefits of this approach and we analyzed the means of implementing web services for fulfilling this goal.

We developed an API for our service which would be consumed inside the mobile application. We decided on using REST web services as they preferred when working with mobile applications. We needed the application to be available on as many mobile phone operating systems as possible, so we continued by analyzing cross platform mobile development solutions. After comparing Titanium development with other development frameworks we decided on using this platform because it offered a series of advantages such as compiling natively and being able to be extended in order to support more advanced functionality available for iOS or Android.

One important requirement was that the cross platform development supports *GPS*. According to [5] we make use of how to implement *GPS* into our application and how to determine *GPS* coordinates with various precisions. We can still determine the approximate user position when *GPS* is not available, such as when the user is located inside a building, which is a very common use case for our system. The way to identify the position of the user in such condition is by *GPS*triangulation. Even without a *GPS* receiver, the cell phone can provide information about your location. A computer can determine the location based on measurements of your signal, such as: its angle of approach to the cell towers, how long it takes the signal to travel to multiple towers and the strength of your signal when it reaches the towers.

The specific system that we are developing allows clients (users) to book vehicles directly from their mobile device without having to call through an operator. Having an app for this use case opens the doors for a wide variety of marketing strategies such as offering promotions, coupons, paying by credit card, offering subscriptions. This allows users to have an alternative to the traditional method of booking a vehicle by phone calling, based on the new and powerful trend of mobile cloud applications.

## 3.1. Functional and Nonfunctional System Characteristics

Software is becoming critical in driving the information-based economy. Time-to-market, robustness, and quality are important factors for measuring the success of systems in competitive economies and environments. There is also a need to evolve and adapt rapidly in an environment of continuous changes of business requirements. Therefore, there are stronger needs for standards and formalizations of the processes by which we specify and capture these requirements. Requirements capture is one of the initial phases to undertake in the system development process.

The functional requirements (FR) have been decomposed into low-level functional specifications that are depicted in Table 2. These specifications have been assigned priorities which are consistent with the iterative approach of development that we are following.

**Table 2.** Functional Requirements.

| | | |
|---|---|---|
| **FR1** | **Booking a vehicle by clients** | High |
| FR1.1 | Ordering based on GPS location | High |
| FR1.2 | Add precise location | High |
| FR1.3 | Remember used locations for suggestions | High |
| FR1.4 | Display map with user location | High |
| FR1.5 | Allow dragging the position marker on the map | Medium |
| FR1.6 | Get GPS location based on wireless | High |
| FR1.7 | Handle cases when GPS location cannot be obtained by allowing only exact address input | High |
| **FR2** | **Vehicle Dispatching** | High |
| FR2.1 | View active orders | High |
| FR2.2 | Respond to active order | High |
| FR2.2.1 | Respond with car id and time until it arrives | High |
| FR2.2.2 | Mark initial car position on a map | Medium |
| FR2.3 | Blink and sound alert on new order | High |
| FR2.4 | Call phone for order not processed within 1 min | Low |
| **FR3** | **Order confirmation** | High |
| FR3.1 | Display vehicle id and time until it arrives | High |
| FR3.2 | Allow order canceling | High |
| FR3.3 | Allow vehicle check-in | Medium |
| FR3.4 | Allow push notification if app is closed | High |
| **FR4** | **Authentication** | High |
| FR4.1 | Allow Facebook authentication | High |
| FR4.2 | Allow authentication with username, password and phone number | High |
| FR4.3 | Verify phone number | Low |
| **FR5** | **App promotion trough social networks** | High |
| FR5.1 | Allow Facebook sharing of app use | High |
| FR5.2 | Prompt for app review after 1 successful ride | High |
| **FR6** | **Feedback** | High |
| FR6.1 | Allow feedback from button in tab bar | High |
| FR6.2 | Allow vehicle check-out | Low |
| **FR7** | **User post-ride functionalities** | High |
| FR7.1 | Allow distance displayed on check out | Low |
| FR7.2 | Prompt user for driver rating on check out | Low |
| **FR8** | **Management Dashboard and Social CRM** | High |
| FR8.1 | Filter data in real time across multiple social networks | High |
| FR8.2 | Get an overall sentiment analysis of the service provided for specific time intervals | High |
| FR8.3 | Data augmentation in real time and Metadata generation | High |
| FR8.4 | Export data to a data store | High |

Non-functional requirements (NFR) are properties and qualities the software system must possess while providing its intended functional requirements or services. These types of requirements have to be considered while developing the functional counterparts. They greatly affect the design and implementation choices a developer may make. They also affect the acceptability of the developed software by its intended users. In the following, we briefly describe the three categories of non-functional requirements that may be imposed on a software system.

**System-related NFRs:** These types of requirements impose some criteria related to the internal qualities of the system under development and the hardware/software context in which this system will operate.

- Operational requirements: The Dispatching Application will be running on iOS and Android phones, and will be using Cloud services for data synchronization and storage.
- Manageability requirements: The manager will be able to administer customer complaints and to scan social networks for potential issues regarding the service. He should also be able to use the information in the system databases regarding clients previous booking in order to direct advertising campaigns and monitor the overall client satisfaction with the service.
- Performance requirements: For our system these requirements are considering the response time of data synchronization.
- The response time to an order is dependent of the other user inserting the response manually (the operator or the driver being a human not a system that can respond automatically). Data synchronization must be assured to take place bellow 2 s.
- Maintainability requirements: The system must be designed in such a way that it allows a modifiable, component based system that allows future modifications and functionality extensions without breaking the present working version. This requirement is especially valid for our mobile application, as different mobile application versions installed on smartphone must communicate effectively with the Cloud-based API. In order to achieve maintainability we relied on API versioning for this specific requirement.
- Portability requirements: The system must work on a variety of mobile OS, of which iOS and Android are mandatory. A cross platform solution must be implemented to allow maximum code reuse with little adaptation.

- Security requirements: The application must use the .NET security framework for assuring authentication and authorization security constraints, and must also allow for SSL communication.

**Process and Project-related NFRs:** These types of NFRs impose criteria to be followed while developing the project.

- Conformance to standards requirements: The standard developing pattern for Titanium applications is MVC, which should be followed in order to assure maximum code reusability and maintainability.
- Development process requirements: The project needs to be developed in an iterative method, allowing for partial system components development and testing.
- Testing requirements: The API for the Cloud infrastructure needs to be tested using a unit testing approach, while the mobile vehicle booking application need to be tested using use-case testing.
- Installation and deployment requirements: The mobile applications need to be deployed to the AppStore and GooglePlay accordingly.

**Human-related NFRs:** These types of requirements deal with constraints related to the stakeholders and the social and societal context in which the system is deployed.

- Usability requirements: The application needs to be easy to understand and use by new users. It must also feature a demo the first time the application is launched.
- Look and Feel requirements: The mobile application needs to adhere to the usual UI components and not define custom components that might reduce the learnability of the system.
- Legal requirements: The application should not allow for malicious uses of personal data required by the application such as mobile phone numbers. This data must be stored on the Cloud and should be accessible only for specific users, if needed.

**Device-related NFRs**

- GPS: The device must feature GPS capable services for approximate user position identification.
- Internet: The device must allow for Internet connection for sending order, receiving responses and for the overall interconnection with the Cloud services.
- Operating system: The device must work with any iOS or Android version.

- Screen resolution: The application must work properly on any screen resolution. The application must be compatible with both the Retina display and the lower resolution display screens.

**Social Network related NFR**

- Completeness: The system must be able to scan for customer feedback across multiple social networks.
- Metadata: The data should be augmented in order to provide location context to the social network posts.
- Usability: The dashboard should be easy to operate and with meaningful.

## 3.2. Technological Perspective

### 3.2.1. Cross Platform Mobile Applications

According to Gartner, at the beginning of 2014, Android had 78.4% market share, while iOS had 15.6% of new worldwide sales. This means that their combined market share is more than 90% of all new smartphone sales. However, even if the two players dominate the market, developing for two frameworks is time consuming as very little work can be reused, the programming language and development environment for *Android* and *iOS* being very different. Also if another *OS* must be targeted in the future, this would require rewriting the application. In order to increase productivity a cross platform approach can be used. There is currently a wide range of cross platform solutions available including *Appcelerator Titanium*, *RhoMobile* and *PhoneGap*. *Appcelerator Titanium* [6] is an open source project and has integrated most common functionalities of *iOS* and *Android*. Developing with Titanium compared to other Cross Platform solutions is that it allows for native development. When using *Titanium* you are programming in *JavaScript* and the framework translates the code into native *Java* or *Objectual-C*. The development environment for Titanium is using its own *IDE* based on *Eclipse*, *Titanium Studio*, and it uses the JavaScript development language. It can also be extended using module in order to offer complete native functionality, which is not supported by the Titanium platform, and the recommended way of development is using a *MVC* pattern.

### 3.2.2. Windows Communication Foundation (Wcf)

Windows Communication Foundation [7] is a framework for building service-oriented applications. Using *WCF*, applications can send data or asynchronous messages from one service endpoint to another. An endpoint can be a client of a service that requests data from a service endpoint. The messages can be as simple as a single character or word sent as XML, or as complex as a stream of binary data. In WCF all the communication details are handled by channel, it is a stack of channel components that all messages pass through during runtime processing. When are calling WCF service through a proxy class on the client side, it will send message (request soap message mainly includes some parameter values of method) and first the message will go through protocol Channels which mainly supports for security, transactions and reliable messaging, and second the message will go through encoder which convert messages into an array of bytes for transport, finally, the encoder message will go through the bottom transport channel which are responsible for transporting raw message bytes. WCF provides a number of transport protocols, including HTTP, TCP, MSMQ, peer-to-peer, and named pipes. In summary, *WCF* is designed to offer a manageable approach to creating Web services and Web service clients.

### 3.2.3. Microsoft Entity Framework

The Microsoft ADO.NET Entity Framework [8] is an Object/Relational Mapping (ORM) framework that enables developers to work with relational data as domain-specific objects, eliminating the need for most of the data access plumbing code that developers usually need to write. Using the Entity Framework, developers issue queries using LINQ, then retrieve and manipulate data as strongly typed objects. The Entity Framework's ORM implementation provides services like change tracking, identity resolution, lazy loading, and query translation so that developers can focus on their application-specific business logic rather than the data access fundamentals.

### 3.2.4. SignalR

Traditionally web applications used a polling technique for getting updates. For the client application this is not feasible as the polling interval is unknown. For example the driver could wait for hours without receiving an order, so he would poll thousands of times to receive one favorable result. Also the polling interval would have to be below 2 s (to offer a response time as low as possible), which would mean a high demand on the server and low scalability.

SignalR [9] is an Asynchronous library for .NET to help build real-time, multi-user interactive applications and is based on long polling techniques. Long polling is a variation of the traditional polling technique and allows emulation of an information push from a server to a client. With long polling, the client requests information from the server in a similar way to a normal poll. However, if the server does not have any information available for the client, instead of sending an empty response, the server holds the request and waits for some information to be available. Once the information becomes available (or after a suitable timeout), a complete response is sent to the client. The client will immediately re-request information from the server, so that the server will always have an available waiting request that it can use to deliver data in response to an event. Long polling is not a push code, but can be used under circumstances where a real push is not possible. Using long polling in the client mobile application gets notified to update its data, and thus to synchronize with the server, exactly as the new data is available. Using a long polling approach there is a very low demand on the server which translates into a high scalability, as new users and drivers are added to the distributed dispatching system.

In the .NET framework SignalR represents an implementation of long polling. However SignalR does not rely only on the long polling technique. SignalR has a concept of transports, each transport decides how data is sent/received and how it connects and disconnects. Transports build into SignalR are: WebSockets, Server Sent Events, Forever Frame, Long polling. SignalR tries to choose the "best" connection supported by server and client.

### 3.2.5. Push Notifications

Mobile apps are allowed to perform only very specific activities in the background, so battery life is conserved. However, it is required that there is a way to alert the user of interesting things that are happening even if the user is not currently inside the app. Mobile OS have provided a solution to this. Instead of the app continuously checking for events or doing work in the background, a server-side component for doing this can be written. When an event of interest occurs, the server-side component can send the app a push notification, which is intended for signaling the app that there are event pending on the server. Push Notifications are not intended for transmitting data to the client app, but are used as a signaling mechanism when the app is not running. Push Notifications makes no guarantee about delivery or the order of messages. Apps need to register with the Notification Service that is APNS (Apple Push Notifications Service) [10] for Apple and C2DN for Android [11]. This assigns a specific ID called device token that the app can send to the server. If the server needs to perform a push notification, it uses this device token to specify the app it want to send the notification to. Device tokens change so it is advisable to perform device token updates on the mobile preferably every time the app is opened. The Notification service offers an API that the server can poll periodically to determine what device tokens are still active. Because communication between the server and the notification Service is not trivial, 3rd party services are available such as Urban Airship [12].

### 3.2.6. Social Network Data Filtering

DataSift [3] is a platform that enables cost efficient and simple retrieval of data cross platform with built in augmentation for data. The main usage of this data at the moment is for marketing purposes, for example a marketer might be interested in how a specific new product is received by the market, the sentiment towards various functional aspects or some specific idea. DataSift bridges all this different data sources and delivers insights, and as this data is created and analyzed in real time, it is possible to respond with very low latency to the current public sentiment. Because some specific search queries might be too complex for search engines, this is the point where search technology can be improved by using crowd-sourced data across a multitude of systems. This data can be combined in order to respond to more complex queries. DataSift can be configured to act as the query engine for answers to question that come from various data sources.

### 3.2.7. Data Sources

Twitter was the first Data Source supported by DataSift and still is the most important. However once the infrastructure was created, DataSift has added more data sources that can be analyzed in real time.

- Facebook—license cost FREE—With more than 1.1 Billion active users, Facebook public data provides a unique view into what the world is watching, sharing and interested in.This data source provides access to the stream of public Facebook status updates, which include text-updates, links, photos and videos. Location names (e.g. restaurants) are added if the status update includes a location or check-in. This provides valuable insights to help market researchers. Author information including full name, profile photo and Facebook user-id is removed in accordance with Facebook's Platform Policies on Data Collection and Usage.

- Twitter—license cost $0.10 per 1000 interaction—The Twitter source delivers the text of Tweets plus more than 40 other pieces of data associated with Tweets. With more than a quarter of a billion Tweets every day, Twitter is an immensely significant source of data, delivering both breadth and depth of coverage. With this source you can receive data such as the author's name and screen name, their location, their preferred language, the number of people they follow on Twitter and how many people follow them. Other examples include filtering for Retweets, or for Tweets sent in reply to a particular author, or for particular keywords in users' bios.

- Wordpress—license cost $0.50 per 1000 interactions—WordPress powers 20 percent of blogs and sites on the web and has more than 1 million posts per day from blogs on wordpress.com, as well as content from sites hosted elsewhere that utilize WordPress as a content management platform if they enable the Jetpack plug-in. Comments and likes are also available from this data source.
- Blogs—license cost $4.00 per 1000 interactions—The Blog data source combines material from a wide variety of sites, ranging from well-known hosts such as Blogger with very large numbers of active users to small, single-user sites that run as blogs or incorporate a blog. You want to count mentions of a competitor's brand across as many social media sites as possible. Activate the Blog data source and use the interaction content target in your filter to capture posts from every available source. By spreading your "net" in this way you can add extra volume to your input data, to make your statistical analysis more significant.

## 3.3. System Use Cases

There are four types of actors that the system supports, each having specific capabilities. We will analyze each actor together with the associated use cases.

The client actor is the user that has the booking application installed on his mobile phone. He uses the application to order taxis by sending his location to the server that consists of the *Cloud*. This is the main functionality of the system, which we will be presenting later on in a more detailed fashion. We note that this use case is composed of two elements: getting the *GPS* position of the user, which is used by the system to identify the address of the user, and it also offers the possibility of fix tuning this location to specify it more precisely, as this location will be sent to the operator or the driver. The User use cases are presented in Table 3.

The vehicle tracking functionality allows the user to see the taxi approaching on a map. In addition to this time estimation will be displayed together with a distance approximation. In case the response to an order comes from the operator, this functionality will not be available, as the taxi will not have GPS capabilities that allow tracking. The Share on Social networks use case allows the user to share the current ride with his friends on social media. This is an element that

**Table 3.** Client Use Case specifications.

| Category | Use case |
|---|---|
| Book vehicle | Access map view of nearby vehicles |
| Book vehicle | Specify exact location |
| Book vehicle | Get time and cost estimates |
| Book vehicle | Specify advance booking time |
| Book vehicle | See vehicle details |
| Track Vehicle | Track vehicle on map |
| Track Vehicle | Get notifications |
| Pay for the ride | In app payment |
| Rate vehicle | Rate vehicle |
| Share on Social Network | Share on social networks |

enhances the marketing potential for the app and a key component in attracting new users. There are two types of services which users can use with the app: Facebook and Twitter. One of the main benefits of using this app is the possibility of accumulating points, as a rewards program envisioned to spur app usage and attract new users. Each time the user will be making orders using the app, he will accumulate points which can be converted into free apps.

The Driver is responsible for responding to incoming orders. It does this by accepting or declining an order using a simple two buttons interface. The orders are assigned to drivers based on the proximity of the client to the driver. In addition to these functionalities, the Driver can also call the client in case he cannot see him at the specified pick up location or if he needs additional information. The driver cannot see the clients phone number, but only a call button. The rate client functionality allows the driver to rate the client based on his behavior. The rating is based on considerations such as: was the client present at the meeting point, did he leave a tip, was he loudly *etc*. The rating is based on a 5 star system subjective to the driver. Future orders placed by the client will show the overall rating that this client has.

The operator is responsible for responding to orders that were not answered by drivers directly. This allows companies to use the traditional mechanism for finding a taxi and send a response to the client. Using this mechanism, the client always gets a response to his order, even if no driver is available in his proximity that is active.

Responding to a client involves two things. First, an identifier for the taxi must be specified. This consists of the car number or some other way for the client to identify the taxi. Also the operator must specify the approximate location where the taxi is at the moment, by selecting it from a map. This creates a more visual context for the client and creates a sense of consistency between orders answered by the driver and the operator. Similar to the driver, the operator can call the client to ask him more details. Distinctly from the driver, the operator can see the users number. As we earlier specified, when a response to an order is set, the operator selects an address from the map which will display the initial taxi position to the client. It is possible for the operator to cancel an order from the client, in which case can write a cancelation message explaining the decision. The operator use cases are illustrated in Figure 1.

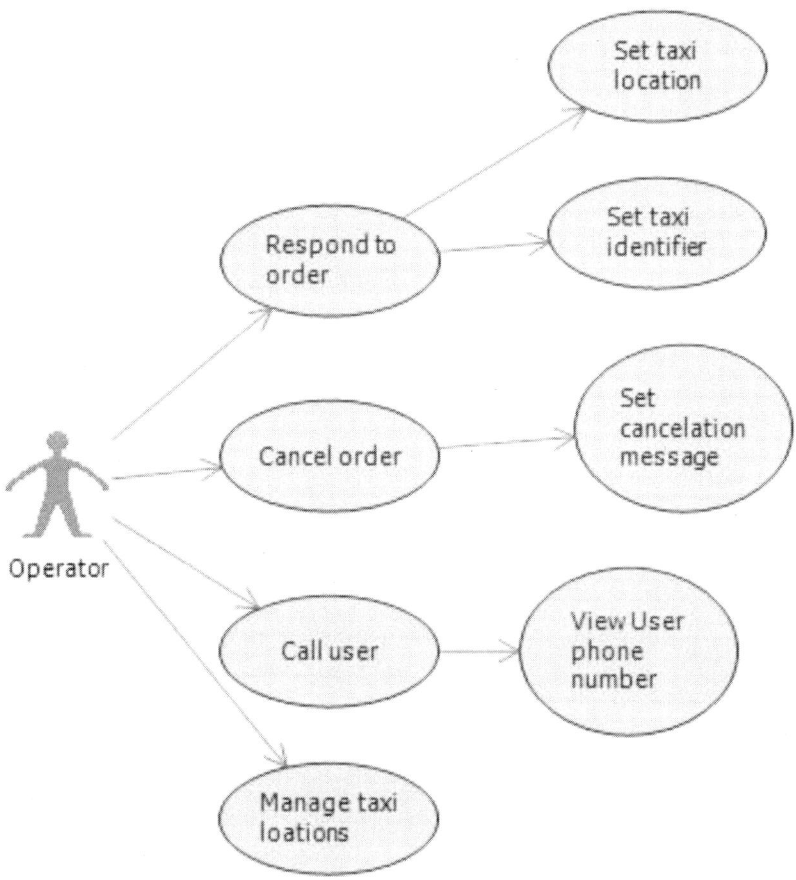


**Figure 1.** Operator use case.

The Manager actor is responsible with registering taxi companies into the system, setting the areas in which they operate, adding drivers and creating operator accounts. The manager is a role comparable with the administrator of the system. It has the power to change accounts, activate or deactivate them.

The Social CRM can provide valuable information regarding the user satisfaction level with the service and the potential direct improvement points. The person responsible for the Social CRM management will have access to a dashboard offering metrics such as overall customer satisfaction levels for specific time intervals, highly negative or positive comments in real time and automation and filtering tools. Also the Social CRM component will augment user data with statistics obtained using DataSift. The list of Social CRM use case is presented in Table 4.

**Table 4.** Social Customer Relationship Management (CRM) Use Case specifications.

| Category | Use Case |
|---|---|
| User data augmentation | See user satisfaction metric |
| User data augmentation | Segment users by activity levels |
| User data augmentation | Identify promotion targets |
| Data filtering | Identify comments in real time |
| Data filtering | React to comments in real time |
| Customer satisfaction | Create promotion |
| Customer satisfaction | Assign to-do items |

Social CRM—React to Comment Use Case Detailed

When a highly positive or negative comment regarding the service is published on the web either on a social media website such as Twitter or Facebook, or through a blog comment or even an article, DataSift will extract that interaction and will deliver it to our application in real time as presented in Figure 2. The complete process through which DataSift is capable of extracting this interactions and augmenting them in real time will be explained in the following section.

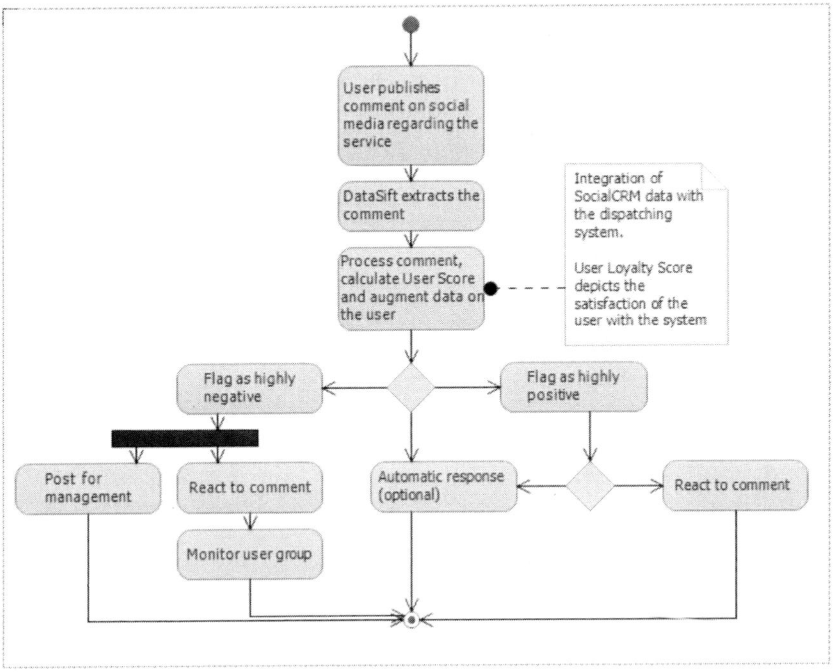


**Figure 2.** Social CRM react to comment use case.

Once the interaction enters our system, it is already augmented with sentiment analysis, which means it can easily be catalogued by our application. The comments that have a sentiment rating between 15 and 20 (20 being the maximum) are tagged as highly positive. Comments having a rating between −20 and −15 (−20 being the minimum) are tagged as highly negative. Both of this categories are extremely important from a marketing perspective.

If a comment is highly positive, the marketer is interested in building on the positive experience of the user and will offer him bonus point or extra credit for inviting new people to the platform.

## 3.4. Conceptual Design

The proposed system is a complex solution which can be decomposed into multiple components. From a high level architectural point of view, the core of the product is represented by the *Cloud Engine*, which is stored on Windows Azure. The Cloud Engine uses a *relational SQL database* for persistence and interacts with third party services. The mobile applications for clients and drivers access the service through the *custom built API*. The *management panel* is also a separate component that is built on the Cloud service. The *social media analysis tool* cuts across both the cloud service and the operator management panel, providing insights and automating social media data augmentation. A high level representation of the system can be observed in Figure 3.

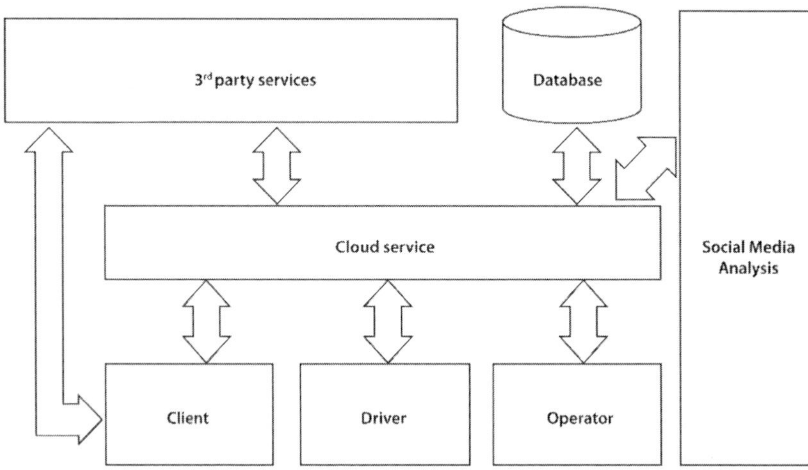


**Figure 3.** The block diagram of the system.

Client and Driver apps and the Operator web interface are the consumers of the *API* exposed by the Cloud service. The Cloud Service acts as the intermediary between all communication that takes place between these components and handles the data synchronization. The Cloud service relies on its functionality on using a database for persisting information such as orders, responses, users *etc*. The Cloud service also interacts with external services for performing specific tasks. Examples of this include sending *push notifications* or *reverse geocoding*. The client mobile applications can also access external services. For example the Client app accesses Facebook and analytics services.

The Cloud service acts as *a hub* and intermediating all communication between the clients. While for a client booking a vehicle seems as a P2P operation, it actually constitutes a client-server operation. As illustrated, numerous operators, divers and Clients can connect to the Cloud, new ones can be added, or some can be removed at any time. For example a taxi driver that terminates his work schedule for the day, can disconnect from the Cloud service and will not receive any new orders until he checks in again with the service.

All data is stored into a proprietary SQL database, and specific tasks that have been delegated to external services are managed by the Cloud service. When a client books a vehicle, the Cloud service checks through the fleet of vehicles that are available on that area at that moment and selects one for being dispatched to the client. In case no vehicle is received, the Cloud service sends the order to a specific vehicle company in order to be processed. Not all mobile applications are required to have a server component. However applications that require a higher degree of complexity need to create their own model and an API for exposing the services. *Cloud* computing is known to be a promising solution for mobile computing due to reasons including mobility, communication, and portability, reliability, security. In the following, we describe how the Cloud can be used to overcome obstacles in mobile computing, thereby pointing out advantages of *Mobile Cloud Computing (MCC)* [15] MCC refers to an infrastructure where both the data storage and the data processing happen outside of the mobile device. Mobile Cloud applications move the computing power and data storage away from mobile phones and into the Cloud, bringing applications and mobile computing to not just smartphone users but also a much broader range of mobile subscribers.

Figure 4 depicts a high level overview of the Social media analysis tool as implemented by DataSift. Facebook, Twitter, Blogs and other online data sources are monitored in real time and processed by the DataSift Engine.

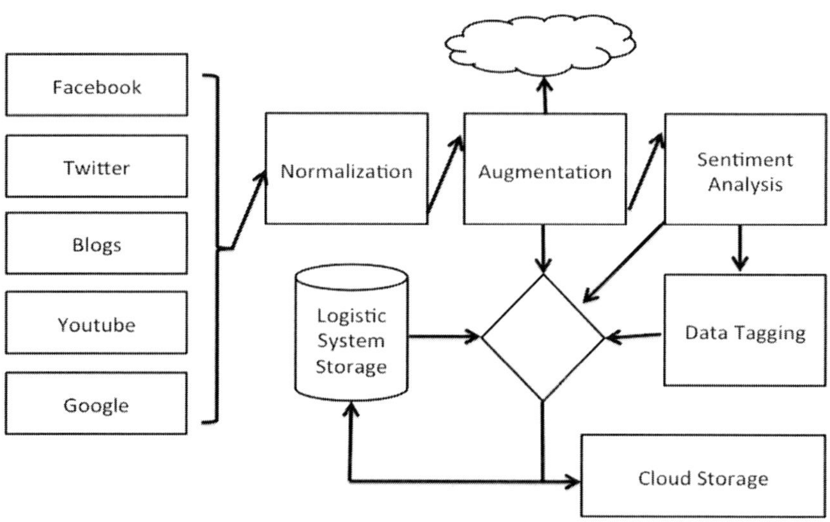


**Figure 4.** Social CRM components built on DataSift.

The process of augmentation of the user data in our system and the insights provided to the customer relationship responsible goes through a pipeline of steps. The normalization step converts all interactions into a similar format independent of their source, whether it is Facebook, Twitter or a blog post. Augmentation provides additional data on the interaction such as location context and fetching of the content of a link. The sentiment analysis tool provides a mean of grading the sentiment associated with a given post on a scale from −20 to +20. The sentiment analysis is provided by a Lexalytics algorithm that is offered as a black box solution. Data integration with the dispatching system is handled in the Logistic System Storage, where the data is stored into one common database.

We have analyzed the theoretical approaches and the frameworks required for implementing the proposed application. In the following chapter we are detailing how we implemented the vehicle booking application.

## 3.5. System Implementation

In this section we will present the system architecture and some implementation deign concerns for all major components. As we have stated in the previous sections, our system consists in a dispatching system which is vertically integrated with a Social CRM system. The Social CRM system is responsible for aggregating information about our users from online data sources and are used for improving the customer relationships or better targeting the users using advertising.

In Figure 5 we have represented the two systems in more detail. The Social CRM system is built on top of the DataSift platform. The dispatching system is responsible for controlling the DataSift platform using the API it exposes. Through the API we can use filters for sifting only the interactions we need, and then integrating the two systems using a common SQL Azure database.

Next we will analyze both of the two systems and the integration between them. First we will address the dispatching system, and in the second half of this chapter we will analyze the DataSift platform in detail.

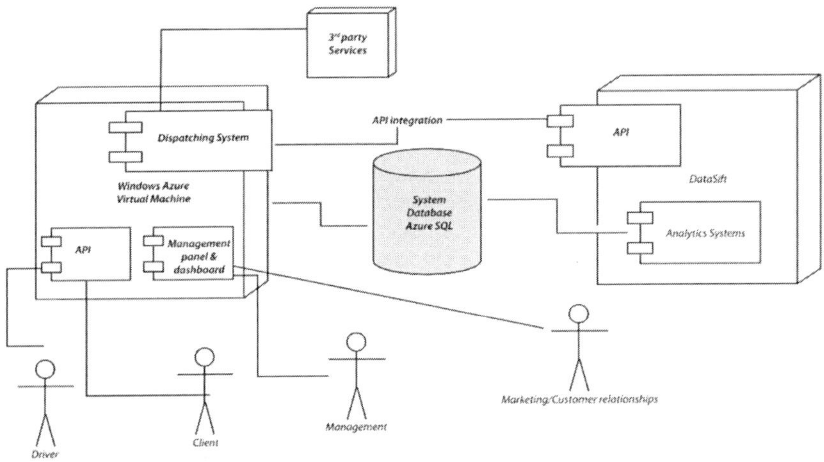


**Figure 5.** System integration.

### 3.5.1. General Mobile Dispatching System Architecture And Implementation

The Dispatching System can operate as a standalone application. There can be identified two types of components. The first type includes the proprietary components. This need to be developed by the developers, are based on specific frameworks and include: the components constituting the Cloud service (designating the service built by the developers), the mobile application, the browser client and the management interface. The second type of components are represented by the 3rd party services (distinctly from proprietary services, 3rd party services or external services are built by other organizations and are made available to the public for use) are exposed trough certain API.

In this example we are using five types of external services: The Notification Service—used for sending Push Notifications (a way of alerting a mobile device), social services that offer integration with Facebook and Twitter, Analytics services for tracking usage patterns, SMS gateway service for sending the user an SMS with the activation code (required by the business rules), and a geocoding and reverse geocoding service for converting GPS position into street address. All of these components will be explained together with their implementation technologies and internal working

A request is serialized as *JSON*, signed using the user key and sent to the server through the server *API*. The server determines the nearest driver to the user, by interrogating the database based on the business logic. Once the nearest driver is determined, the *Signaling Framework* (used to alert the mobile application) is used to determine the selected driver's app to download or update the order sent by the client. After the driver confirms the order, the server uses the same approach to inform the user that his order was responded. All requests sent to the proprietary server components need to use SSL for proving security to the system. The dispatching application exposes *JSON REST* services using *WCF* Framework. Working with *JSON* in the context of *WCF* is easy as the framework automatically serializes *JSON* request and responses and performs data binding between *JavaScript* and *CLR* objects. Once the data is received on the server, the server performs some security check on the request. This usually implies authentication and authorization of the request. As there is no password required for the Taxi Ordering application, signing the data using a key, which is known only by the client and the server, and is unique for each client mobile application, does this.

Figure 6 depicts the integration between the client mobile application and the server. On The client we have the *MVC*pattern. The view sends an event to the controller, which calls the send order operation on the *Model*. The model component responsible for sending the request (implemented in Titanium using an *HTTP Socket*), serializes the data and sends them to the specified service endpoint exposed by the API. Once the request arrives on the server, the reverse process occurs as the JS data objects are translated into *CLR* objects by the *WCF* framework. The security component is responsible for checking the signature of the user in the case of Order Taxi applications. In other applications a username and password approach can be used for obtaining the same result. It is essential to observe that once the request passes the security verification, it is recorded and the registration key for the order is returned to the client. Further on the client uses this registration key for referring to his order. At this point there is no response available for the client yet.

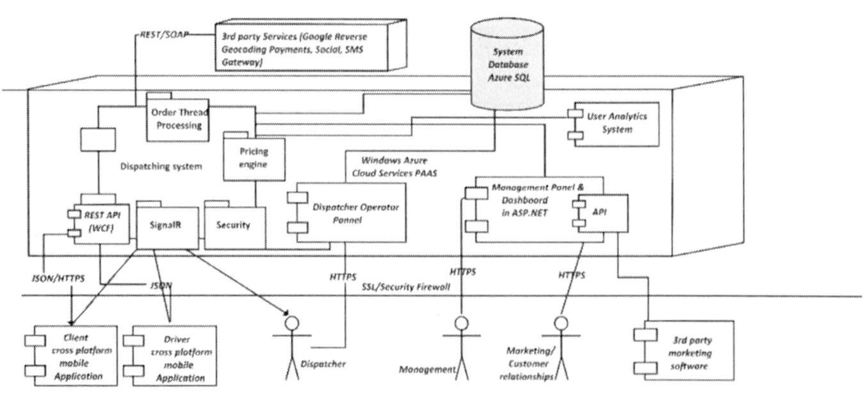


**Figure 6.** General Dispatching System Architecture.

The order placed by the user in the system is assigned to the nearest driver. When the driver confirms the order, a response is sent to the client mobile application. This response can come after a variable amount of time which can be anywhere between a few seconds and 3 min. In consequence *SignalR* is used to inform the client when the response is ready. SignalR is not used to pass the response directly to the user, but rather the user applications download the response once it receives the update signal.

An important characteristic of the service is that it should offer scalability. All the components depicted can be hosted in the *Cloud*. This allows an elastic hosting environment, which can be used easily. For Order Taxi application, we are using *Windows Azure*. Using *Windows Azure* we can easily deploy the server component as it was built completely on the *.NET*framework.

**Location determination.** Titanium offers the possibility of interacting with device capabilities such as using the GPS and allows for specific parameter to be set on the GPS such as the precision of positioning, as a balance between time and required accuracy. When the app starts the coordinates are the ones cached on the device, in other words the ones detected at the last time you used the geolocation on your device. Detecting the current position takes time so if you have an app based on geolocation you might want to take this in account to improve the user experience and avoid to get false results. Titanium.Geolocation [6] provides the necessary methods to manage geolocation.

**Implementation of the Model.** The business logic of the system is implemented in the model. The service model is composed of a set of classes representing the implementation of the domain model. Figure 7 represents the most important objects that constitute the domain model. Because Entity Framework was used for mapping CLR objects to database records, these entities have a corresponding implementation in the SQL server database. We are outlining the most important entities presented in our system:

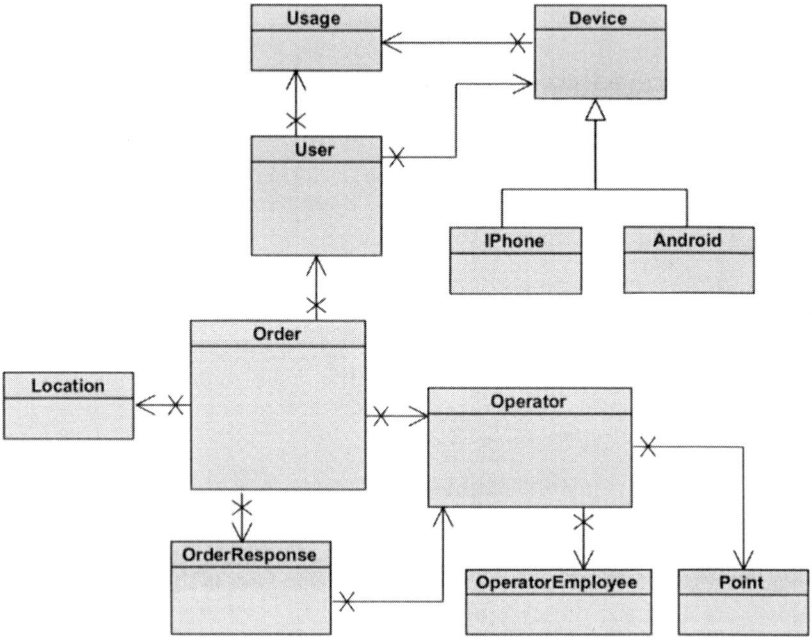


**Figure 7.** The entities of the system model.

*Order*: represents an order placed by the client into the system. The Order has a set of attributes representing:

- State of the order: *IsResolved, IsCanceled, IsPendingResponse*. This attributes are used for identifying the current status of the order.
- Modification time: Each modification of the state of the order also sets a time stamp on the object, which is used by the system. For example when an order is created, it is displayed to the operator together with a label showing how much time has passed since the order was submitted.
- Data associated with an order: Represent information such as the rating of the taxi driver or the feedback of the client following the ride.
- Associated data such as the pick-up location or the owner is represented as references to the specific entities.

*User*: represents the client who is placing orders into the system. The user has the following attributes associated with him:

- Name represents the name chosen by the person submitting orders.

- Registration date the date when this user registered by submitting his phone number and name
- Phone number is used for contacting the person in case he does not show up at the pick-up location
- Phone is validated is used to determine whether the specific user was validated by the validation code sent through the *SMS*.
- The user must be marked as active in order to be able to place orders into the system. A user state can be changed to inactive in case abuse has been observed for this particular user.
- The confirmation code is the activation code sent to the user through *SMS* that is used to determine if the phone number is valid.

*Location*: Represents the position where an order is set. It contains the *GPS* coordinates for the location together with an optional name for it. There is also a property used for counting how often that location is used. The more frequent locations will be displayed first in the location suggestion list.

*Operator:* This entity represents an operator, which might me understood as a taxi company or a collection of taxi companies unified as a group. This entity presents the following properties:

- Activation date and time, when this operator has been registered
- A perimeter that represents where the operator is active, represented by a collection of points.
- Stations represent predefined locations on the map where taxis are expected to be present.

*OperatorEmployee:* This class represents the operator that responds to orders.

The name is the real name of the operator.

*IsActive* property is set to true for those *Operators* which are active, meaning having permission to access the system, permission set the manager.

*OrderResponse:* created by the *OperatorEmployee* and represents the response the user receives for his order. It contains the necessary information required by the client such as the car number, the name of the driver, and the expected waiting time for the user. It also has an *IsRead* property which is used for determining whether the response has been read by the user application. If the Response is not read in a certain amount of time, this means that that the client application is closed and as a consequence the response needs to be delivered using push notifications.

*Point:* This class is used for defining perimeters in which an operator activates. Ay order placed within this perimeter might come to the operator. The number represents the count for the point, so that given a collection of points and their orders, the system can check whether a specific point is inside that perimeter or outside of it.

The entities are mapped by Entity Framework into the CLR classes which are further extended in functionality by means of partial classes, by adding extra functionality.

**Service Database.** The service relies on a SQL rational database. The service database is generated using *Entity Framework*, and we designed the *Entity Framework* entities directly mapped to the tables, and providing the same properties as columns in the rational database.

*UserSet* table represents the client who is placing orders into the system. The most important columns of this table include the name which represents the name chosen by the person submitting orders, the registration date – the date when this user registered by submitting his phone number and name. The phone number is used for contacting the person in case he does not show up at the pick-up location, and is represented as an nVarChar.

We used this representation especially because phone number formats are very different for distinct regions. *IsPhoneValidated* column is used to determine whether the specific user was validated by the validation code sent through SMS. The user must be marked as active in order to be able to place orders into the system, this column being represented as a non-nullable Boolean type. A user state can be changed to inactive in case abuse has been observed for this particular user. The confirmation code is the activation code sent to the user through SMS that is used to determine if the phone number is valid. This column is also represented as an nVarChar.

The table *OrderSet* has the foreign key represented by *User_id* that specifies the User which placed the order inside the system. *OrderSet* and *OrderResponseSet* have a one to one relationship between them. We decided to separate these two tables, even though there is a synonymy relationship between them as there can be order, which do not have a response, such as for example an order that was canceled.

We can observe that there was no case for splitting entities in our model. In this mapping scenario, properties from a single entity in the conceptual model are mapped to columns in two or more underlying tables. In this scenario, the tables must share a common primary key. In our mapping scenario each entity in the conceptual model is mapped to a single table in the storage model. This is the default mapping generated by Entity Data Model tools. Each operator can define multiple stations which represent positions on the map which an associated name (records in the *LocationsSet* Table) that are by the operator to specify the initial taxi position easily, by clicking the marker on the map associated to that specific location. The mapping of a list of stations (defined as actually being of type location) to the *OperatorSet* is done by *EntityFramework* by introducing a new table called *OperatorLocation*, as can be observed in Figure 8.

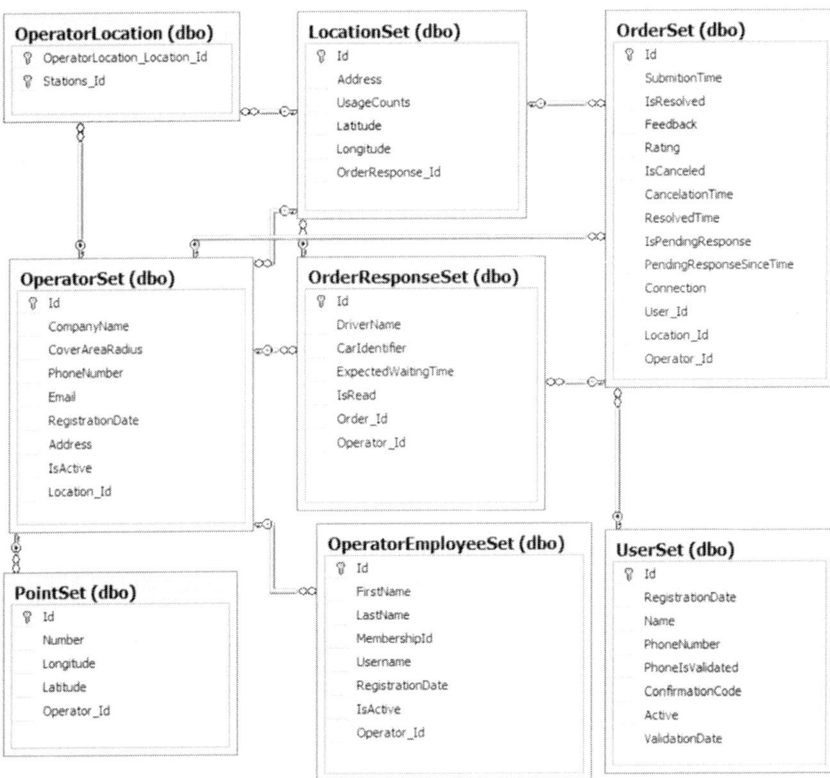


**Figure 8.** The MS-SQL database.

We are using this database model representing the conceptual model of the system inside *SQL Server 2010*. We have decided on implementing our database using Entity Framework generate Database from Model approach, as it offered a productive environment where changes in the model could be easily translated into updates of the database. We also notice that there is a balance between the numbers of read and write operations as every record inserted into the database needs to be read usually just one time, processed and then archived. For example an Order is created, added to the system, it is answered by the operator, and the response is sent back to the client and after this there response is no longer used actively and constitutes solely a history used for creating suggestions such as, for example, suggesting pick up locations.

**System API specification.** The interaction between the client mobile and the server is performed through the means of a *REST* API and we implemented the *REST* API trough WCF. For example, IApi is the interface which is implemented by the API class. IApi exposes multiple methods including: UserOrderNew, UserOrderCancel, UserOrderResponse and UserNew.

*UserOrderNew*—this method is exposed as a resource using the verb POST and is available by invoking the service at the location /Api/user/order/new. The data passed to the method are encoded as JSON and consist of the User name and phone number. Once this data are received on the server the system sends the user an SMS message at the specified phone number. At this moment the user status is set as invalidated. In order to validate the phone number the user needs to send the confirmation code sent to him through SMS by using the next method described, ValidatePhone.

*UserOrderCancel*—this method is used to validate the users phone number by sending using the POST verb the code sent to him by SMS. This rest resource is available at /Api/user/order/cancel. The data needs to be submitted in the JSON format, as with all API calls to our service. When the code reaches the server, it is checked whether the code matches the one in the system. If the code is correct, the user is allowed to submit the order.

*UserOrderResponse*—this method allows for creating a new order inside the system. This is performed by sending the information required the order to the address /Api/user/order/response using the POST verb. Once an order is received on the server, it is recorded inside the database; it gets displayed on a specific operator panel. Once the operator responds to the order, an OrderResponse entry is created and an update signal is sent to the client. Among the attributes in a create order request the most important are:

- The location where the order was sent for. This consists of the GPS position
- The user who submitted the request

- The date and time the order was created
- The device information

*GetOrderResponse*—allows the client to read the response to his order. It is accessible using the GET verb at the address /Api/order/response. The request contains the identity of the order. The response is encoded as JSON and contains the information for the client such as:

- The car number which was assigned for the order
- The information regarding the driver
- The estimated arrival time of the driver

*UserOrderCancel*—allows an order to be canceled by the user. The cancelation is performed by the client, and is accessible at /Api/user/order/cancel. The request verb is POST, as the submitted information contains the identity of the order that should be canceled. We note that we decided on not implementing the DELETE verb combined with the call at /Api/order as some Api best practices recommend as in our case there is no associated delete operation on the server. When an order is canceled what happens is that the IsCanceled property is set for the order, and an update notice is sent to the subscribers, such as the operator.

**Security and Membership Framework.** The API is secured using ASP.NET Membership Framework that handles the authentication and authorization logic of the application. The benefit of the Membership Framework is that a robust and throughout tested framework offers much better security than self-implemented framework. As a consequence, the Security framework was not extended and was allowed to operate as it is. By not extending or close integrating any services of the Membership framework with our system, we decoupled the two subsystems and allowed for further changes.

Also, all API calls are authenticated. The authentication is done using the user id, password and the session id. Each session is started when a user logs in. This prevents users to run the application on multiple devices in parallel and improves the overall security of the system. For the driver application authentication is done using tokens that are valid for a specific time interval. When a token expires, it needs to be renewed. Using tokens we are able to reduce the resource utilization on the server. If a call fails to authenticate, an error code is retuned. All communication is forced to use SSL, which eliminates or reduces the chance of Man in the middle attacks.

**SignalR.** It is not feasible to implement data synchronization using a polling interval, as the polling interval is both unknown and will generate large amount of data and CPU usage. In the .NET framework SignalR represents an implementation of long polling. However SignalR does not rely only on the long polling technique. SignalR has a concept of transports, each transport decides how data is sent/received and how it connects and disconnects. SignalR uses two concepts on the server implementation: *Hubs* and *persistent connections*. The Client app uses *Hubs*. Extending the *Hub* class represents the implementation of a hub on the server. Each method defined inside this class is mapped to a JavaScript implementation at compile time. The JavaScript document is saved on the project root folder and the client must reference it. It is possible to have broadcast events, which alert all the clients or only one in particular. It is also possible to group client and inform a whole group at a time. When the mobile application registers using SignalR, on the server a session ID called client ID is given to it. We are storing this client ID for each order. When a response is available and needs to be sent from the server to the client, we are sending an update request to the mobile app, using the client ID stored earlier.

There are three components of the system that need to be updated from the server. This are the client app, the driver app and the operator panel. The update scenario for the driver app is similar to the one for the client app. We note that the client app and the driver app are components that need to be independently updated, so having groups in this scenario is unnecessarily. However for the operator panel we need multiple operators to be able to respond to an incoming order. In this scenario it is more feasible to group the operators in groups, a group representing one operating company. When a new order is registered into the system the first operator who sees the new order will be able to respond to it.

### 3.5.2. Management Panel For Human Aided Dispatch

Some orders need to be inserted by the dispatcher, or might come from an external API that integrates with other SCM or ERP systems. Management Panel represents a web interface intended for responding to orders through a human actor acting as a dispatcher. The webpage is developed using *ASP.NET* and is secured using *.NET Membership Framework Forms Authentication*. A logged in user will be displayed a panel consisting of the current orders. Color codes are used for different order statuses. Brown is used for canceled orders, Green for orders that were responded successfully. No color is used for orders which have not been responded yet. The webpage uses AJAX techniques for receiving new orders and sending them without requiring complete page reloads. When a new order is inserted into the system, *SignalR* is used to notify the browser webpage to reload its orders panel. Partial page reloads are designed using the *ASP.NET UpdatePanel* and the *AJAX* functionality is built on JQuery. Using the Operator panel website the operator is able to respond to client orders. Whenever a new order that is destined for that operator is inserted into the system, SignalR that the orders grid needs to be updated notifies the webpage. Using an update panel control, as we specified earlier, does the update.

We implemented the operator panel in such a way to allow multiple operators to work on the same set of orders without worrying of responding to the same order. Whenever an operator views the content of an order, the order is marked as pending. When this happens a message is sent to the user notifying him that the operator viewed his order. Also another operator is announced that his colleague is already processing the specific order. If he tries to process the same order he will get an alert.

*Feature usage metrics using Analytics*. Analytics provide the means of measuring user experience inside the app and becomes a key component of the mobile ecosystem. Analytics provide the means of observing how users are interacting with the app and this provides the information required for further updates. Traditionally two analytics were used: *daily active users* and *user session time*. However it has been observed that user engagement falls sharply few days after the app first installation. As a consequence another key metric has become the *user retention level* after one day, one week and one month. Unless the app uses analytics it cannot understand its users base accordingly.

Analytics provide information regarding usage statistics such as new users, active users (which combines new and returning users into one stat), and sessions (how many times your app is used over a time period). You can grow this stat several ways such as acquiring new users, getting existing users to use more often or retaining users longer), session length (Session Length is a key engagement metric. Although different kinds of apps have different average session lengths, you would like this stat to improve over time with each additional update), frequency of use (this stat reveals the intensity with which your app is used), retention level, and app versions. It is also possible to track custom events such as the user clicking a menu button or completing a game level. We are tracking the address textbox editing feature, the map marker move, the amount the map marker is moved, the amount of time spent editing the address textbox, the amount of time until the order is placed.

*Social media integration*. Using Social Networks such as Facebook and Twitter we provide a mean of authentication using *OAuth v2*. For example if the app requires the users email address it can prompt the user to authenticate in the app using his *Facebook* account. If the user agrees to allow *Facebook* to share the email address with the app, the app is authorized to retrieve the users email from the Facebook service using the *Facebook* API. *OAuth* is an open standard for authorization, it allows users to share their private resources stored on one site with another site without having to hand out their credentials, typically supplying username and password tokens instead.

The other common use of *social services* integration is for marketing purposes. Many apps allow users to post messages to *Facebook* or to post on the users behalf. The posted messages should be based on users intention to share them, but they also often serve as a marketing strategy inside the users social network. *Order Taxi* application uses *social services* for marketing purposes by sharing the users ride information with the users consent. In order to use social services, as with most third party *APIs* an *API* key must be obtained by registering on the providers website. For *Facebook* this is available in the developers section of their website. Titanium offers modules for integrating *Facebook* and *Twitter* services and encapsulating the communication with the REST *API*. In our Taxi Ordering Application, we are integrating Facebook in order to allow people to post messages on their wall to inform their friend they are using Order Taxi application. They can also invite friends to join the application and earn points.

*Management and configuration* .There are three types of components that need to be managed: The proprietary server, the mobile client and the third party services. Managing the third party services is usually done by a management panel on the providers' website. A management panel for changes that have a high occurrence rate manages the proprietary server. For example new drivers are added manually to the system from this management panel. The hardest component to be managed is the mobile client application as there is no direct control over it. If major changes to the system are required for implementing new functionalities and this requires a change in the API it is important that API versioning is used to secure reliability for old clients that do not install the last updates. Backward compatibility of the system must always be respected. If the changes made to the system do not require any change in the API, but rather a change in the address, this can be resolved if the client was designed to adapt to such changes. Otherwise an update of the client app is required.

### 3.5.3. Social Crm System Using Datasift

DataSift [3] supports a variety of datasources. However the idea and first implementation addressed just one datasource, which is the most active of them, all that being the Twiter Firehose. Twitter does allow anyone to access its streaming API. However only a subset of all tweets are available through the streaming API, which are less than 1%. Twitter does however have two affiliated companies which get all the tweets through the Twitter Firehose, those being DataSift and Gnip (which is now a subsidiary of Twitter).

In this section we will describe how the DataSift architecture is implemented and build for a massively scalable requirements. DataSift implemented both their software and hardware solution because the large amount of data required to process offered both technical and economic challenges. DataSift runs on Hadoop and has one of the largest Hadoop clusters in the world. By creating their own hardware cluster they were able to take advantage of more low level performance optimizations than if they had used a public cloud provider such as Amazon, Google or Microsoft. Also considering the massive explosion in Big Data over the past few years, their infrastructure is expanding massively which would have been much more costly if they decided to use a public clod solution.

The DataSift architecture can be broken up in three large areas as follows that being *data extraction, filtering and delivering*.

(1) Data Extraction and Preprocessing

We call data preprocessing the act of extracting or receiving data from the defined datasources. Given the multitude of data sources one important aspect of this step is normalizing the data. The Redis Queue is used as a buffer during high peak usage. This allows the DataSift architecture to remain reliable at all times. Data is extracted out and normalized. Twitter data is highly dimensional, it has 30 plus attributes and you get access to them all. These attributes include geolocation, name, profile data, the tweet itself, timestamp, number of followers, number of retweets, verified user status, client type, *etc.*

The Interaction Generation thus acts similar to a JOIN operation over multiple streams of proprietary data structures and formats. As one can see the data sources are received using both Push and Pull HTTP requests and the formats are ranging from JSON and XML to Binary Streams. The result of the Interaction Generation block is a normalized object. This object is further augmented with data extracted from third party sources or by analyzing the data using proprietary or licensed algorithms such as Sentiment analysis or Language Detection. Entity extraction and natural language processing is applied to the tweet. Language is determined, for example, and that result is made available in the meta-data. Each link is resolved and the contents fetched so filters can be applied to content and the links themselves. Data is fully elaborated before the filtering process occurs.

Bringing the datasets into their system they needed to form close partnerships. Their sentiment analysis engine was licensed, made fast, made clusterable, and made suitable to handle 500 million hits a day with low latency. Each service must have < 100 ms response time. After 500 ms it is thrown away. In order to respect this they needed to cache the augmentation data sources locally. Also one in 10 tweets is a link, so the system creates a request for fetching the content of the referenced page in order to allow filters against it. So if a brand is mentioned it can be resolved against the actual content to figure out what it all means. This can provide quick insights into new blog posts or product reviews mentioned on social media.

Metadata Generation.

- Tagging allow adding custom metadata to interactions. For example, a specific car model can be tagged as luxury or economy. This information can be very useful later on into post processing. Adding tags based on conditional rules gives you the power to code business rules directly into your CSDL code. Normalized data is augmented in order to provide more context into the application. By enrichment the interactions will gather more metadata that can be queried using CSDL. The supported Enrichment engines are Demographics, Sentiment, Gender, Entities, Topics and Trends.

- Sentiment scoring allows a computer to consistently rate the positive or negative assertions that are associated with a document or entity. The scoring of sentiment (sometimes referred to as tone) from a document is a problem that was originally raised in the context of marketing and business intelligence, where being able to measure the public's reaction to a new marketing campaign (or, indeed, a corporate scandal) can have a measurable financial impact on your business.

- The Salience Sentiment data source delivers a measure of the positive or negative sentiment in a post. Within DataSift, sentiment is typically scored from −20 to 20 although values outside this range do sometimes occur. A score of zero is neutral, scores below zero indicate negative sentiment, and scores above zero indicate positive sentiment. For example, a score of −1 is mildly negative while a score of 15 is strongly positive.

- The Salience Topics data source lists the topics it finds in a post. Salience Topics are derived from an analysis of all the content in Wikipedia. As such, they allow for robust detection of content that is "about" a particular topic. A major advantage of this approach is that the topics analysis engine can easily be extended. The engine independently analyzes the content and the title.

- The Salience Entities data source lists the entities it finds in a post. Entities are typically proper nouns (people, companies, products, places) but can also include special patterns like URLs, phone numbers, addresses, currency amounts, and quotes. It can also recognize entities that we have never seen before. Each entity has sentiment associated with it so, if there is a Tweet that says "I really like Brand X, but don't like Brand Y", the entity discovery feature will correctly associate the sentiment with the individual entities. Sentiment analysis is also able to understand emoticons and nuances in the language. Only English is available however.
- Classifiers take a large sample of interactions from the platform, manually classify the interactions and use machine learning to learn key signals, which dictate which category interactions should belong to. The result is a set of scoring rules that form the classifier. The resulting classifier can be run against live or historic data ongoing. For example a classifier can be used to asses a user's probability of preaching a specific product or to route specific interactions to specific customer support or marketing teams inside a company.

(2) Filtering the Interactions

The cost of licensing the Twitter Firehose is extremely high and would become an inefficient investment for the majority of companies. Datasift created a declarative language called CSDL is order to filter out the Interaction (such as Tweets, Facebook posts, blog entries *etc.*) you do not want and keep the Interactions you do want. As we have explained in the previous sections the cost of running a queue includes both a licensing fee and a processing fee. The licensing fee is based on the number of interactions that match the defined query.

CDSL language CDSL allows for defining filtering conditions that specify what information the stream will include and augmenting the objects in the stream with data from third-party sites. A filtering condition has three elements: target, operator and argument. The target specifies the operand such as the content of a Twitter post. The operator defines the comparison Datasift should make. For example, it might search for Tweets from authors who have at least 100 followers. More complex filters can be built by combining simple filters using the logical operators: AND, OR, and NOT. Once a result stream has been defined through a filter, it can be reused as part of the definition of another stream by using the stream keyword to combine it with further filtering conditions. The argument can be any value, as long as the type of the argument matches the type of the target.

All interactions matching a filter form a stream. Each stream is assigned an identifier such as "4e8e6772337d0b993391ee6417171b79. Stream identifiers are included in rules to further qualify which tweets should be in a stream. Rules build on filters and other rules: rule "4e8e6772337d0b993391ee6417171b79" and language.tag = "en" This allows filters to grow on one another. DataSift also pushes for public streams which are more cost effective to process because of resource sharing the computation of a specific rule.

In order to create scalable filters DataSift uses a compiler to schedule filters efficiently across a cluster. Rules are made from a combination of filters and can have 1000 s or millions of terms. Millions of rules can be evaluated simultaneously, scheduled across hundreds of machines. Rules can be reused and hierarchically order. Filters include regular expressions, you can filter out tweets based on text in the profile, for example. There are many different targets and operators. The core filter engine is in C++ and is called the Pickle Matrix and is depicted in the Figure 9 below. The filtering engine is implemented using a custom built compiler and virtual machine based on Distributed Complex Event Processing with Query Rewriting.

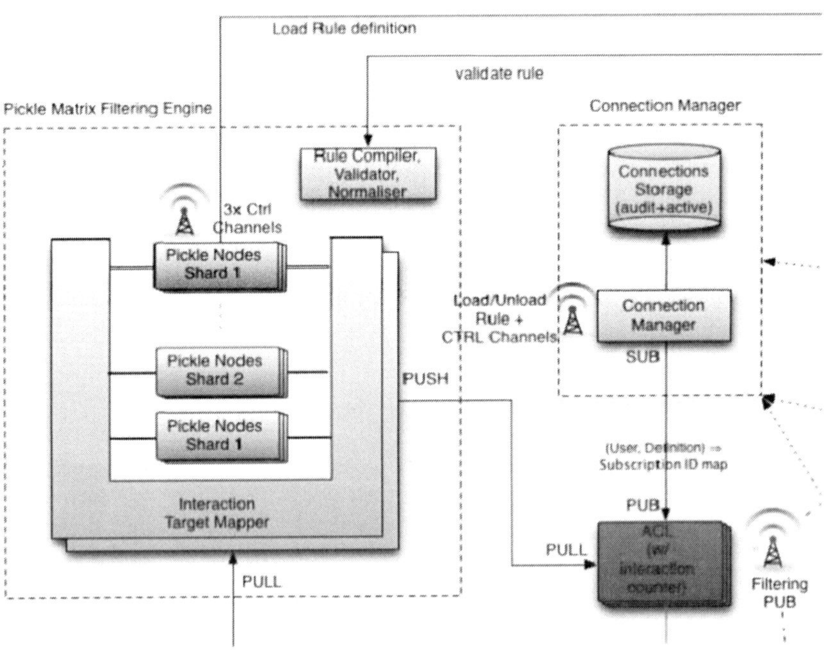


**Figure 9.** Real time filtering of normalized posts based on precompiled rules [3].

A compiler takes filters and targets a Hadoop cluster with a Manager and Node servers. The Manager's job is to determine that if a rule is loaded anywhere else and if can be put somewhere that is highly optimized, like close to someone else that is running a similar stream. Node's job is filter tweets by rules, get a list of matches, and push the matches down the pipeline.

Custom algorithms are built so rules are shared as much as possible. No filter is run in isolation. The filters form a shared space. If there is a filter that filters only for "computer" references then that filter is run on each tweet once and the result is shared between all rules using the same filter. Instead of continually running duplicate filters they are only run once. Rules can be a hierarchical and the compiler is merges them together so that they share rule evaluations. If a node already has a rule then it will attract filters that use that rule. That rule is run just once for all the filters on the node.

By combining workloads of multiple customers together they can exploit any commonality in the filters. DataSift is paid for every operation even though they only run it once. If a regular expression is shared, for example, it is only run once. It cannot always work this way, perhaps a node is loaded so cannot take another client, so it must run on another machine.

The entire configuration dynamically changeable at runtime. The scheduling algorithm is constantly looking at monitoring data. If latency crosses a threshold then the system will be reconfigured. Filters are processed immediately in memory. Each server, for example, can run 10,000 streams. Nodes have a rule cache so they can be shared.

Compiler supports short circuiting to optimize filters. If a regular expression is bigger than an entire machine, for example, then they will automatically load balance across nodes.

The filtering engine is sharded. Each shard receives the full firehose and every "interaction" (*i.e.* a "tweet" or "FB status" or "blog post") is processed by all shards, the results of which are collated before being sent downstream. Each of the N nodes in a single shard (which are replicas of each other) receives 1/N of the hose on a round robin basis. So, supposing there are two shards, with three nodes each, 50% of the filters would be found on each shard. Each node in a shard would receive 1/3 of the hose (and would have 50% of the filters on it). And it would be a replica of the other nodes in that shard. Thus, if a very heavy filter is loaded, that will be balanced by adding more nodes to the shard the heavy rule is loaded into, thus reducing the amount of data that a single node has to process.

A big push is for customers to create reusable public rules to encourage the reusability of data streams. People can use any of the public streams in their own rules. For example, someone could make a word filter that creates a stream. You can build off that stream by using it. Everyone shares that same stream so if a 1000 users are using the dirty word filter the filter is not getting evaluated 1000 times. The filter is getting evaluated once for everyone, which is highly efficient. The platform will thus offer even better performance for a higher number of workloads and become highly scalable with resource usage relative to processing requirement being reduced.

(3) Loading and Delivering the Results

Once the filtering process identifies an interaction that matches the specified query, the interaction is delivered to the specific stream. It is important to mention that DataSift buffers the data it receives for up to one hour. During this time it is possible to request specific interactions from DataSift. The data is stored in Hadoop HBase. However most implementations will require specific custom processing on the results created by DataSift. For example a client might be interested in extracting information such as addresses or mentions of specific users or places and store them later in their own database.

When creating a DataSift Stream running task it is possible to specify a specific output location. Tweets that match the filter are accessible to external applications via a REST API, HTTP Streaming, or Web sockets with a client library exists for: PHP, Ruby, C#, Java, Node.js. The results are JSON objects containing all the data in a normalized, fully augmented format. Augmentations include gender, geolocation, point-of-interest, country, author, the tweet, follower count, Klout score, *etc.* in the stream. There up to 80 fields for each message. Tweets are not guaranteed to arrive in any order and you are not guaranteed to see all the tweets ever sent. This is because Hadoop MapReduce jobs are used to extract the data out of HBase, which involves sharding and thus change the order. However Hadoop does offer solutions for persisting the order of the analyzed data.

## Recording interactions on DataSift

DataSift records the result of the Filtering Task in HBase tables. When data is streamed out of DataSift, Hadoop MapReduce jobs will extract the data in the specific desired format. Most of the time this format will be JSON. DataSift took the decision of storing the normalized data in HBase table instead of pure JSON because it allows further querying if necessarily or exporting it in other formats such as CSV or Excel documents as depicted in the Figure 10. This storage component is fundamental to DataSift for two reasons. First it is used as an Achiever, where all the Interactions that came through the system are stored in a normalized form and can be later processed using the Historic Task Services. The recorder is used for buffering the data until it is transferred to the client in the specified way (live stream, push to a specific data source, download using HTTP *etc.*) The recording table uses entries similar to <interaction ID><recording ID> in order to map the interactions that should be exported to a specific stream.

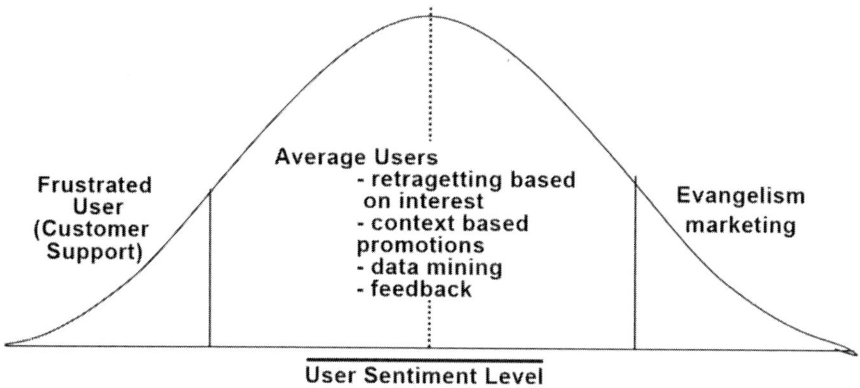


**Figure 10.** Bell Curve of our User Base. Social CRM has the purpose of moving the curve to the right and increasing the number of users.

The content of each interaction is only stored once, and will be archive by DataSift. When DataSift introduced Historic Queues, it bought the data from Twitter for the previous two years. This data amounted to 300 TB, which was delivered over the Internet and normalized according to the way all interaction objects are processed, including augmentations.

## Social CRM integration with the Dispatching System

The dispatching system is offered as a SAAS product to enterprise clients. The Social CRM system builds upon it and has the purpose of aggregating as much information about the users as possible. The most important data that we extract using DataSift and utilize in our system is presented below.

**User sentiment score**—describes the sentiment the user has towards the application. This metric is closely monitored as it groups the users into three major categories.

The first category is composed of users that are neither highly enthusiastic about using the system nor highly negative. They are the regular users and compose 80%–90% of the user base. In general no human interaction with these users is performed. They are advertised and retargeted using their profile and interests, as we will describe bellow. The second category is composed of users that are negative on the system. They have probably experienced either a problem with the system or in the interaction with the driver for example. Whatever the cause, the problem should be addressed so that it will not affect other users or have a spillover effect. The most effective way of dealing with highly negative users is an apologetic customer support phone call during which the user is offered free credit for retrying the system and with the promise that his problem will be addressed as soon as possible.

This method has been used effectively by Uber for monitoring their drivers. The last category is composed of users who are extremely positive on using the system, which we will be calling evangelizers. This category should be enticed to promote the system by offering them a more privileged role that allows better service and social recognition. This method of gamification at the high levels of the customer spectrum has been proven by numerous companies including Foursquare, Path, Quora and StackExchange.

**Interaction History**—this provides anyone interested in a specific user the ability to see the exact posts that constitute the sentiment index, or to identify what the pain points of a highly negative user are. All the interactions provided by DataSift are stored in our database and augment the user profile.

**Promotions History**—all the promotions and advertising campaigns that have ever been targeted to a specific user are recorded. This is for two reasons. One of them is to see the conversion and activation factors of specific campaigns. The other is to aid us in future campaigns by selecting only those users that have or have not been targeted previously within a specific program.

**More information on the users**—by aggregating more information about each user such as age, locations, interests, network of friends *etc.*, we are able to understand the user base better and it helps with categorizing them better. The purpose of the entire Social CRM component is to improve the service and increase the success rate of our marketing campaigns by better targeting which will reduce the total cost. We can thus create online marketing campaigns that can be extremely targeted and still benefit from low CPC rates.

In this section we have detailed the implementation of the proposed system and explained the functionality of the complete architecture by breaking it up into the composing parts. We also analyzed how we managed to integrate the two systems in an efficient and scalable manner by using Windows Azure Cloud Computing as the underlying architecture for our system. We decomposed the system into two large subsystems: the dispatching system and the Social CRM system.

We explained how a cross platform approach can be used to developing mobile application and we have proved the native capacities of the system by using the GPS API. We also presented how the mobile application can be integrated with the Cloud and how the Cloud can act as a data synchronization mechanism between the client mobile application, the driver application and the operator panel. Regarding the Social CRM system, we explained how it can be built to extract and augment the data in our database and bring more value and customer engagement.

# 4. TESTING AND VALIDATION

## 4.1. Mobile based Client Application Testing

Testing of the mobile applications has been performed, covering usability testing and integration testing. Usability testing of software applications developed for mobile devices faces a variety of challenges due to their unique features, such as limited bandwidth, unreliability of wireless networks, as well as the changing context. For assuring the system correctness Use Case Driven Testing of the functionalities of the system must be addressed in various environmental contexts such as no Internet access, no GPS signal *etc*. The client application was designed with these considerations in mind and the testing approach was by using Use Case Driven testing in various conditions. The following issues have been tested:

- **Mobile application context.** It can be defined as "any information that characterizes a situation related to the interaction between users, applications, and the surrounding environment [2]." For our client application we have tested how the app was performing in different times and places, especially how GPS was acting inside buildings and how well wireless networks aided the positioning based on the accuracy of position determination. It is very difficult to select a methodology that can include all possibilities of mobile context in a single usability test. If the user position cannot be obtained and the GPS was turned off, we asked the user to turn it on or input the address manually.

- **Connectivity and Mobile Internet Coverage.** Logistic Systems are characterized by very high availability constraints. Lack of connectivity or slow Internet speed is common with mobile applications. We tested whether the application can identify this situation and alert it to the user, notifying him that the app cannot work properly and he has to either turn on internet (if this is not turn on already), or just report that the app cannot work in the absence of an internet connection. According to Ericsson, 85% of the world population will have access to 3G coverage by 2017. In the European Union, over 95% of the metropolitan areas are covered by 3G. According to the same report from Ericsson, by 2017 50% of the world population will have access to 4G which will enable even richer interactions in terms of data synchronization and reach media content, especially voice and video streaming.
- **UI/UX testing for different screen sizes.** The mobile screen resolution is extremely fragmented. We also realized that many mobile devices that will be used as dispatching terminals will range from small 3 inch diagonal low resolution devices, up to tablets reaching over 10 inch in diagonal. These concerns affect mobile applications. We tested the applications on multiple devices and also used UI elements that can adapt proportionally to screen sizes. We have observed that for some small screens the application was not displayed properly because we have implemented some minimum size attributes in order to display the text completely. In order to resolve the issue we added test cases for small screen displays, and if the screen width was bellow a specific value, we used a smaller font and minimum width, which solved the problem. In order to test the aspect of the application rendered on different devices, virtualization tools such as Samsung Remote Test Lab. The Remote Test Lab is a free service from Samsung Developers. With it, you can access a remote physical device through a network, install an application and test it remotely.
- **CPU and Memory performance considerations.** Mobile devices have a high diversity of performance specifications. As we intend to support old and new devices as well, we need to test how the application performs on different hardware environments. These requirements must be tested especially if the work is not mitigated to the Cloud. For our system this was less of a concern as we perform the processing and storage on the Cloud. The order history and user data are all stored in the Cloud, and is consumed using the service API. Because we do not have access to all hardware devices, we used pCloud platform [18], which allows virtualization of different devices using screen streaming. Using their service we were able to deploy

the application to a large variety of Android handsets and test the behavior of the system on both old and new devices.

## 4.2. API Testing and Validation

The API was implemented using the REST protocol and the JSON data passing format. All communication between the Cloud System and other systems is done using the API (excluding the integration with the Social CRM System which is also done using the database). In the first instance the validation of the service was performed by adding a new project to the solution and creating *Unit Test* classes. Inside this class specific methods for testing functionalities have been defined. Sending JSON requests required a series of step including creating the JSON request data from the CLR object, sending the request using a selected verb, and handling the HTTP specific errors, we defined a method called SendRequest.

Using this method we specified the resource we wanted to test, the verb and the data.

The data object was defined as dynamic to allow for easier operation with encoding and decoding JSON data. We designed the system to return specific error codes for specific errors such as duplicate telephone number. When designing the Unit Test we have tested if this error codes are returned appropriately. For example when creating a new user we tested different combinations of telephone and user name.

As we added new functionality to the system we expended the test scenarios and we rerun the test periodically to ensure that the system remains valid after performing modifications.

## 4.3. Load Testing for Scalability and Synchronization

For Load Testing, we were interested in how the system would reach to a high increase in usage. As we built the System on Windows Azure, we were certain that the scalability aspect will be mitigated effectively as long as we did not have any bottlenecks. Load testing also allowed for an efficient way of discovering errors in the system that occurred in scenarios such as concurrent access to shared resources and overriding of data that was not protected using locks. For Load Testing we first used a number of 10000 concurrent threads that were fired from a virtual machine in the cloud. We used as virtual machine in the Windows Azure Cloud as the communication latency would be minimized and it would help us discovering synchronization issues.

Once we handled all synchronization issues that have arisen through our testing, we needed a better way of testing the scalability beyond what we could have obtained using simple threads. For this we relied on LoadStorm, which is a cloud based tool that can create multiple client virtual machines firing requests at the test server requests can be customized with specific automate trigger based on the received responses. Up to 250 requests/second Windows Azure used just one medium size virtual machine. As the stress on the server reached over 90% CPU usage, automatic scaling was performed, which increased the number of virtual machines and decreased the response time to around 0.5 s. The time required for a virtual machine to launch was around 3–4 min.

## 4.4. Social Media Analysis

For the Social CRM component, the data is received in real time. However delays are to be expected. According to DataSift SLA (Service level agreement), the maximum delay between a Tweet being posted by a user and the time it is processed by DataSift should be less than 4 s. In this respect we analyze what is the average delay we will encounter from a tweet being posted on Twitter and the time it is analyzed by our Social CRM component.

In order to calculate the time delay we fired a number of 300 threads that each posted a message on Twitter. Then we used a stopwatch to obtain the time interval between when the message was posted and the moment the interaction was delivered from DataSift into our system. It is important to understand that the delays between the time the user publishes an interaction on other dataset such as blogs or discussion groups and the time DataSift processes this interaction can be much larger and span up to one hour.

## 4.5. Coverage Ratio of Matching Interactions

While analyzing the processing lag described in the previous paragraph we observed that for the 300 interactions we submitted on twitter using Twitters public API, DataSift received only 248. This means that 52 interactions were not identified by DataSift. Further investigation revealed that the reason why this was happening was because we had a sudden burst in activity that lasted only a few seconds. In this test case we tried to identify if the DataSift platform provides a high enough coverage ratio. For this we fired a number of 1000 Twitter posts over a range of 10 different accounts. Each interaction was submitted at a time interval ranging randomly between 1 and 10 s from the last one. A number of 10 threads were used for posting the threads. In this scenario the number of interactions captured by DataSift have been of 972, which translates into a 97.2% coverage ratio.

In conclusion we have tested the various components of the system and we concluding that the system is valid and works according to the initial functional and non-functional requirements.

# 5. CONCLUSIONS AND FURTHER DEVELOPMENTS

We have detailed the implemented the system according to the specifications. We started by analyzing the requirements for our system by comparing similar applications in order to identify the most important features. We than stated the functionalities which the system was designed to offer and we created the use cases for our actors. We explained the two large subsystems that constitute our project: the dispatching system and the Social CRM system. Before implementation we created the conceptual model and listed the suitable technologies necessarily for meeting our requirements. In this respect we used DataSift as the underlying platform for building the Social CRM engine and Titanium as the best solution for developing cross platform mobile applications We also analyzed what the main threats to REST security are and we have enumerated some actions that we have taken in order to lower the chances of an attacker breaking the system or to help identify and mitigate an attack. We identified what are the main differences in terms of security between running the applications on premise *vs.* Cloud, as this has been a particular controversial topic. We than analyzed what methods can be used to secure REST services.

The Social CRM component of our application was designed in order to augment the information on our users and enhance the performance of our marketing campaigns. For this we used DataSift as the underling platform for extraction of interactions from Social Networks and other online public data sources. We than detailed the implementation of DataSift and how it extracts, normalizes and delivers the data into our system. We also examined some technical challenges that DataSift has encountered and explained the solutions that were applied such as defining time intervals for processing historic content. The Datashift remains a good option which is able to sustain a growing level of scalability for our system.

In conclusion we have tested the various components of the system and we are affirming that the system is valid and works according to the initial specified functional and non-functional requirements. The system is for now up and running [19], but as for any real system there are a lot of further developments and improvements which are determined by production usage.

As further developments, we would like to explore some other aspects for improving the system as elaborating on the dispatch strategy [20], integrating a solution for cruising mile reduction as presented in [21], or even a component for finding potential passengers as proposed in [22]. We also plan in the next release to complement our services with other services such as for example Google traffic API [23] or Skyhook [24] in order to create some new functionalities. Concerning the data, we started the project with relational database, but also we take into account the alternative of transferring the data persistence layer to a noSQL solution (such as for example Redis or Couchdatabase) as a more scalable solution. As a potential problem from a real world environment perspective exploitation of the system, capturing massive data from social networks could represent a possible problem, but designing appropriate filters for data, must be able to solve such a prospective bottleneck.

## AUTHOR CONTRIBUTIONS

This paper was a result of a collaboration between the two authors. Razvan Popa came with the idea and implemented the system software. Cosmina Ivan refined the initial idea, supervised the project and contributed to the writing and editing of the manuscript. Both authors have read and approved the final manuscript.

## CONFLICTS OF INTEREST

The authors declare no conflict of interest.

## REFERENCES


1. Ericsson Mobility Report. 2014. Available online: http://www. ericsson. com/res/docs/2014/ericsson-mobility-report-june-2014.pdf (accessed on 25 September 2014).
2. Sharma, A.; Soni, P. Mobile Cloud Computing (MCC) Open Research Issues. IJIET, 2013. Available online: http://ijiet.com/wp-content/uploads/2013/02/5.pdf (accessed on 29 September 2014).

3. DataSift Guide. Available online: http://dev.datasift.com/docs (accessed on 29 June 2015).
4. Gnip, Social Media in Financial Markets. 2013. Available online: http://gnip.com /docs/social-media-and-markets-the-coming-of-age.pdf (accessed on 15 November 2014).
5. Wilson, T. "How GPS Phones Work". 2011. Available online: http://www. howstuffworks. com/gps-phone.htm(accessed on 15 January 2015).
6. Titanium. Available online: http://www.appcelerator.com/product/ (accessed on 29 June 2015).
7. Microsoft WCF Feature Details. Available online: http://msdn.microsoft.com/en-us/library/ms733103.aspx (accessed on 29 June 2015).
8. Microsoft ADO.NET Entity Framework At-a-Glance. Available online: http://msdn. microsoft.com /en-us/data/aa937709 (accessed on 5 December 2014).
9. ASP.NET SignalR. Available online: http://signalr.net/ (accessed on 29 June 2015).
10. Apple Push Notification Service. Available online: https://developer. apple.com/notifications/ (accessed on 15 December 2014).
11. Android Cloud to Device Messaging. Available online: https://developers .google.com /android/c2dm/ (accessed on 15 January 2015).
12. Urban Airship. Available online: http://urbanairship.com/ (accessed on 29 June 2015).
13. Alonso, G.F.; Casati, F.H.; Kuno, H. Web Services: Concepts, Architectures, Applications; Springer: Berlin, Germany, 2004.
14. Dinh, H.T.; Lee, C.; Niyato, D.; Wang, P. A survey of mobile cloud computing: Architecture, applications, and approaches. Wirel. Commun. Mobile Comput. 2013, 13, 1587–1611.
15. Tyree, J.; Akerman, A. Architecture decisions: Demystifying architecture. IEEE Softw. 2005, 22, 19–27.
16. Schultz-Møller, N.P.; Migliavacca, M. Distributed Complex Event Processing with Query Rewriting, Imperial College London. In Proceedings of the Third ACM International Conference on Distributed Event-Based Systems, Nashville, TN, USA, 6–9 July 2009.
17. Bass, L.; Clements, P.; Kazman, R. Software Architecture in Practice; Wesley: Boston, MA, USA, 2003.
18. Pcloud. Available online: www.pcloud.com (accessed on 29 June 2015).
19. Taxy Army. Available online: www.taxiarmy.com (accessed on 29 June 2015).
20. Hou, Y.; Li, X.; Zhao, Y.; Jia, X.; Sadek, A.W.; Hulme, K.; Qiao, C. Towards efficient vacant taxis cruising guidance. In Proceedings of the 2013 IEEE Global Communications Conference (GLOBECOM), Atlanta, GA, USA, 9–13 December 2013; pp. 54–59.
21. Zhang, D.; He, T. pCruise: An On-demand Cruising Miles Reduction for Taxicab Networks. In Proceedings of the 2012 IEEE 33rd Real-Time Systems Symposium, San Jan, PR, USA, 4–7 December 2012; pp. 85–94.
22. Yuan, N.J.; Zheng, Y.; Zhang, L.; Xie, X. T-finder: A recommender system for finding passengers and vacant taxis. IEEE Trans. Knowl. Data Eng. 2013, 25, 2390–2403.
23. Google Traffic API. Available online: https://developers. google.com/ maps/documentation/javascript/examples/layer-traffic (accessed on 26 June 2015).
24. Skyhook Technology. Available online: http://www.skyhookwireless.com/ (accessed on 26 June 2015).

# Index